Abundance

Abundance

THE ARCHAEOLOGY
OF PLENITUDE

Edited by Monica L. Smith

UNIVERSITY PRESS OF COLORADO

Louisville

© 2017 by University Press of Colorado

Published by University Press of Colorado
245 Century Circle, Suite 202
Louisville, Colorado 80027

First paperback edition 2020

The University Press of Colorado is a proud member of
The Association of University Presses.

The University Press of Colorado is a cooperative publishing enterprise supported, in part, by Adams State University, Colorado State University, Fort Lewis College, Metropolitan State University of Denver, Regis University, University of Colorado, University of Northern Colorado, University of Wyoming, Utah State University, and Western Colorado University.

ISBN: 978-1-60732-593-2 (cloth)
ISBN: 978-1-64642-125-1 (paperback)
ISBN: 978-1-60732-594-9 (ebook)

Library of Congress Cataloging-in-Publication Data

Names: Smith, Monica L., editor.
Title: Abundance : the archaeology of plenitude / edited by Monica L. Smith.
Description: Boulder : University Press of Colorado, 2017. | Includes bibliographical references and index.
Identifiers: LCCN 2016049220| ISBN 9781607325932 (cloth)| ISBN 9781646421251 (pbk) | ISBN 9781607325949 (ebook)
Subjects: LCSH: Economic anthropology—Case studies. | Consumption (Economics)—Social aspects—History—Case studies. | Material culture—Case studies. | Social archaeology—Case studies.
Classification: LCC GN448 .A28 2017 | DDC 306.3—dc23
LC record available at https://lccn.loc.gov/2016049220

Cover illustration by Johnny Clasper

Contents

Figures

Abundance

1

The Archaeology of Abundance

MONICA L. SMITH

When excavating a site or surveying a region, archaeologists are often confronted with thousands or even hundreds of thousands of artifacts and ecofacts. Sometimes this is the result of deflation or other site formation processes that aggregate the remains of many periods onto a single landscape surface. In many cases, however, plenitude was just as obvious to ancient people as to us: every hunter had the experience of killing an animal that was more than could be eaten by one person; every farmer had a harvest in which there was more food than could be eaten at one sitting; every shoreline dweller saw populations of fish and birds that outnumbered the human inhabitants of the landscape; and every urban center had markets and distribution centers that contained more than what any single household could use. Contexts ranging in time from Paleolithic deposits to ancient cities thus provide evidence of vast quantities of objects, indicative of conditions in which individuals recognized, generated, and gravitated toward plenitude.

In this volume, we choose the term *abundance* to describe the mass quantities that were perceived as part of ancient human-environmental interactions and cultivated as part of human social landscapes. Our use of the word *abundance* as a neutral term is taken in deliberate counterbalance to the pejorative and subjective term *excess*, with its connotations of waste, greed, and inequality (e.g., Oka and Kuijt 2014; Wilk 2014), or *surplus*, which implies inherent political power in the allocation of resources or the deliberate manipulation of labor and raw materials for exchange (Groot and Lentjes 2013; Morehart and De Lucia 2015). Similarly, concepts of *scarcity* as the dominant

DOI: 10.5876/9781607325949.c001

explanatory economic paradigm obscure conditions of plenitude in which items can become more desirable even as they become more abundant (Guerzoni and Troilo 1998; Silverstein and Fiske 2005; Smith 2012). We propose that the ability to characterize natural and culturally produced items as scarce, excess, and surplus is rooted in the more fundamental capacity to recognize the relative effect of mass quantities and their potential for positive and negative effects.

Scholars have philosophized about the ways human-made objects have shaped social relationships, as seen in seminal works including those by Thorstein Veblen (1899), Daniel Miller (1985), and Sheena Iyengar (2010). Artifacts have been a component of individual development and collective activities since the origin of our species, and materiality has been the mechanism by which cognition and linguistic virtuosity have profoundly impacted the surrounding environment (Karlin and Julien 1994; Martin 1998; Shipman 2010). The mutually constituted relationships sustained between people and objects over the past million years have been variously characterized as "engagements" (Masquelier 1997; Renfrew 2001), "interactions" (Schiffer 1992); "enchainment" (Chapman 2000), and "entanglements" (Hodder 2012). Although these scholarly treatments have definitively demonstrated the essential nature of objects for human social life, they have generally addressed only the *concept* of objects as inanimate phenomena and have set aside the critical consideration of object *quantity*. In this volume, we address the distinct effects of object plenitude as seen in the archaeological record of both natural objects and deliberately created artifacts.

An explicit understanding of object quantity allows us to address two undertheorized aspects of the material record: singular finds and abundant ones. Singular finds are treated as statistical outliers whose interpretive importance varies according to the contexts in which they are found (Zedeño 2009). Particularly for the earliest human cultural phases, unique items are viewed as "leading-edge" developments of material culture in which there is a "low number of finds because initial creative efforts were the result of individual actions" (Marshack 1990:460). Low find-density is also attributed to the existence of a small number of sites for the most ancient time periods, the vagaries of survey and excavation methods, or taphonomic and site formation processes that result in infrequent preservation. Commentators on the recovery of single finds of ordinary goods often include the caveat that more research would surely turn up additional items. The exception to the apologetic treatment of singular finds is when such finds are perceived to have been deliberately created as items of distinction through the use of unusual raw materials or high levels of labor investment. These singular finds are interpreted as evidence for elite activities, in which the low frequency of archaeological recovery is regarded as a faithful representation of the object's prevalence in antiquity.

Like singular and unique finds, abundant ones have heretofore been interpreted through ad hoc and context-dependent criteria. Within a site, a plenitude of durable items may be recorded as the result of formation processes such as deflation and erosion or as a compressed palimpsest of ancient activities perceptible only to the archaeologist who conducts a stratigraphic investigation. Mass quantities resulting from incremental processes, such as the filling of a well with discards, are viewed as having had a cumulative effect that was invisible or inconsequential to ancient people. Mass quantities associated with industrial-scale production, as evidenced at sites of iron and pottery production, are perceived as having effects on the landscape that were incidental to the role of finished products. When mass quantities are interpreted as purposeful accumulations, such as the presence of large number of objects in a burial, they are analyzed from the perspective of craft specialization, ritual deposition, or the elite control of wealth in which plenitude is viewed as supporting an interpretation of special-purpose activities distinct from living contexts.

A focus on abundance provides the opportunity to evaluate large quantities as a consistent component of human-material engagements that permeated daily life and were not limited to elites. Large quantities prompted individual and collective responses, in which objective assessments of plenitude were transformed into subjective assessments that the amount of a particular item was too much, insufficient, or just right for present circumstances. The authors of the chapters in this volume address the quantification of ancient objects and artifacts at both site-specific and regional scales. The first step of analysis is the recognition of large quantities and the extent to which those quantities were perceived by the ancient inhabitants of the sites they studied. This is followed by an assessment of the role of abundant goods in social groups of varying sizes and a consideration of the ways in which plenitude prompted social responses: sometimes people gravitated toward abundance, and in other cases they shunned it.

The evaluation of abundance has implications not only for the study of the meaning of objects in the past but also for approaches to artifact study in the present. Perhaps one reason archaeologists have undervalued abundance is that although we excavate items in large quantities, their display in museums is done with a focus on singularity in which one or two items represent an entire category in a glassed-in case. This display tactic renders individual artifacts as the partible "approved document" of representation. A similar distillation effect is seen in scholarly publications in which items are selected for illustration on a one-by-one basis, separated from data tables that provide information about quantification in numerical rather than visual form. Recognition that artifacts were originally manufactured and used in quantity reorients our assessment of ancient materialized contexts as far more populated than the spare aesthetic of museums and publications.

Ours is not the only data-driven field to place differential interpretive weights on singular finds relative to mass quantities. Like archaeologists, biologists seem to have under-theorized abundance to date, as noted by Anton Pauw (2013:31) who has commented that studies of floral communities "seem to be biased towards studying the low-density end of the spectrum." Biologists' focus on minimum rather than maximum numbers is driven by considerations for species decline, the specter of extinction, and the pressing need to ascertain minimum thresholds of viability while creating reserves and corridors. Biologists do, however, emphasize quantitative effects when discussing mass migrations and invasive species, two phenomena that could be further evaluated as providing comparative perspectives for theory building. A potential model is provided by the citizen science mass-data project eBird, for which researchers note that "abundance" can be characterized in a variety of ways that result in new understandings of the dynamics of environmental systems (Sullivan et al. 2014).

The recognition of mass quantities as having both emic and etic value is critical to our field's increasing use of large data sets to address broad research questions. Contemporary "big-data" approaches include compilations of heritage data (e.g., Kintigh et al. 2014; Peterson and Drennan 2012), new initiatives of information collection through citizen science (Bonacchi et al. 2014; Smith 2014), and open-access data sources that are providing mass data sets such as the Alexandria Archive and the Digital Archaeology Record (tDAR). The resultant data sets will not only render comparative analysis more robust but will enable the assessment of both the variability and quantity of archaeological phenomena as they were experienced by ancient people.

THE HUMAN HISTORY OF ABUNDANCE

Our earliest ancestors were endowed with the same survival strategies as other mobile, omnivorous species: they gravitated toward locations replete with desirable resources such as food, shelter, water, and potential mating opportunities. In the relatively underpopulated landscape of early foragers, abundance was not the exception but rather the norm of human expectations. Communal hunts would have produced piles of recognizable discards, as Sandra Olsen (2010:529) describes for Upper Paleolithic Solutré, where generations of hunters would have encountered a landscape replete with horse bones. Demonstrable abundance in food became intertwined with conceptualizations of "the good life." Extremely large prey appears to have provided an opportunity for provisioning that was symbolic rather than practical (Waguespack and Surovell 2003). Daily acts of symbolism were also manifested in the cumulative effects of small-size food units: trees full of nuts, plants full of berries, and streams full of fish.

Our ancestors' engagement with abundant artifacts was an outgrowth of a cognitive propensity to recognize quantitative value, in which accumulation was a purposeful, recognized, and deliberate aspect of human activities. The earliest durable evidence for artifact production comes from the Oldowan period, dating to 2.6 mya in East and South Africa, where some sites have thousands of artifacts and manuports (Kuman 2014). The earliest tool manufacturing was accompanied by large numbers of waste flakes, as exemplified by the 1.6 mya MNK "factory site" at Oldovai where a 2 meter × 5 meter excavation area produced about 30,000 pieces of debitage (Stiles 1991). Like the accumulations of manufactured objects, the heaps and scatters of waste material from production would have presented a visible record of plenitude forming part of the community's experiential landscape. When our ancestors began to make more elaborate stone tools such as hand axes incorporating bilateral symmetry and repeated hammer blows of manufacture, the quantities we find in the archaeological record suggest not only a practical but also a symbolic investment of labor (Klein 2009:95).

Our ancestors' engagement with crafted goods extended beyond utilitarian tools to the use of decorative items such as beads, pendants, and ochre as early as 130,000 years ago in Africa (McBrearty and Brooks 2000). As Mary Stiner (2014) has argued, early ornamentation was standardized across large areas, indicative of communication and contact among groups about style and manufacture. Quantity was an important part of that display, such that the number of beads worn by an individual enabled the person to modify the amplitude, or "loudness," of communication (Stiner 2014:61). Quantities of decorative objects are certainly evident in a variety of forager contexts worldwide, such as the Upper Paleolithic gravesite of Sungir where burials contain over 3,000 ivory beads per individual (Soffer 1985:259), the prehistoric coastal fisher/forager settlement of Khok Phanom Di in Thailand in which 120,000 shell beads were recovered from a single grave (Bentley et al. 2007:303), and the prehistoric Pacific Northwest fishing camp in which the investigators recovered extraordinary amounts of stone and shell beads, including 350,000 beads from one burial alone (Coupland et al. 2016:302).

The deliberate pursuit of food abundance appears to have underwritten the diversified approach to provisioning starting in the Upper Paleolithic period. In contrast to earlier interpretations that the "broad spectrum revolution" was the response to population surpluses or food shortfalls, Melinda Zeder (2012) has argued that it was not the scarcity of food but its abundance that conditioned the location of early migratory populations. What made our ancestors distinct from other migratory species, however, is that they not only moved toward locations of plenitude, but they also collected, consolidated, and augmented that plenitude through the selective acquisition, transportation, and curation of distinctive items to create a notion of plenty through human actions. The worldwide phenomenon of shell middens indicates the extent to which discards were not merely an afterthought of consumption but constituted visible forms of place-making by forager groups (McNiven 2012; Moore and Thompson 2012).

Expressions of plenitude were scaled up as social configurations grew more complex, accompanied in many cases by sedentism and the domestication of plants and animals. Food-production activities enabled humans to become active agents in the creation of "natural" abundance as they weeded, tended, fertilized, and watered plants and experienced seasonal harvests. Those moments of plenitude were counterbalanced with an expectation that harvested foods had to last for a long period of subsequent consumption, a factor that prompted both the symbolic and substantive management of the harvest through feasts and long-term storage (Halstead and O'Shea 1989; see also Bogaard et al. 2009; Smith 2015). The abundances afforded by food production were paralleled by a surfeit of material objects and an incremental discard of waste that signaled the passage of time and the growth of the community. For the Khartoum Neolithic, Randi Haaland (2007) has reported a site in which 30,000 pieces of grinding stone were recovered in only 140 square meters of excavated area, suggesting a stockpiling and use of tools far beyond their necessary uselife. Craft making through new technologies such as metallurgy resulted not only in an increase of finished products but also in vast quantities of discards, such as the hundreds of thousands of tons of slag and hundreds of thousands of crucible fragments cited by Joyce White and Elizabeth Hamilton (2014:816) for the sites of Non Pa Wai and Nil Kham Haeng occupied during the first millennium BC in central Thailand.

In addition to serving as an economic indicator, abundance was a marker of social cohesion and ritual affirmation. Pilgrimages to ancient sacred sites were marked by mass dedicatory caches and animal sacrifices whose accumulations reinforced individuals' depositional acts (e.g., Hartman et al. 2013). Burials and ritual spaces became the focal points of activities in which the individual placement of items resulted in visible, incremental accumulations constituting intentional acts of place-making through deposition (e.g., Osborne 2004; Rajan 2008:45). Individuals' incremental placement of artifacts enabled them to transform modest contributions into monumentality through accumulations that often became strikingly large. From the Fourth to Sixth Dynasties in Egypt, people discarded millions of miniature vessels as part of mortuary ritual (2550–2150 BC; Allen 2006). At the third-millennium BC site of Shijiahe in China, archaeologists recovered hundreds of thousands of red-cup ritual vessels (Fuller and Qin 2009:101). Accumulations in a landscape were significant not only to those who placed them but also to those who came long afterward and repurposed ancient abundance into their own contemporary meaning, as seen in the case of Egyptian religious sites on which later

Ptolemaic and Roman visitors left graffiti "in extraordinary numbers" (Gates-Foster 2012:204; see also Champion 2012).

Ritual deposition is only one form of large-scale participation in shared material culture. The acquisition of repetitive objects from a particular place constitutes another form of collective engagement, including souvenirs emanating from a particular locality or event (cf. "necrolithic theatrics" in Carter 2007:96, 100). Souvenirs, whether natural or manufactured, are often abundant in their source locale and subsequently become dispersed along trade routes by their collectors. Although we cannot decipher the idiosyncratic experience of any particular individual, the archaeological record shows the results of collective efforts that could have been "read" by subsequent visitors who then added their own material or graphic donations to existing accumulations. Similar social (or anti-social) expressions are seen in the "trash magnet" effect identified in public spaces by Richard Wilk and Michael Schiffer (1979) and in the private realms of object collection that enable individuals to create and sustain identity through the accumulation of material objects (Bianchi 1997).

In agriculturally sustained population centers, abundance became a distinguishing characteristic of social stratification as well as a marker of social cohesion. At the North American site of Cahokia, for example, the Mound 72 burial contained over 10,000 shell beads (Ambrose, Buikstra, and Krueger 2003:221). But at Cahokia we also see evidence for events that enabled larger and larger proportions of the community to participate in handling mass quantities of materials, such as the discarded remains of hundreds of carcasses and thousands of pots associated with feasting (Pauketat and Emerson 2007:112). At other chiefly sites as well, an increase in per capita portable objects was matched by an increase in the scale of built spaces meant to attract large numbers of people, indicative of labor investment in mound building and monumental architecture. In some cases, large architecture was intended to replicate domesticity on a grand scale (as seen in the Pacific Northwest; see Ames et al. 1992). In other cases, structures were intended to provide an altogether new type of architecture that had no analogue in ordinary domestic life but that represented social power through sheer size: Stonehenge, Göbekli Tepe, the menhirs of Atlantic France, and the moai of Easter Island.

The highest echelons of political authority demonstrated their power not only through hierarchical consumption but also through displays of magnanimity and largesse. Brian Hayden (1990) has suggested that one impetus for the development of agriculture was the desire of aggrandizers to generate sufficient food for feasts. And in countless texts of social authority, leaders portray themselves as generous with provisions to wealthy and poor alike. In Mesopotamia, iconography provided visual reminders of largesse in which "abundance [w]as the result of divine beneficence brokered by the state apparatus" (Winter 2007:117; for more abstract visual expressions of plenitude, see Porter 2011). Unlike household-level food storage, which was often meant to be private (cf. Bogaard et al. 2009), institutional storage facilities are meant to convey magnitude (e.g., Gremillion 2011:106–9). Central storehouses, such as the ones on Inca roads and in Cretan palaces, were physical manifestations of the *intent* of abundance in provisioning, even if those storehouses were never actually filled.

Political leaders could represent their symbolic control of abundance through intangibles such as ritual performances, song, dance, and music. Even "empty" spaces could reinforce leaders' association with plenitude when they created plazas and other open areas to accommodate large numbers of people as a metaphor of largesse materialized in architecture. Much of the plenitude of complex societies, however, consists of ordinary goods that were manufactured and used in mass quantities. The Roman world presents strikingly strong and well-studied evidence for mass-production, mass-consumption phenomena, ranging from the distinctive glossy redware pottery that is ubiquitous throughout the Mediterranean (Fulford and Durham 2013) to the 40 million discarded amphorae at the single Roman site of Monte Testaccio (Bailey 1965). Archaeologically investigated urban centers worldwide have similar levels of discards, and the producer-consumer interaction that resulted in these massive quantities of objects has left its traces throughout the landscape at kilns, metal furnaces, waste dumps, urban households, port sites, and shipwrecks that illustrate the volume of manufacturing and exchange.

DEFINITIONS

Scarcity, sufficiency, and abundance are relative and situational parameters, the exact boundaries of which are conditioned by individual perceptions and in comparison with the sum total of desired available materials. What might be sufficient food for one type of occasion (such as a routine family meal) might be insufficient for a feast with extended family and guests. What might be a shortage of manufactured items might become an oversupply when fashions or technological needs change. Nonetheless, some definitions serve to place abundance in the context of other relative assessments for comparison and analysis.

Scarcity in the physical realm results from both variability in distribution and the inherent qualities of particular phenomena relative to demand or need (see discussion in Smith 2012). For example, some geological elements are rare because they occur in limited areas, while some animals are rare because they have low reproduction rates, require large areas of territory, or have characteristics that limit their capacity to compete with other species. In human societies, scarcity can also be a constructed quality in which some individuals restrict access to otherwise plentiful supplies, whether through sumptuary laws or by elite decree. Enforced scarcity need not always be material; for example, restrictions on services, hairstyles, modes of speech, songs, or bodies of knowledge can also be enforced within a group and constitute markers of distinction. Scarcity can be universally perceived or relative: even when items are few in number, some individuals in a group may have large quantities of them.

The threshold of *sufficiency* cannot be abstracted to a single numerical value (e.g., "two of everything makes a household") but instead refers to context within a complete repertoire of individual and household possessions. Like scarcity, sufficiency is conditioned by both biological and social parameters; although there is a minimum biological threshold of viability with reference to calories and hydration, different sectors of society might well have varying assessments of what constitutes "sufficient" amounts of food and drink. Unexpectedly large numbers within a repertoire may be a result of stockpiling relative to the frequency of manufacturing and loss rather than of the expectation of simultaneous use (see Varien and Potter 1997:196).

The notion of sufficiency applies to the lowest echelons of society as well as to the uppermost. An illustration is provided by the site of Cerén in El Salvador, where the study of three architecturally modest households showed the existence of a fairly standardized repertoire of objects: "an incensario, a celt, about five obsidian prismatic blades in use and another five in storage, a scraper, a macroblade, a mano and metate, a hammerstone, two to three donut stones, an antler tapiscador (maize husker), a few bone needles, a few lajas as portable grinding stones, and a few smoothing stones" (Sheets and Simmons 2002:180). While this repertoire can be keyed to the number of adult hands likely to be present in the living space, pottery at Cerén stands out as an object with what appears to be elevated numbers suggestive of culturally constructed ideals of sufficiency: "Each household had about a dozen or more polychrome serving vessels, a much larger number than we would have expected" (Sheets and Simmons 2002:181).

The archaeological record of numerically large quantities can be categorized by the term *abundance*, a value-neutral term that describes accumulations that are quantitatively large and/or diverse in their composition. A focus on abundance provides the opportunity to understand the dynamics of the "found" world and the "created" world of material culture interaction as consistent factors in societies at all levels of complexity. Abundance is a condition that can exist naturally through the repetitive appearance of both individual items (such as trees) and a diversity of interconnected biota (such as a forest with its trees, grasses, and animals). These diverse and plentiful locales represented resource zones that provided niches to which humans were attracted. As a mobile apex predator, humans' use of the surrounding landscape modified preexisting natural demographies, resulting in altered profiles of mortality as well as incremental effects on population sizes. Some slow-maturing species might have been initially abundant but dwindled under the pressure of human predation; some species might have been initially infrequent but encouraged through low-intensity practices of landscape management to produce greater and greater quantities (cf. B. Smith 2001). Human effects on the environment for the creation of new forms of materiality through artifact manufacture permitted a deliberate alteration of the natural world: craft manufacturing beyond the capacity of any individual to handle or use simultaneously and animal husbandry as a practice to bring control over natural processes of birth and death. Storage as a mechanism for the temporary or permanent accumulation of desired items enabled individuals and households to create abundance through the curation of windfalls and harvests, as well as through the incremental stockpiling of food, ornaments, and tools.

In urbanized societies and in territorially expansive states and empires, an increasing number of people and an increasing diversity of production strategies often resulted in increasing numbers and types of goods. Cities in particular are places where there is a higher diversity of goods and a more rapid turnover of styles compared to rural areas, with a resultant increase in discard frequency as items are replaced prior to the end of their uselife (Smith 2012). Strategies used at a household level for risk management and in support of community needs, such as storage, were scaled up by central agencies that commissioned extra-large vessels or constructed prominent warehouses and storerooms. Centralized authorities also influenced and exhorted increases in production through a variety of mechanisms, such as the forced movement of people for agricultural production (e.g., Kolata 2013), the sponsorship of irrigation works and other landesque capital (e.g., Shaw and Sutcliffe 2003), or the management of tax regimes and production quotas to guide the cumulative effect of household production (e.g., Sinopoli 2003). Recognized as "surplus" that could be put to political use (cf. Morehart and De Lucia 2015), the abundances that resulted from state-sponsored activities nonetheless were understood in the same cognitive context that had long shaped individual and household responses to the natural and social world.

CHAPTERS IN THIS VOLUME

The authors of this collection of chapters identify and analyze the effects of abundance throughout the spectrum of social complexity, ranging from forager societies through the most expansive historical empires. Their data sets illustrate the ways abundance can be documented in the archaeological record and the many crosscutting themes of analysis supported by an abundance perspective.

In focusing on the creation of hunter-gatherer wealth, María Nieves Zedeño examines northern North America starting ca. 1,100 years ago. At that time, climate, ecology, and demography resulted in optimal conditions for bison herds and their increasingly specialized human predators along the northern Rocky Mountain foothills. Researchers in Canada and the United States are mapping bison and people at large scales to determine landscape use, political boundaries, and the reach of interregional trade, as well as to re-conceptualize the relationships between bison abundance and organizational complexity. The material record of abundance among pre-contact bison-hunting societies on the northwestern Plains had both short-term and long-term impacts on social and political systems in which there was a dynamic relationship between bison and the generation of different kinds of wealth within the rhythms of everyday life.

Christopher R. Moore and Christopher W. Schmidt's chapter examines forager economies in eastern North America to consider the ways Archaic hunter-gatherers in the lower Ohio Valley experienced a "giving environment" and how this interpretation of the Archaic lifeworld contributes to more nuanced understandings of health, site use, and artifact distribution patterns. Explanations of Archaic settlement patterns often juxtapose these "rich" zones with areas that had fewer or less diverse (i.e., scarcer) resources, such that hunter-gatherers were either pushed out of these zones or pulled toward the resource-rich zones by changing climatic conditions. Moore and Schmidt instead argue that the material and biocultural records of Archaic peoples in this region indicate healthy populations and little to no evidence of scarcity in either subsistence resources or material goods.

Shifting to the analysis of prehistoric agricultural societies, Mark D. Varien, James M. Potter, and Tito E. Naranjo integrate archaeological and ethnographic perspectives in their examination of the American Southwest. This region has typically been viewed as a landscape of scarcity because of limited precipitation and relatively short growing seasons. Despite this view, Pueblo people have thrived in the region and have used a variety of social strategies to create circumstances of abundance through practices such as feasting associated with ceremonialism and community social organization. In contrast to other parts of the world, communal feasting in the northern Southwest involves common, everyday "abundant" resources—such as ceramic bowls, maize, and rabbits—rather than rare, valuable, or feasting-specific resources. Inhabitants also used bountiful intangibles such as innovations and repetition of motifs in the increasing elaboration of artifact assemblages associated with both feasting and daily domestic life, such as decorated serving bowls.

The challenges of early agricultural societies are examined from a different perspective by Katheryn C. Twiss and Amy Bogaard, who consider the circumstances that occur when agricultural and husbandry produce "bumper crops." They note that abundance may be a generally good thing, but in early agricultural societies the stochastic variation of food presents a variety of challenges. Individuals or groups who produce or acquire an abundance of resources must determine how to physically preserve and socially deploy that largesse while maintaining at least some appearance of equality and integration. They explore possible strategies for coping with resource abundances using the case study of Neolithic Çatalhöyük in central Anatolia, in which management strategies included concealment, dispersal within a production group, and distribution across broader segments of society.

Payson Sheets examines the integration of economies and social worlds among the Maya, where settlements ranged in size from isolated farming households through small and large villages to the large urban site of San Andres during the middle of the Classic period in El Salvador's Zapotitan Valley. Among these, he focuses on Cerén, buried by volcanic ash about AD 630. Although Cerén was a very small settlement, each Cerén household "overproduced" something for exchange with other households and thus avoided the need to be economically self-sufficient. Autonomy and the goal of abundance guided household-level decisions about production and consumption even as households engaged in communal activities. Local individuals were responsible for construction and maintenance of the *sacbe* (road), for example, but they had considerable discretion in how they achieved their goals within the parameters of cultural acceptability. Sheets's contribution illustrates the transitions whereby hierarchical sociopolitical configurations became increasingly apparent as societies became more complex and the fact that those hierarchies were integrated with daily life through household-level initiatives.

Traci Ardren evaluates abundance in the largest settlements of the Classic Maya period, with a focus on the site of Chunchucmil, which was located in an agriculturally marginal area but adjacent to a rich savannah. Archaeological studies of ancient Maya trade have long acknowledged the movement of products among different environmental zones as a cornerstone of Classic period economies. One of the most important circulations was between the long coastline of the Yucatan Peninsula and the many inland urban centers of the Classic period. In addition to the transportation of long-distance trade goods such as obsidian, traders moved savannah products including organic materials such as palm thatch and other often overlooked plant fiber technologies essential to household and political economies of the Classic northern lowlands. A consideration of the abundance of savannah resources provides a new perspective on initial settlement and eventual urban migrations to this unusual ancient center.

The relationship of natural resources and abundant manufactured goods is the focus of the contribution by Elizabeth Klarich, Abigail Levine, and Carol Schultze, who examine obsidian trade at the Andean sites of Pukara and Taraco. During the Middle and Late Formative periods (500 BC–AD 300), Taraco and Pukara became major centers in the northern Lake Titicaca Basin of Peru. Both sites imported obsidian from the Chivay source located 200 kilometers to the west. Although it is exotic to the basin, obsidian is ubiquitous in recently excavated contexts at both Taraco and Pukara, and its purposeful accumulation corresponds with increased investment in corporate architecture and supra-household food sharing. In addition, analysis of obsidian debitage indicates that "cavalier" craftspeople made few attempts to conserve or recycle obsidian during the preliminary stages of manufacture, a pattern that can be linked with resource abundance. The authors propose that this intentionally wasteful behavior further reflects the status of settlements as primary nodes in region-wide obsidian exchange networks.

Justin St. P. Walsh's chapter makes use of big-data approaches to archaeological science by examining the incremental and subtle links of ethnic groups as determined by the distribution of everyday wares in the ancient Greek Mediterranean world. Using more than 20,000 whole and fragmentary Greek vases from 233 sites, he employs ArcGIS to evaluate patterns that illustrate the presence of different networks of provisioning and consumption among different "Celtic" and "Iberian" ethnic groups in the areas now encompassed in the countries of Portugal, Spain, Italy, Switzerland, and France. Large-scale data analysis also illustrates the effects of agency, as ancient groups' adoption of Greek materials was a deliberate and strategic acquisition that cannot be predicted by simple economic criteria, such as distance to the source or the presence of easy trade routes.

Production, globalization, and distribution experienced accelerated integration through the process of colonialism. In considering the deliberate creation and local adoption of "excessive economies" in West Africa, François G. Richard proposes an alternative understanding of colonial practices as one that does not follow the standard narratives of elite control over property, production, economic surplus, and long-distance trade. In this region, the widespread availability of land combined with relatively small, mobile populations, resulting in a mosaic of consumption patterns in which conventional notions of dispossession, scarcity, and accumulation fall short of capturing the subtleties of political economy rooted in a broad ethos of abundance, such as collective ownership, horizontal redistribution, wealth in people/knowledge, and compositional forms of consumption for both wealthy and modest households. Using Bataille's concept of "general economy," which draws on ideas of excess, dissipation, waste, and sacrifice, Richard examines broad trends in the relationship among labor, wealth, and social power in northern Senegal during the past millennium and how these relationships were materialized in archaeological landscapes of local plenitude.

Manufacturing and distribution are prime signals of "globalized" trade activities that emerged numerous times in the pre-modern world, with one of the most spectacular examples that of the growth of Chinese porcelain trade starting ca. AD 1300, as seen in Stacey Pierson's chapter. For foreign consumers, the development of maritime trade from as early as the Tang dynasty ensured that they could acquire and use large quantities of Chinese porcelain. Throughout the subsequent Yuan, Ming, and Qing dynasties, porcelains were made in vast quantities at Jingdezhen for domestic and foreign consumption using large amounts of raw materials, labor, and energy. The evidence of abundance is visible today in the huge sherd heaps at imperial kilns, the textual records of vast orders for specific occasions, and the deforestation of entire areas of south China. Artisans and consumers engaged with porcelains that also included a visual dimension of plenitude through the often dense and repetitive decoration that can be seen from the fourteenth century onward.

CONCLUSION

Throughout the volume, the authors emphasize that abundance is not a passive condition but an actively managed component of individual and social interactions. The masses of artifacts evident at sites of many different time periods indicate that plenitude was the sought-after norm throughout human history and that the desire for and perception of abundance influenced the entire material spectrum, from production and distribution to consumption and discard. Abundance was an economic and political phenomenon, but it was also an aesthetic that was materialized in both tangible everyday goods and the performance of ritual. From the Paleolithic to the present, humans have responded to abundance by gravitating toward it and by creating it, resulting in a relationship to material culture in which "too much is not enough."

REFERENCES CITED

Allen, Susan. 2006. "Miniature and Model Vessels in Ancient Egypt." In *The Old Kingdom Art and Archaeology (Proceedings of the Conference Held in Prague, May 13–June 4, 2004)*, edited by Miroslav Bárta, 19–24. Prague: Czech Institute of Egyptology.

Ambrose, Stanley H., Jane Buikstra, and Harold W. Krueger. 2003. "Status and Gender Differences in Diet at Mound 72, Cahokia, Revealed by Isotopic Analysis of Bone." *Journal of Anthropological Archaeology* 22 (3): 217–26. http://dx.doi.org/10.1016/S0278 -4165(03)00036-9.

Ames, Kenneth M., Doria F. Raetz, Stephen Hamilton, and Christine McAfee. 1992. "Household Archaeology of a Southern Northwest Coast Plank House." *Journal of Field Archaeology* 19 (3): 275–90.

Bailey, D. M. 1965. "A Sherd with a Painted Inscription from Monte Testaccio in Rome." *British Museum Quarterly* 30 (1–2): 40–41. http://dx.doi.org/10.2307/4422919.

Bentley, R. Alexander, Nancy Tayles, Charles Higham, Colin Macpherson, and Tim C. Atkinson. 2007. "Shifting Gender Relations at Khok Phanom Di, Thailand: Isotopic Evidence from the Skeletons." *Current Anthropology* 48 (2): 301–14. http://dx.doi.org/10.1086/512987.

Bianchi, Marina. 1997. "Collecting as a Paradigm of Consumption." *Journal of Cultural Economics* 21 (4): 275–89. http://dx.doi.org/10.1023/A:1007457219775.

Bogaard, Amy, Michael Charles, Katheryn C. Twiss, Andrew Fairbairn, Nurcan Yalman, Dragana Filipović, G. Arzu Demirergi, Füsun Ertuğ, Nerissa Russell, and Jennifer Henecke. 2009. "Private Pantries and Celebrated Surplus: Storing and Sharing Food at Neolithic Çatalhöyük, Central Anatolia." *Antiquity* 83 (321): 649–68. http://dx.doi.org/10.1017/S0003598X00098896.

Bonacchi, Chiara, Andrew Bevan, Daniel Pett, Adi Keinan-Schoonbaert, Rachael Sparks, Jennifer Wexler, and Neil Wilkin. 2014. "Crowd-Sourced Archaeological Research: The MicroPasts Project." *Archaeology International* 17: 61–68. http://dx.doi.org/10.5334/ai.1705.

Carter, Tristan. 2007. "The Theatrics of Technology: Consuming Obsidian in the Early Cycladic Burial Arena." In *Rethinking Craft Specialization in Complex Societies: Archaeological Analyses of the Social Meaning of Production*, edited by Zachary X. Hruby and Rowan K. Flad, 88–107. Archeological Papers of the American Anthropological Association 17. Washington, DC: American Anthropological Association. http://dx.doi.org/10.1525/ap3a.2007.17.1.88.

Champion, Matthew. 2012. "The Medium Is the Message: Votive Devotional Imagery and Gift Giving amongst the Commonality in the Late Medieval Parish." *Peregrinations* 3 (4): 103–23.

Chapman, John. 2000. *Fragmentation in Archaeology: People, Places, and Broken Objects in the Prehistory of South Eastern Europe*. New York: Routledge.

Coupland, Gary, David Bilton, Terence Clark, Jerome S. Cybulski, Gay Frederick, Alyson Holland, Bryn Letham, and Gretchen Williams. 2016. "A Wealth of Beads: Evidence for Material Wealth–Based Inequality in the Salish Sea Region, 4000–3500 cal. BP." *American Antiquity* 81 (2): 294–315.

Fulford, Michael, and Emma Durham, eds. 2013. *Seeing Red: New Economic and Social Perspectives on Terra Sigillata*. London: Institute of Classical Studies, University of London.

Fuller, Dorian Q., and Ling Qin. 2009. "Water Management and Labour in the Origins and Dispersal of Asian Rice." *World Archaeology* 41 (1): 88–111. http://dx.doi.org/10.1080/00438240802668321.

Gates-Foster, Jennifer. 2012. "The Well-Remembered Path: Roadways and Cultural Memory in Ptolemaic and Roman Egypt." In *Highways, Byways, and Road Systems in the Pre-Modern World*, edited by Susan E. Alcock, John Bodel, and Richard J.A. Talbert, 202–21. Chichester: John Wiley and Sons. http://dx.doi.org/10.1002/9781118244326.ch10.

Gremillion, Kristin. 2011. *Ancestral Appetites: Food in Prehistory*. Cambridge: Cambridge University Press. http://dx.doi.org/10.1017/CBO9780511976353.

Groot, Maaike, and Daphne Lentjes. 2013. "Studying Subsistence and Surplus Production." In *Barely Surviving or More than Enough? The Environmental Archaeology of Subsistence, Specialisation and Surplus Food Production*, edited by Maiike Groot, Daphne Lentjes, and Jørn Zeiler, 7–27. Leiden: Sidestone.

Guerzoni, Guido, and Gabriele Troilo. 1998. "Silk Purses Out of Sows' Ears: Mass Rarefaction of Consumption and the Emerging Consumer-Collector." In *The Active Consumer: Novelty and Surprise in Consumer Choice*, edited by Marina Bianchi, 174–97. London: Routledge.

Haaland, Randi. 2007. "Porridge and Pot, Bread and Oven: Food Ways and Symbolism in Africa and the Near East from the Neolithic to the Present." *Cambridge Archaeological Journal* 17 (2): 165–82. http://dx.doi.org/10.1017/S0959774307000236.

Halstead, Paul, and John O'Shea. 1989. "Introduction: Cultural Responses to Risk and Uncertainty." In *Bad Year Economics: Cultural Responses to Risk and Uncertainty*, edited by Paul Halstead and John O'Shea, 1–7. Cambridge: Cambridge University Press. http://dx.doi.org/10.1017/CBO9780511521218.002.

Hartman, Gideon, Guy Bar-Oz, Ram Bouchnick, and Ronny Reich. 2013. "The Pilgrimage Economy of Early Roman Jerusalem (1st Century BCE–70 CE) Reconstructed from the $\delta15N$ and $\delta13C$ Values of Goat and Sheep Remains." *Journal of Archaeological Science* 40 (12): 4369–76. http://dx.doi.org/10.1016/j.jas.2013.07.001.

Hayden, Brian. 1990. "Nimrods, Piscators, Pluckers, and Planters: The Emergence of Food Production." *Journal of Anthropological Archaeology* 9 (1): 31–69. http://dx.doi.org/10.1016/0278-4165(90)90005-X.

Hodder, Ian. 2012. *Entangled: An Archaeology of the Relationships between Humans and Things*. Malden, MA: Wiley-Blackwell. http://dx.doi.org/10.1002/9781118241912.

Iyengar, Sheena. 2010. *The Art of Choosing*. New York: Twelve.

Karlin, C., and M. Julien. 1994. "Prehistoric Technology: A Cognitive Science?" In *The Ancient Mind: Elements of Cognitive Archaeology*, edited by Colin Renfrew and Ezra B.W. Zubrow, 152–64. Cambridge: Cambridge University Press. http://dx.doi.org/10.1017/CBO9780511598388.016.

Kintigh, Keith W., Jeffrey H. Altschulb, Mary C. Beaudry, Robert D. Drennan, Ann P. Kinzig, Timothy A. Kohler, W. Fredrick Limp, Herbert D.G. Maschner, William K.

Michener, Timothy R. Pauketat, Peter Peregrine, Jeremy A. Sabloff, Tony J. Wilkinson, Henry T. Wright, and Melinda A. Zeder. 2014. "Grand Challenges for Archaeology." *PNAS* 111 (3): 879–80. www.pnas.org/cgi/doi/10.1073/pnas.1324000111.

Klein, Richard. 2009. "Hominin Dispersals in the Old World." In *The Human Past*, edited by Chris Scarre, 84–123. New York: Thames and Hudson.

Kolata, Alan L. 2013. *Ancient Inca*. Cambridge: Cambridge University Press.

Kuman, Kathleen. 2014. "Oldowan Industrial Complex." In *Encyclopedia of Global Archaeology*, edited by Claire Smith, 5560–70. New York: Springer. http://dx.doi.org/10.1007/978-1-4419-0465-2_652.

Marshack, Alexander. 1990. "Early Hominid Symbol and Evolution of the Human Capacity." In *The Emergence of Modern Humans: An Archaeological Perspective*, edited by Paul Mellars, 457–98. Ithaca, NY: Cornell University Press.

Martin, Alex. 1998. "Organization of Semantic Knowledge and the Origin of Words in the Brain." In *The Origin and Diversification of Language*, edited by Nina G. Jablonski and Leslie C. Aiello, 69–88. Memoirs of the California Academy of Sciences 24. San Francisco: California Academy of Sciences.

Masquelier, Adeline. 1997. "Vectors of Witchcraft: Object Transactions and the Materialization of Memory in Niger." *Anthropological Quarterly* 70 (4): 187–98. http://dx.doi.org/10.2307/3317225.

McBrearty, Sally, and A. S. Brooks. 2000. "The Revolution That Wasn't: A New Interpretation of the Origin of Modern Human Behavior." *Journal of Human Evolution* 39 (5): 453–563. Medline:11102266 http://dx.doi.org/10.1006/jhev.2000.0435.

McNiven, Ian J. 2012. "Ritualized Middening Practices." *Journal of Archaeological Method and Theory* 20 (4): 552–87. http://dx.doi.org/10.1007/s10816-012-9130-y.

Miller, Daniel. 1985. *Artefacts as Categories*. Cambridge: Cambridge University Press.

Moore, Christopher R., and Victor D. Thompson. 2012. "Animism and Green River Persistent Places: A Dwelling Perspective of the Shell Mound Archaic." *Journal of Social Archaeology* 12 (2): 264–84. http://dx.doi.org/10.1177/1469605311431518.

Morehart, Christopher T., and Kristin De Lucia, eds. 2015. *Surplus: The Politics of Production and the Strategies of Everyday Life*. Boulder: University Press of Colorado. http://dx.doi.org/10.5876/9781607323808.

Oka, Rahul, and Ian Kuijt. 2014. "Introducing an Inquiry into the Social Economies of Greed and Excess." *Economic Anthropology* 1: 1–16.

Olsen, Sandra L. 2010. "Response to Pat Shipman: The Animal Connection and Human Evolution." *Current Anthropology* 51 (4): 528–29.

Osborne, Robin. 2004. "Hoards, Votives, Offerings: The Archaeology of the Dedicated Object." *World Archaeology* 36 (1): 1–10. http://dx.doi.org/10.1080/0043824042000192696.

Pauketat, Timothy R., and Thomas E. Emerson. 2007. "Alternative Civilizations: Heterarchies, Corporate Polities, and Orthodoxies." In *Hierarchy and Power in the History of Civilizations Third International Conference Selected Papers*, 107–17. Moscow: Center for Civilizational and Regional Studies of the RAS.

Pauw, Anton. 2013. "Can Pollination Niches Facilitate Plant Coexistence?" *Trends in Ecology and Evolution* 28 (1): 30–37. Medline:22951227 http://dx.doi.org/10.1016/j.tree.2012.07.019.

Peterson, Christian A., and Robert D. Drennan. 2012. "Patterned Variation in Regional Trajectories of Community Growth." In *The Comparative Archaeology of Complex Societies*, edited by Michael E. Smith, 88–137. Cambridge: Cambridge University Press.

Porter, Benjamin W. 2011. "Feeding the Community: Objects, Scarcity and Commensality in the Early Iron Age Southern Levant." *Journal of Mediterranean Archaeology* 24 (1): 27–54. http://dx.doi.org/10.1558/jmea.v24i1.27.

Rajan, K. 2008. "Situating the Beginning of Early Historic Times in Tamil Nadu: Some Issues and Reflections." *Social Scientist* 36 (1–2): 40–78.

Renfrew, Colin. 2001. "Symbol before Concept: Material Engagement and the Early Development of Society." In *Archaeological Theory Today*, edited by Ian Hodder, 122–40. Cambridge: Polity.

Schiffer, Michael B. 1992. *Technological Perspectives on Behavioral Change*. Tucson: University of Arizona Press.

Shaw, Julia, and John Sutcliffe. 2003. "Water Management, Patronage Networks and Religious Change: New Evidence from the Sanchi Dam Complex and Counterparts in Gujarat and Sri Lanka." *South Asian Studies* 19 (1): 73–104. http://dx.doi.org/10.1080/02666030.2003.9628622.

Sheets, Payson, and Scott E. Simmons. 2002. "Household Production and Specialization at Cerén." In *Before the Volcano Erupted: The Ancient Cerén Village in Central America*, edited by Payson Sheets, 178–83. Austin: University of Texas Press.

Shipman, Pat. 2010. "The Animal Connection and Human Evolution." *Current Anthropology* 51 (4): 519–38. http://dx.doi.org/10.1086/653816.

Silverstein, Michael J., and Neil Fiske, with John Butman. 2005. *Trading Up: Why Consumers Want New Luxury Goods–and How Companies Create Them*, revised ed. New York: Portfolio.

Sinopoli, Carla M. 2003. *The Political Economy of Craft Production*. Cambridge: Cambridge University Press. http://dx.doi.org/10.1017/CBO9780511489648.

Smith, Bruce D. 2001. "Low-Level Food Production." *Journal of Archaeological Research* 9 (1): 1–43. http://dx.doi.org/10.1023/A:1009436110049.

Smith, Monica L. 2012. "Seeking Abundance: Consumption as a Motivating Factor in Cities Past and Present." *Research in Economic Anthropology* 32: 27–51. http://dx.doi.org/10.1108/S0190-1281(2012)0000032006.

Smith, Monica L. 2014. "Citizen Science in Archaeology." *American Antiquity* 79 (4): 749–62. http://dx.doi.org/10.7183/0002-7316.79.4.749749.

Smith, Monica L. 2015. "Feasts and Their Failures." *Journal of Archaeological Method and Theory* 22 (4): 1215–37. http://dx.doi.org/10.1007/s10816-014-9222-y.

Soffer, Olga. 1985. "Patterns of Intensification as Seen from the Upper Paleolithic of the Central Russian Plain." In *Prehistoric Hunter-Gatherers: The Emergence of Cultural Complexity*, edited by T. Douglas Price and James A. Brown, 235–70. Orlando: Academic. http://dx.doi.org/10.1016/B978-0-12-564750-2.50014-7.

Stiles, Daniel. 1991. "Early Hominid Behaviour and Culture Tradition: Raw Material Studies in Bed II, Olduvai Gorge." *African Archaeological Review* 9 (1): 1–19. http://dx.doi.org/10.1007/BF01117214.

Stiner, Mary C. 2014. "Finding a Common Bandwidth: Causes of Convergence and Diversity in Paleolithic Beads." *Biological Theory* 9 (1): 51–64. http://dx.doi.org/10.1007/s13752-013-0157-4.

Sullivan, Brian L., Joceyln L. Aycrigg, Jessie H. Barry, Rick E. Bonney, Nicholas Bruns, Caren B. Cooper, Theo Damoulas, André A. Dhondt, Tom Dietterich, Andrew Farnsworth, et al. 2014. "The eBird Enterprise: An Integrated Approach to Development and Application of Citizen Science." *Biological Conservation* 169: 31–40.

Varien, Mark D., and James M. Potter. 1997. "Unpacking the Discard Equation: Simulating the Accumulation of Artifacts in the Archaeological Record." *American Antiquity* 62 (2): 194–213. http://dx.doi.org/10.2307/282506.

Veblen, Thorstein. 1899. *Theory of the Leisure Class: An Economic Study in the Evolution of Institutions*. New York: Macmillan.

Waguespack, Nicole M., and Todd A. Surovell. 2003. "Clovis Hunting Strategies, or How to Make Out on Plentiful Resources." *American Antiquity* 68 (2): 333–52. http://dx.doi.org/10.2307/3557083.

White, Joyce C., and Elizabeth G. Hamilton. 2014. "The Transmission of Early Bronze Technology to Thailand: New Perspectives." In *Archaeometallurgy in Global Perspective*, edited by Benjamin W. Roberts and Christopher P. Thornton, 805–52. New York: Springer. http://dx.doi.org/10.1007/978-1-4614-9017-3_28.

Wilk, Richard. 2014. "Poverty and Excess in Binge Economies." *Economic Anthropology* 1: 66–79.

Wilk, Richard, and Michael B. Schiffer. 1979. "The Archaeology of Vacant Lots in Tucson, Arizona." *American Antiquity* 44 (3): 530–36. http://dx.doi.org/10.2307/279551.

Winter, Irene J. 2007. "Representing Abundance: A Visual Dimension of the Agrarian State." In *Settlement and Society: Essays Dedicated to Robert McCormick Adams*, edited by Elizabeth C. Stone, 117–38. Los Angeles: Cotsen Institute of Archaeology.

Zedeño, María Nieves. 2009. "Animating by Association: Index Objects and Relational Taxonomies." *Cambridge Archaeological Journal* 19 (3): 407–17. http://dx.doi.org/10 .1017/S0959774309000596.

Zeder, Melinda A. 2012. "The Broad Spectrum Revolution at 40: Resource Diversity, Intensification, and an Alternative to Optimal Foraging Explanations." *Journal of Anthropological Archaeology* 31 (3): 241–64. http://dx.doi.org/10.1016/j.jaa.2012.03.003.

2

Rethinking the Impact of Abundance on the Rhythm of Bison Hunter Societies

María Nieves Zedeño

Hear now, you Chief of Mountains, you who stand foremost: listen, I say, to the mourning of the people. Now are the days truly become evil and are not as they were in ancient times. But you know. You have seen the days. Under your fallen garments the years are buried. Then were the days full of joy, for the buffalo covered the prairie, and the people were content. Warm dwellings had they then, soft robes for coverings, and feasting was without end.

    Blackfoot Prayer, J. W. Schultz (Grinnell 1887:442)

In the northern Plains, bison hunter archaeology is about bone and stone; it generally lacks conventional indicators of abundance and economic differentiation, such as grave offerings, exotic or elaborate objects, or housewares other than food-processing tools. Yet careful scrutiny of the archaeological record through the light of historical accounts and early ethnographies (e.g., Schultz 1962) reveals that hunters of the last millennium had access to immense supplies of bison meat, grease, and hide. Late Prehistoric period (AD 1000–1750) bison-hunting complexes considered ancestral to the Blackfoot speakers cover vast stretches of upland prairie along the Rocky Mountain Front, often terminating above meters-thick layers of butchered bone (Kornfeld, Frison, and Larson 2010; Peck 2011). Processing sites associated with these bone beds contain the remains of dozens of cooking fires (perhaps hundreds in some localities; Brink 2008). Likewise, camp-sites dating to this period also contain large numbers of stone structures that were

DOI: 10.5876/9781607325949.c002

the foundation of bison hide tents known as tipis. Memorial monuments and stone effigies are found alone or interspersed with the more mundane hunting, processing, and living spaces (Brace 2005; Brumley 1988; Kehoe and Kehoe 1959, 1979; Mirau 1995; Vickers and Peck 2009).

Many of these sites may have been erected earlier than AD 1000; however, social and ecological conditions of the Late Prehistoric period were ripe for production specialization, economic intensification, and the development of mechanisms of integration and differentiation among bison hunter groups (Reher and Frison 1983). Investment in landscape modifications that mark these historical processes, particularly the size and density of hunting and domestic sites, can be seen from southern Alberta to central Montana, extending east into Saskatchewan (figure 2.1) (e.g., Aaberg, Crofutt, and Green 2009; Brink 2008; Carlson 2011; Cooper 2008; Fawcett 1987; Kehoe 1960, 1967; Kehoe and Eynman 1973; Kennedy and Reeves 2013; Peck 2011; Zedeño, Ballenger, and Murray 2014). Such investment was, at least in part, encouraged by unparalleled opportunities to engage in robust trade with tribes near and far, providing specialized hunters with the opportunity to acquire goods of recognized prestige or value as well as starch-rich staples such as roasted tubers and corn in exchange for bison (Binnema 2004; Brink and Dawe 1989; Schultz and Donaldson 1930; Zarrillo and Kooyman 2006).

Indicators of status and wealth, including elk tusks and *Dentalia* shell, often depicted in portrait paintings by George Catlin (Catlin, Dippie, and Gurney 2002) and Karl Bodmer (Wood, Potter, and Hunt 2007) as well as in countless photographs, attest to the importance of wealth accumulation through trade with western tribes and the social prestige associated with its display (figure 2.2). After 1730, horses and people—particularly women—were captured (e.g., Keyser, Sundstrom, and Poetschat 2006) and purchased or sold at known regional centers, notably the Dalles of the Columbia River (Ruby and Brown 1993). Ceremonial items, too, could be obtained through trade: red-stone pipes (present in archaeological contexts, e.g., Zedeño, Ballenger, and Murray 2014), woven bags and pouches used to keep bundle contents (Scriver 1990:196, 220, 235), medicinal roots, and certain animal parts were the more durable goods; less tangible things, such as esoteric knowledge that accompanied ceremonial items and medicines, could travel among individuals and groups across considerable distances (McClintock 1999; Wissler and Duvall 1912).

Each of the goods just enumerated signifies a given trajectory toward the accumulation of valuables that can be identified as economic wealth. Using northern Plains historical and ethnographic evidence of the manipulation of goods and valuables—notably painted tipi hides, bundles, pipes, and items of personal adornment—as reference, I explore the relationships between those economic pursuits

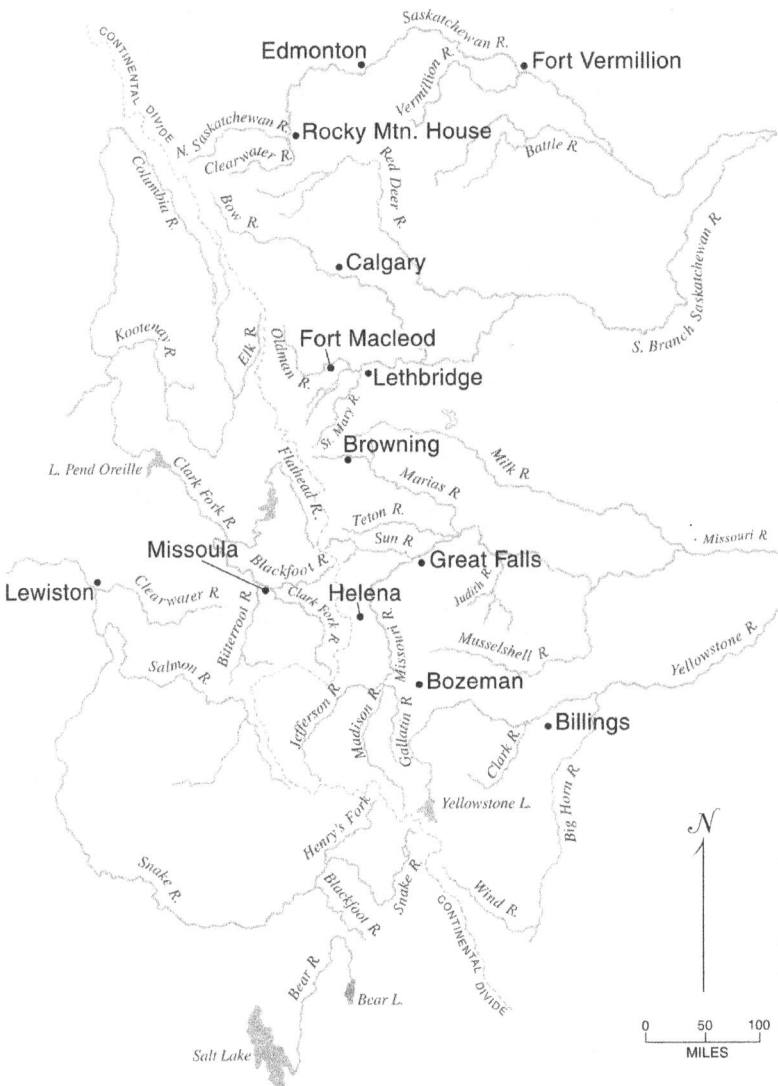

FIGURE 2.1. Blackfoot Aboriginal territory and hunting range (after Jackson 2000).

and the acquisition of social, political, and spiritual power by individuals and corporate groups. The goal is to illustrate how, under conditions of ecological abundance and promising intergroup relationships, tangible and intangible goods could be accumulated by mobile hunters and manipulated in the quest for prosperity.

FIGURE 2.2. Kills Inside. Photo by Edward S. Curtis, 1926. *Courtesy*, Museum of Photographic Arts.

ABUNDANCE AND BISON WEALTH

Abundance can be characterized as the product of three interrelated processes associated with supply and demand. First, abundance may result from securing direct and dependable access to quantities of a desired resource and to the requisite means of extraction. Second, abundance may also derive from the capacity to transform accessible resources into valuables, where a resource's value is measured by its capacity to bring economic gain, social prestige, or spiritual power. And third, abundance may arise from the possession of knowledge or resources that others want badly. Value, in contrast, hinges on people's ability to manipulate perception about an object or resource.

Among the ancestral Blackfoot hunters of the northwestern Plains (Old Women's phase, AD 1000–1750), abundance resulted not only from access to bison but also from the ability to process enormous quantities of meat into lightweight, nutritious, and durable pemmican that could be transported over long distances (Brink 2008; Verbicky-Todd 1984).

Social networks with close and distant groups were key to Blackfoot prosperity, not only during the Prehistoric period but also, perhaps even more so, during the Historic period. For decades, North American archaeologists have followed Braun and Plog's (1980) seminal argument that tribal social networks evolved to buffer uncertainty and scarcity (e.g., Borck et al. 2015). We have paid far less attention to the role of social networks during times of abundance. The mobile Blackfoot maintained contact with people from the Northwest as well as those living downstream on the Missouri River and south along the Rocky Mountains; they could mobilize bison by-products as well as other valuables across this vast area. These networks were furthermore a key to the success of the trade in European goods, notably horses (Mitchell 2013; Wood and Thiessen 1985). In times when fresh bison meat was scarce, the Blackfoot could fall back on stored pemmican and dried meat as well as on the trade in durable goods, such as feathers, paint, and bison hides, that brought in starchy foods. Beyond commodity trade, their ritual system allowed for the distribution of resources among the less prosperous, thus providing temporary relief during hard times. The ritual system was effective in generating valuables well beyond staples as well as promoting or relieving social scarcity.

To procure large quantities of meat, hunters built numerous driveline systems in strategic localities to kill dozens of animals at once. For instance, driveline systems dating to the Old Women's phase in the Two Medicine River Valley, north-central Montana, were built in clusters at evenly spaced locations and facing one another across the valley to maximize the opportunity for success. Hunting sites often had more than one terminus (a "jump"), each with a pair of drivelines; the resulting investment can be measured in square kilometers containing thousands of individual stone features (Zedeño, Ballenger, and Murray 2014). Carcass processing had to be addressed quickly because bisons' body temperature is high and the hide is very thick; thus, there was a risk of losing the hunt to decomposition even in winter. Given the size and number of bison killed in communal hunts and the weight of meat and fresh hides, a large labor pool composed of men, women, and able children was needed to clean the carcasses, dry and pound or roast the meat, break long bones and boil them to render fat, gather berries for pemmican, and clean and dress hides (Brink 2008; Quigg 1997). A magnetic survey performed on the Kutoyis processing site in Montana revealed a dense distribution of heat features covering the floodplain below the kill site; excavations uncovered extensive evidence of bone processing, meat roasting, pounding, and fat rendering (Bethke et al. 2016).

Campsites dating to this period are commensurately large. Along the Rocky Mountain Front, where wintering grounds were located, it is not uncommon to find campsites containing hundreds of structures. From contact period accounts (e.g., Haig 1991), it is possible to estimate an average of 6–8 people per structure. Surely, some of these structures were not strictly contemporaneous; however, even a small occupation (30–40 tipis) could have housed a minimum of 150–200 people. These estimates accord well with demographic data from early ethnographers that reported the size of historic Blackfoot bands at 100–500 people each, with the Pikani, or Missouri River Blackfoot, the most numerous (Schaeffer and Schaeffer 1934). An important ceremony, such as the Okan or Blackfoot Sun Dance, or a very large hunt could bring various bands together in gatherings of more than 100 pitched tipis and, in Schultz's (1962:30) personal experience, as many as 400.

How did Old Women's phase hunters manage to feed their numbers and produce a surplus for storage and exchange? In the northwestern Plains, the environmental conditions of the period known as the Little Ice Age (ca. AD 1250–1850) promoted grassland expansion that attracted bison herds toward the Rocky Mountain foothills (Cooper 2008; Peck 2004). Nature was aided to an extent by human grassland management. It has long been accepted that bison hunters used fire on the prairie to both enhance the growth of nutritious grasses and manipulate game (Boyd 2002; Oetelaar 2014). Yet direct evidence of anthropogenic fires is difficult to obtain. Nevertheless, the geomorphology and radiocarbon columns of paleofires along the Two Medicine River Valley clearly show that a regular fire regime and concomitant post-fire erosion episodes began at the time the valley was colonized by specialized bison hunters (~AD 1200), were especially pronounced during the height of valley-wide occupation (~AD 1350–1650), and ended with the decommissioning of communal hunting facilities (~AD 1850) (Roos, Zedeño, and Hollenback 2014).

Management by fire strongly suggests that people expected to return to areas they had previously burned. Through the construction of permanent hunting facilities and implementation of fire regimes, hunters structured opportunities for future success. Contact period fur trader Peter Fidler, who traveled with Blackfoot hunters in 1796 (Haig 1991), noted that the Blackfoot knew where bison jumps were located all across their territory so they could hunt anywhere while traveling alone or during seasonal moves. However, he also noted that bison hunting implied, at least to the untrained eyes of the fur trader, a regimen of feast or famine (cf. Varien, Potter, and Naranjo, this volume). Bison move very fast, and there were days when none could be located or successfully driven to their deaths. But the brief historical observations do not represent as accurately as does archaeology the longevity and significance of bison procurement by increasingly large groups.

As Gremillion (2011:93) notes, controlling access to staple resources by a sector of the group promotes social differentiation and differential wealth accumulation; this was not the case among bison hunters. Communal hunting complexes, located in bison wintering grounds, were owned by the band. Tools and weapons were individually owned. However, access to bison products was not socially restricted; hunters each took a share of meat, hides, and fat to feed their families, and the elderly or weak also received their share in times of abundance or scarcity (Verbicky-Todd 1984). Yet from contact period accounts it is known that among the Blackfoot, control over ritual means of production was a source of upward social mobility (Tyrell 1916). Within the hunters' ritual system, valuables could be created and manipulated not only to propitiate the group's success and well-being but also to achieve prestige, which could potentially translate into economic wealth.

VALUE AND RITUAL WEALTH

The performance of rituals aimed at propitiating game fertility, predicting the location of herds, and ensuring hunting success is a central part of aboriginal societies worldwide. In North America, value systems anchored in the animal world of temperate latitudes are clearly visible in Late Archaic societies 3,000 years ago, although components of these systems date as far back as the Paleoindian period (Bement 1999; Claassen 2010). In the northwestern Plains these developments are characterized by stone architecture (monuments or "medicine wheels"), as well as the use of red ocher, pipes, tobacco, and possibly of sacred bundles containing animal bodies and parts. The Beaver Bundle, which contains the essential components of the Blackfoot landscape (Lokensgaard 2010), may date as early as the Archaic period, but this date has not been confirmed. This bundle is at the core of Blackfoot identity and territory and thus may relate to the group's ethnogenesis.

Other than red ochre used to consecrate objects and people, a singular manifestation of bison-specific rituals in the northern Plains is the use of ammonites and novaculites that the Blackfoot call Iniskim, or buffalo stones (Peck 2002; Reeves 1993). Iniskim, most commonly associated with Old Women's phase sites (Peck 2002), are imbued with diverse forms of power. Oral traditions and practices recorded by early ethnographers, most notably Duvall (1908), indicate that these fossils had the power to charm bison, to call in a favorable wind speed when needed, and to aid in divination. Iniskim are an indispensable component of the Beaver Bundle and, in turn, the Beaver Bundle is indispensable to the bison-calling rituals (McClintock 1999; Wissler and Duvall 1912).

Iniskim are commonly found in the upper Cretaceous formations that extend across the northern Plains; among the Blackfoot, individuals keep them as amulets even though their owners might not be familiar with all the rituals associated with them. But in the past the possession and use of Iniskim was mostly restricted to certain individuals who owned ceremonial bundles or who had the right to carry them in their personal war bundles and medicine bundles. People were instructed to turn in Iniskim they found to the appropriate bundle holder. For Iniskim to achieve their true power, they had to be animated with red ocher, and this was also done by a bundle holder. Painted Iniskim could also be given as gifts (Duvall 1908; Schaeffer and Schaeffer 1934; Wissler and Duvall 1912).

Another critical aspect of the hunt—rights to bow-and-arrow making—was also imbued with sacred origins and ritual and belonged in certain bundles (Duvall 1908). The origins of the bow and arrow belong in the Star Stories complex; these stories tell how the culture hero Scarface received the gift of a bow and arrow during his journey to the Sun. Star Stories are closely associated with Blackfoot ethnogenesis and contain ancient social mores held by the group. The special significance of the bow and arrow carried on into modern times, as a set was kept in the Thunder Medicine Pipe Bundle that belonged to the late Blackfeet elder Iron Pipe (J. R. Murray, personal communication, 2013).

Rights to use Iniskim for magical purposes, to hold bundles, to possess and paint tipis, and to paint objects and people in ceremonial contexts were achieved, first and foremost, through individual dreams and visions in which the visionaries made an alliance with the spirits and obtained their instructions. It was through these individual visions that certain institutions, including bundles, painted lodges, group ceremonies, and secret societies, originally emerged (Duvall 1908; Wissler and Duvall 1912). Through the suffering individuals undertook in their quests, they also acquired rights to particular objects and liturgical orders and practices. Sanctions against emulators were severe, and transgression could cause illness, disgrace, and even death (McClintock 1999:217). Thus, the social pressures to respect the rights of others kept ritual knowledge in the hands of the few; however, there was some opportunity to obtain such rights through formal transfers.

An individual made a vow to a bundle holder or any other owner of ritual knowledge and objects to care for these valuables and to abide by the rules that accompanied them (McClintock 1999). He or she brought gifts to demonstrate the seriousness of the vow; if this was accepted, then a date was set for the transfer and a method of payment. Depending on the antiquity and power of what was being transferred, payment was made in horses, guns, blankets, feathers, hides, money, or anything the holder desired. Today, the transfer of a powerful pipe can fetch as much as $5,000, and the new holders must also acquire many other objects that go into the pipe bundle. For his or her part, the holder was enriched not only by the gifts and payment but also by the spiritual power and prestige acquired from this transfer. Valuable liturgical and practical knowledge about rituals associated with the transferred bundle was retained, even though the specific bundle ceremonies could no longer be performed. The holder could then obtain new rights to sacred things through visions or transfers, thus expanding his or her ability to accumulate ritual wealth.

In Lokensgaard's (2010) view, Blackfoot bundles circulated as gifts in the classic anthropological sense of the term; they only became commodities in the eyes of white men. I think the value system associated with formal transfers is more reminiscent of Weiner's (1992) "inalienable possession." Inalienable possessions circulate in a paradoxical context, in which the holder simultaneously keeps at least a portion of this wealth and gives it away. I use the term *wealth* because this system enriches the original holder in three ways: through spiritual power accumulated while holding rights to the bundle, the social prestige incurred through the transfer, and the economic wealth collected as payment. To be sure, bundle holders and powerful individuals also had numerous obligations toward the community; but they had a privileged place in society.

Yet another important aspect of the Blackfoot value system was the possibility to participate in multiple facets of ceremonialism at once. In addition to bundles, notably the Beaver Bundle and several pipe bundles, individuals could own the rights to painted lodges. The designs on painted tipis were exclusive to the owner and could not be copied. Further, they could not be painted without the owner having first acquired the design from the spirits or through a formal transfer (McClintock 1999:217). These tipis could also be inherited within the family. Some designs were so powerful that they could be found repeated through generations—there was no stipulation as to the uniqueness of a vision or a spirit helper. Thunder lodges, for example, recurred through time, but each design was unique.

Among the myriad tipi designs recorded over the centuries, the most closely associated with the bison hunt were the Crow, Black Buffalo, and Yellow Buffalo Lodges. Duvall (1908) and Hellson (n.d.) recorded the most detailed information about their origin and role in bison hunting. Two men obtained the designs from the underwater people. The Black Buffalo Lodge owner also possessed the Iniskim bundle, and members of the community generally returned the Iniskim they came across to this person. Each lodge had its special altar and bundle. The Black and Yellow Buffalo Lodges were pitched near the bison drivelines to perform bison-calling rituals.

McClintock (1999) once recorded that only 35 painted lodges could be found in an Okan camp of 350 tipis; thus, only about 10 percent of the aggregated Blackfoot population actually owned them. Painted lodges advertised their owners' spiritual power. They were generally associated with chiefs and medicine men who, in turn, could hold other bundles or take membership in esoteric societies. Bundle owners, too, advertised their power by exhibiting their bundles to the Sun. An outsider, such as Schultz (1962:30), could easily recognize who the chiefs were by looking at

FIGURE 2.3. Blackfoot painted tipi with bundles exposed to the sun. *Courtesy*, Glenbow Museum, na-668-11, Calgary, AB.

the painted tipis or the bundles hanging from tripods outside the tipis (figure 2.3). I suggest that this outward expression of connection with the spirits was a form of aggrandizing and securing a prominent place in society. Archaeological expressions of aggrandizing included the "death lodge" monuments, which were built on the lodge of a prominent individual after death by erecting radiating stone lines from the ring, each line pointing to a great deed. Individuals who thought highly of themselves were also known to have built their own monuments (Dempsey 1956; Kehoe 1954).

Esoteric societies with exclusive and expensive membership contributed their own elements to the value system. These corporate institutions, common across the Great Plains, had unique expressions among the Blackfoot. Of interest here are those societies that had a direct impact on communal bison hunting: the Matoki, or Buffalo Women, Society, and the Old Bull, or Bull Chaser, Society (Duvall 1908; Wissler 1916). The origin of these societies, particularly the Matoki, has not been revealed to outsiders. The Bull Chaser Society, according to Duvall (1908), was established soon after a Blackfoot woman received the revelation of the Iniskim. Regardless of their origins, societies were already in place by first contact (Tyrell 1916). These institutions controlled the hunt insofar as they co-opted ritual knowledge associated with bison fertility and calling rituals, driveline construction, use of fire in the hunt, and corral construction, among many other aspects of social life (Zedeño, Ballenger, and Murray 2014).

The societies regulated large-scale communal hunts that took place in the cold months of the year, as well as the seasonal moves to and from wintering grounds. I further suggest that societies likely neutralized the political power of individual aggrandizers by focusing on organizational areas that served the common good. As Friesen (2007) notes, dynamic tensions among individuals and corporate organizations are common in junctures of emerging complexity where the society as a whole struggles to maintain an appearance of equality in the face of conditions that favor differentiation and unequal accumulation of wealth. Blackfoot esoteric societies were geopolitically integrative, in that their membership crosscut bands and divisions scattered across a huge territory while at the same time fostering and perpetuating social and economic differences within bands. Society members could also accumulate wealth and prestige by individually procuring ritual and healing "services" or transferring their membership to another.

Thus, it becomes clear how each element of the value system played a given role in a given context but was not necessarily limited to a single role; the Iniskim and Beaver Bundles were also significant in the tobacco-planting ceremony, as were the pipe bundles (Duvall 1908). The pipe bundles, in turn, were brought into society ceremonies. Each of these bundles interacted with painted lodges and their own bundles. Yet it was the communal bison hunt that brought all valuables into the center of society, illustrating the dialectical relationship of socially induced scarcity to natural abundance.

WEALTH AND TRADE

People around the world regard trade and exchange of goods as the glue that binds society together. *Good* is an inclusive term that denotes tangible and intangible things, such as natural resources, manufactured objects, knowledge, and services. Just as goods are diverse, so are the mechanisms and rationales that circulate them. Throughout the twentieth century, anthropologists dwelled on the differences between gift and commodity exchange. They divided goods according to two general mechanisms of circulation: gift and commodity (e.g., Appadurai 1986; Bird-David 1990; Godelier 1999; Gregory 1982). Gifts are typically circulated in social trade networks, in which the social capital associated with reciprocal good exchange is more valuable than the good itself. Commodities, in contrast, circulate in a market economy where the main goal is not to attain prestige or fulfill a social obligation but to incur economic gain.

Clearly, gift and commodity are essentialized categories that mask a huge range of circulation mechanisms. These categories also obscure the various roles certain goods may play in any given trade community. There are fundamental differences between gifts and commodities, on the one hand, and inalienable possessions, on the other. The most significant difference is that gifts and commodities are consumed as they change hands (in other words, they are lost to the giver), whereas inalienable possessions are conserved or even multiplied in the act of exchange (kept by the giver). Furthermore, inalienable possessions, such as esoteric knowledge associated with craft production, are transferred within closed learning systems (Hollenback 2012). Gifts, commodities, and inalienables often coexist and can be circulated simultaneously within a single network. Research on the cultural significance of birds, bird parts, and bird knowledge among several Missouri River tribes, for example, suggests that these categories are not mutually exclusive (Zedeño, Murray, and Chandler 2014).

Bundles, as Lokensgaard (2010) and I (Zedeño 2008) explain, are regarded as non-human persons, capable of social interaction and able to exert influence on their holders and other people. As persons, bundles are inalienable possessions in one sense, although they also circulate as gifts, albeit within very strict rules. Yet a deeper analysis of all the components of bundles reveals that these, too, are complex things whose parts have different biographies, roles, and exchangeable potential. For example, the Blackfoot regard ritual knowledge (songs, protocols, origin stories, and social sanctions associated with a bundle) as inalienable; as long as people retain this knowledge, tangible things that are lost, destroyed, gifted, or exchanged can always be replaced.

Particular objects have more or less value depending on their origin and life histories; for example, the Long Time Pipe has been passed on for untold generations (McClintock 1999:427). But others could be acquired, if needed, and then consecrated. Components in a bundle (e.g., certain animal skins and woven bags) could be purchased without ceremony. Other items had to be collected by the bundle holder; sometimes they, too, could be purchased. Thus, there is a continuum between inalienable possession and commodity that essentialized categories cannot fully encompass. Inomata (2013) suggests that true inalienable possessions are so difficult to demonstrate that only through a close examination of the roles and life histories of tangible and intangible things can they be truly identified. A discussion of interregional trade in the prehistoric and historic periods may further clarify this point within the context of abundance.

Specialized bison hunters and farmers were involved in the systematic extraction, modification, and exchange of knowledge and goods, interacting under comparable valuation systems and mechanisms of social control (Mitchell 2013; Wood and Thiessen 1985). Running from the Rocky Mountains to the Mississippi, the Missouri River was an avenue of movement that played a pivotal role in the peopling of the Plains and in the evolution of economic and social networks across and

beyond the Plains. Long-distance connections between Plains and eastern societies are insinuated in the archaeological record of the Middle Precontact, or Plains
Woodland, period (Brink and Dawe 1989), flourishing during the last millennium
before present.

In addition to the expansion of bison in the northwestern Plains during the
Little Ice Age, one major event marked the expansion of Late Prehistoric economic networks in the region: the abandonment of Cahokia after AD 1300. It is
difficult not to see the domino effect of this event, as the resultant diaspora altered
the demographic structure of prairie societies linked directly or indirectly to the
Mississippian polity and stimulated the formation of ancestral Mandan farming
communities on the Middle Missouri River (Fenn 2014; Mitchell 2013). Given the
subsequent close contact between Middle Missouri and northwestern Plains populations (Binnema 2004; Walde 2006), Blackfoot ancestors colonized and occupied
valleys previously occupied only sporadically. As noted earlier, this colonization can
be seen in the impact of anthropogenic fires on valleys where intensive hunting
took place.

By the fifteenth century, Mandan and Blackfoot ancestors had developed successful means to manage the production of staples: the Mandan by nucleating near
the best farmland and the Blackfoot by building large-scale communal hunting
complexes in bison wintering grounds located on the same upper tributaries of the
Missouri River as the ones just described. Both the Mandan and Blackfoot were cultivating corn and harvesting bison above their subsistence needs. With abundance
came challenges, opportunities, and responsibilities (see also Twiss and Bogaard,
this volume). Middle Missouri enclaves were living among the Blackfoot in the
Protohistoric period, indicating a close relationship between the two groups (Peck
2011). Unfortunately, the Blackfoot are often left out of the reconstructed trade networks across the northern Plains (e.g., Wood and Thiessen 1985).

In addition to staples, other goods circulated in different realms of exchange.
Historical accounts and early ethnographies explain that people went to great
lengths to obtain paints, animals and animal parts, medicinal plants, and certain
minerals and rocks to restock their bundles and manufacture prestige items. When
items could not be procured directly, people recurred to additional ceremonial
transfers or trade. Paints, pipestone, and birds, in particular, could be obtained
through established trade networks, as they could through ceremonial transfers.
These items were purchased from specialists in the procurement of minerals and
birds. McClintock (1999:214) noted that given the abundant use of paint among
the Blackfoot, collecting and preparing paints was "a business in itself."

The Missouri River is a major bird migration pathway, as well as the habitat of
myriad resident birds. Raptors, waterfowl, passerines, and gallinaceous birds are

everywhere and, with few exceptions, were also available in the past. Dozens of these bird species were used by the Missouri River tribes in bundles, ritual paraphernalia, and personal adornment or were incorporated into their traditional stories. Both the Blackfoot and the Mandan had extensive ornithological knowledge (Bowers 2004; Chandler et al. 2017; Schaeffer 1950) and harvested a great variety of birds. At the Mandan site known as Scattered Village, Falk (2002) identified bones representing 34 bird species, 10 orders, and at least 15 families. There is no comparable bone assemblage from Blackfoot sites, but their Beaver Bundles reveal a range of valuable birds rivaling Scattered Village's inventory (Scriver 1990).

While individuals handled birds that were personal spirit helpers, the handling of the most sacred birds, specifically eagles, was restricted to specialists who owned the rituals and the technology to catch eagles and preserve their skins and parts. Eagles and eagle parts were conduits of Thunderbird power and as such were required for individual and group ceremonies and valued as insignias of bravery and social power. Eagle trapping stands out as the most specialized and highly ritualized resource extraction activity (Murray 2011). And yet, eagle feathers were a trade good, too, so commonly circulated in Native markets and rendezvous that they could be easily considered a kind of currency. According to Grinnell (1962:236), "Before the Whites came to Blackfoot country, the Indian standard of value was the eagle tail-feathers."

Eagle trapping among the Mandan and Hidatsa has been thoroughly documented by Wilson (1928), Bowers (1992, 2004), and most recently Murray (2011). Transfer of eagle-trapping rights is a long-term process of exchange between owner and apprentice; over a period of many years, the apprentice provides gifts and commodities to the owner in exchange for portions of the collective rights until the transfer is complete. Cultural protocols dictate that eagle-trapping rights can only be transferred four times over the course of a lifetime, after which the owner loses the authority to make such transfers. In this example, the transfer of an inalienable possession can bring a great deal of wealth to the giver and social capital to both giver and receiver. The inalienable qualities that characterize bird parts in this context, however, do not preclude the same types of objects from being treated as gifts or commodities in another context (Zedeño, Murray, and Chandler 2014).

Although both bald and golden eagles were trapped, the latter was more valuable. Not all tribes trapped eagles, so the Blackfoot and the Mandan were well positioned to profit from this trade. In 1738, Pierre Varennes de la Verendrye visited the Mandan towns and described in detail their bustling trade activity (Wood 1980). He noted that the Mandan traded eagle feathers and headdresses (among many other feathered items) to the Assiniboine. For their part, the Blackfoot lived in golden eagle country; possible eagle-trapping pits are scattered around the river bluffs, ridges, and mountain slopes, particularly in the northern portion of their territory (Kennedy and Reeves 2013). Although there are detailed descriptions of Blackfoot trapping practices (Grinnell 1962; McClintock 1999), their transfer protocols have not been documented, as have those of the Mandan and Hidatsa.

In the past, entire family lineages supported themselves through eagle procurement, manufacture of war bonnets and other objects, and trade of feathers. Eagle war bonnets were bestowed only on the bravest warriors and the holy people; they required large numbers of tail feathers and thus were highly expensive goods. Golden eagles were more abundant in the north than in the southern portion of Blackfoot country. Brings-down-the-Sun, "a celebrated medicine man of the north," supported his family through eagle trapping and feather trading with the Pikani in the south, who used the items for regalia and ceremonial objects (McClintock 1999:428).

With the introduction of horses and objects of European manufacture, trade in Native valuable and staple goods took a new turn. Horses were acquired by the Blackfoot in the early 1700s, and though they were never as horse-wealthy as the Crow or the Cheyenne, they nonetheless kept large herds that they obtained mainly through raiding but also through trade (Ewers 1955). Because of their value, golden eagle feathers played a significant role in the Blackfoot horse trade. Under given circumstances, this special eagle feather could purchase a horse; three to five tail feathers were usually required for this trade (Chandler et al. 2017). Horses were also a currency and the preferred payment for the acquisition of sacred objects and bundle transfers. Catlin (1989) related an incident when the Blackfoot found out that the Mandan had a white buffalo robe in their possession. The well-to-do Blackfoot pulled together 150 horses to purchase the robe. Their emissaries were to bargain 50 horses at a time, but the Mandan would not part with the robe because it was destined for Lone Man's shrine.

Horses brought an element of change to abundance, value, and wealth among the Blackfoot. Although a detailed discussion of the impact of the horse is outside the scope of this chapter, it is important that horses, as personal property, deeply increased the ability to accumulate considerable economic wealth among individuals who could purchase them, for instance, eagle trappers (Ewers 1955; Hämäläinen 2003; Nugent 1993). The horse, and the acquisitive power afforded by participation in the American bison hide trade in the nineteenth century, led to the development of a network organization (sensu Feinman 2000) through which individuals established long-distance or local partnerships that neutralized the power of corporate institutions to regulate the circulation of valuables and wealth. Communal pedestrian hunts lost favor to mounted roundup hunts in which rifles were used as much as traditional weapons. As the bison herds diminished, differences in wealth distribution among the Blackfoot became highly pronounced, with the horse and not the bison the new focus of abundance.

CONCLUSION

Abundance has tangible and intangible dimensions, encompassing both quantity and quality. Abundance may be directly tied to the availability of staple resources but can also be fabricated through the manipulation of the value of both widely available and scarce resources. Manipulations of value, in turn, are encoded within social and ritual systems that are pragmatic and result-oriented (Joyce 2013; Ortner 1978). Broadening measures of abundance to include these dimensions is particularly important in the archaeology of pre-state societies, where cultural systems of valuation mediate the production of abundance and accumulation of wealth along a continuum ranging from spiritual power to social prestige and from to economic gain to political influence. A reevaluation of the usefulness of categories of value such as gift, commodity, and inalienable possession is necessary to unpack the complex system of production, accumulation, and circulation of resources, knowledge, and services; in the Blackfoot case, powerful institutions such as esoteric societies, as well as individual sources of power, could alter the perception of value and thus the quality of abundance.

REFERENCES CITED

Aaberg, Stephen A., Chris Crofutt, and Jayme Green. 2009. "First Peoples Buffalo Jump State Park: Results of Archaeological Survey of Portions of the Park." Report prepared for the Montana Department of Fish, Wildlife, and Parks Foundation. Billings, MT: Aaberg Cultural Resource Consulting Service.

Appadurai, Arjun. 1986. "Introduction: Commodities and the Politics of Value." In *In the Social Life of Things: Commodities in a Cultural Perspective*, edited by Arjun Appadurai, 3–63. Cambridge: Cambridge University Press. http://dx.doi.org/10.1017/CBO9780 511819582.003.

Bement, Leland C. 1999. *Bison Hunting at Cooper Site: Where Lightning Bolts Drew Thundering Herds*. Norman: University of Oklahoma Press.

Bethke, Brandi, María Nieves Zedeño, Geoffrey Jones, and Matthew Pailes. 2016. "Complementary Approaches to the Identification of Bison Processing for Storage at the Kutoyis Site, Montana." *Journal of Archaeological Science: Reports*. http://dx.doi.org /10.1016/j.jasrep.2016.05.028.

Binnema, Theodore. 2004. *Common and Contested Ground*. Norman: University of Oklahoma Press.

Bird-David, Nurit. 1990. "The Giving Environment: Another Perspective on the Economic System of Gatherer-Hunters." *Current Anthropology* 31 (2): 189–96. http://dx.doi.org /10.1086/203825.

Borck, Lewis, Barbara J. Mills, Matthew A. Peeples, and Jeffery J. Clark. 2015. "Are Social Networks Survival Networks? An Example from the Late Prehispanic Southwest." *Journal of Archaeological Method and Theory* 22 (1): 33–57. http://dx.doi.org/10.1007/s10 816-014-9236-5.

Bowers, Alfred W. 1992. *Hidatsa Social and Ceremonial Organization*. Lincoln: University of Nebraska Press.

Bowers, Alfred W. 2004. *Mandan Social and Ceremonial Organization*. Chicago: University of Chicago Press.

Boyd, Matthew. 2002. "Identification of Anthropogenic Burning in the Paleoecological Record of the Northern Prairies: A New Approach." *Annals of the Association of American Geographers* 92 (3): 471–87. http://dx.doi.org/10.1111/1467-8306.00300.

Brace, G. Ian. 2005. *Boulder Monuments of Saskatchewan*. Saskatoon: Saskatchewan Archaeological Society.

Braun, David P., and Stephen Plog. 1980. "Evolution of 'Tribal' Social Networks: Theory and North American Evidence." *American Antiquity* 47: 504–25.

Brink, Jack W. 2008. *Imagining Head-Smashed-In*. Edmonton, AB: Athabasca University Press.

Brink, Jack W., and Robert Dawe. 1989. *Final Report of the 1985 and 1986 Field Season at Head-Smashed-In Buffalo Jump, Alberta*. Edmonton: Alberta Archaeological Survey.

Brumley, John H. 1988. *Medicine Wheels on the Northern Plains: A Summary and Appraisal*. Archaeological Survey of Alberta Manuscript Series 12. Edmonton: Alberta Culture and Multiculturalism Historical Resources Division.

Carlson, Kristen. 2011. "Prehistoric Bison Procurement: Human Agency and Drive Lane Topography on the Northwestern Plains." MA thesis, Northern Arizona University, Flagstaff.

Catlin, George. 1989. *North American Indians*. Ed. Peter Matthiessen. New York: Penguin Group.

Catlin, George, Brian W. Dippie, and George Gurney. 2002. *George Catlin and His Indian Gallery*. Produced and edited by the Smithsonian American Art Museum and Renwick Gallery. Washington, DC: Smithsonian Institution Press.

Chandler, Kaitlyn, Wendi Murray, María Nieves Zedeño, Samrat Clements, and Robert Jones. 2017. *The Winged: An Ethno-ornithology of the Upper Missouri River*. Anthropological Papers 78. Tucson: University of Arizona.

Claassen, Cheryl. 2010. *Feasting with Shellfish in the Southern Ohio Valley: Archaic Sacred Sites and Rituals*. Memphis: University of Tennessee Press.

Cooper, Judith. 2008. "Bison Hunting and Late Prehistoric Subsistence Economies in the Great Plains." PhD dissertation, Southern Methodist University, Dallas, TX.

Dempsey, Hugh A. 1956. "Stone 'Medicine Wheels'—Memorials to Blackfoot War Chiefs." *Journal of the Washington Academy of Sciences* 46 (6): 177–82.

Duvall, David C. 1908. Papers, vol. 1, typed manuscripts. New York: American Museum of Natural History.

Ewers, John. C. 1955. *The Horse in Blackfeet Indian Culture: With Comparative Material from Other Western Tribes.* Smithsonian Institution Bureau of American Ethnology, Bulletin 159. Washington, DC: Government Printing Office.

Falk, Carl. 2002. "Fish, Amphibian, Reptile, and Bird Remains." In *Prehistory on First Street NE: The Archaeology of Scattered Village, Mandan, North Dakota,* edited by Stanley Ahler, 7.1–7.25. Submitted to the City of Mandan and the North Dakota Department of Transportation. Flagstaff, AZ: Paleo Cultural Research Group.

Fawcett, William Bloys, Jr. 1987. "Communal Hunts, Human Aggregations, Social Variation, and Climatic Change: Bison Utilization by Prehistoric Inhabitants of the Great Plains." PhD dissertation, University of Massachusetts, Amherst.

Feinman, Gary. 2000. "Corporate/Network New Perspectives on Political Action in the Pueblo Southwest." In *Social Theory in Archaeology,* edited by Michael B. Schiffer, 31–51. Salt Lake City: University of Utah Press.

Fenn, Elizabeth. 2014. *Encounters at the Heart of the World—a History of the Mandan People.* New York: Hill and Wang.

Friesen, T. Max. 2007. "Hearth Rows, Hierarchies and Arctic Hunter-Gatherers: The Construction of Equality in the Late Dorset Period." *World Archaeology* 39 (2): 194–214. http://dx.doi.org/10.1080/00438240701249686.

Godelier, Maurice. 1999. *The Enigma of the Gift.* Chicago: University of Chicago Press.

Gregory, Chris A. 1982. *Gifts and Commodities.* London: Academic.

Gremillion, Kristen J. 2011. *Ancestral Appetites: Food in Prehistory.* Cambridge: Cambridge University Press. http://dx.doi.org/10.1017/CBO9780511976353.

Grinnell, George B. 1887. "Rock Climbers I." *Forest and Stream* 29 (3) (December 29).

Grinnell, George B. 1962. *Blackfoot Lodge Tales.* Lincoln: University of Nebraska Press.

Haig, Brian, ed. 1991. *Journal of a Journey Overland from Buckingham House to the Rocky Mountains in 1792 and 93.* Lethbridge, AB: Historical Research Centre.

Hämäläinen, Pekka. 2003. "The Rise and Fall of Plains Indian Horse Cultures." *Journal of American History* 90 (3): 833–62. http://dx.doi.org/10.2307/3660878.

Hellson, John. n.d. "The Black and Yellow Painted Buffalo Tipis: Mythology and History Informant's Account." Manuscript in the author's possession.

Hollenback, Kacy L. 2012. "Disaster, Technology, and Community: Measuring Responses to Smallpox Epidemics in Historic Hidatsa Villages, North Dakota." PhD dissertation, University of Arizona, School of Anthropology, Tucson.

Inomata, Takeshi. 2013. "Negotiation of Inalienability and Meanings at the Classic Maya Center of Aguateca, Guatemala." In *The Inalienable in the Archaeology of Mesoamerica*, edited by Brigitte Kovachevich and Michael C. Callahan, 128–41. Archeological Papers of the American Anthropological Association 23. Hoboken, NJ: Wiley and Sons. http://dx.doi.org/10.1111/apaa.12020.

Jackson, John C. 2000. *The Piikani Blackfeet*. Missoula, MT: Mountain Press.

Joyce, Rosemary. 2013. "Religion in a Material World." Paper presented at the 112th Annual Meeting of the American Anthropological Association, Chicago, November 23.

Kehoe, Alice B., and Thomas F. Kehoe. 1979. *Solstice-Aligned Boulder Configurations in Saskatchewan*. Mercury Series, Canadian Ethnology Service Paper 48. Ottawa: National Museum of Man.

Kehoe, Thomas F. 1954. "Stone 'Medicine Wheels' in Southern Alberta and the Adjacent Portion of Montana: Were They Designed as Grave Markers?" *Journal of the Washington Academy of Sciences* 44 (5): 133–37.

Kehoe, Thomas F. 1960. "Stone Tipi Rings in North-Central Montana and the Adjacent Portion of Alberta, Canada." *Bureau of American Ethnology Bulletin* 173: 421–73.

Kehoe, Thomas F. 1967. "The Boarding School Bison Drive Site." *Plains Anthropologist* 12 (35): 1–165.

Kehoe, Thomas F., and Frances Eynman. 1973. *The Gull Lake Site: A Prehistoric Bison Drive Site in Southwestern Saskatchewan*. Milwaukee, WI: Milwaukee Public Museum.

Kehoe, Thomas F., and Alice B. Kehoe. 1959. "Boulder Effigy Monuments in the Northern Plains." *Journal of American Folklore* 72 (284): 115–28. http://dx.doi.org/10.2307/538474.

Kennedy, Margaret, and Brian O.K. Reeves. 2013. "Plains Rocks in a Row: Some Ideas about Rock Alignments in the Northern Plans." Paper presented at the 71st Annual Plains Anthropological Conference, Loveland, CO, October 3

Keyser, James D., Linea Sundstrom, and George Poetschat. 2006. "Women in War: Gender in Plains Biographic Rock Art." *Plains Anthropologist* 51 (197): 51–70. http://dx.doi.org/10.1179/pan.2006.003.

Kornfeld, Marcel, George Frison, and Mary Lou Larson. 2010. *Prehistoric Hunter-Gatherers of the High Plains and Rockies*. Walnut Creek, CA: Left Coast.

Lokensgaard, Kenneth H. 2010. *Blackfoot Religion and the Consequences of Commoditization*. Burlington, VT: Ashgate.

McClintock, Walter. 1999. *The Old North Trail: Life, Legends and Religion of the Blackfeet Indians*. Lincoln: University of Nebraska Press.

Mirau, Neil A. 1995. "Medicine Wheels on the Northern Plains: Contexts, Codes, and Symbols." In *Beyond Subsistence: Plains Archaeology and the Post-Processual Critique*, edited by Philip Duke and Michael C. Wilson, 193–210. Tuscaloosa: University of Alabama Press.

Mitchell, Mark. 2013. *Crafting History in the Northern Plains*. Tucson: University of Arizona Press.

Murray, Wendi Field. 2011. "Feathers, Fasting, and the Eagle Complex: A Contemporary Analysis of the Eagle as a Cultural Resource in the Northern Plains." *Plains Anthropologist* 56 (218): 143–53.

Nugent, David. 1993. "Property Relations, Production Relations, and Inequality: Anthropology, Political Economy, and the Blackfeet." *American Ethnologist* 20 (2): 336–62. http://dx.doi.org/10.1525/ae.1993.20.2.02a00070.

Oetelaar, Gerald. 2014. "Better Homes and Pastures: Human Agency and the Construction of Place in Communal Bison Hunting on the Northwestern Plains." *Plains Anthropologist* 59 (229): 9–37. http://dx.doi.org/10.1179/2052546X13Y.0000000004.

Ortner, Sherry B. 1978. *Sherpas through Their Rituals*. Cambridge: Cambridge University Press. http://dx.doi.org/10.1017/CBO9780511621796.

Peck, Trevor R. 2002. "Archaeologically Recovered Ammonites: Evidence for Long-Term Continuity in Nitsitapii Ritual." *Plains Anthropologist* 47 (181): 147–64.

Peck, Trevor R. 2004. *Bison Ethnology and Native Settlement Patterns during the Old Women's Phase on the Northwestern Plains*. BAR International Series 1278. Oxford: Archaeopress.

Peck, Trevor R. 2011. *Light from Ancient Campfires: Archaeological Evidence for Native Lifeways on the Northern Plains*. Edmonton, AB: Athabaska University Press.

Quigg, J. Michael. 1997. "Bison Processing at the Rush Site, 41TG346, and Evidence for Pemmican Production in the Southern Plains." *Plains Anthropologist* 42 (159): 145–61.

Reeves, Brian O.K. 1993. "Iniskim: A Sacred Nitsitapii Religious Tradition." In *Kunaitupii: Coming Together on Native Sacred Sites: Their Sacredness, Conservation and Interpretation: A Native and Non-Native Forum*, edited by Brian O.K. Reeves and Margaret A. Kennedy, 194–259. Proceedings of the First Joint Meeting of the Archaeological Society of Alberta and the Montana Archaeological Society, Waterton Lakes National Park, Alberta, Canada, May 2–6, 1990. Calgary: Archaeological Society of Alberta.

Reher, Charles A., and George C. Frison. 1983. "The Vore Site, 48CK302, a Stratified Buffalo Jump in the Wyoming Black Hills." *Plains Anthropologist* Memoir 16.

Roos, Christopher, María Nieves Zedeño, and Kacy Hollenback. 2014. "Alluvial and Colluvial Records of Multi-Centennial Fire Histories from Blackfoot Country." Paper presented at the 72nd annual Plains Anthropological Conference, Fayetteville, AK, October 30.

Ruby, Robert H., and John A. Brown. 1993. *Indian Slavery in the Pacific Northwest*. Spokane, WA: Arthur H. Clark.

Schaeffer, Claude E. 1950. "Bird Nomenclature and Principles of Avian Taxonomy of the Blackfeet Indians." *Washington Academy of Sciences* 40 (2): 37–46.

Schaeffer, Claude E., and Mrs. Schaeffer. 1934. *Field Work among Blackfeet Indians, Montana: Correspondence and Field Notes*. Calgary, AB: Glenbow Museum.

Schultz, James W. 1962. *Blackfeet and Buffalo*. Norman: University of Oklahoma Press.

Schultz, James W., and Louise Donaldson. 1930. *The Sun God's Children*. Helena, MT: Riverbend.

Scriver, Bob. 1990. *Blackfeet Artists of the Northern Plains*. Kansas City: Lowell.

Tyrell, Joseph Burr, ed. 1916. *David Thompson's Narrative of His Explorations in Western America, 1784–1812*. Toronto: Champlain Society.

Verbicky-Todd, Eleanor. 1984. *Communal Buffalo Hunting among the Plains Indians: An Ethnographic and Historic Review*. Occasional Paper 24. Edmonton: Archaeological Survey of Alberta.

Vickers, J. Roderick, and Trevor Peck. 2009. "Identifying the Prehistoric Blackfoot: Approaches to Nitsitapii (Blackfoot) Culture History." In *Painting the Past with a Broad Brush: Papers in Honor of James Valliere Wright*, edited by David L. Keenlyside and Jean-Luc Pilon, 473–97. Canadian Museum of Civilization Mercury Series Paper 170. Gatineau, Quebec: Canadian Museum of Civilization.

Walde, Dale. 2006. "Sedentism and Pre-Contact Tribal Organization on the Northern Plains: Colonial Imposition or Indigenous Development?" *World Archaeology* 38 (2): 291–310. http://dx.doi.org/10.1080/00438240600694032.

Weiner, Annette. 1992. *Inalienable Possessions: The Paradox of Keeping While Giving*. Berkeley: University of California Press. http://dx.doi.org/10.1525/california/9780520076037.001.0001.

Wilson, Gilbert. 1928. "Hidatsa Eagle Trapping." *Anthropological Papers of the American Museum of Natural History* 30 (4): 99–245.

Wissler, Clark. 1916. "Societies and Dance Associations of the Blackfoot Indians." In *Societies of the Plains Indians*, edited by Clark Wissler, 359–460. Anthropological Papers of the American Museum of Natural History, vol. 11. New York: Trustees.

Wissler, Clark, and David Duvall. 1912. *Social Organization and Ritualistic Ceremonies of the Blackfoot Indians*. New York: AMS.

Wood, W. Raymond, ed. 1980. *The Explorations of the La Vérendryes in the Northern Plains, 1738–1743, by G. Hubert Smith*. Lincoln: University of Nebraska Press.

Wood, W. Raymond, Joseph C. Potter, and David Hunt. 2007. *Karl Bodmer's Studio Art: The Newberry Library Bodmer Collection*. Chicago: University of Illinois Press.

Wood, W. Raymond, and Thomas D. Thiessen, eds. 1985. *Early Fur Trade on the Northern Plains: Canadian Traders among the Mandan and Hidatsa Indians, 1738–1818*. Norman: University of Oklahoma Press.

Zarrillo, Sonia, and Brian P. Kooyman. 2006. "Evidence for Berry and Maize Processing on the Canadian Plains from Starch Grain Analysis." *American Antiquity* 71 (3): 473–99.

Zedeño, María Nieves. 2008. "Bundled Worlds: The Roles and Interactions of Complex Objects from the North American Plains." *Journal of Archaeological Method and Theory* 15 (4): 362–78. http://dx.doi.org/10.1007/s10816-008-9058-4.

Zedeño, María Nieves, Jesse A. Ballenger, and John R. Murray. 2014. "Landscape Engineering and Organizational Complexity among Late Prehistoric Bison Hunters of the Northwestern Plains." *Current Anthropology* 55 (1): 23–58. http://dx.doi.org/10.1086/674535.

Zedeño, María Nieves, Wendi F. Murray, and Kaitlyn Chandler. 2014. "The Inalienable-Commodity Continuum in Plains Indian Trade and Politics." Paper presented at the 72th Annual Meeting of the Plains Anthropological Conference, Fayetteville, AK, October 31.

3

Abundance in the Archaic

A Dwelling Perspective

CHRISTOPHER R. MOORE AND CHRISTOPHER W. SCHMIDT

Archaic period studies in eastern North America typically address resource avail-ability and abundance in environmental terms. Patches or ecotones are considered resource-rich if they exhibit a high diversity of available resources or relatively high yields of particularly productive resources (Brown 1985; Jefferies, Thompson, and Milner 2005; Zeder 2012). Explanations of Archaic settlement patterns often juxta-pose these "rich" zones with areas characterized by fewer or less diverse (i.e., scarcer) resources, arguing that hunter-gatherers were either pushed out of these zones or pulled toward the resource-rich zones by changing climatic conditions (Brown 1985, 1986; Dye 1996; Munson 1986). In this chapter we examine hunter-gatherer sites in and around the lower Ohio River Valley and propose that the material and bio-cultural records of Archaic peoples in this region indicate healthy populations and little to no evidence of scarcity in either subsistence resources or material goods. Rather, hunter-gatherers appear to be well stocked with abundant foodstuffs, raw materials, and tools. Contrasting the assumption of scarcity common in many Archaic period studies, this chapter adopts Tim Ingold's (2000) concept of a dwell-ing perspective and examines the degree to which Archaic hunter-gatherers in the lower Ohio Valley experienced a "giving environment" and how this interpretation of the Archaic lifeworld contributes to more nuanced understandings of site use, human health, and artifact distribution patterns.

The Archaic hunter-gatherers of the Green and lower Ohio River Valleys of the midwestern United States were healthy populations with ready access to food,

DOI: 10.5876/9781607325949.c003

shelter, lithic tool stone, and life's other material necessities (figure 3.1). Changing environmental conditions certainly impacted mobility options, but population densities were low and the river valleys quite large. For example, a survey of 611 ha of the Cypress Creek drainage (a tributary of the Green River) in western Kentucky by Jefferies and colleagues (2005) yielded only 9.5 archaeological components per 1,000 years during the Early Archaic (ca. 10,000 to 8000 BP), 9.7 components per 1,000 years during the Middle Archaic (ca. 8000 to 5000 BP), and 21.5 components per 1,000 years during the Late Archaic (ca. 5000 to 3000 BP). If numbers of components (defined by each time period represented by a temporally diagnostic hafted biface at a site) can act as a proxy for population, then it appears that population was increasing in the Cypress Creek drainage throughout the Archaic, a trend evident in the Ohio River Valley as a whole (Jefferies 2008). While some areas like the Middle Green River Valley, the Falls of the Ohio River region, and the lower Wabash River Valley were more intensively used than others, there is currently no evidence that Archaic populations experienced sustained periods of resource stress (Gremillion 2004:227; Smith and Yarnell 2009:6566; Zeder 2012) even as populations were increasing.

Furthermore, bioarchaeological evidence indicates little long-term food stress and an ability to care for even the sickest and most disabled individuals well into middle and old age (Casserly et al. 2013; Ward 2005). As Mary Lucas Powell (1996:126) observes, "The general picture of nutrition in Archaic peoples of the Green River region suggests a well-balanced array of food resources hunted and gathered from forests and freshwater streams." While it is likely that short-term environmental perturbations periodically caused Archaic individuals and groups to experience stress, these same individuals were connected through trade and intermarriage with other groups over large regions and could effectively respond through mobility (e.g., Jefferies 1997; Moore 2010). By all measures, the Archaic cultures of the Green and lower Ohio River Valleys experienced long periods of material abundance.

In this chapter we take a three-part approach to the question of abundance in the Archaic. First, we draw on the work of Tim Ingold, Nurit Bird-David, and others to establish why we believe Archaic hunter-gatherers perceived their lifeworlds in terms of abundance. Next, we establish the material basis for an abundance perspective, describing just a handful of the material and bioarchaeological correlates of abundance. Finally, we examine the articulation of Archaic perceptions of their environments and material abundance to explore the historical process of entanglement. Specifically, we explore the socio-spatial outcomes of abundance, or the degree to which abundance structured long-term site use and the creation of cultural landscapes.

FIGURE 3.1. Map of Ohio River Valley and its tributaries depicting Archaic sites and cultures. Illustration by Christopher R. Moore.

HUNTER-GATHERERS AND ABUNDANCE

Marshal Sahlins's (1972) paper "The Original Affluent Society" was the first highly influential anthropological application of concepts of abundance to hunter-gatherers. In that paper Sahlins pointed out that ethnographic research and early reports by explorers indicated that hunter-gatherers spent a relatively small amount of time hunting, collecting, and processing foodstuffs and that this work yielded ample returns with significant time remaining for leisure. The classic perception of hunter-gatherers as leading meager lives of hardship and want, Sahlins contended, was rooted in a "Bourgeois ethnocentrism" based on market economics and an assumption of scarcity. While Sahlins's (1972) interpretation simplifies the food quest in unrealistic ways that fail to account for the true effort expended in the full gamut of social, ideological, and technological aspects of hunting and collecting, his paper does illustrate the degree to which some hunter-gatherers perceive of food as abundant.

The perceptions and dispositions Sahlins (1972) captured in his notion of "the original affluent society" are further developed in Bird-David's (1990) discussion of "the giving environment." According to Bird-David, certain immediate-return hunter-gatherers like the Nayaka of South India conceive of "nature as parent" rather than "nature as ancestor." Hunter-gatherers whose social relations are based on presumptions of giving rather than assumptions of reciprocity tend to have very little personal property, and the property they do have has value derived from the social relations it evokes rather than from some inherent worth arising from perceptions of scarcity. For these groups, the lifeworld provides all the resources they need, and objects are abundant (Bird-David 1990).

Not all hunter-gatherers think this way; certainly, there are recorded examples of so-called complex hunter-gatherers whose political economies were structured by unequal access to resources and for whom abundance led to socially imposed scarcities (e.g., Hayden 1994; Kim and Grier 2006; Sassaman 2004). But for much of human history, it is likely that most hunter-gatherers maintained significant political autonomy (Crothers and Bernbeck 2004; Ingold 1988, 1999; Kelly 1995; Leacock and Lee 1982). For these groups, the food quest was as much about relations with animals, spirits, and other non-human persons as it was about social relations among people (Ingold 2000; see also Zedeño, this volume). Among some hunter-gatherers, perceptions of abundance are linked to behavior, in that abundance is the predictable outcome of properly maintaining relationships with other organism-persons. In a giving environment, however, expectations of abundance are even stronger and not always predicated on assumptions of conduct. Just as parents are expected to provide for their children regardless of how they behave, in a giving environment where nature is parent, nature is always an abundant provider who has no expectations of receiving anything in return (Bird-David 1990).

Perceiving of nature as a giving parent has profound implications. For archaeologists, it means that neoclassical models based on the notion that humans have unlimited wants cannot be uncritically applied to the past. If nature is giving and objects abundant, then scarcity must be imposed. Models that assume scarcity in the absence of institutionalized hierarchies will have no relevance (Dugger and Peach 2009; Hoeschele 2010). For hunter-gatherers, a perception of abundance modifies the human-object relationship; rather than perceiving this relationship in economic terms, humans are free to enter into social relationships with things. A perception of abundance articulates well with an animic ontology wherein actions are more important than ownership and objects are often agents (Bird-David 1999; Ingold 2006; VanPool and Newsome 2012).

KNOWLEDGE

For hunter-gatherers for whom objects of worth link individuals to others both past and present (e.g., Bird-David 1990:193), there is no value in accumulating personal possessions for their own sake. When strategic resources such as food and tool stone are freely available and shared by all, there is little logic in accumulating goods that are naturally concentrated or processed in bulk and shared communally. Rather than invest in the accumulation of goods or the construction of facilities, these groups invest in knowledge—knowledge of the land, knowledge of the spirits, knowledge of stories and myths, knowledge of all kinds (Crothers and Bernbeck 2004; Ridington 1982). Objects of worth are often social persons, and no two are alike; true value derives from one's knowledge.

Situating knowledge and perceptions as central to analysis is a defining characteristic of a dwelling perspective. Defined by Ingold (2000:153) as "a perspective that treats the immersion of the organism-person in an environment or lifeworld as an inescapable condition of existence," a dwelling perspective recognizes that hunter-gatherers often do not perceive of themselves as separate and distinct from their environments but instead consider themselves part of an integrated lifeworld that is always in the process of becoming (Ingold 2000; Moore and Dekle 2010; Moore and Thompson 2012). Ingold (2000) contrasts this with a "building perspective," the classical anthropological idea that worlds are constructed both mentally and physically before they are lived in. Whereas a building perspective conceives of persons and environments as partible phenomena, a dwelling perspective is a relational perspective wherein humans, landscapes, and other organism-persons are interdependent and indivisible; "each component enfolds within its essence the totality of its relations with each and every other" (Ingold 2000:191).

Hunter-gatherers in an abundant environment appear not to perceive the world in dualistic terms of mind versus body or culture versus nature; rather, the mind is at the "cutting edge" of the emergence of the organism-in-its-environment. Thoughts are embodied, and perceptions are projected as part of an ecology of dwelling. Rather than nature existing as an external and opposing presence or backdrop against which humans act, the environment emerges in an entangled relationship with the dividuated person (Bird-David 1999; Fowler 2010; Hodder 2012; Ingold 2000; Strathern 1988). There is but one lifeworld, "saturated with personal powers, and embracing both humans, the animals and plants on which they depend, and the features of the landscape in which they live and move" (Ingold 2000:47).

Techniques are transported in the mind and deployed using local materials; the artifacts so produced are the "products of knowledge and will" (Ridington 1982:477). They are deployed in the process of creating and maintaining social relations, for among hunting societies, animals are perceived as allowing themselves to be taken. For these groups, tools are not a means of control but a means of divining the intent of the animal with whom one wishes to enter into a social relationship through the food quest (cf. Shipman 2010). In this sense, tools are like gifts in that they "mediate an active, purposive engagement between persons and their environments" (Ingold 2000:319).

According to Eduardo Viveiros de Castro (1998, 2004), this relational ontology, central to a dwelling perspective, characterizes Native peoples throughout North and South America. Amerindians, Viveiros de Castro contends, conceive of a uniformity of the spirits or souls of all beings. This idea, referred to as Amerindian Perspectivism, posits that at their core, beings are identical in form; they are differentiated only on the basis of corporeality. While identical in substance, different organisms have different corporeal experiences and affects that provide them with unique perspectives and capabilities. Knowledge is not something that one possesses but something that one feels; it consists of "skills, sensitivities and orientations that have developed through the long experience of conducting one's life in a particular environment" (Ingold 2000:25). In fact, among mobile hunter-gatherers like the Athapaskan Dunne-za (Beaver Indians), material culture is a burden and technology consists of knowledge rather than objects. For these groups, knowledge is powerful, and a person who "knows something" is a person of power (Ridington 1982, 1988).

Knowledge of organisms and their varied perspectives permits certain individuals (typically shamans and other ritual specialists) to utilize certain objects as a means of directly engaging non-human organism-persons and, through shamanic transformations, adopting their perspectives (Conneller 2004; Eliade 1964; Guenther 1999; VanPool 2009; Zedeño, this volume). Objects do not merely represent the world (any more than shamans in costumes are "representing" animal-persons). Rather, they construct the world through interactions and, like other organism-persons, contribute to the construction of the web of relations that is the lifeworld. Agency is not assigned to objects by humans; all objects are inherently invested with the potentiality for personhood. The degree to which that potentiality is realized and held to be significant by humans is variable; nevertheless, objects are agents, beings-in-the-world (Alberti and Marshall 2009; Ingold 2006, 2007; Olsen 2003; VanPool and Newsome 2012).

For hunter-gatherers like those discussed by Viveiros de Castro, the world is animate and composed of entangled relationships among animals, people, landscapes, spirit beings, and meteorological and astronomical phenomena (Bird-David 1999; Ingold 2000, 2006; Knight 2012). Animate beings are those who breathe, transform, and move or who resemble those who do (Jordan 2001). The process of "being alive" itself is emergent; beings "come alive" through interactions with other beings in the process of dwelling (Alberti and Marshall 2009; Ingold 2006). This understanding of the world as composed of relationships, or what Ingold (2000, 2006) refers to as an animic ontology, is widespread among hunter-gatherers and other non-Western societies. For these groups, success in life equates to success in maintaining relationships by conducting oneself appropriately while interacting with others.

Creating and maintaining relationships with other people and organism-persons is a process in which all members of society participate in different ways, but it inevitably has a material component. For instance, John Knight (2012) argues that hunters must develop personal relationships with what he describes as Animal Spirits to ensure their success on the hunt. Among the Khanty of Siberia, this means disposing of or consuming elk and bear remains in particular ways or at special places such as deep pools or holy sites (Jordan 2001, 2003). Among the Dunne-za, animals had to give themselves to hunters in dreams before they could be killed. Furthermore, social relations were intertwined such that acting bad toward one's kin damaged relations with animals, and treating animals inappropriately created bad relations among kin (Ridington 1982). Similarly, hunter-gatherers of the Pacific Northwest systematically dismantled fishing weirs and traps after a successful harvest as an intentional means of managing social relations with salmon organism-persons (Losey 2010). While objects and resources may be abundant, the world does not consist solely of people and things. People must strategically deploy their knowledge of other organism-persons and the specific objects associated with them if they are to be successful persons characterized by power and abundant meaningful social relations with other organism-persons (Bird-David 1990; Ridington 1982, 1988).

ABUNDANCE

Animals, plants, and tools used to process them were abundant in the Green and lower Ohio River Valleys during the Archaic. Medium- to high-quality chert resources available both locally and regionally include the Ste. Genevieve, Wyandotte, Muldraugh, Vienna, and St. Louis chert types (Cantin 2008; DeRegnaucourt and Georgiady 1998; Gatus 2005), access to which was available by way of the region's many riverine transportation routes. Sandstone and siderite used to manufacture a variety of plant-processing tools are also abundant in the Green and Ohio River Valleys (Janzen 2008; Moore 2011). Access to more socially valued objects such as marine shell and copper masks, headgear, necklaces, and other kinds of ornamentation may have been more restricted because of a lack of access to these non-local items, but the recovery of these objects with burials of biological males and females and individuals of all ages suggests that, contra Winters (1968), access was not systematically restricted to particular classes of individuals (Rothschild 1979; Watson 2005).

Evidence for the abundance and lack of restricted access to resources is perhaps best exemplified by the quantity of lightly used artifacts found at large shell and dirt/rock midden sites in the region. For instance, excavation of approximately 8,900 ft^2 of the Late Archaic Chiggerville (15Oh1) shell midden in Ohio County, western Kentucky, by the Works Progress Administration (WPA) without the use of screens resulted in the recovery of 1,485 chipped stone, 388 groundstone, and 1,275 bone and antler artifacts (Moore 2011; Webb and Haag 1939). Excavation of 60,000 ft^2 at the much larger and multi-component Middle to Late Archaic Indian Knoll (15Oh2) shell midden, just downstream from Chiggerville, yielded a stunning 13,806 chipped stone, 3,270 groundstone, and 12,769 bone and antler artifacts (Rolingson 1967; Webb 1974). This pattern is repeated throughout the Green and lower Ohio Valleys, where dozens of sites have yielded large quantities of artifacts, many of which were discarded long before their use-lives were completely expended (Janzen 2008; Jefferies 2008; Watson 2005). For example, 137 diagnostic Late Archaic Saratoga points from Chiggerville ranged in length from 21 mm to 87 mm, with blade lengths ranging from 8 mm to 75 mm. The mean blade length of these points was 33 mm ± 14.2 mm, indicating that the average Saratoga point discarded at Chiggerville still had as much as 2.5 cm of usable blade available when it was deposited in the midden (Moore 2011:508).

Food resources were also abundant, as evidenced by the large and diverse quantity of plant and animal remains found at Archaic sites with good preservation. From the subsistence and coprolite evidence, important dietary resources during the Archaic included deer, raccoons, squirrels, rabbits, turkeys, turtles, catfish, freshwater drum, mussels, acorns, hickory nuts, black walnuts, and a variety of fleshy fruits and starchy and oily seeds (Cassidy 1984; Crawford 2005; Crothers 2005; Glore 2005; Patch 2005; Simon 2009; Styles, Ahler, and Fowler 1983; Styles and Klippel 1996; Wagner 1996). These resources may at first seem disparate, but most share a common trait—they were readily available over wide areas.

Dental micro-wear texture analysis of human teeth indicates that the foods were poorly processed and highly abrasive, which led to severe tooth wear and antemortem tooth loss (Schmidt 2001). However, the diet was not particularly cariogenic, so those with dental disease were older people who had accumulated more tooth wear over time. The data also indicate that males and females had very similar diets. Stable carbon and nitrogen isotopic evidence indicates that meat from terrestrial animals made up a sizable portion of the diet. Overall, as with many hunter-gatherer groups living in resource-rich zones (e.g., Zeder 2012), the eastern North American Archaic diet was broad and founded on abundant resources.

The Archaic diet was abundant, but it had to be collected or hunted, which means injuries, particularly lower-limb fractures, were common. Scarcity was situational and when it did occur, resources were channeled to those in need, as seen in the care of those who would have been unable to provide for themselves (see also Varien, Potter, and Naranjo, this volume). For those who did suffer injury or became ill through infection, significant evidence indicates that the infirm were well cared for. Access to medical knowledge, healing, and healthcare was unrestricted. For instance, two mortuary sites in southern Indiana have adult males who suffered traumatic leg injuries. The first comes from the Late Archaic Kramer Mound site (12Sp7), where an individual fractured his femur just below the femoral neck (Bergman, Peres Lemons, and Schmidt 2014). The fracture spiraled inferiorly and completely separated the proximal end from the rest of the bone. Over time the fracture healed; however, it did not return to its normal anatomical position, and tension from the muscles of the thigh pulled the lower part of the bone up so the two broken aspects slightly overlapped. This person would have been in severe pain and almost completely immobile for weeks; yet he survived and lived well into adulthood.

An adult male from the Firehouse site (12D563) likely fell and fractured both his right tibia and fibula in two places, just below the proximal end and just above the distal end. Again, the bones healed, but they were slightly out of alignment. Like the individual from Kramer Mound, this man would have been in severe pain for an extended period of time. On average, bones heal over a period of about six weeks, which is ample time for a person to expire from starvation or dehydration; yet both men fully recovered and lived on for years.

Finally, a young adult female from the Meyer site (12Sp1082) suffered from a significant infectious condition that altered the appearance of her mid-face, causing her to lose all of her upper incisors and eroding away much of her lower jaw. In fact, her entire skeleton was extremely gracile, indicating that her daily activities were greatly restricted. The condition lasted for approximately ten years, and although the woman did eventually succumb to the disease, there is no doubt that she was fed and cared for throughout (Casserly et al. 2013).

Importantly, the diversity of artifactual and ecofactual remains recovered from Archaic sites in the Green and lower Ohio River Valleys testifies to the abundance of local knowledge possessed by the region's hunter-gatherers. Archaic peoples knew the kinds of animal resources available to them in the region and possessed the technical know-how to manufacture and construct tools to harvest those resources. They had knowledge of the region's plant resources and knew which plants were edible; which could be used to manufacture twine, matting, and baskets; and which could be used for poultices and medicines. They had access to transportation technologies and knowledge of local geography; they knew where the rivers ran and who lived in those areas, and likely they could predict when streams would rise and fall. It is also not hard to imagine that Archaic peoples had access to abundant social and ideological knowledge related to the passing of the seasons, the distribution of kinship networks, and the presence of spirits and other supernatural entities (Moore and Thompson 2012).

ENTANGLEMENT

The socio-spatial outcome of dwelling in an abundant environment is the creation of a cultural landscape infused with meaning and all the sentimental values of home. We contend that the Archaic peoples of the Green and lower Ohio River Valleys were the inhabitants of an ancient landscape ripe with cultural memories that were passed on from generation to generation and that created a shared sense of identity and a connection to place (Moore 2015). Middens at sites such as Chiggerville and Indian Knoll contained the bodies of the ancestors, whose spirits were likely alive in the landscape. Burial grounds, hickory groves, and mussel shoals were persistent places where groups aggregated to fish, laugh, find marriage partners, and exchange knowledge and goods (see also Claassen 2016). These events structured future gatherings and created a temporal rhythm that connected the present to the past and the past to the future (Moore and Dekle 2010; Moore and Thompson 2012).

The region's natural abundance facilitated this social process, probably from the moment people first began to colonize it. As Monica Smith (2012) points out, humans are drawn to abundance; naturally abundant locations near transportation hubs like the Green and Ohio River mussel shoals would have quickly become desirable sites of human occupation. As objects and evidence of past human-animal-plant interactions increased throughout the Archaic, so did evidence of the region's abundance. Persistent places became marked by the accumulation of trash, including discarded food refuse, artifact manufacturing debris, and minimally used artifacts (Smith 2011, 2012). But the ethnographic record of later hunting-and-gathering societies suggests that this was not just any trash—it was deployed in the creation of meaningful relationships between Archaic inhabitants and other organism-persons; after it was discarded, the ancestors were buried in it, people lived on it, it became places of power recorded in stories and myths. The middens reified in material form the abundant lifeworlds of the hunter-gatherers who lived there.

This process of the material, social, and ideological becoming intertwined and indistinguishable facets of human life is a central quality of dwelling. Ian Hodder (2012) refers to it as entanglement, a concept that encapsulates the interconnectedness of humans and things. According to Hodder, humans both depend on things to achieve goals and become dependent on things, thus limiting or constraining their

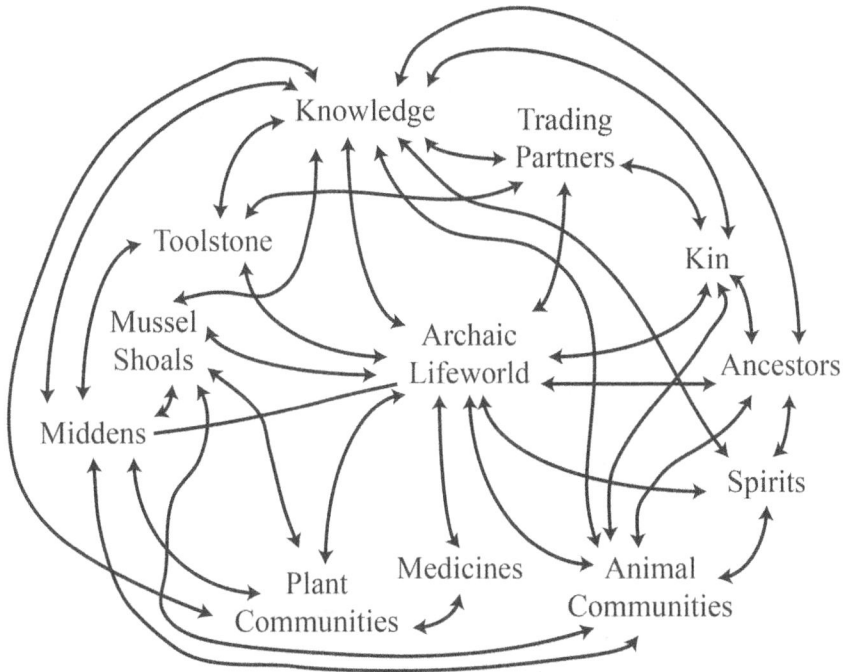

FIGURE 3.2. Ohio Valley Archaic tanglegram. Illustration by Christopher R. Moore, inspired by Hodder (2012).

options. Sometimes these entanglements are the product of history and sometimes they are the product of choice, but in either case the structuring nature of increased entanglement makes maintaining one's material and social interconnections appear inevitable (Hodder 2012). So long as resources remained abundant, so long as the giving environment continued to give, the Archaic hunter-gatherers of the Green and lower Ohio River Valleys continued to maintain their connections to place and their social relations with one another, with the spirits, and with the landscape (figure 3.2).

If this interpretation of Archaic lifeways is correct, then evidence of increasing entanglement and perceptions of abundance should be traceable to the region's earliest Paleoindian or Early Archaic inhabitants. Examples might include the dozens of large (ranging in length from 8 cm to 19 cm) bifaces and adzes recovered from Sloan and other Dalton period sites in Arkansas (Morse 1997), the increasing diversity and abundance of plant remains evident in Paleoindian and Archaic contexts at Dust Cave in Alabama (Hollenbach 2009), and the overwhelming quantity of debitage and minimally used bifaces (i.e., complete, un-retouched points and preforms) at the Early Archaic Swan's Landing site in Indiana (Smith 1995).

Accessing the region's resources made resource-rich areas meaningful places, and discarding debitage and tools at places provided a visible material connection between people and place, past and present. Individual ties to places and things extended outward through kinship networks, friendships, trade partnerships, and other social connections to link entire groups to one another. Stories, myths, burials, and objects linked these groups to the landscape. Animals were not just food but partners. The forest was not just home but caregiver. If you had need, the spirits provided. If you injured yourself, your friends and family were there to take care of you. Material necessities were abundant. An entangled lifeworld bred security and comfort; life was good.

CONCLUSION

The archaeological record of the Green and lower Ohio River Valleys of the midwestern United States indicates that the region's Archaic hunter-gatherers had ample access to material resources such as tool stone and food. This condition structured the Archaic lifeworld, contributing to the construction of a material landscape marked by evidence of abundance—large shell and dirt/rock midden sites containing the remains of food refuse, tool manufacturing debris, minimally used artifacts, and the bodies of the ancestors. By using and reusing these persistent places, the region's Archaic peoples infused them with meaning and embedded them in their memories, creating a robust and dynamic cultural landscape of interconnected peoples, places, and things—an entangled lifeworld.

So, what happened? At different times and in different places over several hundred years following the end of shell and dirt/rock midden formation along the Green and lower Ohio Rivers, Woodland groups began to settle in more permanent villages, giving up degrees of autonomy in exchange for more structured leadership positions and creating new cultural landscapes centered on other places. While we do not yet know all the factors involved in this process, some likely contenders include (1) social changes that developed from more complex entanglements originating in increasingly complex long-distance trade networks and growing populations (e.g., Crothers 2008), (2) environmental changes that introduced stressors and challenged perceptions of nature as a giving parent (Anderson 2001; Kidder 2006; Thompson 2010), and (3) population movements that resulted in conflicts evident in increasing evidence of interpersonal violence during this time (Mensforth 2001; Schmidt et al. 2010). Whatever the factors involved, they never completely modified the Archaic lifeworld, as shamanic practices and an animic ontology continue to be evident in ethnohistoric and early ethnographic accounts of midwestern Native peoples.

REFERENCES CITED

Alberti, Benjamin, and Yvonne Marshall. 2009. "Animating Archaeology: Local Theories and Conceptually Open-Ended Methodologies." *Cambridge Archaeological Journal* 19 (3): 344–56. http://dx.doi.org/10.1017/S0959774309000535.

Anderson, David A. 2001. "Climate and Culture Change in Prehistoric and Early Historic Eastern North America." *Archaeology of Eastern North America* 29: 143–86.

Bergman, Christopher A., Tonya Peres Lemons, and Christopher W. Schmidt. 2014. "Scientific Recovery Investigations at the Kramer Mound (12Sp7): Prehistoric Artifact Assemblages, Faunal and Floral Remains, and Human Osteology." *Indiana Archaeology* 9 (1): 13–101.

Bird-David, Nurit. 1990. "The Giving Environment: Another Perspective on the Economic Systems of Gatherer-Hunters." *Current Anthropology* 31 (2): 189–96. http://dx.doi.org/10.1086/203825.

Bird-David, Nurit. 1999. "'Animism' Revisited: Personhood, Environment, and Relational Epistemology." *Current Anthropology* 40 (S1): S67–91. http://dx.doi.org/10.1086/200061.

Brown, James A. 1985. "Long-Term Trends to Sedentism and the Emergence of Complexity in the American Midwest." In *Prehistoric Hunter-Gatherers: The Emergence of Cultural Complexity*, edited by T. Douglas Price and James A. Brown, 201–31. Orlando: Academic. http://dx.doi.org/10.1016/B978-0-12-564750-2.50013-5.

Brown, James A. 1986. "Food for Thought: Where Has Subsistence Analysis Gotten Us?" In *Foraging, Collecting, and Harvesting: Archaic Period Subsistence and Settlement in the Eastern Woodlands*, edited by Sarah W. Neusius, 315–30. Carbondale: Southern Illinois University.

Cantin, Mark. 2008. *Provenience, Description, and Archaeological Use of Selected Chert Types of Indiana*. Technical Report no. 05–01. Terre Haute: Indiana State University Anthropology Laboratory.

Casserly, Anna-Marie, Rebecca Van Sessen, Amber Osterholt, and Christopher W. Schmidt. 2013. "Evidence of Dietary Adjustments for a Severely Ill Individual in the Middle Archaic." Paper presented at the 128th Annual Meeting of the Indiana Academy of Science, Indianapolis, March 8–9.

Cassidy, Claire Monod. 1984. "Skeletal Evidence for Prehistoric Subsistence Adaptation in the Central Ohio River Valley." In *Paleopathology at the Origins of Agriculture*, edited by George J. Armelagos and Mark N. Cohen, 307–45. Orlando: Academic.

Claassen, Cheryl. 2016. "Abundant Gifts of Stone and Bone." *Midcontinental Journal of Archaeology* 41 (3): 274–94.

Conneller, Chantal. 2004. "Becoming Deer: Corporeal Transformations at Star Carr." *Archaeological Dialogues* 11 (1): 37–56. http://dx.doi.org/10.1017/S1380203804001357.

Crawford, Gary W. 2005. "Plant Remains from Carlston Annis (1972, 1974), Bowles, and Peter Cave." In *Archaeology of the Middle Green River Region, Kentucky*, edited by William H. Marquardt and Patty Jo Watson, 181–212. Gainesville: University of Florida.

Crothers, George M. 2005. "Vertebrate Fauna from the Carlston Annis Site." In *Archaeology of the Middle Green River Region, Kentucky*, edited by William H. Marquardt and Patty Jo Watson, 295–314. Gainesville: University of Florida.

Crothers, George M. 2008. "From Foraging to Farming: The Emergence of Exclusive Property Rights in Kentucky Prehistory." In *Economies and the Transformation of Landscape*, edited by Lisa Cliggett and Christopher Pool, 127–47. Lanham, MD: Altamira.

Crothers, George M., and Reinhard Bernbeck. 2004. "The Foraging Mode of Production: The Case of the Green River Archaic Shell Middens." In *Hunters and Gatherers in Theory and Archaeology*, edited by George M. Crothers, 401–22. Carbondale: Southern Illinois University.

DeRegnaucourt, Tony, and Jeff Georgiady. 1998. *Prehistoric Chert Types of the Midwest*. Greenville: Western Ohio Podiatric Medical Center.

Dugger, William M., and James T. Peach. 2009. *Economic Abundance: An Introduction*. Armonk, NY: M. E. Sharpe.

Dye, David H. 1996. "Riverine Adaptations in the Midsouth." In *Of Caves and Shell Mounds*, edited by Kenneth C. Carstens and Patty Jo Watson, 140–58. Tuscaloosa: University of Alabama Press.

Eliade, Mircea. 1964. *Shamanism: Archaic Techniques of Ecstasy*. Trans. Willard R. Trask. Princeton, NJ: Princeton University Press.

Fowler, Chris. 2010. "From Identity and Material Culture to Personhood and Materiality." In *The Oxford Handbook of Material Culture Studies*, edited by Dan Hicks and Mary C. Beaudry, 352–85. Oxford: Oxford University Press.

Gatus, Thomas W. 2005. "A Preliminary Reconnaissance of Some West Central Kentucky Chert Resources." In *Archaeology of the Middle Green River Region, Kentucky*, edited by William H. Marquardt and Patty Jo Watson, 431–51. Gainesville: University of Florida.

Glore, Michael T. 2005. "Vertebrate Faunal Remains from the Carlston Annis Site (15Bt5): An Evaluation of Cultural Stratigraphy." In *Archaeology of the Middle Green River Region, Kentucky*, ed. William H. Marquardt and Patty Jo Watson, 315–37. Gainesville: University of Florida.

Gremillion, Kristen J. 2004. "Seed Processing and the Origins of Food Production in Eastern North America." *American Antiquity* 69 (2): 215–33. http://dx.doi.org/10.2307/4128417.

Guenther, Mathias. 1999. "From Totemism to Shamanism: Hunter-Gatherer Contributions to World Mythology and Spirituality." In *The Cambridge Encyclopedia of*

Hunters and Gatherers, edited by Richard B. Lee and Richard Daly, 426–33. Cambridge: Cambridge University Press.

Hayden, Brian. 1994. "Competition, Labor, and Complex Hunter-Gatherers." In *Key Issues in Hunter-Gatherer Research*, edited by Ernest S. Burch and Linda J. Ellanna, 223–42. Oxford: Berg.

Hodder, Ian. 2012. *Entangled: An Archaeology of the Relationships between Humans and Things*. Malden, MA: Wiley-Blackwell. http://dx.doi.org/10.1002/9781118241912.

Hoeschele, Wolfgang. 2010. *The Economics of Abundance: A Political Economy of Freedom, Equity, and Sustainability*. Farnham, England: Gower.

Hollenbach, Kandace D. 2009. *Foraging in the Tennessee River Valley, 12,500 to 8,000 Years Ago*. Tuscaloosa: University of Alabama Press.

Ingold, Tim. 1988. "Notes on the Foraging Mode of Production." In *Hunters and Gatherers*, vol. 1: *History, Evolution, and Social Change*, edited by Tim Ingold, David Riches, and James Woodburn, 269–85. Oxford: Berg.

Ingold, Tim. 1999. "On the Social Relations of the Hunter-Gatherer Band." In *The Cambridge Encyclopedia of Hunters and Gatherers*, edited by Richard B. Lee and Richard Daly, 399–410. Cambridge: Cambridge University Press.

Ingold, Tim. 2000. *The Perception of the Environment: Essays in Livelihood, Dwelling, and Skill*. London: Routledge. http://dx.doi.org/10.4324/9780203466025.

Ingold, Tim. 2006. "Rethinking the Animate, Re-animating Thought." *Ethnos* 71 (1): 9–20. http://dx.doi.org/10.1080/00141840600603111.

Ingold, Tim. 2007. "Materials against Materiality." *Archaeological Dialogues* 14 (1): 1–16. http://dx.doi.org/10.1017/S1380203807002127.

Janzen, Donald E. 2008. *Unearthing the Past: The Archaeology of the Falls of the Ohio River Region*. Louisville, KY: Butler Books.

Jefferies, Richard W. 1997. "Middle Archaic Bone Pins: Evidence of Mid-Holocene Regional-Scale Social Groups in the Southern Midwest." *American Antiquity* 62 (3): 464–87. http://dx.doi.org/10.2307/282166.

Jefferies, Richard W. 2008. *Holocene Hunter-Gatherers of the Lower Ohio River Valley*. Tuscaloosa: University of Alabama Press.

Jefferies, Richard W., Victor D. Thompson, and George R. Milner. 2005. "Archaic Hunter-Gatherer Landscape Use in West-Central Kentucky." *Journal of Field Archaeology* 30 (1): 3–23. http://dx.doi.org/10.1179/009346905791072422.

Jordan, Peter. 2001. "The Materiality of Shamanism as a 'World-View': Praxis, Artefacts, and Landscape." In *The Archaeology of Shamanism*, edited by Neil Price, 87–104. London: Routledge.

Jordan, Peter. 2003. "Investigating Post-Glacial Hunter Gatherer Landscape Enculturation: Ethnographic Analogy and Interpretative Methodologies." In *Mesolithic on the Move: Papers Presented at the Sixth International Conference on the Mesolithic in Europe*,

Stockholm 2000, edited by Lars Larsson, Hans Kindgren, Kjel Knutsson, David Loeffler, and Agneta Åkerlund, 128–38. Oxford: Oxbow Books.

Kelly, Robert L. 1995. *The Foraging Spectrum: Diversity in Hunter-Gatherer Lifeways.* Washington, DC: Smithsonian Institution Press.

Kidder, Tristram R. 2006. "Climate Change and the Archaic to Woodland Transition (3000–2500 cal BP) in the Mississippi River Basin." *American Antiquity* 71 (2): 195–231. http://dx.doi.org/10.2307/40035903.

Kim, Jangsuk, and Colin Grier. 2006. "Beyond Affluent Foragers." In *Beyond Affluent Foragers: Rethinking Hunter-Gatherer Complexity*, edited by Colin Grier, Jangsuk Kim, and Junzo Uchiyama, 192–200. Oxford: Oxbow Books.

Knight, John. 2012. "The Anonymity of the Hunt: A Critique of Hunting as Sharing." *Current Anthropology* 53 (3): 334–55. http://dx.doi.org/10.1086/665535.

Leacock, Eleanor, and Richard Lee. 1982. "Introduction." In *Politics and History in Band Societies*, edited by Eleanor Leacock and Richard Lee, 1–20. Cambridge: Cambridge University Press.

Losey, Robert. 2010. "Animism as a Means of Exploring Archaeological Fishing Structures on Willapa Bay, Washington, USA." *Cambridge Archaeological Journal* 20 (1): 17–32. http://dx.doi.org/10.1017/S0959774310000028.

Mensforth, Robert P. 2001. "Warfare and Trophy Taking in the Archaic Period." In *Archaic Transitions in Ohio and Kentucky Prehistory*, edited by Olaf H. Prufer, Sara E. Pedde, and Richard S. Meindl, 110–38. Kent, OH: Kent State University Press.

Moore, Christopher R. 2010. "A Macroscopic Investigation of Technological Style and the Production of Middle to Late Archaic Fishhooks at the Chiggerville, Read, and Baker Sites, Western Kentucky." *Southeastern Archaeology* 29 (1): 197–221. http://dx.doi.org/10.1179/sea.2010.29.1.013.

Moore, Christopher R. 2011. "Production, Exchange, and Social Interaction in the Green River Region of Western Kentucky: A Multiscalar Approach to the Analysis of Two Shell Midden Sites." PhD dissertation, University of Kentucky, Lexington.

Moore, Christopher R. 2015. "Hunter-Gatherer Histories: The Role of Events in the Construction of the Chiggerville Shell Midden." In *The Enigma of the Event: Moments of Consequence in the Ancient Southeast*, edited by Zachary I. Gilmore and Jason M. O'Donoughue, 62–76. Tuscaloosa: University of Alabama Press.

Moore, Christopher R., and Victoria G. Dekle. 2010. "Hickory Nuts, Bulk Processing, and the Advent of Early Horticultural Economies in Eastern North America." *World Archaeology* 42 (4): 595–608. http://dx.doi.org/10.1080/00438243.2010.517675.

Moore, Christopher R., and Victor D. Thompson. 2012. "Animism and Green River Persistent Places: A Dwelling Perspective of the Shell Mound Archaic." *Journal of Social Archaeology* 12 (2): 264–84. http://dx.doi.org/10.1177/1469605311431518.

Morse, Dan F. 1997. *Sloan: A Paleoindian Dalton Cemetery in Arkansas*. Washington, DC: Smithsonian Institution Press.

Munson, Patrick J. 1986. "What Happened in the Archaic in the Midwestern United States?" *Revista de Antropologia* 13: 276–82.

Olsen, Bjørnar. 2003. "Material Culture after Text: Re-Membering Things." *Norwegian Archaeological Review* 36 (2): 87–104. http://dx.doi.org/10.1080/00293650310000650.

Patch, Diana Craig. 2005. "The Freshwater Molluscan Fauna: Identification and Interpretation for Archaeological Research." In *Archaeology of the Middle Green River Region, Kentucky*, edited by William H. Marquardt and Patty Jo Watson, 257–78. Gainesville: University of Florida.

Powell, Mary Lucas. 1996. "Health and Disease in the Green River Archaic." In Of Caves and Shell Mounds, edited by Kenneth C. Carstens and Patty Jo Watson, 119–31. Tuscaloosa: University of Alabama Press.

Ridington, Robin. 1982. "Technology, World View, and Adaptive Strategy in a Northern Hunting Society." *Canadian Review of Sociology and Anthropology. La Revue Canadienne de Sociologie et d'Anthropologie* 19 (4): 469–81. http://dx.doi.org/10.1111/j.1755-618X.1982.tb00875.x.

Ridington, Robin. 1988. *Trail to Heaven: Knowledge and Narrative in a Northern Native Community*. Iowa City: University of Iowa Press.

Rolingson, Martha Ann. 1967. "Temporal Perspectives on the Archaic Cultures of the Middle Green River Region, Kentucky." PhD dissertation, University of Michigan, Ann Arbor.

Rothschild, Nan A. 1979. "Mortuary Behavior and Social Organization at Indian Knoll and Dickson Mounds." *American Antiquity* 44 (4): 658–75. http://dx.doi.org/10.2307/279105.

Sahlins, Marshall. 1972. *Stone Age Economics*. Chicago: Aldine Atherton.

Sassaman, Kenneth E. 2004. "Complex Hunter-Gatherers in Evolution and History: A North American Perspective." *Journal of Archaeological Research* 12 (3): 227–80. http://dx.doi.org/10.1023/B:JARE.0000040231.67149.a8.

Schmidt, Christopher W. 2001. "Dental Microwear Evidence for a Dietary Shift between Two Nonmaize-Reliant Prehistoric Human Populations from Indiana." *American Journal of Physical Anthropology* 114 (2): 139–45. Medline:11169903 http://dx.doi.org/10.1002/1096-8644(200102)114:2<139::AID-AJPA1013>3.0.CO;2-9.

Schmidt, Christopher W., Rachel Lockhart Sharkey, Christopher Newman, Anna Serrano, Melissa Zolnierz, Jeffrey A. Plunkett, and Anne Bader. 2010. "Skeletal Evidence of Cultural Variation: Mutilation Related to Warfare." In *Human Variation in the Americas: The Integration of Archaeology and Biological Anthropology*, edited by Benjamin M. Auerbach, 215–37. Carbondale: Southern Illinois University.

Shipman, Pat. 2010. "The Animal Connection and Human Evolution." *Current Anthropology* 51 (4): 519–38. http://dx.doi.org/10.1086/653816.

Simon, Mary L. 2009. "A Regional and Chronological Synthesis of Archaic Period Plant Use in the Midcontinent." In *Archaic Societies: Diversity and Complexity across the Midcontinent*, edited by Thomas E. Emerson, Dale L. McElrath, and Andrew C. Fortier, 81–114. Albany: State University of New York Press.

Smith, Bruce D., and Richard A. Yarnell. 2009. "Initial Formation of an Indigenous Crop Complex in Eastern North America at 3800 BP." *Proceedings of the National Academy of Sciences of the United States of America* 106 (16): 6561–66. Medline:19366669 http://dx .doi.org/10.1073/pnas.0901846106.

Smith, Edward E., Jr. 1995. "The Swan's Landing Site (12HR304): An Early Archaic (Kirk Horizon) Site in Harrison County, South-Central Indiana." *Midcontinental Journal of Archaeology* 20 (2): 192–238.

Smith, Monica L. 2011. " 'I Discard, Therefore I Am': Identity and Leaving-Taking of Possessions." In *Identity Crisis: Archaeological Perspectives on Social Identity*, edited by Lindsay Amundsen-Pickering, Nicole Engel, and Sean Pickering, 132–42. Calgary, AB: Chacmool Archaeological Association, University of Calgary.

Smith, Monica L. 2012. "Seeking Abundance: Consumption as a Motivating Factor in Cities Past and Present." In *Political Economy, Neoliberalism, and the Prehistoric Economies of Latin America*, edited by Ty Matejowsky and Donald C. Wood, 27–51. Vol. 32 of Research in Economic Anthropology. Bingley, UK: Emerald. http://dx.doi.org /10.1108/S0190-1281(2012)0000032006.

Strathern, Marilyn. 1988. *The Gender of the Gift*. Berkeley: University of California Press.

Styles, Bonnie W., Steven R. Ahler, and Melvin L. Fowler. 1983. "Modoc Rock Shelter Revisited." In *Archaic Hunters and Gatherers in the American Midwest*, edited by James L. Phillips and James A. Brown, 261–97. New York: Academic.

Styles, Bonnie W., and Walter E. Klippel. 1996. "Mid-Holocene Faunal Exploitation in the Southeastern United States." In *Archaeology of the Mid-Holocene Southeast*, edited by Kenneth E. Sassaman and David G. Anderson, 115–33. Gainesville: University Press of Florida.

Thompson, Victor D. 2010. "The Rhythms of Space-Time and the Making of Monuments and Places during the Archaic." In *Trend, Tradition, and Turmoil: What Happened to the Southeastern Archaic?* edited by David H. Thomas and Matthew C. Sanger, 217–28. New York: American Museum of Natural History.

VanPool, Christine S. 2009. "The Signs of the Sacred: Identifying Shamans Using Archaeological Evidence." *Journal of Anthropological Archaeology* 28 (2): 177–90. http://dx.doi.org/10.1016/j.jaa.2009.02.003.

VanPool, Christine S., and Elizabeth Newsome. 2012. "The Spirit in the Material: A Case Study of Animism in the American Southwest." *American Antiquity* 77 (2): 243–62. http://dx.doi.org/10.7183/0002-7316.77.2.243.

Viveiros de Castro, Eduardo. 1998. "Cosmological Deixis and Amerindian Perspectivism." *Journal of the Royal Anthropological Institute* 4 (3): 469–88. http://dx.doi.org/10.2307/3034157.

Viveiros de Castro, Eduardo. 2004. "Exchanging Perspectives: The Transformation of Objects into Subjects in Amerindian Ontologies." *Common Knowledge* 10 (3): 463–84. http://dx.doi.org/10.1215/0961754X-10-3-463.

Wagner, Gail E. 1996. "Botanizing along the Green River." In *Of Caves and Shell Mounds*, edited by Kenneth C. Carstens and Patty Jo Watson, 88–93. Tuscaloosa: University of Alabama Press.

Ward, Steven C. 2005. "Dental Biology of the Carlston Annis Shell Mound Population." In *Archaeology of the Middle Green River Region, Kentucky*, edited by William H. Marquardt and Patty Jo Watson, 489–503. Gainesville: University of Florida.

Watson, Patty Jo. 2005. "WPA Excavations in the Middle Green River Area: A Comparative Account." In *Archaeology of the Middle Green River Region, Kentucky*, ed. William H. Marquardt and Patty Jo Watson, 515–628. Gainesville: University of Florida.

Webb, William S. 1974. *Indian Knoll*. Knoxville: University of Tennessee Press.

Webb, William S., and William G. Haag. 1939. *The Chiggerville Site, Site 1, Ohio County, Kentucky*. Lexington: University of Kentucky.

Winters, Howard D. 1968. "Value Systems and Trade Cycles of the Late Archaic in the Midwest." In *New Perspectives in Archeology*, edited by Sally R. Binford and Lewis R. Binford, 175–221. Chicago: Aldine.

Zeder, Melinda A. 2012. "The Broad Spectrum Revolution at 40: Resource Diversity, Intensification, and an Alternative to Optimal Foraging Explanations." *Journal of Anthropological Archaeology* 31 (3): 241–64. http://dx.doi.org/10.1016/j.jaa.2012.03.003.

4

Water, Wind, Breath

Seeking Abundance in the Northern American Southwest

MARK D. VARIEN, JAMES M. POTTER, AND TITO E. NARANJO

> May ye Great Ones
> Keep plains and mountains alive
> With grass and game
> May I continue to be loved and liked
> May I catch up with that
> For which I am always yearning
> May I gain
> Life of Abundance

TEWA PRAYER: RECORDED BY LASKI (1959)

The concept of scarcity has played a fundamental role in traditional economic theory (Robbins 1932; Smith 2012:29). Stated in its simplest terms, traditional theoretical perspectives view scarcity as inherent to human economic life because people are seen as having unlimited wants that cannot be satisfied as they live in a world of limited resources. William Dugger and James Peach (2009:1–19) discuss an equally long historical thread where economists have contemplated an alternative economy of abundance in which resources are not viewed as inherently finite and fixed because they can be transformed and multiplied by advances in knowledge and technological progress. Monica Smith (2012, this volume) is one of the first archaeologists to join this debate. She challenges the dominant paradigm that privileges scarcity as an economic concept and instead argues that humans, since

DOI: 10.5876/9781607325949.c004

the time of our earliest ancestors, have sought out and experienced abundance in their engagement with the material world (Smith 2012:27–37). As a result, she argues that abundance can be considered a fundamental aspect of human cognition.

It is important to debate the concepts of scarcity and abundance because economics, more than any other branch of social science, influences the policy developed by contemporary governments and global institutions. It is also important because it attributes to humans specific and inherent qualities and predispositions. As Smith (2012:31) points out, archaeology has much to offer this debate: archaeology alone examines the deep history of human beings' interaction with their material world. This deep, cross-cultural perspective gives us the opportunity to view the concepts of scarcity and abundance in a wider frame than does the relatively recent and perhaps myopic lens of capitalist economic theory. In this chapter we examine the concepts of scarcity and abundance by considering Pueblo Indian society of the southwestern United States, both the ancestral Pueblo Indians who occupied the region for millennia and their modern descendants who continue to live in Pueblo communities in New Mexico and Arizona today. In particular, we focus on the seven-century occupation of the Mesa Verde region of southwestern Colorado (AD 600–1300) (figure 4.1). We provide a context for this archaeological case study by including the perspective of modern Tewa-speaking Pueblo people of the northern Rio Grande region of New Mexico. Important for our study, a direct historical link between the ancestral Pueblo people of our Mesa Verde study area and the Tewa-speaking Pueblo people of today has been demonstrated by Scott Ortman (2012) using data from archaeology, oral tradition, physical anthropology, and linguistics.

The northern American Southwest is often viewed as a landscape of scarcity because of its limited precipitation and relatively short growing seasons. This perspective of inherent scarcity is in turn applied to ancestral Pueblo Indian societies, who based their subsistence economy on maize farming (Cordell 1984:189; Plog 1974:160). Despite this view, Pueblo people have thrived in the region for thousands of years. This dichotomy—in which a remarkable culture has thrived for thousands of years in an austere landscape of seemingly scarce resources—provides an intriguing setting for our examination of the concepts of scarcity and abundance. Because both scarcity and abundance have been argued to be inherent properties of the lives of humans in general and Pueblo Indians in particular, we thought it was important to begin this chapter by asking whether Pueblo people themselves view their world as characterized by scarcity or abundance. Our coauthor Tito E. Naranjo, who is from Santa Clara Pueblo, provides a Pueblo perspective on this question.

But we want to go beyond examining abundance as an abstract, philosophical concept and find ways to measure scarcity and abundance in Pueblo society. Were there aspects of Pueblo people's world that became scarcer or more abundant over

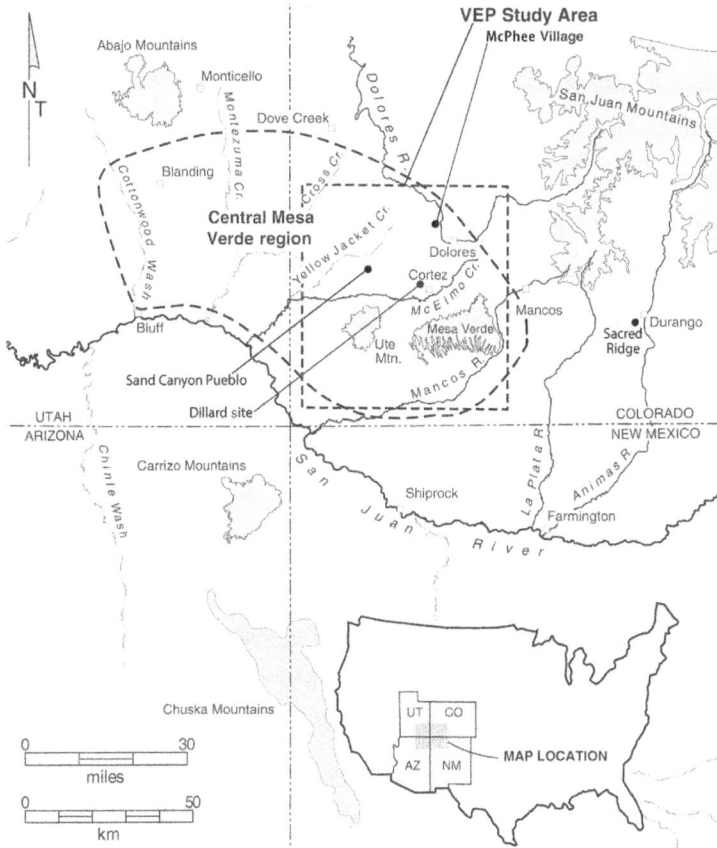

FIGURE 4.1. Map showing location of the central Mesa Verde region, the Village Ecodynamics Project study area, and the major sites discussed in text. *Courtesy,* Crow Canyon Archaeological Center, Cortez, CO.

time? To answer this question we examine three important aspects of Pueblo life: agricultural production, the accumulation of artifacts, and communal feasting at ceremonial events.

To evaluate agricultural production, we draw on recent results by the Village Ecodynamics Project (VEP), which uses computer modeling to reconstruct ancestral Pueblo agricultural yields in the Mesa Verde region. We demonstrate that Pueblo agricultural production in this area was indeed characterized by periodic scarcity, but we also show that abundant yields were just as common. Given this observation, we ask how scarcity and abundance were woven together in the lives of Pueblo people, both ancestral Pueblo people and their living descendants. Further, we explore how the concept of abundance, while not typically associated with Pueblo groups, provides insights into the dynamics that characterize Pueblo society, This perspective allows us to illustrate how Pueblo people's experiences in the Mesa Verde region produced a long-term impact on their social memory and shaped social strategies employed to this day.

To further examine material abundance, we also measure the accumulation of artifacts, focusing on pottery assemblages. We assess whether the pottery vessels in household assemblages became more numerous and more diverse over time. We begin by showing how bowls, which were relatively scarce in the earliest pottery assemblages, became exponentially more common through time. In addition, distinct size classes of bowls eventually developed. We further discuss how new vessel forms other than bowls and jars were added to the household pottery assemblage over time. These analyses show without question that Pueblo households in the Mesa Verde region did produce more abundant pottery assemblages over time.

Finally, we examine the practice of feasting associated with ceremonial events, using architecture, artifacts, and faunal remains as evidence. Clearly, feasting can be viewed as an expression of abundance, but we discuss how this episodic expression of abundance was structured in part by the threat of periodic scarcity. We show how Pueblo feasting is different from feasting that occurred elsewhere. In contrast to other parts of the world, communal feasting in the northern Southwest involved common, everyday resources, such as maize and rabbits, rather than rare, valuable, or feasting-specific resources. We show how ancestral Pueblo feasting occurred at ceremonial events that only took place at certain sites and in association with particular buildings and open spaces. Further, we discuss how feasting included the use of pottery vessels, including larger vessels and some with distinct types of decoration. We suggest that these feasts communicated messages of abundance while often being provisioned under conditions of scarcity or the threat of scarcity; because the feasts occurred in the context of public ritual, they can be viewed as performances of abundance. Our study shows that the scale of these rituals varied greatly but in general increased through time, which may be considered another aspect of increasing abundance in these communities.

A PUEBLO VIEW OF ABUNDANCE

We begin by exploring the concepts of abundance and scarcity from a modern but historically informed Pueblo perspective. For this we draw upon Naranjo's knowledge as a Tewa[1] elder from Santa Clara Pueblo. His Pueblo perspective views these concepts—abundance and scarcity—as two parts of a greater whole: one cannot exist without the other, and they occur in cycles. This is similar to the observation made by Smith in her review of abundance as an economic principle and archaeological concept: she views the perception of something as scarce or abundant as situational and relative, with one defined in part by reference to the other (Smith 2012, this volume).

We believe the perspective that follows would apply broadly to all Pueblo groups, but Tito cautions that he is speaking specifically about the Tewa-Pueblo worldview he knows best. In Tito's view, the concepts of scarcity and abundance are best understood in reference to deeper, more fundamental aspects of ideation that include Pueblo philosophical concepts and values. Perhaps the most central tenet of Tewa philosophy is a concept called "seeking life," and abundance is best understood with reference to this concept. Seeking life refers to the Tewa belief that a life force is present in all aspects of creation—including matter that a scientific perspective would classify as both animate and inanimate—and that all of creation is interconnected through this life force. The Tewa word for this life force is *p'o wa ha*, which literally translates to "water, wind, breath."

When Tewa people speak of seeking life, they are referring to seeking a connection to this life force, and they view this as the most important goal of one's life. Tewa people use a variety of expressions to speak of searching for and finding the life force, with *woatsi tuenji* referring to seeking life, *woatsi shaa* as finding life, and *woatsi maegi* as giving life. According to Tewa understanding, the concepts of an interconnected life force and seeking life developed during the deep Pueblo past, including their time in the Mesa Verde region of southwestern Colorado (AD 600–1285).

A connection to the life force can only be achieved by living one's life according to Tewa values. There are many core Tewa values. They include the importance of community, respecting elders and their knowledge of traditions, nurturing children, hard work, and displaying generosity by sharing with others. Tito understands abundance in terms of this formula: living one's life in accordance with Tewa values brings one into contact with the life force, and contact with the life force ensures abundance. In this way, abundance is not a standalone concept in Tewa thought but is instead an integral component of Tewa values and connecting with the life force that underlies creation. In this way, for Tewa people, abundance is not only material but also spiritual.

AGRICULTURAL PRODUCTIVITY: CYCLES OF SCARCITY AND ABUNDANCE

Economists and other social scientists—especially those concerned with issues of social justice and sustainability—have criticized the central role scarcity plays in modern economic theory (Dugger and Peach 2009; Hoeschele 2010). They point out that rather than intrinsic to economic systems—especially capitalist economies—scarcity is often socially constructed to the advantage of some and the detriment of others. Socially constructed scarcity is an important aspect of theorizing economic systems, including pre-capitalist economies, but as Smith (this volume) notes, not all scarcity and abundance is socially constructed. True scarcity and true abundance exist and largely result from the inherent qualities of particular phenomena. We believe the inherent properties of ancestral Pueblo agricultural production did result in true scarcity and abundance, and so we begin our attempt to measure scarcity and abundance in Pueblo Indian society by estimating the agricultural productivity in the Mesa Verde region.

Despite the fact that Mesa Verde Pueblo people farmed a variety of crops, hunted wild animals, and collected wild plants (Adams and Bowyer 2002; Driver 2002), maize farming was by far the most important component of their subsistence economy. Bone chemistry studies that examine stable carbon and nitrogen isotopes have been used to reconstruct the reliance on maize and consumption of animal protein; these studies indicate that ancestral Pueblo people got at least 70 percent of their calories from maize (Chisholm and Matson 1994; Coltrain and Janetski 2013:4713; Coltrain, Janetski, and Carlyle 2006, 2007:314; Matson and Chisholm 1991:452–56). The results of these bone chemistry analyses are supported by analyses of coprolites, pollen, and plant macrofossils (Aasen 1984; Geib 2011:225–29; Lepofsky 1986) and by the analysis of groundstone (Hard, Mauldin, and Raymond 1996). Pueblo people relied on maize for the vast majority of their calories from the time of their first appearance in the Four Corners region at about 500 BC until they migrated from the area at the end of the thirteenth century.

Focusing on maize farming as the starting point for our examination of scarcity and abundance makes even more sense when we consider the minimum precipitation and growing season requirements for Pueblo varieties of maize. A minimum threshold for precipitation is 30 cm, or about 12 inches, per year (Benson 2011a, 2011b; Benson and Berry 2009). By comparison, the average precipitation during the historic period for the town of Cortez, Colorado, which is in the center of our Mesa Verde region study area, is 12.6 inches, or 32 cm (Shaw, Sprague, and Dudley 1988). Pueblo maize also has a minimum temperature requirement; in technical studies this is measured as growing degree days (GDD), and the minimum threshold is 1,800°F GDD (Bellorado 2007; Benson and Berry 2009). Although not precisely equivalent to GDD, it is easier to understand the temperature requirement for maize when it is expressed as the length of the frost-free growing season. On average, varieties of maize indigenous to the greater Southwest require a 128-day growing season, with a range of 111 to 144 days (Adams et al. 2006:47–48). This compares to 125 days for the average growing season for Cortez. These data indicate that average conditions in our Mesa Verde study area were just above the minimum thresholds for growing maize, and annual fluctuations in precipitation and temperature could therefore result in either crop failure or abundant harvests. It is possible that socially constructed dimensions of maize production also affected the way Pueblo people obtained this crop, which was critical to their survival, but any socially constructed conditions would have derived from the yields determined by these inherent properties of maize farming. An understanding of these inherent properties and their effects on agricultural production provides an important foundation for examining scarcity and abundance in ancestral Pueblo society.

The research program known as the Village Ecodynamics Project uses computer modeling to estimate agricultural productivity in the Mesa Verde region (Kohler and Varien 2012). The VEP methods for modeling maize-farming yields are likely the most rigorous yet developed for reconstructing agricultural production in any ancient society, and they are broken down into steps and reported in detail (Kohler 2012:86–108; Varien et al. in press). The VEP model begins by using tree-ring analysis to get precipitation and temperature estimates for each year between AD 600 and the present. Then the study area is divided into 4-hectare cells—there are over 110,000 of these—and the elevation and the characteristics of the soils in each cell are measured, including the moisture-holding capacity of the soils. Precipitation and soil properties are combined to calculate the accumulated soil moisture for each cell during each year (Palmer 1965). The statistical relationship between this measure and crop yields is calculated for the historic period and subsequently retrodicted back to AD 600. These results were systematically modified to take into account changes in technology, differences between historic and indigenous maize varieties and planting strategies, the effects of elevation on production, and the possible effects of soil nutrient depletion. The result is an estimate of maize yields for every cell in the VEP study area for every year between AD 600 and 1300.

Figure 4.2 presents the results of the VEP analysis, showing annual variation in maize yields standardized as z scores. The horizontal black line at zero is the 700-year average production; the lighter, dashed horizontal black lines are 1 standard deviation above and below this long-term mean. The vertical black bars show individual years that are within 1 standard deviation of the mean, or years when yields were closest to the long-term average. These conditions prevailed during 493 years, or 70 percent of the time, of the 700-year Pueblo occupation of the region. These likely represent years when Pueblo farmers were able to obtain harvests, although figure 4.2 shows that yields would have fluctuated considerably even during those years. There were 230 years when the yields were above the long-term mean and 263 years when they were below average. Even during the times that were closest to the long-term average, Pueblo people would have experienced a constant swing between relatively abundant and relatively scarce yields.

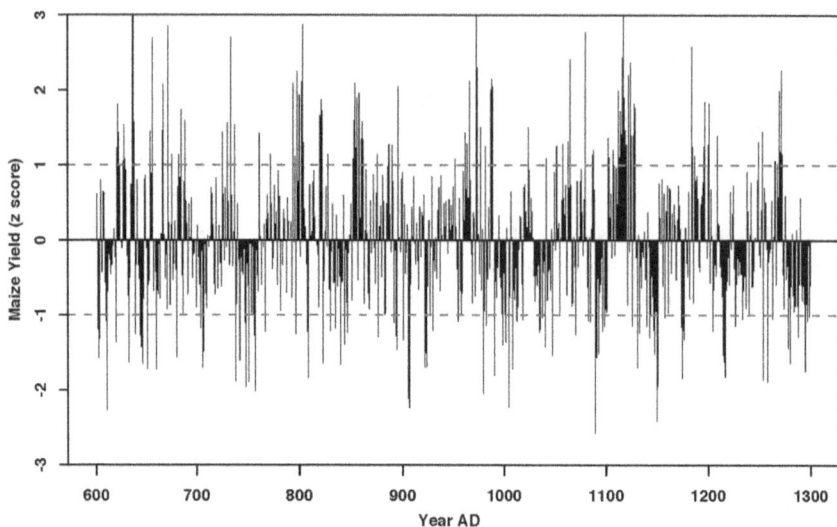

FIGURE 4.2. Annual estimates of maize productivity for the VEP II study area, AD 600–1300 (standardized to z scores). Bars more than 1 standard deviation above the mean are unusually wet years with high productivity and more than 1 standard deviation below the mean are unusually dry years with low productivity. *Courtesy*, Crow Canyon Archaeological Center, Cortez, CO.

The gray vertical bars in figure 4.2 show years that are more than 1 standard deviation above or below the mean. Years below this 1 standard deviation threshold are times of exceptionally low precipitation, extreme cold, or both. These conditions produced extremely low yields or in some cases complete crop failure. There are 104 years—about 1 year in 7—when Pueblo farmers would have experienced extreme scarcity in food production. There are also 140 extremely wet years with adequate temperature and sufficient growing seasons that produced yields 1 standard deviation above the mean. These would have been years with unusually abundant harvests. These data illustrate that unusually abundant and scarce harvests occurred relatively regularly and in the same frequency, reinforcing Tito's observation that a constant oscillation between abundance and scarcity did in fact characterize the lives of Pueblo people.

ACCUMULATING ABUNDANCE: PUEBLO POTTERY ASSEMBLAGES

Next, we examine abundance by focusing on the accumulation of artifacts. As Smith (2012, this volume) notes, as a measure of abundance, artifact accumulation includes per capita increases in the same type of artifact or increases in the diversity of objects. We investigate this form of abundance by examining the pottery assemblages of Mesa Verde Pueblo households and begin by focusing on the accumulation of bowls. We measure how the accumulation of bowls changed through time at thirty-two tree-ring-dated sites from the VEP study area.

A brief history of pottery use in the study area provides the basic context for this analysis. The earliest use of pottery by Pueblo groups in the northern Southwest dates to about AD 300 when a plain utilitarian ware, usually brownish in color, first appeared (Geib 2011:280). These early vessels were jars used primarily for cooking or storage. Pottery sherds from these early brown ware vessels were few in number, and in fact they were not present at many excavated habitation sites dating between AD 300 and the late AD 500s. Brown wares were largely replaced by gray wares and white wares in the late AD 500s, and pottery sherds became much more numerous and uniformly present at habitation sites by about AD 600, when the VEP study area was first settled by large numbers of Pueblo farm families.

There is a clear functional distinction between gray and white wares beginning with the first appearance of this pottery. Early gray wares were mostly cooking jars (Blinman 1988:458, 1993:18) but also included some storage vessels; gray wares become increasingly specialized as cooking pots over time. In contrast, most early white ware vessels were storage jars (Blinman 1993), but for the first time bowls used as serving vessels also occurred in low but consistent numbers at habitation sites. Red ware pottery that primarily included storage jars and bowls first appeared at about AD 780. Red ware vessels were produced in areas outside our Mesa Verde study area but were traded into southwestern Colorado in relatively small numbers and appeared at sites dating between AD 780 and 1300. In the analysis that follows, we focus on gray ware cooking jars, bowls that are predominantly white wares, and red ware bowls when present.

We measure changes in the abundance of bowls by calibrating them against the accumulation of cooking pot sherds. Elsewhere we have demonstrated that cooking pot sherds accumulated at a relatively constant rate (Varien 1999:73–80; Varien and Mills 1997; Varien and Ortman 2005; Varien and Potter 1997). The accumulation rate for cooking pots is largely a result of the regular use of these vessels, and the relationship among use, breakage, and uselife of cooking pots has been documented in experimental, archaeological, and ethnoarchaeological studies (Bronitsky 1986; Bronitsky and Hamer 1986; Nelson 1991; Pierce 1999, 2005; Rice 1987; Rye 1976; Schiffer et al. 1994; Steponaitis 1983, 1984; Tani 1994; Varien and Mills 1997; West 1992). The regular accumulation rate of cooking pots is further demonstrated by examining the relationship between cooking pot sherds and chipped stone debris from screened assemblages at sites dating between AD 600 and 1280 (figure 4.3). Even though their use, discard, and rate of accumulation were governed by entirely

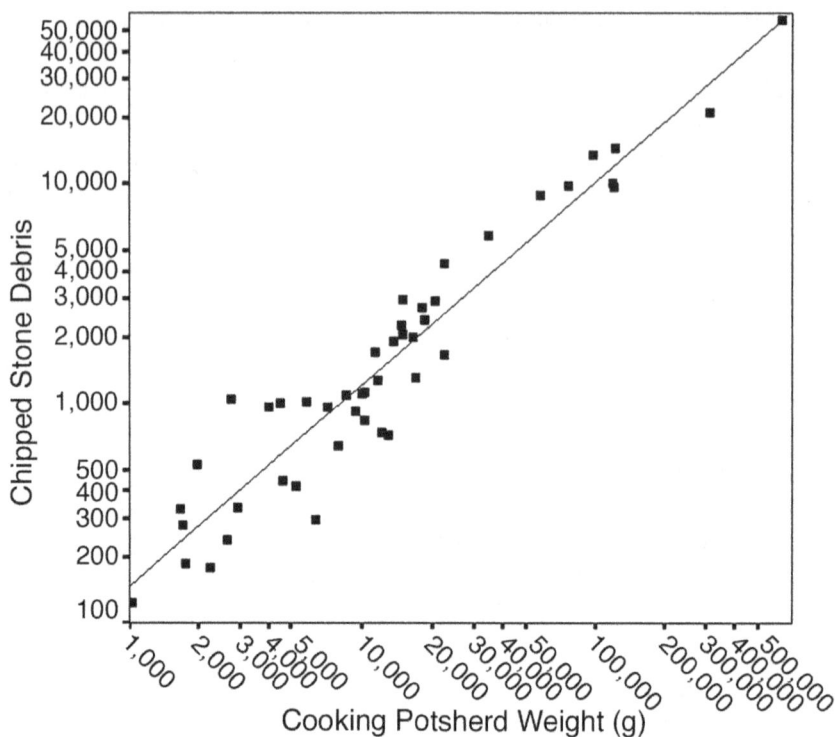

FIGURE 4.3. Scatterplot showing the relationship between discard of cooking pot sherds and chipped stone debris from screened assemblages at forty-five sites dating between AD 600 and 1300 in the central Mesa Verde region VEP II study area (Rsq 0.97). Sites were excavated by the Crow Canyon Archaeological Center or the Dolores Archaeological Program. *Courtesy*, Crow Canyon Archaeological Center, Cortez, CO.

different behaviors, Pueblo people discarded chipped stone debris and broken cooking pots as a result of daily domestic activities. The strong correlation seen here could only result if these functionally unrelated artifact types accumulated at regular rates through time. The fact that we have a good understanding of the use, breakage, and discard of cooking pottery and can demonstrate that this pottery accumulated at a constant rate through time means that it can be used to examine how the accumulation rate of other artifact categories changed (or did not change) through time.

Here, we used the constant accumulation rate of cooking jars to identify changes in the accumulation of pottery bowls. We examined the relationship between the accumulation of pottery sherds from cooking pots and bowls at thirty-two sites dating between AD 600 and 1280. These sites are located in the VEP study area and

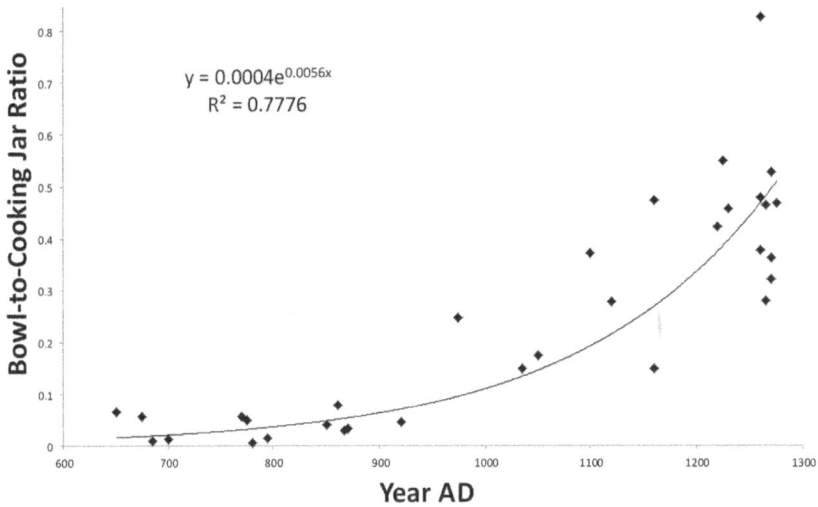

The equation shown on the chart: $y = 0.0004e^{0.0056x}$, $R^2 = 0.7776$

FIGURE 4.4. Ratio of bowl-to-cooking jar pottery sherds from screened assemblages at thirty-two tree-ring–dated sites in the central Mesa Verde region VEP II study area (ratio calculated using sherd weights). *Courtesy*, Crow Canyon Archaeological Center, Cortez, CO.

were selected because they are precisely dated with tree-ring analysis and they have screened deposits. This analysis shows that the accumulation of bowls increased exponentially over time, with an average growth rate of about 0.6 percent per year (figure 4.4). Clearly, household bowl inventories increased through time, and by the end of the sequence households had many more bowls in their pottery inventories, which serves as a direct measure of increasing abundance in the lives of Mesa Verde Pueblo people.

Rim-arc measurements of bowls can be used to estimate the volumes of these vessels, and this analysis shows that two distinct sizes of bowls developed in the AD 1200s in the central Mesa Verde region (Ortman 2000). The volume of small bowls is about a liter, while large bowls hold about 5 liters (Ortman 2000:paragraph 45, figure 1). Small bowls were likely used by individuals to consume food, while large bowls were used to serve food to individuals; the difference in their size suggests that household groups numbered about five people. Several lines of data indicate that these bowls were produced in most, if not all, households by non-specialist potters (Pierce et al. 1999). A similar analysis also shows that household pottery assemblages came to include different-size cooking jars through time (Ortman 2000:paragraph 46, figure 2). These data show a more continuous distribution of vessel sizes, so rather than producing distinct size categories, potters in Mesa Verde households produced a range of vessels of different sizes to meet their needs.

FIGURE 4.5. Whole and partial pottery vessels left behind by the household that occupied Block 500 at Sand Canyon Pueblo. Photo by David Grimes. *Courtesy,* Crow Canyon Archaeological Center, Cortez, CO.

The development of distinct size classes in both bowls and cooking jars is an example of household pottery assemblages becoming more diverse through time, and this diversity is another measure of increasing abundance in Pueblo society. Although few in number relative to bowls, households also added new forms of decorated white ware vessels through time, for example, ladles, mugs, and specialized seed jars known as kiva jars that also occur in different sizes. Here again, greater diversity is a measure of increasing abundance through time. By the AD 1200s, Pueblo families had numerous and diverse household inventories. This is illustrated in figure 4.5, which shows the vessels left behind when a house at Sand Canyon Pueblo was abandoned at about AD 1285.

Ortman examined the frequencies of vessel size categories at both small and large sites that date to the AD 1200s. His analysis shows that large vessels—both cooking pots and bowls—occur in greater numbers at villages and are fewer in number at small farmsteads (Ortman 2000:paragraphs 43–58). He argues this may be a result of the fact that specific activities took place in villages that did not occur at smaller sites. This includes the use of larger vessels during feasts that accompanied communal ceremonies conducted at the large villages. We elaborate on this pattern in the section that follows.

PERFORMING ABUNDANCE

The use of food and ritual to create relationships beyond the family—what we refer to as feasting—is well documented cross-culturally in small-scale societies (Dietler and Hayden 2001; Goody 1982; Gremillion 2011; Monaghan 1990; Weissner and Schiefenhovel 1996). In the Southwest, feasting is understood as one of the primary mechanisms whereby small-scale agriculturalists of the past increased the social, demographic, and political scale of their societies (Blinman 1989; Ford 1972; Graves and Spielmann 2000; Phillips and Sebastian 2004; Potter 2000; Potter and Ortman 2004; Spielmann 2002, 2004; Wills and Crown 2004). In contrast to the majority of small-scale societies around the world, though, communal feasting in Pueblo contexts was less overtly political and less lavish, and for the most part it involved the same suite of artifacts and food resources generally used for the preparation of domestic-style meals rather than rare or special items and foods. This has prompted Potter and Ortman (2004:175) to suggest that communal feasts at Pueblos are a metaphorical extension of the domestic meal. In this way, Pueblo feasts differ from many other feasting contexts around the world in which the ideological significance of communal feasting derives from its articulation with more authoritarian and sometimes masculine realms, for example, warfare, competitive politics, and hunting (de Garine 1996; Dietler 1996; Hayden 1995, 2001; Weissner 2001; Young 1971).

Another unique aspect of Pueblo feasts is that they are generally financed by the participating families rather than a single "big man" or political leader (Potter 2000). Thus, feasts have been described more as potluck than potlatch events (Blinman 1989). Food is prepared in homes and then brought to the communal gathering place, often a large structure or plaza, and shared among the participants. Households that have fared better provide greater quantities of food, and this is distributed—often by masked and anonymous *katchinas*—to less fortunate families. These events ensure that household scarcity and abundance are evened out (to the extent that they can be) and that household abundance is translated to communal abundance or at least sufficiency. As discussed above, food resources in the Southwest are episodically scarce when annual precipitation was too low or the growing season too short to produce maize. Hunted game, particularly deer, became scarce as a result of sedentism, population growth, and resultant overhunting (Driver 2002). Yet even during times of scarcity, the performance of the feast and associated ceremony celebrated and acknowledged abundance through the active display and exchange of food and gifts among community members.

Evidence indicates that these performances occurred at villages (i.e., settlements containing nine or more aggregated households [Wilshusen and Potter 2010]) rather than at smaller sites such as single-family farmsteads or small hamlets. This is exemplified by four cases presented below—the Dillard site, Sacred Ridge, McPhee Village, and Sand Canyon Pueblo—all of which are villages surrounded by smaller contemporaneous settlements. In addition to being associated with larger settlements, feasting is also typically associated with specific types of buildings and open space at these villages: great kivas, oversized pit structures, multi-wall structures, and plazas.

- Great kivas are large, circular structures that are at least partly subterranean and greater than 10 m in diameter; some are much larger. They can be either roofed or unroofed, tend to contain relatively few floor features (although ritual features are present), and often incorporate a bench encircling the perimeter of the structure. Great kivas were truly communal structures in that they could accommodate the entire (or a large segment of the) community at once, but the visibility of the activities conducted in them was variable depending on whether they were roofed. Domestic activities were not typically conducted in great kivas.
- Oversized pit structures, in contrast, functioned both as communal gathering places and as domestic residences of what were likely to have been high-status, important, or large households. Oversized pit structures resemble domestic pit structures in their basic morphology but are larger—on average about 8–10 m in diameter—and usually have more elaborate ritual features compared with smaller, domestic pit houses.
- Multiple-wall structures are buildings with concentric walls that define the outside of the structure; the space between these concentric walls is divided by cross walls that create numerous rooms around the perimeter of the building. A small kiva or kivas are usually located in the interior of the building. Multiple-wall structures typically occur in two variations: D-shaped bi-walls that were most common in the central Mesa Verde region of southwestern Colorado and circular tri-walls that were most common in the middle San Juan region of northwestern New Mexico. Multi-wall structures are often interpreted as elite residences and generally did not house large communal gatherings but rather more exclusive rituals.
- Finally, plazas are the most inclusive public space found in Pueblo villages at which feasting occurred. Their size and configuration varies widely as determined by the standing architecture that defines their boundaries, but access to them, both physical and visual, tends to be open.

We examine the evidence for ritual and feasting at several sites in our study area at which this practice has been documented in association with these various types of architecture: the Dillard site during the AD 600s, Sacred Ridge during the late 700s and early 800s, McPhee Village in the late 800s, and Sand Canyon Pueblo in the late 1200s. Our study shows that the scale of these rituals varied greatly but in general increased through time, which may be considered another aspect of increasing abundance in Pueblo communities.

The Dillard Site

The earliest evidence for public ceremony and communal feasting in the Mesa Verde region appears at the Dillard site, a village of the Basketmaker III period located just west of Cortez, Colorado, and dating to the AD 600s. Investigations at this site are ongoing by the Crow Canyon Archaeological Center. The site is centered on a great kiva that is the earliest and only known great kiva in the Mesa Verde region. The Dillard site is unusual because most of the sites dating to this time period are single-household farmsteads; Dillard, by contrast, is a village with at least a dozen pit structures concentrated in two clusters, one north and one south of the great kiva. Kari Schleher and others (2013) have documented relatively high proportions of serving bowl sherds in association with the great kiva at this site, presumably because of the communal serving and consumption of food during ceremonies performed in and around this structure. Data on the types of foods served have not yet been recovered, but presumably stews and boiled foods prepared in cooking pots and in domestic contexts were served in these bowls.

The great kiva is a very large communal structure that served the ritual needs of the village and perhaps a larger, more dispersed Basketmaker III population. This marks the initiation of a long tradition of the use of great kivas as communal structures and a context for feasting, one that began in the northern Southwest during the late AD 500s or early 600s and continued for the next 700 years. Although some archaeologists argue that great kivas disappeared from the Pueblo record at about AD 1300, we view great kivas as the best analogy for the kivas that continue to be used in Pueblo communities today.

Sacred Ridge

Located on a tributary of the Animas River, the early Pueblo I (AD 700–825) settlement Sacred Ridge occupied a large knoll at the west end of Ridges Basin. The village contained twenty-two pit structures, dozens of burials, and a complex of ritual features at the apex of the knoll consisting of a two-story surface structure, a large circular surface room, and a palisade enclosure. Five of the pit structures were unusually large, or "oversized," and contained features similar to those found in smaller pit structures, such as a hearth and a wing wall. But they also contained additional ritual floor features and immense wraparound benches. Ritual floor features include small circular holes analogous to *sipapus* directly behind the central hearth and large conical pits offset from the hearth, all of which were plastered and, when closed, filled with clean sand and capped with a layer of clay. Averaging 8 m in diameter (50 m² in roofed area), these oversized pit structures were two to five times the size of the smaller, household-level pit structures. Feasting has been argued to have occurred in these structures based on their large capacity, the disproportionately high numbers of serving bowl sherds, and the relatively high frequencies of artiodactyl (deer) and lagomorph (rabbit) remains associated with them (Allison 2010; Potter and Edwards 2008). Thus, stews and roasted game appear to have been served and consumed in these contexts.

Sacred Ridge was one of a number of contemporaneously occupied early Pueblo I sites in Ridges Basin, thirty-four of which were excavated as part of the Animas–La Plata Reservoir project from 2002 to 2005 (Potter 2010). These sites were much smaller than Sacred Ridge, consisting of one to four pit structures. As indicated, though, Sacred Ridge was not only larger than these sites, but it also contained (1) the only communal architecture in the community (in the form of oversized pit structures); (2) the only architectural complex comprising unique architectural forms, such as a two-story tower and a circular surface room, all enclosed by a palisade; (3) the only evidence of feasting in the community; and (4) the highest relative frequency of serving bowl sherds and artiodactyl remains in the community. It is doubtful that feasts at Sacred Ridge were truly communal in scale and as inclusive as those associated with great kivas; this interpretation is based on the large size of the community (i.e., over fifty households at peak population levels), the comparatively small size of oversized pit structures, and the direct association of the oversized pit structures with particular households.

McPhee Village

McPhee Village was an aggregated community in the Dolores River Valley that was occupied during AD 850–900; an earlier component exists but is not part of an aggregated community (Kane and Robinson 1988). It was composed of twenty-one spatially discrete but contemporaneous roomblocks, each with associated pit structures. Like Sacred Ridge, the site lacked a great kiva but contained a number of oversized pit structures that have been interpreted as communal ritual structures. Three oversized pit structures associated with three different roomblocks (5MT4475, 5MT4477, and 5MT5107) in this community had roofed areas greater than 30 m^2 (67 m^2, 64 m^2, and 37 m^2, respectively) and contained an array of floor features comparable to historic "chief kivas" (Mindeleff 1891:134), including complex sipapus, lateral vaults, sand-filled pits as sockets to support altars, possible prayer-stick holes in structure floors, and floor vaults with wooden covers interpreted as foot drums (Wilshusen 1989). These structures differ markedly from those at Sacred Ridge in the number and complexity of floor features associated with them that were likely related to the performance of ritual.

Another distinction at McPhee is that the oversized pit structures are associated with U-shaped roomblocks. The construction of U-shaped roomblocks created small, semi-enclosed spaces that enveloped the oversized pit structures and formed some of the earliest known architecturally bounded plazas. In at least one case, a wall closed off the open end of the surrounding U-shaped roomblock, restricting access to the oversized pit structure and surrounding plaza to an even greater degree (Brisbin, Kane, and Morris 1988:234–35). This suggests that feasts held in these plazas and the rituals conducted in these structures were even more exclusive than were the feasts at Sacred Ridge.

Eric Blinman (1989) has demonstrated a significant correlation at McPhee Village between roomblocks associated with oversized pit structures and high relative frequencies of red ware bowls, which were imported into the area during the ninth century AD. He suggests that the communal ceremonial behaviors associated with these structures account for the inflated frequencies of red ware bowls, both because of their value as imported commodities and because of their use in serving and consuming food during feasts. Likewise, James Potter (1997) noted the high proportion of rabbit and deer remains associated with oversized pit structures within the community, as well as inordinate frequencies of wild and carnivore remains, arguing that these patterns are a result of the performance of communal feasting and ritual. This is supported by Timothy Kohler and Charles Reed's (2011) analysis that indicates that McPhee Village and other large settlements in the Dolores River Valley emphasized deer hunting and located their villages to ensure successful hunts. Again, data suggest that roasted game, in addition to stewed and boiled foods, were served and consumed in these contexts and that participation (both physical and visible) was relatively restricted within the community.

Sand Canyon Pueblo

The late Pueblo III site Sand Canyon Pueblo dates from about AD 1250 to 1285; with 400 to 600 residents, it was one of the largest villages inhabited during the final decades of Pueblo occupation in the Mesa Verde region (Kuckelman 2007). Prior inhabitants in the area had reduced local game populations; the developed sociopolitical landscape also made it difficult for people to range widely in search of game (Driver 1993, 2002; Schollmeyer and Driver 2011, 2013; Varien 1999). Intensified ritual and ceremonial feasting at the site is suggested by the presence of a variety of communal architectural spaces: a plaza, an unroofed great kiva, and a D-shaped bi-wall structure.

This architectural evidence is complemented by the differences in the sizes and decoration of cooking pots and serving bowls discussed above (Ortman 2000;

Ortman and Bradley 2002). A higher proportion of very large cooking pots was deposited at Sand Canyon Pueblo than at earlier and contemporaneous smaller sites around the village. These vessels are larger than needed for family meals, and Scott Ortman and Bruce Bradley (2002) argue that the larger cooking pots were used to prepare food for communal meals and that the meals were consumed in public view around the plaza and in the great kiva. Large serving bowls were also present in greater numbers than those found at smaller sites. In addition, a higher percentage of the larger serving vessels at Sand Canyon were decorated on their exteriors (Ortman 2000:paragraphs 59–61). The exterior decoration on these vessels has been interpreted as evidence of intentional display of social identity in public contexts, as these intricate decorations would have been visible even when the bowls were full of food (Ortman and Bradley 2002:68; Robinson 2005). This strongly suggests that communicating social identity was important in these contexts and that these events were likely multi-community in scale.

The depleted nature of the local environment, a high frequency of grinding implements, and a low proportion of faunal remains, especially deer, compared to Pueblo I contexts (Potter and Ortman 2004:table 10.1) all suggest that cuisine at Sand Canyon Pueblo was dominated by agricultural products such as corn and beans rather than by hunted game. By extension, serving and consuming prepared agriculturally based cooked food was likely emphasized in communal feasting contexts, and roasted and stewed fauna deemphasized. Moreover, the high proportion of cooking pots and serving bowls (particularly compared to Pueblo I villages) indicates that boiling was the preferred preparation method (rather than roasting, for example).

FEASTING AND ABUNDANCE: A SUMMARY

Communal ritual accompanied by food sharing is a practice that extends deep into the Pueblo past. By sharing food surpluses at public ceremonies, community members performed and experienced abundance, perhaps even in the face of production shortfalls and scarcity. This performed abundance provided food to needy families, but these rituals also produced long-term social relations of reciprocity, debt, and obligation.

The scale of these events, and the network of social relations facilitated by them, varied but tended to increase through time. Two very different communal ritual traditions operated in the northern Southwest, one that was truly communal—the great kiva tradition—and one that was restricted to certain households within the community—the oversized pit structure tradition. The great kiva was the longest-lived tradition. It began in the Basketmaker III period at the Dillard site and other early villages (e.g., Cummings 1953; Gilpin and Benallie 2000; Haury 1928; Roberts

1929; Wills and Windes 1989) and continued through the sequence until 1285, as exemplified by Sand Canyon Pueblo. Even during the Pueblo I period, when some villages adopted the oversized pit structure ritual tradition, great kivas were still in use in some communities. A great kiva at Grass Mesa Village in the Dolores River Valley, for example, was in use between AD 760 and 810, the same time as the oversized pit structures at Sacred Ridge (Lightfoot 1988; Lightfoot, Emerson, and Blinman 1988). This great kiva measured 22.6 m in diameter and had a floor area of approximately 400 m², making it 16 times the size of the contemporaneous structures that surrounded it.

By contrast, the oversized pit structure tradition was relatively short-lived. There are examples of oversized Basketmaker III pit houses (Hurst 2011; Lux-Harriman 1982), but it is not clear if they are analogous to the later oversized pit structures discussed above, with these examples limited to the period AD 750–900. In addition, communities with oversized pit structures were short-lived and volatile (Wilshusen and Potter 2010). Occupation at Sacred Ridge, for example, ended in a community-wide massacre involving at least thirty-five victims (Potter and Chuipka 2010). We suggest that this was in part the result of a contradiction between the communal practice of potluck feasts that occurred in the plazas and open spaces at these villages and the more exclusive ritual practices that occurred in the oversized pit structures. The smaller, more exclusive structures may have been less effective at integrating culturally diverse village populations than were the more communal and inclusive great kiva feasts. Not only do great kivas (and the rituals associated with them) persist after 900, but more inclusive and visible contexts for ritual performance—the plaza and the unroofed great kiva—become more common as well.

We also see a shift from primarily hunted resources being shared at feasts in earlier villages to agricultural products in later contexts (Kohler and Reed 2011; Potter 1997; Potter 2000). Unlike hunted meat, corn and beans can be stored for long periods of time. Thus, the timing of corn-based feasts is not dependent on the timing of resource acquisition—these feasts can occur, for example, during times of the year in which household stores are low and consequently can facilitate the redistribution of food surpluses across households, as Richard Ford (1972) has documented for the historic Tewa. Maize-based feasts would not have been as dependent on the timing of resource acquisition and could have occurred during times of the year when individual household stores were low, redistributing food across households.

But storable foods can also encourage surplus accumulation among households or communal storage of surpluses (Gremillion 2011; Twiss and Bogaard, this volume). Surplus accumulation is one of the principal factors cited in evolutionary models of the development of political leadership and social inequality in middle-range societies (Blitz 1993; Feinman 2000; Smith 2012:30–31), and it appears that surplus accumulation was an important dimension of the social dynamic at Sand Canyon Pueblo (Lipe 2002). One of the buildings in the village appears to have been a communal storage facility located in the plaza, and adjacent to this structure was a D-shaped building that appears to have functioned as both a high-status residence and a setting for secretive ritual (Lipe 2002:225; Ortman and Bradley 2002:67). This raises the possibility that community surpluses were controlled by the community's political leadership. Community leaders at Sand Canyon Pueblo appear to have had greater access to larger quantities of stored food resources such as corn, and redistributing those resources in the context of public rituals would have solidified their position as leaders—a scenario more in line with the potlatch model of feasting than the potluck model.

As noted, large bowls of a standardized size were added to the pottery assemblage in the thirteenth century, and at late villages with public architecture a greater percentage of these bowls have exterior decoration, serving as statements of identity in public contexts. The need to convey identity in this manner suggests that people from beyond the immediate community attended these events; this would further extend the network of social relations at play during communal rituals at these late villages. Thus, feasts grew in both scale and political import as surpluses—the consequences of periodic abundance—were publicly shared. The shift to corn-based feasts not only allowed for increased abundance but also facilitated greater wealth distinctions among households and opportunities to display that variation in a public context.

CONCLUSION

It seems clear that ancestral Pueblo people understood and sought out abundance. This is indicated by years when agricultural harvests were unusually bountiful, by the increasing accumulation of pottery bowls and other vessel forms through time, and by communal ceremony and feasts where abundance was performed. We have also shown how these three aspects of abundance were woven together: harvested maize was cooked and consumed in pottery vessels, bountiful harvests were the basis for ceremonial feasts, and special oversized cooking pots and large bowls with exterior decoration were manufactured for use in these feasting events. But this expression of Pueblo abundance was framed by an equally intimate understanding of scarcity, structured in part by a heavy dependence on maize agriculture in circumstances where episodic drought and cold temperatures resulted in years when maize harvests were extremely scarce or entirely absent (Bocinsky 2014; Bocinsky and Kohler 2014).

Tito notes that there is no Tewa word for feast or feasting; however, there is a Tewa word for starvation: *haa'chu*, which translates as "life-breath death." For Tito, this indicates that Tewa people have a profound understanding of scarcity, one derived from direct experience and a social memory rooted deep in the Pueblo past. Tito views the dual Pueblo understanding of abundance and scarcity as central to modern Tewa public ceremonies in which community members and costumed dancers exchange food. This performed ritual of abundance reinforces the fundamental Tewa values of community and sharing and the establishment of an extended web of social relations—one's *maa tú*—upon which Tewa people depend. Ford (2014) translates maa tú literally as "next of kin," but he notes that this can extend beyond one's biological relatives who are reckoned bilaterally to include a wider network of relationships. Similarly, Tito views maa tú as referring to both one's blood relatives and the larger social network created by events such as the participation in performed ceremonies of abundance noted above. Ford (2014) notes that one's maa tú is named, and individuals use this name to connect with individuals in distant villages who are part of a similarly named maa tú, establishing fictive kin relations with socially distant people.

Pueblo communal feasts and ceremonies, as social and performed expressions of abundance, differ from similar practices in small-scale societies elsewhere in the world. It seems likely that these practices were connected to the development of social inequality in ancestral Pueblo society, but here, too, the Pueblo case seems more nuanced when compared with the more straightforward relationship among feasts, ceremony, and inequality in societies elsewhere in the world. This is especially true when we compare the evidence for these practices in ancestral Pueblo societies with the relationship among feasting, reciprocity, ritual, and inequality in modern Pueblo societies. There appears to be a transformation in Pueblo society that occurred during the late thirteenth and fourteenth centuries AD, the time when vast areas of the ancestral Pueblo world, including those in the Mesa Verde region, were depopulated and the modern Pueblos began to take shape. This transformation produced a modern Pueblo world in which this relationship among feasting, ceremony, and inequality is even more nuanced and muted. For modern Pueblo people this nexus of practices, so interesting from an anthropological perspective, is less important than the relationship among the fundamental concept of seeking life, the values of community and reciprocity, and the ability to gain a life of abundance.

NOTE

1. Pueblo Indian culture is composed of people with distinct histories and languages. The linguistic groups include Hopi, Zuni, Keres, and three distinct Tanoan languages: Towa, Tewa, and Tiwa (which has distinct northern and southern dialects). The Pueblo perspectives Tito shares in this chapter come from his understanding as a Tewa-Pueblo person.

REFERENCES CITED

Aasen, Diane K. 1984. "Pollen, Macrofossil, and Charcoal Analyses of Basketmaker Coprolites from Turkey Pen Ruin, Cedar Mesa, Utah." Master's thesis, Washington State University, Pullman.

Adams, Karen R., and Vandy E. Bowyer. 2002. "Sustainable Landscape: Thirteenth-Century Food and Fuel Use in the Sand Canyon Locality." In *Seeking the Center Place: Archaeology and Ancient Communities in the Mesa Verde Region*, edited by Mark D. Varien and Richard H. Wilshusen, 123–42. Salt Lake City: University of Utah Press.

Adams, Karen R., Cathryn M. Meegan, Scott G. Ortman, R. Emerson Howell, Lindsay Werth, Deborah A. Muenchrath, Michael K. O'Neill, and Candice Gardner. 2006. "MAÍS (Maize of American Indigenous Societies) Southwest: Ear Descriptions and Traits That Distinguish 27 Morphologically Distinct Groups of 123 Historic USDA Maize (Zea mays L. ssp. mays) Accessions, and Data Relevant to Archaeological Subsistence Models." Unpublished report submitted to the James S. McDonnell Foundation 21st Century Research Award/Studying Complex Systems, Arizona State University, Tempe, JSMF Grant #21002035. http://farmingtonsc.nmsu.edu/documents /maissouthwestcopyrightedmanuscript1.pdf.

Allison, James R. 2010. *Animas–La Plata Project: Ceramic Studies*. SWCA Anthropological Research Papers 10, vol. 14. Phoenix: SWCA Environmental Consultants.

Bellorado, Benjamin. 2007. "Breaking down the Models: Reconstructing Prehistoric Subsistence Agriculture in the Durango District of Southwestern Colorado." Master's thesis, Northern Arizona University, Flagstaff.

Benson, Larry V. 2011a. "Factors Controlling Pre-Columbian and Early Historic Maize Productivity in the American Southwest, Part 1: The Southern Colorado Plateau and Rio Grande Regions." *Journal of Archaeological Method and Theory* 18 (1): 1–60. http://dx.doi.org/10.1007/s10816-010-9082-z.

Benson, Larry V. 2011b. "Factors Controlling Pre-Columbian and Early Historic Maize Productivity in the American Southwest, Part 2: The Chaco Halo, Mesa Verde, Pajarito Plateau/Bandelier, and Zuni Archaeological Regions." *Journal of Archaeological Method and Theory* 18 (1): 61–109. http://dx.doi.org/10.1007/s10816-010-9083-y.

Benson, Larry V., and Michael S. Berry. 2009. "Climate Change and Cultural Response in the Prehistoric American Southwest." *Kiva* 75 (1): 87–117. http://dx.doi.org/10.1179/kiv .2009.75.1.005.

Blinman, Eric. 1988. "Ceramic Vessels and Vessel Assemblages in Dolores Archaeological Program Collections." In *Dolores Archaeological Program: Supporting Studies and Reductive Technologies*, edited by Eric Blinman, Carl J. Phagan, and Richard H. Wilshusen, 449–82. Denver: Bureau of Reclamation, Engineering and Research Center.

Blinman, Eric. 1989. "Potluck in the Protokiva: Ceramics and Ceremonialism in Pueblo I Villages." In *The Architecture of Social Integration in Prehistoric Pueblos*, edited by William Lipe and Michelle Hegmon, 113–24. Occasional Paper 1. Cortez, CO: Crow Canyon Archaeological Center.

Blinman, Eric. 1993. "Anasazi Pottery: Evolution of a Technology." *Expedition* 35 (1): 14–22.

Blitz, John. 1993. "Big Pots for Big Shots: Feasting and Storage in a Mississippian Community." *American Antiquity* 58 (1): 80–96. http://dx.doi.org/10.2307/281455.

Bocinsky, R. Kyle. 2014. "Landscape-Based Null Models for Archaeological Inference." PhD dissertation, Washington State University, Pullman.

Bocinsky, R. Kyle, and Timothy A. Kohler. 2014. "A 2,000-Year Reconstruction of the Rain-Fed Maize Agricultural Niche in the US Southwest." *Nature Communications* 5. Medline:25472022 http://dx.doi.org/10.1038/ncomms6618.

Brisbin, Joel M., Allen E. Kane, and James N. Morris. 1988. "Excavations at McPhee Pueblo (5MT4475), a Pueblo I and Early Pueblo II Multicomponent Village." In *Dolores Archaeology Program: Anasazi Communities at Dolores: McPhee Village*, compiled by Allen E. Kane and Christine K. Robinson, 63–401. Denver: US Department of the Interior, Bureau of Reclamation, Engineering and Research Center.

Bronitsky, Gordon. 1986. "The Use of Materials Science Techniques in the Study of Pottery Construction and Use." In *Advances in Archaeological Method and Theory*, vol. 9, edited by Michael B. Schiffer, 209–76. Cambridge, MA: Academic. http://dx.doi.org/10.1016/B978-0-12-003109-2.50008-8.

Bronitsky, Gordon, and Robert Hamer. 1986. "Experiments in Ceramic Technology: The Effects of Various Tempering Materials on Impact and Thermal Shock Resistance." *American Antiquity* 51 (1): 89–101. http://dx.doi.org/10.2307/280396.

Chisholm, Brian, and R. G. Matson. 1994. "Carbon and Nitrogen Isotopic Evidence on Basketmaker II Diet at Cedar Mesa, Utah." *Kiva* 60 (2): 239–55. http://dx.doi.org/10.1080/00231940.1994.11758268.

Coltrain, Joan B., and Joel C. Janetski. 2013. "The Stable and Radio-Isotope Chemistry of Southeastern Utah Basketmaker II Burials: Dietary Analysis Using the Linear Mixing Model SISUS, Age and Sex Patterning, Geolocation and Temporal Patterning." *Journal of Archaeological Science* 40 (12): 4711–30. http://dx.doi.org/10.1016/j.jas.2013.07.012.

Coltrain, Joan B., Joel C. Janetski, and Shawn W. Carlyle. 2006. "The Stable and Radio-Isotope Chemistry of Eastern Basketmaker and Pueblo Groups in the Four Corners Region of the American Southwest: Implications for Anasazi Diets, Origins, and Abandonments." In *Stories of Maize: Multidisciplinary Approaches to the Prehistory, Biogeography, Domestication, and Evolution of Maize (Zea Mays)*, edited by John E. Staller, Robert H. Tykot, and Bruce F. Benze, 275–87. San Diego: Elsevier. http://dx.doi.org/10.1016/B978-012369364-8/50272-2.

Coltrain, Joan B., Joel C. Janetski, and Shawn W. Carlyle. 2007. "Stable and Radio-Isotope Chemistry of Western Basketmaker Burials: Implications for Early Puebloan Diets and Origins." *American Antiquity* 72 (2): 301–21. http://dx.doi.org/10.2307/40035815.

Cordell, Linda S. 1984. *Prehistory of the Southwest*. New York: Academic.

Cummings, Byron. 1953. *First Inhabitants of Arizona and Southwest*. Tucson: Cummings Publication Council.

de Garine, Igor. 1996. "Food and the Status Quest in Five African Cultures." In *Food and the Status Quest: An Interdisciplinary Perspective*, edited by Polly Weissner and Wolf Schiefenhovel, 193–218. Oxford: Berghahn Books.

Dietler, Michael. 1996. "Feasts and Commensal Politics in the Political Economy: Food, Power, and the Status Quest in Prehistoric Europe." In *Food and the Status Quest: An Interdisciplinary Perspective*, edited by Polly Weissner and Wolf Schiefenhovel, 87–125. Oxford: Berghahn Books.

Dietler, Michael, and Brian Hayden. 2001. *Feasts: Archaeological and Ethnographic Perspectives on Food, Politics, and Power*. Washington, DC: Smithsonian Institution Press.

Driver, Jonathan C. 1993. "Early to Late Prehistoric Lithic and Faunal Assemblages, Site DjPp–8, Alberta." *Canadian Journal of Archaeology* 17: 43–58.

Driver, Jonathan C. 2002. "Faunal Variation and Change in the Northern San Juan Region." In *Seeking the Center Place: Archaeology and Ancient Communities in the Mesa Verde Region*, edited by Mark D. Varien and Richard Wilshusen, 143–60. Salt Lake City: University of Utah Press.

Dugger, William M., and James T. Peach. 2009. *Economic Abundance: An Introduction*. Aromonk, NY: M. E. Sharpe.

Feinman, Gary. 2000. "Corporate/Network: A New Perspective on Leadership in the American Southwest." In *Hierarchies in Action: Cui Bono?* edited by Michael Diehl, 152–80. Center for Archaeological Investigations, Occasional Paper 27. Carbondale: Southern Illinois University.

Ford, Richard I. 1972. "An Ecological Perspective on Eastern Pueblos." In *New Perspectives on the Pueblos*, edited by Alfonso Ortiz, 1–18. Santa Fe: School of American Research Press.

Ford, Richard I. 2014. "Maatu'in: The Bridge between Kinship and Clan in the Tewa Pueblos of New Mexico." Paper presented at the 10th Annual Meeting of the Society for Anthropological Sciences, Albuquerque, March 18–22.

Geib, Phil R. 2011. *Foragers and Farmers of the Northern Kayenta Region*. Salt Lake City: University of Utah Press.

Gilpin, Dennis, and Larry Benallie Jr. 2000. "Juniper Cove and Early Anasazi Community Structure West of the Chuska Mountains." In *Foundations of Anasazi Culture: The Basketmaker-Pueblo Transition*, edited by Paul F. Reed, 161–73. Salt Lake City: University of Utah Press.

Goody, Jack. 1982. *Cooking, Cuisine, and Class: A Study in Comparative Sociology.* Cambridge: Cambridge University Press. http://dx.doi.org/10.1017/CBO9780 511607745.

Graves, William, and Katherine A. Spielmann. 2000. "Leadership, Long Distance Exchange, and Feasting in the Protohistoric Rio Grande." In *Alternative Leadership Strategies in the Greater Southwest*, edited by Barbara J. Mills, 45–59. Tucson: University of Arizona Press.

Gremillion, Kristen J. 2011. *Ancestral Appetites: Food in Prehistory.* Cambridge: Cambridge University Press. http://dx.doi.org/10.1017/CBO9780511976353.

Hard, Robert J., Raymond P. Mauldin, and Gerry R. Raymond. 1996. "Mano Size, Stable Carbon Isotope Ratios, and Macrobotanical Remains as Multiple Lines of Evidence of Maize Dependence in the American Southwest." *Journal of Archaeological Method and Theory* 3 (3): 253–318. http://dx.doi.org/10.1007/BF02229401.

Haury, Emil W. 1928. "The Succession of House Types in the Pueblo Area." MA thesis, University of Arizona, Tucson.

Hayden, Brian. 1995. "Pathways to Power: Principles for Creating Socioeconomic Inequalities." In *Foundations of Social Inequality*, edited by T. Douglas Price and Gary Feinman, 15–86. New York: Plenum. http://dx.doi.org/10.1007/978-1-4899-1289-3_2.

Hayden, Brian. 2001. "Fabulous Feasts: A Prolegomenon to the Importance of Feasting." In *Feasts: Archaeological and Ethnographic Perspectives on Food, Politics, and Power*, edited by Michael Dietler and Brian Hayden, 23–64. Washington, DC: Smithsonian Institution Press.

Hoeschele, Wolfgang. 2010. *The Economics of Abundance: A Political Economy of Freedom, Equity, and Sustainability.* Farnham, UK: Gower.

Hurst, Winston. 2011. "A Tale of Two Villages: Basketmaker III Communities in San Juan County, Utah." *Blue Mountain Shadows* 44: 7–18.

Kane, Allen E., and Christine K. Robinson. 1988. *Dolores Archaeological Program: Anasazi Communities at Dolores: McPhee Village.* Denver: US Department of the Interior, Bureau of Reclamation, Engineering and Research Center.

Kohler, Timothy A. 2012. "Modeling Agricultural Productivity and Farming Effort." In *Emergence and Collapse of Early Villages: Models of Central Mesa Verde Region Archaeology*, edited by Timothy A. Kohler and Mark D. Varien, 85–112. Berkeley: University of California Press. http://dx.doi.org/10.1525/california/9780520270145.003.0006.

Kohler, Timothy A., and Charles Reed. 2011. "Explaining the Structure and Timing of Formation of Pueblo I Villages." In *Sustainable Lifeways: Cultural Persistence in an Ever-Changing Environment*, edited by Naomi F. Miller, Katherine M. Moore, and Kathleen Ryan, 150–79. Philadelphia: University of Pennsylvania Museum of Archaeology and Anthropology.

Kohler, Timothy A., and Mark D. Varien, eds. 2012. *Emergence and Collapse of Early Villages: Models of Central Mesa Verde Region Archaeology*. Berkeley: University of California Press. http://dx.doi.org/10.1525/california/9780520270145.001.0001.

Kuckelman, Kristin A. 2007. "The Archaeology of Sand Canyon Pueblo: Intensive Excavations at a Late-Thirteenth Century Village in Southwestern Colorado." Accessed November 14, 2014. www.crowcanyon.org/.

Laski, Vera. 1959. *Seeking Life*. American Folklore Society, vol. 50. Philadelphia: American Folklore Society.

Lepofsky, Dana. 1986. "Preliminary Analysis of Flotation Samples from the Turkey Pen Ruin, Cedar Mesa, Utah." Manuscript on file. Vancouver: Laboratory of Archaeology, University of British Columbia.

Lightfoot, Ricky R. 1988. "Roofing an Early Anasazi Great Kiva: Analysis of an Architectural Model." *Kiva* 53 (3): 253–72. http://dx.doi.org/10.1080/00231940.1988.11758097.

Lightfoot, Ricky R., M. Alice Emerson, and Eric Blinman. 1988. "Excavations in Area 5, Grass Mesa Village (Site 5MT23)." In *Dolores Archaeological Program: Anasazi Communities at Dolores: Grass Mesa Village*, edited by William D. Lipe, James N. Morris, and Timothy A. Kohler, 561–766. Denver: US Department of the Interior, Bureau of Reclamation, Engineering and Research Center.

Lipe, William D. 2002. "Social Power in the Central Mesa Verde Region, AD 1150–1290." In *Seeking the Center Place: Archaeology and Ancient Communities in the Mesa Verde Region*, edited by Mark D. Varien and Richard H. Wilshusen, 203–32. Salt Lake City: University of Utah Press.

Lux-Harriman, Deborah. 1982. "Site 5DL297: A Basketmaker III Site North of Cahone, Colorado." In *Testing and Excavation Report, MAPCO's Rocky Mountain Liquid Hydrocarbons Pipeline, Southwest Colorado*, prepared by Jerry E. Fetterman and Linda Honeycutt, 6–6 to 6–21. San Francisco: Woodward-Clyde Consultants.

Matson, R. G., and Brian Chisholm. 1991. "Basketmaker II Subsistence: Carbon Isotopes and Other Dietary Indicators from Cedar Mesa, Utah." *American Antiquity* 56 (3): 444–59. http://dx.doi.org/10.2307/280894.

Mindeleff, Victor. 1891. *A Study of Pueblo Architecture in Tusayan and Cibola: Eighth Annual Report of the Bureau of Ethnology to the Secretary of the Smithsonian Institution, 1886–1887*. Washington, DC: Smithsonian Institution.

Monaghan, John. 1990. "Reciprocity, Redistribution, and the Transaction of Value in the Mesoamerican Fiesta." *American Ethnologist* 17 (4): 758–74. http://dx.doi.org/10.1525/ae.1990.17.4.02a00090.

Nelson, Ben A. 1991. "Ceramic Frequency and Use Life: A Highland Mayan Case in Cross-Cultural Perspective." In *Ceramic Ethnoarchaeology*, edited by William A. Longacre, 162–81. Tucson: University of Arizona Press.

Ortman, Scott G. 2000. "Artifacts." In *The Archaeology of Castle Rock Pueblo: A Thirteenth-Century Village in Southwestern Colorado [HTML title]*, edited by Kristin A. Kuckelman. Accessed November 14, 2014. http://www.crowcanyon.org/castlerock.

Ortman, Scott G. 2012. *Winds from the North: Tewa Origins and Historical Anthropology.* Salt Lake City: University of Utah Press.

Ortman, Scott G., and Bruce A. Bradley. 2002. "Sand Canyon Pueblo: The Container in the Center Place." In *Seeking the Center Place: Archaeology and Ancient Communities in the Mesa Verde Region*, edited by Mark D. Varien and Richard Wilshusen, 41–78. Salt Lake City: University of Utah Press.

Palmer, Wayne C. 1965. *Meteorological Drought.* Research Paper 45. Washington, DC: US Weather Bureau.

Phillips, David A., and Lynn Sebastian. 2004. "Large-Scale Feasting and Politics." In *Identity, Feasting, and the Archaeology of the Greater Southwest*, edited by Barbara J. Mills, 233–58. Boulder: University Press of Colorado.

Pierce, Christopher D. 1999. "Explaining Corrugated Pottery in the American Southwest: An Evolutionary Approach." PhD dissertation, University of Washington, Seattle.

Pierce, Christopher D. 2005. "The Development of Corrugated Cooking Pottery in Southwestern Colorado." *Kiva* 71 (1): 79–100. http://dx.doi.org/10.1179/kiv.2005.71.1.004.

Pierce, Christopher D., Mark D. Varien, Jonathan C. Driver, G. Timothy Gross, and Joseph W. Keleher. 1999. "Artifacts." In *The Sand Canyon Archaeological Project: Site Testing*. Accessed November 19, 2014. http://www.crowcanyon.org/sitetesting.

Plog, Fred T. 1974. *The Study of Prehistoric Change.* New York: Academic.

Potter, James M. 1997. "Communal Ritual and Faunal Remains: An Example from the Dolores Anasazi." *Journal of Field Archaeology* 24 (3): 353–64.

Potter, James M. 2000. "Pots, Parties, and Politics: Communal Feasting in the American Southwest." *American Antiquity* 65 (3): 471–92. Medline:17086659 http://dx.doi.org/10.2307/2694531.

Potter, James M. 2010. *Animas–La Plata Project: Final Synthetic Report.* SWCA Anthropological Research Paper 10, vol. 16. Phoenix: SWCA Environmental Consultants.

Potter, James M., and Jason P. Chuipka. 2010. "Perimortem Mutilation of Human Remains in an Early Village in the American Southwest: A Case for Ethnic Violence." *Journal of Anthropological Archaeology* 29 (4): 507–23. http://dx.doi.org/10.1016/j.jaa.2010.08.001.

Potter, James M., and Joshua S. Edwards. 2008. "Vertebrate Faunal Remains." In *Animas–La Plata Project: Environmental Studies*, edited by James M. Potter, 243–85. SWCA Anthropological Research Paper 10, vol. 10. Phoenix: SWCA Environmental Consultants.

Potter, James M., and Scott G. Ortman. 2004. "Community and Cuisine in Prehispanic American Southwest." In *Identity, Feasting, and the Archaeology of the Greater Southwest*, edited by Barbara J. Mills, 173–91. Boulder: University Press of Colorado.

Rice, Prudence M. 1987. *Pottery Analysis: A Sourcebook*. Chicago: University of Chicago Press.

Robbins, Lionel. 1932. *An Essay on the Nature and Significance of Economic Science*. London: Macmillan.

Roberts, Frank H.H. 1929. *Shabik'eschee Village, a Late Basket Maker Site in the Chuco Canyon, New Mexico*. Frank H.H. Roberts Jr. Bulletin 92. Washington, DC: Bureau of American Ethnology.

Robinson, Hugh Lobdell. 2005. "Feasting, Exterior Bowl Decoration, and Public Space in the Northern San Juan AD 1240–1300." MA thesis, Washington State University, Pullman.

Rye, Owen S. 1976. "Keeping Your Temper under Control: Materials and the Manufacture of Papuan Pottery." *Archaeology and Physical Anthropology in Oceania* 11 (2): 106–37.

Schiffer, Michael B., James M. Skibo, Tamara C. Boelke, Mark A. Neupert, and Meredith Aronson. 1994. "New Perspectives on Experimental Archaeology: Surface Treatments and Thermal Response of the Clay Cooking Pot." *American Antiquity* 59 (2): 197–217. http://dx.doi.org/10.2307/281927.

Schleher, Kari, Kevin Brown, and Jamie Gray. 2013. "Experimentation in Pottery: A Preliminary Analysis of Basketmaker III Pottery Production in the Mesa Verde Region." Poster presented at the 78th Annual Meeting of the Society for American Archaeology, Honolulu, April 3–7.

Schollmeyer, Karen Gust, and Jonathan C. Driver. 2011. "Deer in Prehistory in the Southwestern United States." *Deer, the Journal of the British Deer Society* (Autumn): 20–24.

Schollmeyer, Karen Gust, and Jonathan C. Driver. 2013. "Settlement Patterns, Source-Sink Dynamics, and Artiodactyl Hunting in the Prehistoric US Southwest." *Journal of Archaeological Method and Theory* 20 (3): 448–78. http://dx.doi.org/10.1007/s10816-012 -9160-5.

Shaw, Robert H., George F. Sprague, and John Wesley Dudley. 1988. "Climate Requirement." *Corn and Corn Improvement* 3: 609–38.

Smith, Monica L. 2012. "Seeking Abundance: Consumption as a Motivating Factor in Cities Past and Present." *Research in Economic Anthropology* 32: 27–51. http://dx.doi.org /10.1108/S0190-1281(2012)0000032006.

Spielmann, Katherine A. 2002. "Feasting, Craft Specialization, and the Ritual Mode of Production." *American Anthropologist* 104 (1): 195–207. http://dx.doi.org/10.1525/aa .2002.104.1.195.

Spielmann, Katherine A. 2004. "Communal Feasting, Ceramics, and Exchange." In *Identity, Feasting, and the Archaeology of the Greater Southwest*, edited by Barbara J. Mills, 210–32. Boulder: University Press of Colorado.

Steponaitis, Vincas P. 1983. *Ceramics, Chronology, and Community Patterns: An Archaeological Study at Moundville*. New York: Academic.

Steponaitis, Vincas P. 1984. "Technological Studies of Pottery from Alabama: Physical Properties and Vessel Function." In *The Many Dimensions of Pottery*, edited by Sander E. van der Leeuw and Alison C. Pritchard, 79–122. Amsterdam: University of Amsterdam.

Tani, Masakasu. 1994. "Why Should More Pots Break in Larger Households? Mechanisms Underlying Population Estimates from Ceramics." In *Kalinga Ethnoarchaeology: Expanding Archaeological Method and Theory*, edited by William A. Longacre and James M. Skibo, 51–70. Washington, DC: Smithsonian Institution Press.

Varien, Mark D. 1999. *Sedentism and Mobility in a Social Landscape: Mesa Verde and Beyond*. Tucson: University of Arizona Press.

Varien, Mark D., and Barbara J. Mills. 1997. "Accumulations Research: Problems and Prospects for Estimating Site Occupation Span." *Journal of Archaeological Method and Theory* 4 (2): 141–91. http://dx.doi.org/10.1007/BF02428057.

Varien, Mark D., and Scott G. Ortman. 2005. "Accumulations Research in the Southwest United States: Middle-Range Theory for Big-Picture Problems." *World Archaeology* 37 (1): 132–55. http://dx.doi.org/10.1080/0043824042000329603.

Varien, Mark D., Scott G. Ortman, Paul Ermigiotti, and Timothy A. Kohler. In press. "Modeling Agricultural Potential in the Mesa Verde Region: Combining Computer Simulation with Experimental Gardening." In *Dendroarchaeology in the Southwest*, edited by Ronald H. Towner. Salt Lake City: University of Utah Press.

Varien, Mark D., and James M. Potter. 1997. "Unpacking the Discard Equation: Simulating the Accumulation of Artifacts in the Archaeological Record." *American Antiquity* 62 (2): 194–213. http://dx.doi.org/10.2307/282506.

Weissner, Polly. 2001. "Of Feasting and Value: Enga Feasts in Historical Perspective." In *Feasts: Archaeological and Ethnographic Perspectives on Food, Politics, and Power*, edited by Michael Dietler and Brian Hayden, 115–43. Washington, DC: Smithsonian Institution Press.

Weissner, Polly, and Wolf Schiefenhovel. 1996. *Food and the Status Quest: An Interdisciplinary Perspective*. Oxford: Berghahn Books.

West, Steven M. 1992. "Temper, Thermal Shock, and Cooking Pots; A Study of Tempering Materials and Their Ethnographic, Archaeological, and Physical Significance in Traditional Cooking Pottery." Masters thesis, University of Arizona, Tucson.

Wills, Wirt H., and L. Patricia Crown. 2004. "Commensal Politics in the Prehispanic Southwest." In *Identity, Feasting, and the Archaeology of the Greater Southwest*, edited by Barbara J. Mills, 153–72. Boulder: University Press of Colorado.

Wills, Wirt H., and Thomas C. Windes. 1989. "Evidence for Population Aggregation and Dispersal during the Basketmaker III Period in Chaco Canyon, New Mexico." *American Antiquity* 54 (2): 347–69. http://dx.doi.org/10.2307/281711.

Wilshusen, Richard H. 1989. "Unstuffing the Estufa: Ritual Floor Features in Anasazi Pit Structures and Pueblo Kivas." In *The Architecture of Social Integration in Prehistoric Pueblos*, edited by William D. Lipe and Michelle Hegmon, 89–111. Occasional Papers 1. Cortez, CO: Crow Canyon Archaeological Center.

Wilshusen, Richard H., and James M. Potter. 2010. "The Emergence of Early Villages in the American Southwest: Cultural Issues and Historical Perspectives." In *Becoming Villagers: Comparing Early Village Societies*, edited by Matthew S. Bandy and Jake R. Fox, 165–83. Tucson: University of Arizona Press.

Young, Michael. 1971. *Fighting with Food: Leadership, Values, and Social Control in Massim Society*. Cambridge: Cambridge University Press.

5

Abundance in the Ancient Maya Village of Cerén?

During the Classic period, AD 300–900, the Maya occupied southeastern Mexico and northwestern Central America and reached their maximum expansion into El Salvador during the middle of the period. Following the Ilopango eruption and the ecological recovery in El Salvador, people re-colonized the area (Dull, Southon, and Sheets 2001). The Zapotitan Valley in central El Salvador was colonized largely by Maya peoples (Sheets 2009), including a few families who founded the small village of Cerén adjacent to the river that drains the valley (Sheets 2002).

Prior to the eruption of a nearby volcanic vent, Cerén was much like a few dozen other small villages in the valley. We find no aspects of Cerén that were unusual or unique before its summary interment. The opening of the nearby Loma Caldera volcanic vent at about the AD 660s caused the emergency evacuation and ensured the site's good preservation. The community was attending and participating in the harvest celebrations/rituals at Structure 10, and members did not have time to return to their domiciles or storehouses to grab valuables (evidence: the front doors were still tied shut with agave twine from when people left their homes to attend the ceremony, and small valuable items were left inside). The result is essentially complete household inventories of artifacts in their in situ locations of use or storage. The volcanic ash assisted in the preservation of organic materials such as stored food, thatch roofs, and plants in gardens and agricultural fields. We were often surprised by the large numbers of artifacts households owned, such as pottery vessels, obsidian prismatic blades, and gourds, and at first

DOI: 10.5876/9781607325949.c005

discovery we did consider them "abundant." But were they perceived as abundant by ancient Cerénians?

Cerén provides an unusually complete synchronic window on material culture and the landscape. Most other sites provide longitudinal samples of material culture that are impoverished by gradual abandonments and multiple post-abandonment processes. A key to understand some difficulties in assessing abundance at Cerén is therefore the issue of modes of abandonment (Cameron and Tomka 1993). Cerén was abandoned under emergency conditions with no possibility of return and was preserved by the Loma Caldera tephra (volcanic ash, cinders, lava bombs, and other airborne particles) such that virtually entire household assemblages are available for archaeological documentation. The gradual abandonment of other households, villages, and settlements in the valley or area resulted in such different assemblages that it is difficult to achieve reliable comparisons. Cerén is strikingly different from most archaeological sites. It is more like an ethnographic experience of entering a suddenly abandoned village right after the villagers left in haste.

DEFINITIONS AND CONSIDERATIONS OF ABUNDANCE

Abundance and surplus are at one end of an economic spectrum, with scarcity anchoring the other end. I view the difference between abundance and surplus as follows. Abundance is having so much of something that one does not worry about having more of it. A surplus of something is having more than one needs for individual or household consumption and is thus available for other uses, such as exchange. As Monica Smith (2012) observes, scarcity has received the predominance of attention by recent scholars. She defines abundance as "the recognition and/or creation of a large quantity of items" (2012:34). Her definition includes qualitative and quantitative elements. In chapter 1 of this volume she focuses on an "overwhelming quantity of artifacts" frequently collected by archaeologists on large projects. Archaeologists are often swamped by vast numbers of ceramic and lithic artifacts, especially when excavating large sedentary settlements, and they can readily view them as abundant. This is an etic concept. According to *Webster's Seventh New Collegiate Dictionary* (1969:4), abundance is an ample or overflowing quantity, profusion, affluence, and a relative degree of plentifulness. This definition emphasizes quantitative over qualitative aspects. Kerry Hull (2005:12) provides the Ch'orti' Maya word for abundance, *b'oro*, its definition in Spanish and English, and its use in a sentence. In this Ch'orti' definition the quantitative predominates: "**B'oro**. Apt. *Multiplicar, abundar, aumentar, rendir, producir.* Abound, multiply, increase, produce, yield. *B'oro me'yra nar twa' uk'uxi e jab' xe' numuy. Abundo mucho maiz para comer el año que paso.* Last year corn was in abundance for eating."

In this chapter I present both quantitative and qualitative aspects as we have documented and interpreted the material culture of the ancient Maya village of Cerén. The qualitative aspects can be differentiated into emic and etic components. What elements of their culture do *we* see as abundant, and what elements did *they* perceive as abundant? The former is not difficult to answer, but I argue that our perception of abundance may not be all that meaningful. Searching for what Cerénians perceived as abundant is more challenging, but at least in a few instances it is not impossible; and in the harvesting of great amounts of manioc, villagers apparently faced an irony or a dilemma when abundance created a scarcity, more specifically when material abundance created a labor scarcity (see below). Because the village was buried by a sudden explosive volcanic eruption, the record is of an instant of time; therefore, what we do not have is a longitudinal sample of changes and developments. It must be recognized that the agricultural production entombed and preserved that particular year may have been above or below average, and we have no way of measuring that annual variation. That annual variation would have directly affected emic and etic components of the abundance/surplus-scarcity agricultural spectrum. The study of abundance in any society is facilitated by a comparative framework that can be longitudinal or synchronic. Perceptions of abundance can be multi-scalar, from individuals through households to larger components of the society. Here we lack the longitudinal samples, but we can make some comparisons among households at Cerén and make limited comparisons with other households in the Zapotitan Valley. The latter comparisons are hampered by the lack of good preservation beyond the tephra blanket of the Loma Caldera eruption. Toward the end of this chapter I make brief comparisons of Cerén households to other valley households that were not covered by volcanic ash, in spite of the poor preservation of the latter.

Sample sizes should be kept in mind when dealing with data and interpretations in this chapter. The valley survey intensely covered only 15 percent of the entire area (Black 1978), and only twelve structures have been excavated at Cerén to date (Sheets 2002; figure 5.1). The most effective means of exploring abundance and the abundance-to-scarcity spectrum at Cerén would be to have other village sites with their households excavated that are contemporary and other village sites that preceded and postdated it, all with comparable preservation. Then detailed comparisons could be made of durables, perishables, kitchen garden plants, and seed and root crops in the agricultural fields. The problem, of course, is that those other well-preserved sites have yet to be discovered and investigated. Internally within the village we can perceive artifacts, architectural aspects, and crops that appear to be abundant, based on our expectations. An example is the high number of ceramic vessels per household that surprised us: about seventy (Beaudry-Corbett 2002:123). Over 20 percent of

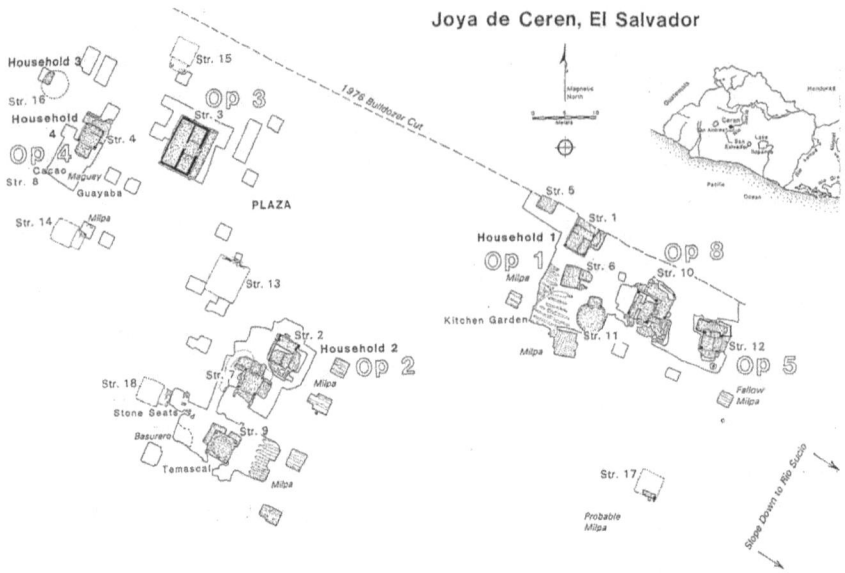

FIGURE 5.1. Map of the Cerén site, El Salvador.

each household's ceramics were polychrome decorated wares used for serving liquids and solid foods and obtained from markets at one of the elite centers in the valley.

Most of the polychromes at Cerén were made in the Copan Valley and exported to elite settlements in the Zapotitan Valley near Cerén. Cerénians must have had sufficient surplus production of foodstuffs or basic goods, or collected firewood or thatching, or provided labor to obtain their polychrome vessels. The other 80 percent of their ceramics was locally made, within the village or very close, and they were used for cooking, water and hard-food storage, and storage of small valuable items. It is tempting at first glance to label this large number of ceramic vessels as abundant. But interpretive caution is needed here, as we need to know if that number is unusually large for other contemporary households in the Zapotitan Valley or elsewhere in Mesoamerica. It is important to point out that our surprise was grounded more in our ignorance than in either etic or emic knowledge of ceramic abundance. Did other households in the valley have similar large numbers per household? If so, the reason for our surprise is simply our lack of knowledge of widespread conditions at that time. Even within Cerén and its fine preservation, it is challenging to detect residents' perception of abundance (an emic perception). However, when compared with the relatively complete floor-contact ceramic assemblages recovered from Xochicalco and Aguateca, described below, it is striking how many ceramic vessels commoner households owned at Cerén.

Excavations at three Epiclassic extended-family households at Xochicalco encountered an average of 71 whole ceramic vessels (with a wide range of 45 to 91) preserved by a catastrophic attack and rapid abandonment (Hirth 2006:27–47). The average number of vessels is strikingly close to that at Cerén, but the social contexts are considerably different. The Xochicalco residences were more like compounds, with 11–17 rooms in each, probably housing multiple families or households that were relatively affluent and thus fundamentally different from the nuclear family–based households in Cerén. Takeshi Inomata (2014:272) encountered complete and re-constructable ceramic vessels at Aguateca, also as a result of an attack and sudden abandonment. A total of 367 vessels were recovered from six structures, with a range of 16 to 95 per structure and a mean of 61. They date to the Late Classic, and most are royal or elite structures, with a few of a lower social class.

Two examples of possible emic judgments of abundance made by ancient Cerénians are briefly offered here. An example of a possible emic perception is in deciding that abundant or at least sufficient land was under cultivation so they could leave some arable land uncultivated (Sheets and Dixon 2011). During excavations south of the village, a few plots of land cultivated in previous years were left fallow for the agricultural season prior to the eruption. We could detect no evidence that soil erosion or nutrient leaching was the cause of the fallowing. Rather, it appeared the villagers decided that they had sufficient land under cultivation to produce sufficient food if precipitation was adequate. However, it is possible that the fallowing was for soil regeneration.

A more compelling case of emic abundance may be in the discovery of root crop productivity, harvesting, and processing. The tons of manioc tubers harvested from plots south of the village may have been perceived as emic abundance, especially when one notes how much was left behind in the raised beds. Manioc is developed in more detail below. It appears that agricultural productivity was sufficient to feed household members and provide a surplus in good years. That surplus was probably used for exchanges with other households in the Cerén village, in other villages nearby, and in the marketplaces in the valley where specialized products were available.

There are a number of cases where individual households had unusually large numbers of a certain commodity, and it would be tempting to identify those cases as abundances. However, close contextual examination has usually shown that the apparent abundance is the result of a special activity such as part-time craft specialization, to "overproduce" something relative to household needs to exchange within the community or valley (Sheets 2000). Each household had a functional specialization, a division of labor that produced tools or containers or vegetative products for local or distant exchange in an integrated regional economy. Cerén commoners maintained considerable agency in that regional economy in deciding what, where, and why they would engage in those exchanges. An unusual number of items in a household can also represent a service relationship by that household for a special facility or religious feasting ceremony. For example, the plethora of metates in Household 1 is revealing of a service relationship with the community ceremonial building.

Studies of personal satisfaction/happiness in contemporary Western societies have found that satisfaction/happiness is based not so much on absolute wealth (income and possessions) but rather on the comparisons people make with their peers, neighbors, relatives, and friends (Park 2010). Researchers found that people are happier if they perceive that they are wealthier than the group to which they compare themselves, in other words, their perception of ranking. Melanie Greenberg (2012) argues that relative wealth can be more important to happiness and satisfaction than can absolute wealth. The universality of wealth ranking and happiness is questionable when applied to traditional cultures. The cargo system functioning in many traditional highland Maya communities today can effectively redistribute wealth by having a family that has done better than others take on the expensive sponsorship of religious and social events. For example, Ruben Reina (1966:103, 122–29) documents how economically more prosperous individuals are chosen to serve one-year positions in the *cofradias* and how considerable their expenditures are. The system performs a leveling, homogenizing function. The family that experiences a decrease in wealth because of such a sponsorship can, however, experience an increase in prestige, status, respect, and appreciation through a conversion of tangibles to intangibles.

SHARING, FOOD, AND AGRICULTURE

The nature and implications of sharing as a form of exchange were innovatively explored by Michelle Hegmon (1991). Apart from the market exchanges that occurred in the Zapotitan Valley, many of her observations are applicable to activities within and among households in Cerén. She presents a spectrum of sharing ranging from none whatsoever in independent households through restricted sharing to pooling as complete sharing. She found that the most effective strategy to minimize risks of food shortages was restricted sharing, in which a household maintains storage in private and only shares what it deems as surplus. She uses Marshall Sahlins's (1972) distinctions of generalized versus balanced reciprocity, in which generalized reciprocity is socially embedded and the returning of sharing may or may not be done or even expected. Balanced reciprocity involves obligations to return food or goods and is the form of reciprocity that predominates in

FIGURE 5.2. Polychrome jar made in the Copan Valley, imported by elites, and available in a marketplace for commoners.

sedentary agricultural societies. The return can be immediate or delayed but certainly not forgotten (e.g., Vogt 1969). The evidence unearthed at Cerén indicates that households participated in a well-developed system of balanced reciprocity in surplus and possibly abundant artisanal products, specialty foods, and vegetative items (figure 5.2).

Varien, Potter, and Naranjo (this volume) describe the seasonal oscillation from scarcity to late-summer food abundance in the semiarid US Southwest and the resultant feasting that symbolized communal abundance. There, feasting involved common resources including maize and rabbits, and they were served in quotidian ceramic vessels. Although Cerén is in a tropical wet environment (mean precipitation 1,700 mm ± 300), it too was highly seasonal, with a six- month rainy season followed by a half year of very dry months (Sheets 2006:3). Maize was and still is planted in mid- to late May and matures in August. Then as now, it is not harvested all at once; rather, when the ear is mature, the stalk is bent over so the ear is upside-down and dries in the field. So maize was and still is harvested ear-by-ear only when needed, and that can be over many weeks or months.

FIGURE 5.3. Manioc planting beds, with walkways between. Their irregular surfaces resulted from harvesting shortly before the eruption.

Maize at Cerén is in contrast with the root crop manioc, which was cultivated in intensive plots 200 m south of the village (Sheets et al. 2012; figure 5.3). The mono-cropping was done in a highly structured area with field boundaries rigorously set by land lines (Sheets and Dixon 2011). Beyond the manioc beds, flat platforms were constructed, presumably for processing the harvest. Within the excavated fields at least four different farmers had cultivated manioc in raised and sloping beds for about a year. From that area over 10 metric tons of manioc tubers were harvested in a very short time, about a week or two just before the eruption. How much more than 10 tons is unknown, as we have discovered only two boundaries of the manioc fields. This certainly seems like a true emic and etic abundance. However, one needs to consider the labor intensity needed for pulling the tubers out of the ground and removing the cortex, as well as the great amount of labor needed for each form of processing. Manioc tubers spoil after a few days of being harvested, so one or most of the processing tasks need to be done promptly.

What could Cerénians have done with so much manioc? There are five potential uses: consumption, exchange, storage as flour, fermentation, and glue (Sheets et al. 2012). Tubers could have been carried to markets 5 km to the south or another 5 km to the north or to other nearby villages for exchange. Some must have been consumed, but a village of only 200 people would have had trouble consuming that much in just a few days. Another use is as glue (e.g., a binder for the white and red paint on Structures 10 and 12), but that would have used up only a tiny fraction of the harvest. The moderate degrees of wear of the paint indicate that the painting was done much earlier than the harvest, so no manioc juice glue was used from the harvest just before the eruption.

The only way manioc can be stored is if it is sliced into thin sections (disks), sun-dried for eight days, ground into flour, and kept dry. This process is very labor-intensive. Fermentation into a mild alcoholic beverage is also possible, as is done in many other areas of the world (Jennings et al. 2005), and it would have been appropriate during the ceremonies that were ongoing at Structure 10. Therefore, the abundance of manioc tubers harvested must have clashed with a scarcity of labor in doing the harvesting, hauling, decortication, and multiple modes of processing under a time crunch. About one out of six manioc tubers were missed in the harvesting and left in the ground, which I take as an emic abundance of manioc productivity. It would have taken only a slight bit more effort to dig into the planting bed to find the tubers that broke off the plant when the stalk was pulled up with most of the tubers attached. The soft, elevated planting beds would not even have required a digging stick to extract the remaining tubers. They merely could have dug in by hand, found them, and pulled them out. The fact that they did not spend the small additional effort to find and pull up the remaining tubers indicates that what came up with the pulling represented plentitude, in which a 1/6 wastage rate was acceptable given the harvest achieved and the available labor. I believe the reason for leaving so much manioc unharvested was the scarcity of labor for processing and consumption. The peak-load labor scarcity is reflected in the unharvested tubers. Might a similar situation have existed with the bison kills on the Great Plains (Nieves Zedeño, this volume)? Might the issue of waste noted by Klarich and colleagues (this volume) be pertinent?

Ironically, the abundance of manioc, with so much harvested that residents did not worry about the amount, may have created a scarcity in the labor needed for processing and use. The worry was directed more toward what to do with all of it. Abundance is not an unqualified "good," as Twiss and Bogaard (this volume) also discuss. Nonetheless, as in the US Southwest (Varien, Potter and Naranjo, this volume), the harvest was celebrated at Cerén. The village-wide celebration was held at Structure 10, a building constructed just for that purpose, with sacred artifacts symbolizing the fertility of nature. The building and its contents are examined later in this chapter.

WHAT CERÉN HOUSEHOLDS HELD IN COMMON

Each household at Cerén evidently built and maintained its own buildings (Sheets 2002, 2006). Each had a domicile, a kitchen, and a storehouse. Each building was placed on a platform to facilitate drainage away from the interior, and, with the exception of the kitchen, the clay surface of the platform was fired for durability. The kitchens had replaceable floors of volcanic ash to absorb spills. Walls were wattle and daub, with vertical poles approximately every 20–25 cm reinforcing the mudded portions and extending upward to support the thatch roofs. The horizontal reinforcements inside the mudded portions were spaced 20 cm apart, with the net result of vernacular architecture that was among the most highly seismically resilient anywhere in the world. The thatch roofs of domiciles and storehouses extended for a meter or more beyond the walls, creating covered work spaces and areas for provisional storage. Based on artifacts, activity areas, and limited sleeping spaces in the domiciles, it appears that the households were occupied by nuclear families. Ethnographers understand that nuclear families can take advantage of new opportunities more readily than can more encumbered extended families (Dennis McGilvray, personal communication, 2014), and this seems particularly appropriate in the colonizing situation after ecological recovery from the Ilopango eruption when people came back into the area and founded the Cerén village. Given preservation of the thatch roofs and also the drip lines on the ground surrounding them, we can calculate that Household 1 had 89.25 m^2 under roofs (961 ft^2). The household also had a ramada-style building (Structure 5) that increased the under-roof area to 94.25 m^2 (1,015 ft^2). The estimated time two people would need to construct their three buildings is fifty days (Victor Manuel Murcia, personal communication, 1995). My etic appraisal evaluates such architecture for nuclear families as abundant in space, quality, and environmental appropriateness.

A striking commonality among all households at Cerén is incense burners (Sheets 2006). Not only did every household possess an *incensario*, but every household *building* had one. Every domicile, storehouse, and kitchen had one, and each tested positive for copal incense. They must have been used for family religious purposes, probably including contacting the spirits of deceased ancestors, accessing deities, exploring future situations, and likely petitioning for abundance in future agricultural cycles. Because no incensario was found in the public political building, the village feasting structure, the sauna, or the shaman's building, it is clear that incensarios were specifically made and used for intra-household religious activities.

Found at each household was a relatively standard set of lithic, ceramic, and organic artifacts (Sheets 2002). In the category of organics each household had a few baskets, about a dozen plain gourds (largely for storing wood ash) and a few painted gourds, an antler *tapiscador* (cornhusker), various bone tools, lots of agave fiber twine and rope, net bags, many mats, and cotton fabric. Households stored considerable amounts of food in maize granaries and in ceramic vessels and particularly in the fields.

The chipped stone artifacts were all of obsidian and all from the nearby immense Ixtepeque source 75 km to the northwest. Each household had about a dozen prismatic blades, about half of which were in difficult-to-access storage high in the thatch roof and the other half in use. The ones in use were in convenient storage in easy-to-reach, predictable locations in the thatch roof. Such storage protects sharp cutlery and child-proofs homes. Each household had a scraper or two and a macroblade. All were obtained at a market; the only lithic fracturing activity was resharpening scrapers and perhaps macroblades.

An apparent abundance in the obsidian blades is how robust and therefore durable they were, in contrast to the blades in the Maya lowlands and beyond. By robust I mean they were relatively thick compared with their lowland cousins, and we developed a quantitative measure of this called the cutting-edge-to-mass ratio, or CE/M (Sheets and Muto 1972). Prismatic blades in western El Salvador during the Classic period, including Cerén, had an average of about 2.7 cm of cutting edge per gram of obsidian. In contrast, seven Classic period sites in Peten and Belize averaged 5.9 cm per gram (Sheets 1978), more than twice the length of cutting edge per gram. The highest measured length in that small study was 8.3 cm/g at Tres Zapotes, more than three times the cutting edge per gram of obsidian than at Cerén. One could try to argue that at Tres Zapotes consumers experienced an abundance of cutting edge relative to the amount/weight of obsidian they had, but to achieve it they produced very thin and thus very fragile blades. In the Zapotitan Valley, an abundance of obsidian allowed manufacturers to create durable thick blades. The primary factor here, of course, is distance from the source. Cerén is only 75 km from the Ixtepeque source, while the lowland sites are hundreds of kilometers from the sources. Lowland manufacturers "stretched" the obsidian into thinner blades to economize on a scarcer material. I doubt that at any of the localities, whether close or at a great distance from the source, there was a general emic perception of abundance of either material or cutting edge. Rather, at each household I think both would have oscillated in numbers with blades that were familiar in thickness to the residents: as blades were used and discarded, the people would have perceived an impending scarcity and taken action to obtain more.

In the category of groundstone, each household had a mano-metate set and a few donut stones used for a variety of purposes. Each household also had a single jade ax, surely the most expensive item a household obtained from a market. Every household also had a few *lajas* (flat-fractured andesite slabs), small grinding stones, and a few smoothing stones—probably for architectural construction and renovation. Households also had pigments, primarily hematite and limonite but also some cinnabar (mercuric sulfide), and they shared many agricultural similarities, beginning with kitchen gardens and the variety of food and medicinal species (Sheets and Woodward 2002). Surrounding each household was a high-performance milpa (Wilken 1971) that had been planted in maize at the beginning of the rainy season and matured in August, at which moment the Loma Caldera tephra buried it. The maize plants grew on carefully constructed ridges that followed the architectural orientation of the village (at 30° east of north) or its perpendicular. The dry-weight productivity of maize in these near-household fields was considerable indeed, probably because of greater care in cultivation and fertilization by kitchen scraps and human excreta and the lowered chance of passers-by removing ears in an unauthorized manner. Had the Loma Caldera eruption occurred a few weeks later, we presumably would have found evidence of beans and squash having been planted. The structures and surrounding agricultural fields give the impression of a highly ordered landscape and likely household pride in creating and maintaining it.

Beyond the architectural area of the village is what we are calling the intermediate zone, where a farmer's plot does not visually connect with household buildings and neat fields (Sheets and Dixon 2011). The variation in field maintenance was striking, ranging from ridging almost as well done as the near-household ones to only mounding around each maize plant cluster to no micro-topographic management whatsoever. We interpret the greater range of variation in this outside-village area as resulting from less social pressure to conform to the ideal, so farmers had greater latitude in choices. The farmer who did no micro-topographic field management did save time but suffered slightly in decreased maize productivity per unit area. We nicknamed him "*el perezoso*" (the lazy one). Farmers strategically made use of the potential for increased productivity in this zone at the cost of investing greater labor. Here, as with so many human endeavors, there is a tradeoff relationship between a desired abundance of productivity and a scarcity of labor. We detected no differences in weeding among these farmers.

HOW CERÉN HOUSEHOLDS DIFFERED: PARTICULAR "ABUNDANCES" AND THEIR INTERPRETATIONS

Each household excavated at Cerén to date has provided evidence of producing something in excess of its own consumptive needs (details in Sheets 2000). While excavating and noting those unusual numbers of items in each household, our first reaction was that they represented abundance. However, we quickly realized otherwise, for instance, that the large numbers of manos and metates and the tools to manufacture them were there for good reasons in Household 1 and were not necessarily etic or emic abundance. Rather, they represented a balanced reciprocity in the sense of Sahlins (1972) and Hegmon (1991). One mano-metate set was manufactured and in use as the primary grinding stone on the floor of the kitchen, and others were manufactured to exchange with other households when both supplier and receiver reached an agreement. Household 1 maintained the tools for manufacture, primarily hammerstones, and the knowledge about how and where to obtain the andesite with the proper vesicularity and rough shape. That household also manufactured, used, and exchanged donut stones. In addition, most of the spindle whorls recovered at the site to date were found in this household, indicating a large amount of cotton fiber production. Because of the weight of metates, they were likely only exchanged within the community, but donut stones and cotton thread or fabric were likely exchanged in a market for the obsidian tools, jade ax, pigments, and polychrome vessels the household desired and owned.

Tracy Sweely (1999) ingeniously used the location and positioning of the metates in Household 1 to infer subtle power relationships among the women presumably using them. The metate on the floor in the kitchen (Beaudry-Corbett, Simmons, and Tucker 2002) clearly was in quotidian use, as evidenced by the deep use-wear it sustained and its location adjacent to the hearth and to the pot that soaked maize overnight. The other four metates sustained the same amount of only slight use-wear, and three of the four were mounted on *horquetas* (thick forked sticks) that supported them so grinding could be done by a standing person. The Loma Caldera tephra packed around the metates and supported them in their original positions, even though the sticks decomposed and left hollow spaces after the eruption. Because a person would have stood behind the more elevated end of the metate while grinding, pushing the maize dough off the lower end, Sweely determined who could have seen whom and thus inferred a power hierarchy. She argued that the woman who could see all the others was the most powerful of the group.

So, why did Household 1 have so many metates? Why does it seem like there was such an abundance of metates at Household 1 when a household only needs one? I believe the answer lies in the service relationship between this household and Structure 10 (Brown and Gerstle 2002), the community ritual-ceremonial building adjacent to it. The household evidently looked after the building in terms of maintenance and loaned the building many of its ceramic vessels and cornhuskers for feasting (Sheets 2006). The horqueta-mounted metates must have been used just to grind maize for the harvest festival, and therefore what appeared to be an abundance of metates may not have been at all. One of the metates was upside-down, in between the horquetas, which I interpret as women making the decision that sufficient maize could be ground with the three mounted ones, so the fourth was left in its storage position. In this case what appeared to be abundance was apparently judged by the women as sufficient for that occasion. In not mounting the last metate, I think they decided to avoid an overabundance of ground maize dough. An apparent abundance, when the social context is understood, might well not be abundance at all but might be interpreted as a socially risky endeavor (see Twiss and Bogaard, this volume).

Structure 7, the storehouse of Cerén's Household 2 (McKee 2002), contained an unusual number of pottery *ollas* for water and an unusual amount of firewood. The proximity of the storehouse to the sauna, only 6 m to the south, suggests a service relationship rather than an abundance of either of these items. It appears that household members provided firewood for the sauna's firebox and water to pour over the firebox to make steam as well as for drinking and rinsing off after exiting. Household 4's part-time specialization was vegetative commodities (Gerstle and Sheets 2002; Sheets 2006). They grew seventy agave (maguey) plants to supply all their household needs for fiber for twine and rope and much, if not all, of the community's needs as well. They also grew and processed cacao and grew the cane poles used in wattle-and-daub vertical pole reinforcements, which also functioned to support the roof. A line of mature chili plants ran to the west of the building, supplying many households. I suspect these chili plants supplied all the chilies needed for the entire village.

THE VILLAGE FEASTING CEREMONIAL CENTER

By focusing on the broader issue of activities at Structure 10, the village feasting facility that was celebrating the harvest, I suggest we can perceive an important domain: the community effort to give thanks for the actual abundance of the harvest and to lay the supernatural groundwork for abundance to characterize the next agrarian cycle. Irene Winter (2007) explored the visual aspects of highly stratified ancient Mesopotamian states that desired divine beneficence in food production, clearly on the "writ-large" scale, and at Cerén we can see the same desire and related activity "writ-small" in this village of Maya commoners. The structure consists of two rooms on a formal platform making up the superstructure, an entrance corridor, and a large anteroom enclosure (Brown and Sheets 2001; Sheets 2002, 2006). The building functioned to store ceremonial paraphernalia and to process and serve festival food. Community ceremonies were produced in and around the building, with the latter evidenced by the extremely hard-packed surfaces to the building's east and especially its north (figure 5.4). Dances and theatrical/musical performances likely took place beyond those sides of the building. A person authorized to enter the building did so by opening a pole door and passing through a narrow corridor that ran along the north side of the building. Two hearths and a metate mounted on horquetas, with an open bowl below the lower end to catch the masa, were located in that corridor.

Maize was de-husked with three deer antlers and deer bone tools, and discarded corncobs were mute testimony to shelling the corn. No antler de-huskers were

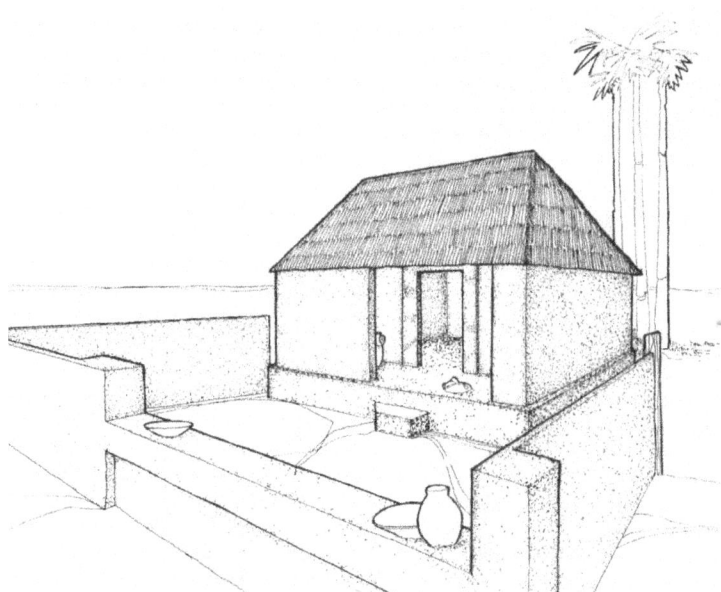

FIGURE 5.4. Artist's rendition of Structure 10, built for ceremonies celebrating the harvest.

found in Household 1, so I suspect that these three were loaned from there as part of the service relationship. Passing through the corridor one entered the anteroom, loaded with food in vessels accompanied by serving vessels. The anteroom was an active area of food preparation and serving, in contrast to the upper two rooms. A total of thirty-six vessels were recovered, and a similar number probably remain under the unexcavated fallen walls at the building's southeast corner. Five of the ceramics were polychrome food-serving vessels. It is possible that people brought their own gourd vessels to receive food and drink. Painted gourds, likely made in Household 2, were also used for food serving. Judging from the amount of food still in the twenty jars, the harvest ritual was almost half completed when the volcanic eruption struck.

Ritual and unique artifacts were stored in the front (east) room of the structure. I believe the most sacred item was a deer skull headdress stored on the high shelf that ran the full length of the middle of the building. The skull was painted red, with some white and blue, and still has the twine used to secure it to the wearer's head during performances. Next to the deer skull headdress was an obsidian blade that tested positive for human hemoglobin (Sheets 2006:110). It must have been used for bloodletting in rituals. A large jar full of achiote seeds was on the floor below the skull. Achiote is a powerful (in both physical and supernatural senses) red pigment that symbolizes human blood and the *ch'ulel* (soul-spirit) in it, and it was used to decorate bodies and artifacts during rituals in ancient and contemporary times (McGee 1990). Deer scapulae and numerous other items made from deer bones (beads and unusually shaped artifacts) were apparently part of the ritual paraphernalia used in ceremonies. This front room of the main building, on the platform, had walls and lower pilasters painted white, with red paint on the upper part of the pilasters. The red was hematite, and the white was extra–fine-grained Ilopango volcanic ash attached with a binder, likely manioc juice. The painting emphasizes the importance of the structure's purpose: to obtain divine beneficence for the next agrarian cycle.

The predominance of deer bone and antler paraphernalia in this structure, especially the painted deer skull headdress, indicates a focus on the fertility of nature (Schlesinger 2001:182). The view was presumably bi-directional, giving thanks for the harvest immediately past and simultaneously asking for supernatural assistance for the upcoming growing season and harvest. Clearly, large amounts of food were prepared in the corridor, stored in the anteroom, and dispensed to participants over the half-height wall. Drinks were likely served, although we have no direct evidence of them. The most likely drinks are water and chicha made from maize or manioc. No beverage serving vessels were found, but almost half of the anteroom has yet to be excavated, and cylinder vessels could be in that area. Or people could well have brought gourds into which beverages were poured.

The harvest ceremonies can be interpreted as the community desiring abundance in the future harvest by giving thanks for the present harvest and invoking the supernatural domain to achieve it. Of course, Cerénians were well aware of the weather/climatic cycles that resulted in variable harvests, and they requested divine intervention to assist in bountifulness. In this domain I am confident that we can see desired emic abundance.

ISOLATED HOUSEHOLDS IN THE ZAPOTITAN VALLEY

The attempt in this chapter to make comparisons with other valley households was stimulated by Smith's (2012:27) observation that "the earliest urban centers were attractive places of settlement because they represented a greater variety of jobs and objects compared to the rural countryside." Of course, the scale in the Zapotitan Valley is dramatically smaller than the cities of South Asia and the Near East, but at a much smaller scale we can make at least a partial comparison of households in the Cerén village with isolated households in the surrounding valley and discern some significant differences.

The 1978 archaeological survey of the Zapotitan Valley encountered eighteen "hamlets" and one isolated residence within the 82 km² covered, representing 15 percent of the entire valley (Black 1978:73–74). Collections from surface surveys represent different sampling strategies than do excavated samples, thus limiting the robustness of comparisons. Nevertheless, some generalizations may be possible. About half of the "hamlets" were so small that they were probably separate individual households. Although none of them were buried catastrophically by tephra in a way that would have provided a comparable level of preservation with Cerén, sufficient artifacts were present to date them and get some idea of how they functioned. All of them showed evidence of making their own metates and manos. The evidence was the finding of numerous hammerstones and fragments of manos and metates that were broken in manufacture. An observer could comment that isolated families had an abundance of tools to make ground-stone implements and probably an abundance of the implements themselves compared to the average Cerén household. However, that would be a misperception, as it appears that isolated households had to produce their own heavy grinding stones. Although this is not definitive, these data might be a proxy for isolated households having to make a higher proportion of the other goods, such as utilitarian ceramics, they used in their houses than did households in villages. At Cerén, a household would have overproduced something and exchanged for other commodities with another household only minutes away. Isolated households needed to be more self-sufficient and therefore to maintain the knowledge and implements needed to make a wider range of consumer goods. Isolated households went to marketplaces and engaged in exchanges much like Cerén households. But they did not have the advantage of other nearby households engaging in part-time productive specializations and therefore had to produce a wider range of goods for themselves than did the interrelated Cerén households.

The Cerén village households were considerably more economically integrated than the isolated households. The Cerén households give the appearance of a compressed rural settlement, with each household's agricultural fields surrounding its buildings and abutting on its neighbors' fields. Crowding relative to the isolated families may have been perceived, but the isolated households may have enjoyed a relative abundance of arable land. The part-time craft specializations of each village household confer an artisanal efficiency and complementarity because each household did not need to maintain the knowledge, experience, and manufacturing tools required to make all the needed commodities. And each household was only a five-minute walk from the others to make the exchanges. The negotiations involved in the exchanges surely developed a rich social network in the village, occasionally resulting in conflict but often working to the economic and social advantage of the components of the community.

But there was a tradeoff as the households clustered into a village, and that unfortunately was the risk of theft (Sheets 2006:47). The storehouse of Household 1 was undergoing renovation just prior to the eruption by removing the mudded portions of the walls and replacing the vertical poles and horizontal reinforcements. They had completed renovation of only the east wall and doorway and had only replaced the vertical poles on the other three sides. Thus, there were spaces between the poles averaging about 20 cm. All the valuable items that were smaller than 20 cm had been moved into temporary storage in the domicile, an apparent perception of the risk of theft. Items larger than the gaps between the poles were still in the storehouse. The other households' storehouses contained small valuable items, which seems to have been the cultural pattern when that building was complete.

CONCLUSION

From this small sample of Zapotitan Valley households during the Classic period, we can perceive a correlation between settlement size and the division of labor. The isolated households produced a wider range of commodities because the greater distance to other households inhibited regular exchanges, in contrast to the households in villages. At least with groundstone tools, each isolated household manufactured its own. In the Cerén village each household exchanged surplus food, part-time artisanal goods, or vegetative specialties. Those exchanges occurred within the village, with other nearby villages, and in marketplaces. Household 1 manufactured its own metates and manos and exchanged its surplus production for the commodities available from other households. Household 2 did polychrome decoration of gourds, and Household 4 produced prodigious amounts of agave fiber, chili, and cacao.

Two of the households undertook service relationships. Household 2 maintained the sauna by stocking sufficient firewood for its firebox and water for creating steam, for rinsing, and for drinking. Household 1 supported the community feasting and rituals celebrating the harvest at nearby Structure 10. In a sense, one could argue that each household had sufficient or abundant time to put into those activities.

Identifying with confidence what ancient people perceived as abundant versus surplus is challenging for archaeologists. Perhaps the easiest domain in which to perceive abundance is the supernatural, where people were requesting divine intervention to support the fertility of nature. The harvest ceremony and feasting that was in process at Structure 10 is the example at Cerén. It is not surprising that the ancient Maya developed rituals focused on maize rather than manioc, as maize is highly sensitive to temperature and moisture. Manioc is drought-adapted and very durable, and it produces prodigious amounts of food regularly; therefore, it does not need divine intervention. The impressive tonnage of production, probably perceived as abundance at the time, ironically resulted in a scarcity of labor required for harvesting, decortication, and processing.

Acknowledgments. The predominance of support for research at Cerén has come from the archaeology program at NSF, for which I am immensely grateful. The advice and counsel of John Yellen is particularly appreciated. Dennis McGilvray provided ethnographic insights. My colleagues at the University of Colorado in Boulder provided astute critiques of weak or confusing sections, and I express my appreciation here. They are Art Joyce, Cathy Cameron, Steve Lekson, John Hoffecker, Gerardo Gutierrez, and Scott Ortman. My good Salvadoran friend Victor Manuel Murcia provided insights into traditional life in his country and carefully calculated estimates of the time needed to construct the wattle-and-daub structures. I acknowledge Monica Smith for inviting me to participate in her SAA symposium and to provide this chapter in her book. Her copyediting certainly improved the text. My colleagues Ken Hirth and Takeshi Inomata assisted my comparisons of ceramics per household or compound.

REFERENCES CITED

Beaudry-Corbett, Marilyn. 2002. "Ceramics and Their Use at Cerén." In *Before the Volcano Erupted: The Ancient Cerén Village in Central America*, edited by Payson Sheets, 117–38. Austin: University of Texas Press.

Beaudry-Corbett, Marilyn, Scott Simmons, and David Tucker. 2002. "Ancient Home and Garden: The View from Household 1 at Cerén." In *Before the Volcano Erupted: The Ancient Cerén Village in Central America*, edited by Payson Sheets 45–57. Austin: University of Texas Press.

Black, Kevin. 1978. "The Zapotitan Valley Archeological Survey." In *Archeology and Volcanism in Central America: The Zapotitan Valley of El Salvador*, edited by Payson Sheets 62–97. Austin: University of Texas Press.

Brown, Linda, and Andrea Gerstle. 2002. "Structure 10: Feasting and Village Festivals." In *Before the Volcano Erupted: The Ancient Cerén Village in Central America*, edited by Payson Sheets, 97–103. Austin: University of Texas Press.

Brown, Linda, and Payson Sheets. 2001. "The Material Correlates of Village Ceremony: Two Ritual Structures at the Cerén Site, El Salvador." In *Fleeting Identities: Perishable Material Culture in Archaeological Research*, edited by Penelope Drooker, 114–36. Occasional Paper 38. Carbondale: Center for Archaeological Investigations, Southern Illinois University.

Cameron, Catherine, and Steve Tomka, eds. 1993. *Abandonment of Settlements and Regions: Ethnoarchaeological and Archaeological Approaches*. Cambridge: Cambridge University Press. http://dx.doi.org/10.1017/CBO9780511735240.

Dull, Robert, John Southon, and Payson Sheets. 2001. "Volcanism, Ecology, and Culture: A Reassessment of the Volcan Ilopango TBJ Eruption in the Southern Maya Realm." *Latin American Antiquity* 12 (1): 25–44. http://dx.doi.org/10.2307/971755.

Gerstle, Andrea, and Payson Sheets. 2002. "Structure 4: A Storehouse-Workshop for Household 4." In *Before the Volcano Erupted: The Ancient Cerén Village in Central America*, edited by Payson Sheets, 74–80. Austin: University of Texas Press.

Greenberg, Melanie. 2012. "Is Money the Secret to Happiness?" *Psychology Today*, September 10. Accessed September 9, 2014. https://www.psychologytoday.com/blog/the-mindful-self-express/201209/is-money-the-secret-happiness.

Hegmon, Michelle. 1991. "The Risks of Sharing and Sharing as Risk Reduction: Interhousehold Food Sharing in Egalitarian Societies." In *Between Bands and States*, edited by Susan Gregg, 309–29. Occasional Paper 9. Carbondale: Center for Archaeological Investigations, Southern Illinois University.

Hirth, Kenneth. 2006. "Households and Plazas: The Contexts of Obsidian Craft Production at Xochicalco." In *Obsidian Craft Production in Ancient Central Mexico: Archaeological Research at Xochicalco*, edited by Kenneth Hirth, 18–62. Salt Lake City: University of Utah Press.

Hull, Kerry. 2005. *An Abbreviated Dictionary of Ch'orti' Maya: Report*. Los Angeles: Foundation for the Advancement of Mesoamerican Studies, Los Angeles County Museum of Art.

Inomata, Takeshi. 2014. "Synthesis of Data from the Rapidly Abandoned Buildings." In *Life and Politics at the Royal Court of Aguateca: Artifacts, Analytical Data, and Synthesis*, edited by Takeshi Inomata and Daniela Triadan, 271–319. Salt Lake City: University of Utah Press.

Jennings, Justin, Kathleen L. Antrobus, Sam J. Atencio, Erin Glavich, Rebecca Johnson, German Loffler, and Christine Luu. 2005. "'Drinking Beer in a Blissful Mood': Alcohol Production, Operational Chains, and Feasting in the Ancient World." *Current Anthropology* 46 (2): 275–303. http://dx.doi.org/10.1086/427119.

McGee, Jon. 1990. *Life, Ritual, and Religion among the Lacandon Maya*. Belmont, CA: Wadsworth.

McKee, Brian. 2002. "Household 2 at Cerén: The Remains of an Agrarian and Craft-Oriented Corporate Group." In *Before the Volcano Erupted: The Ancient Cerén Village in Central America*, edited by Payson Sheets, 58–71. Austin: University of Texas Press.

Park, Alice. 2010. "Study: Money Isn't Everything—but Status Is!" *Time*, March 23. Accessed September 9, 2014. http://content.time.com/time/health/article/0,8599,1974718,00.html.

Reina, Ruben. 1966. *The Law of the Saints: A Pokomam Pueblo and Its Community Culture.* Indianapolis: Bobbs-Merrill.

Sahlins, Marshall. 1972. *Stone Age Economics.* Chicago: Aldine.

Schlesinger, Victoria. 2001. *Animals and Plants of the Ancient Maya: A Guide.* Austin: University of Texas Press.

Sheets, Payson. 1978. "From Craftsman to Cog: Quantitative Views of Mesoamerican Lithic Technology." In *Papers on the Economy and Architecture of the Ancient Maya,* edited by Raymond Sidrys. Monograph 8. Los Angeles: Institute of Archaeology, University of California.

Sheets, Payson. 2000. "Provisioning the Cerén Household: The Vertical Economy, Village Economy, and Household Economy in the Southeastern Maya Periphery." *Ancient Mesoamerica* 11 (2): 217–30. http://dx.doi.org/10.1017/S0956536100112039.

Sheets, Payson. 2006. *The Cerén Site: An Ancient Village Buried by Volcanic Ash in Central America.* Belmont, CA: Thompson Wadsworth.

Sheets, Payson. 2009. "Who Were Those Classic Period Immigrants into the Zapotitan Valley, El Salvador?" In *The Ch'orti' Maya Area: Past and Present,* edited by Brent Metz, Cameron McNeil, and Kerry Hull, 61–77. Gainesville: University Press of Florida. http://dx.doi.org/10.5744/florida/9780813033310.003.0005.

Sheets, Payson, ed. 2002. *Before the Volcano Erupted: The Ancient Cerén Village in Central America.* Austin: University of Texas Press.

Sheets, Payson, and Christine Dixon, eds. 2011. "Maya Agriculture South of the Cerén Site, El Salvador, 2011." Accessed October 21, 2014. https://anthropology.colorado.edu/dir ectory/faculty-bios/payson-sheets/.

Sheets, Payson, David Lentz, Dolores Piperno, John Jones, Christine Dixon, George Maloof, and Angela Hood. 2012. "Ancient Manioc Agriculture South of the Cerén Village, El Salvador." *Latin American Antiquity* 23 (3): 259–81. http://dx.doi.org/10.7183 /1045-6635.23.3.259.

Sheets, Payson, and Guy R. Muto. 1972. "Pressure Blades and Total Cutting Edge: An Experiment in Lithic Technology." *Science* 175 (4022): 632–34. Medline:17808802 http://dx.doi.org/10.1126/science.175.4022.632.

Sheets, Payson, and Michelle Woodward. 2002. "Cultivating Biodiversity: Milpas, Gardens, and the Classic Period Landscape." In *Before the Volcano Erupted: The Ancient Cerén Village in Central America,* edited by Payson Sheets, 184–91. Austin: University of Texas Press.

Smith, Monica L. 2012. "Seeking Abundance: Consumption as a Motivating Factor in Cities Past and Present." *Research in Economic Anthropology* 32: 27–51. http://dx.doi.org /10.1108/S0190-1281(2012)0000032006.

Sweely, Tracy. 1999. "Gender, Space, People, and Power at Cerén, El Salvador." In *Manifesting Power: Gender and the Interpretation of Power in Archaeology*, edited by Tracy Sweely, 155–71. London: Routledge. http://dx.doi.org/10.4324/9780203279663.

Vogt, Evan. 1969. *Zinacantan: A Maya Community in the Highlands of Chiapas.* Cambridge, MA: Belknap Press, Harvard University. http://dx.doi.org/10.4159/harvard .9780674436886.

Webster's Seventh New Collegiate Dictionary. 1969. Springfield, MA: G&C Merriam.

Wilken, Gene. 1971. "Food-Producing Systems Available to the Ancient Maya." *American Antiquity* 36 (4): 432–48. http://dx.doi.org/10.2307/278462.

Winter, Irene. 2007. "Representing Abundance: A Visual Dimension of the Agrarian State." In *Settlement and Society*, edited by Elizabeth C. Stone, 117–38. Los Angeles: Cotsen Institute of Archaeology, University of California at Los Angeles.

6

Savanna Products and Resource Abundance

Asking the Right Questions about Ancient Maya Trade and Urbanism

TRACI ARDREN

Archaeological studies of ancient Maya trade have long acknowledged that the movement of products between different environmental zones was a cornerstone of Classic period economies. One of the most important circulations was between the long coastline of the Yucatan Peninsula and the many inland urban centers of the Classic period (AD 200–900). In addition to the transportation of goods such as obsidian that originated at only a few inland sources, traders moved a large variety (and likely large quantities) of plant products, including "phantom" or "invisible artifacts" such as cloth, basketry, and other often overlooked plant fiber technologies essential to household and political economies of the Classic Maya lowlands. Current models for Classic Maya trade systems derive from a resource scarcity paradigm because identification of the movement of relatively rare materials such as obsidian or jade has dominated our approach to understanding long-distance trade and the parties involved in its execution. Ever since William L. Rathje (1972) modeled the origin of social complexity in the Maya area around the exchange of select highland and lowland goods, the long-distance trading economy of the ancient Maya has been conceptualized as driven by the movement of scarce objects over long distances. Even when Rathje's model was largely disproven, Maya trade continued to be discussed as the movement of rare durable goods under the control of small numbers of elites.

Sixteenth-century Spanish sources seem to problematize this conceptualization, as the Franciscans described an active trading economy in such merchandise as

DOI: 10.5876/9781607325949.c006

cotton cloth, apiary goods (such as beeswax and honey), slaves, and plant fiber products (Gates 1937 [1566]). However, given the vagaries of the archaeological record in the tropics, ancient trade in such materials is difficult to document quantitatively (cf. Álvarez and Peniche May 2012), and so-called soft technologies have been largely overlooked in models of economic exchange. This study explores the analytical value of centering our focus on the abundance—in the sense of both a wide variety and a large quantity—of natural resources, particularly plant fibers but also other savanna products, within the catchment area of one unusual Classic Maya city.

SOFT TECHNOLOGY

Following the work of Liam Frink and others who have explored the technologies of soft storage, it is clear that archaeologists have used preservation issues to avoid careful consideration of how soft technologies such as skins, cloth, and basketry were used for the storage of food surpluses, a basic component of most complex societies (Frink and Giordano 2015; Smith 2013; Soffer et al. 2000). Monica Smith (2013:147) has questioned the designation of soft storage artifacts such as textiles as perishable, given their long use life and relative durability compared to more brittle artifacts (that preserve well) such as ceramics or flaked stone. Frink claims that cross-cultural ethnographic data support a general pattern in which durable goods such as stone and metal artifacts are generally produced by men while perishable artifacts such as textiles and basketry are often produced by women (Frink and Giordano 2015; Murdock and Provost 1973). While there are important exceptions to this generalization, the presumed association of durable goods with male producers has a long history in archaeological interpretation and has positioned such artifacts as the more visible and prestigious examples of technology as a manifestation of culture (Dobres 2010). Thus, when economic models of past societies are built around primarily durable goods, such models are androcentric and can undervalue the contributions of women, children, and elderly craft producers to their economic systems.

Issues of preservation are not a sufficient reason to overlook fiber technologies. In the Maya area there are artifacts long associated with the production of perishable crafts, such as bark beaters and spindle whorls, well documented in the archaeological record yet mostly neglected in our economic analyses. The rich ethnographic record of plant fiber use by contemporary Maya people likewise argues for plant fiber technology as a central component of the ancient economy and ethnobotanical knowledge base. The writings of the sixteenth-century Franciscan bishop Diego de Landa and other ethnohistoric documents such as the Motul and Vienna dictionaries confirm that sixteenth-century Maya craftspeople used plant fibers for a rich assortment of goods, or what Landa described as "an infinity of things," during the contact period. Baskets, mats, rope, and nets are all well represented in the artistic corpus of the Classic period and earlier (Clark and Houston 1998; Follensbee 2008; Gates 1937 [1566]:102).

The sheer scale of plant fiber usage and exchange, as discussed below, suggests that models of ancient Maya trade that rely on a scarcity framework may be ill equipped to accommodate or explain data on plant fiber technologies. Likewise, since these models derive from data on elite exchange of rare goods, they would be unlikely to accurately represent the cultural characteristics that resulted from the management of a substantial trade in plant fiber raw materials and finished products. The harvest and transport of plant fibers likely required relatively common manual skills but a high degree of social cooperation given the perishable nature of the materials, their bulk, and the lack of pack animals for transport in ancient Mesoamerica. Did social collectivities manage these tasks? Were extended kin networks mobilized for work parties, or did individual households provide tribute payments to administrative units? The study of abundance and especially the acknowledgment that elites often justified their privilege in complex societies through the provisioning and performance of abundance provide a welcome reorientation to ancient Maya economic systems.

A CITY AT THE EDGE

Chunchucmil, a large urban Classic Maya center, was located in an agriculturally marginal area of rocky, poor soils in northwestern Yucatan, Mexico (figure 6.1). This large urban center with a peak population estimated at 30,000–40,000 was situated adjacent to a rich savanna zone that borders the Gulf of Mexico. The savanna is a seasonally inundated tropical open grassland that contrasted dramatically with the bedrock and cactus landscape of urban Chunchucmil. Traditional models in Maya studies of agricultural self-sufficiency fail for this particular city, which relied instead on trade and exchange (Ardren 2015; Beach 1998; Dahlin and Ardren 2002; Dahlin et al. 2005; Hutson, Dahlin, and Mazeau 2010; Magnoni et al. 2014). Most scholars working at ancient Maya urban centers utilize some variant of the regal-ritual model to theorize the city-states of the Classic period (Chase and Chase 1998; Demarest 2005; Houston and Inomata 2009; McAnany 2010; Sanders and Webster 1988). A key component of this model is the lack of a well-developed economy (acknowledging that no consensus exists on a definition of this term for ancient Mesoamerica) and a reliance on local provisioning for subsistence needs. Such centers were primarily venues for the exchange and consumption of prestige goods rather than the production or distribution of crafts or commodities. Evidence for craft specialization, large-scale storage, or markets is scarce at most

FIGURE 6.1. Location of Chunchucmil in the Maya lowlands. Map by Traci Ardren.

Classic Maya cities. Production of utilitarian items for exchange is also scarce, and daily commodities such as pottery, textiles, and tools were generated in outlying residential settlements. Likewise, there is little evidence for storage or redistribution of agricultural goods in Maya urban centers, leading most scholars to believe that in general, each city was largely agriculturally self-reliant and autonomous.

Located inland from the second-largest natural saltworks in Mesoamerica, the 25 km² urban population of Chunchucmil grew to its largest extent in the Early Classic period (AD 200–700), a period of intensive interregional trade throughout the region. It survived into the Late Classic and Terminal Classic periods (AD 700–1200), but with a reduced population and less architectural construction. Despite the poverty of the soils in this zone of the peninsula, Chunchucmil had a strategic location that facilitated the control and movement of coastal resources, especially salt and trade goods, to interior population centers; this location was the motivation for the settlement of Chunchucmil and its long-term success (Hutson 2016). Research has demonstrated that the agricultural needs of the city, which functioned as a port of trade and gateway center, were met through market-based exchange of salt, obsidian, and other goods in a down-the-line form of exchange (cf. Renfrew 1975; Hutson 2016). While earlier publications have emphasized the importance of salt and Gulf Coast trade items in the non-agricultural economy of Chunchucmil, in this chapter I focus on the role of savanna resources, especially plant fiber products, in the city's success.

A cornerstone of the research agenda at Chunchucmil was the rich supplementary resource base of the savanna that to all of us working at the site clearly provided subsistence insurance against the harsh conditions and poor soils of the urban center. Bruce Dahlin and Traci Ardren (2002) wrote about resource diversification as one of the key mechanisms for the success of the Terminal Classic state centered at Chichen Itza and considered the uncultivable savanna a significant limitation on the ability of the ancient population at Chunchucmil to sustain itself agriculturally (Dahlin et al. 2005). The 20 km band of wetlands to the west of Chunchucmil was a constant factor in earlier models developed to explain the rise of this unique urban center, both as a limit on arable land and as a source of other resources. Yet little attention has been paid to investigating one class of savanna products that is certain to have been heavily exploited—the palms and other vegetal fibers used in woven plant technology.

PLANT FIBER TECHNOLOGY IN YUCATAN

Today, the Yucatan Peninsula is home to expert plant fiber artisans who preserve local traditions of plant fiber processing and use. Within the peninsula is a rich and diverse tradition of plant fiber technology, and products from many different plant species are used in a wide variety of woven forms and purposes (Rasmussen, Arroyo, and Terán 2010). Yucatecan artisans are famous for specialized products made of henequen and jipijapa, both of which require elaborate processing and expert weaving skills (Fadiman 2001). The bejuco vine is used for a variety of forms, and there are at least seven varieties of palms whose leaves are used to make basketry, rope, and thatch (Rodriguez Lazcano and Torres Quintero 1992:13). The role of this superabundant soft technology in models of domestic economies within the Classic Maya lowlands has been overlooked and under-theorized.

What can we say, then, about how the unique resources of the Chunchucmil savanna were used within Classic period systems of plant fiber technology and crafting? First we must establish that plant fiber technologies are not necessarily less complex or sophisticated than others but are simply under-studied in the Maya area. The skills needed to identify and harvest the correct plants, process them to extract usable fibers, and then weave or construct usable items are numerous and highly specific. Basketry alone can be classified into three main technologies of twining, coiling, and plaiting; and the potential number of technological subtypes within each class is relatively great (Adovasio 1977:1). Ethnographic studies have shown that rarely do cultural groups reproduce the exact same types of baskets, and while technological attributes are standardized, they are also culturally determined, and no class of artifacts presents a greater diversity of culturally visible attributes than does basketry (Adovasio 1977:4; Flechsig 2004:78). Given most Western archaeologists' unfamiliarity with fiber technologies and their relative scarcity in the archaeological record of the tropics, it has been easy to consider them simple technologies requiring little expertise, skill, or value in Classic Maya economies.

Today, Maya children begin learning to manufacture simple tools with plant fibers at a very early age and progress to more complicated forms given their individual abilities—evidence that certain plant fiber expertise requires years of apprenticeship to master (Rodriguez Lazcano and Torres Quintero 1992:15). While many apprenticeship processes are highly gendered in modern Maya societies, such as instruction in back-strap weaving, which is limited to young girls, the variety of forms and products made from plant fibers allows access to training for all children who have an aptitude. The social relationships generated and circulated during the plant fiber apprenticeships of modern Yucatan center on family units and crosscut age and gender groups, although certain classes of soft technology such as woven mats and baskets are more often produced by women, especially the elderly with assistance from children (Fadiman 2001; Flechsig 2004; Snoddy Cuellar 1993). Weavers who make their living working with plant fibers to make high-quality "Panama" hats (a misnomer) spend nine hours a day in a human-made underground cave that keeps fibers supple and pliable, but they earn less than one-tenth of the final selling price because of modern marketing strategies (Fadiman 2001:544). These highly skilled weavers have invested significant time in training and learning complex technologies not easily mastered. The materials they utilize are easily cultivated in Yucatan, but few people understand how to work the palm fibers while they are pliable or the complex weaves necessary to create a waterproof and durable hat with up to 1,000 weaves per square inch. The range of plant fiber products made in Yucatan today, and the variety of skills needed to produce such a range of products, suggests that while in the past many people may have possessed the ability to make simple ropes and utility baskets, other forms of craft making such as supple mats, cloth, and ceremonial items were likely the product of specialized craftspeople who possessed the knowledge of intricate weaving patterns and sophisticated plant fiber processing technologies.

PLANT FIBER PRODUCTS IN CLASSIC MAYA ECONOMIES

Imagery from elite ceramic vessels and carved stone monuments suggest a wide range of uses for plant fibers during the Classic period. Many forms of baskets are shown with offerings of food and other substances, and they mirror certain domestic forms of woven technology produced today (figure 6.2). Carrying devices, such as net bags, tump lines, and bundles, are also common in the iconographic record and likewise are used today (figure 6.3). Rope, twine, and cordage of all types are shown, as are codices or books made of lime-covered bark paper. Modest domestic structures covered in palm thatch are shown in monumental elite architecture in a metaphorical equation of elite and commoner domestic architecture (figure 6.4). Even clothing, hats, headdresses, and capes were made of plant fibers, according to Classic iconography. Mats, for covering both stone surfaces and walls, were obviously ideologically significant as well as ubiquitous symbols of privilege (figure 6.5).

Research has shown that Classic Maya people managed forest resources in a sustainable manner, for consistent yields and access, at least during the majority of the Classic period (Faust 1998; Ford and Nigh 2009, 2015; Gómez-Pompa et al. 2003). Earlier theories (Abrams and Rue 1988; Paine and Freter 1996) that deforestation may have played a significant role in the collapse or cessation of new construction late in the history of southern Maya lowland cities such as Copan have recently been challenged with new data (McNeil, Burney, and Burney 2010). Normal forest management yielded a modest surplus for exchange, as demonstrated by the presence of forest products such as jaguar pelts, parrot feathers, and hardwoods in multiple contexts at nearly all major Classic Maya cities, even those far from forest zones. The difficulty of finding evidence for these highly perishable materials outside of tombs or iconographic illustrations has likely resulted in an underestimation of the movement of forest products across regions. Bark paper made from the fig tree, natural rubber used for balls and ritual offerings, and cacao beans are all ephemeral organic forest products that textual and iconographic indications suggest were crucial materials produced for exchange. Patricia McAnany, for example,

FIGURE 6.2. Rollout of Classic Maya painted vase showing woven baskets holding tribute payments in a royal court. Used with permission, © Justin Kerr.

suggests that cacao production zones could have been controlled as "chocolate factories" through a system of tribute exchange at the heart of Classic Maya palace economies (2010:294).

Because of their relative inaccessibility and inundation, the coastal savannas of the Yucatan Peninsula are virtually unoccupied today and thus are reserves of high forest biodiversity (Martinez-Ballesté, Martorell, and Caballero 2008). Plants and animals that might have been present across the peninsula at one time have retreated to these environments in recent decades, and certain resources are significantly more plentiful in the savannas because of their rich soils and moisture. Palms of all species grow well here, and today the savannas, with their associated islands of higher ground fed by freshwater springs, are important economic resources in part for their ability to provide thatching material for traditional Maya domestic structures, a commodity that has become increasingly difficult to obtain in certain parts of the peninsula.

To examine in detail one of the most dominant forms of woven plant technology in Classic Maya economies, we need look no further than thatch. The architectural remains of Classic period domestic structures across the Maya lowlands support a hypothesis that the vast majority of living structures were covered with thatch roofing in a manner very similar to the way traditional Yucatec Maya homes are

FIGURE 6.3. Classic Maya carved bowl showing the Merchant God carrying goods in a woven back rack. Illustration by Traci Ardren.

roofed today. The dimensions of Classic period structures are easily accommodated by perishable roofing. The absence of evidence for an alternative manner of roofing in most archaeological contexts and iconographic depictions of small domestic structures that show in detail the use of palm thatch provide additional evidence supporting an extensive use of plant technology in living structures of the past (see figure 6.4).

FIGURE 6.4. Monumental Arch at the Classic Maya city of Labna, decorated with depictions of thatched Maya domestic structures. Photograph by Dan Griffin.

AN ABUNDANCE OF THATCH

Aline Magnoni's (2007) careful analysis of settlement pattern data generates a population estimate useful for understanding the importance of thatch in the economy of a Classic Maya urban center. Based on a detailed calculation of mean family size from ancient, historic, and modern data, Magnoni identified structures in the range of 18 m² as likely domestic buildings, eliminating smaller structures as likely storage or animal pens and larger structures as multi-use facilities. Within the 25 km² of continuous ancient settlement at Chunchucmil, she identified between 7,871 and 8,555 simple domestic structures, accounting for the change in structural density in the outermost periphery (Magnoni 2007:163)—a number range we can simplify to suggest that there were approximately 8,000 thatched-roofed domestic structures at the site.

Using figures from modern domestic construction techniques in Yaxunah, Yucatan, which utilize similar dimensions as ancient structures and so represent a reasonable proxy for thatching techniques of the past, a conservative estimate of 4,000 guanos or palm leaves would be required to thatch an 18 m² domestic structure. This type of roof would have been under constant maintenance and repair, with the entire set of fronds replaced after approximately ten years. This process of replacement would have occurred piecemeal as individual sections degraded, indicating a continuous and enduring engagement with thatch procurement

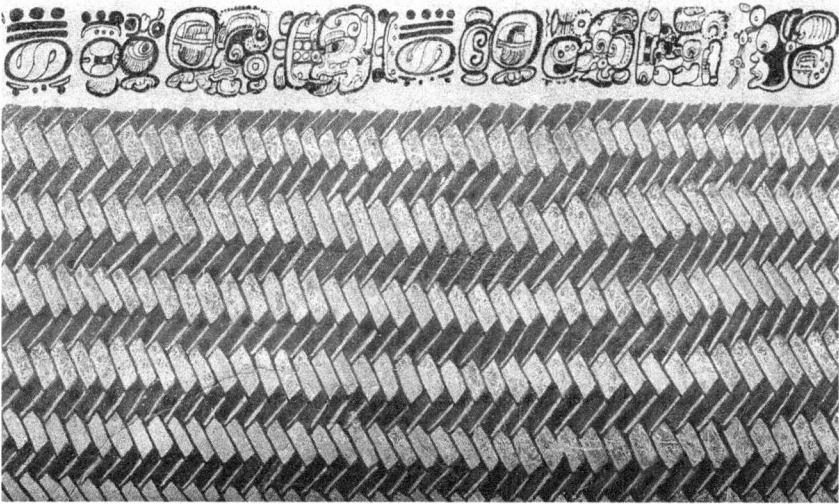

FIGURE 6.5. Elite Classic Maya cylindrical ceramic vase painted to resemble a woven basket (detail). Used with permission, © Justin Kerr.

and technology. Using Magnoni's data on the number of domestic structures at Chunchucmil, which we know from extensive residential sampling date largely to the Early Classic period, 32 million palm leaves were required at any given time for domestic architecture alone. If we think about this figure for the entire Early Classic period, 200–700 CE, a 500-year period in which domestic thatched roofs would have been replaced approximately forty times, the total amount of palm thatch necessary is 1.28 billion fronds for Chunchucmil alone. Studies of *Sabal mexicana* and *Sabal yapa* (*palma de guano* in Spanish and *xa'an* in Yucatec Maya) in the Yucatan have shown that these palms produce only about six–twelve leaves per year, when managed in a sustainable manner according to traditional Maya forest management techniques used across the peninsula (Martinez-Ballesté, Martorell, and Caballero 2008:1322). These techniques are aggressive, and they harvest all but a single frond once a year, in part because these palm species regenerate faster when harvested at this rate compared to a less aggressive harvesting regime or when not harvested at all (Martinez-Ballesté, Martorell, and Caballero 2008:1323). However, this still results in the need for a staggering amount of palms in the forests of the peninsula to accommodate this one particular usage of palm fronds.

The ancient inhabitants of Chunchucmil would have been situated advantageously for the procurement of thatch, a commodity that today has a clear market value in Yucatan. Sabal palms are ubiquitous across the various microenvironments of the peninsula, but they grow best in the wet, rich soils and closed canopy of the savanna zones (Pulido and Caballero 2006). The shift to more intensive agricultural practices, smaller forests, and increased demand for thatch in the tourist facilities of the Caribbean coast has contributed to the scarcity of thatch in some parts of the peninsula today.

While today thatch can be harvested for free by modern villagers of Chunchucmil, as many of them maintain rights of access to the savanna, traditional Maya in the center of the peninsula within the village of Yaxunah pay as much as 4 pesos a frond to purchase the raw materials necessary to construct a thatched roof. The cost of a new roof can be over US$1,000, which negatively impacts the choice of traditional building methods and practices today when the daily minimum wage in Mexico remains approximately US$5. While monetary considerations are a relatively recent development in the history of plant fiber technology within the Maya area, ancient families still had to calculate either labor investments for procurement or exchange value in other goods. Demand was also much higher in the past, when other roofing materials used today such as aluminum or tarpaper were not available. The differential access to thatch between modern Yucatec people in Chunchucmil versus those in Yaxunah is still a relevant model for the prehistoric period, in which Chunchucmileños and other near-coast residents certainly had enhanced access to this very necessary commodity.

SAVANNA PRODUCTS AND THE CHUNCHUCMIL ECONOMY

The valuable products of the savanna and associated estuary zone include palm fibers and other plant materials such as hardwoods and medicinal flora but also an abundance of animal resources, such as migratory birds, reptiles, deer, jaguars, sea turtles, and fish. Procurement and trade in these materials is believed to have been a central part of the market economy of ancient Chunchucmil, and the isotopic studies of Eugenia Mansell and colleagues demonstrate that the inhabitants of the city ate a more diverse diet than did most ancient Maya people of the region (Mansell et al. 2006). Thus the movement of people, both traders and regular citizens, back and forth from the city to the coast was a regular part of the experience of living at ancient Chunchucmil. The savanna and its distinct landscape of forest and wetland features must have been a familiar background to the frequent expeditions to the coast undertaken by many of the city's inhabitants.

Based on Landsat satellite photographs and radar imagery, David Hixson located two previously identified campsites within the western wetlands and surveyed their microenvironments (Hixson 2005, 2011). Using the remote data to identify similar microenvironments, Hixson was able to verify the presence of prehistoric habitation in a number of locations throughout the savanna. Small hamlets are found on many pockets of higher ground in the wetlands, and ancient field houses are found even in the most isolated locations within the swamp (Hixson 2005:4). Rock alignments of human manufacture but unknown function were also documented in the savanna by the Pakbeh Regional Archaeological Project members. These alignments are the physical manifestation of Chunchucmil's regional communication and trade network, outlining a dendritic system of local and regional pathways.

The concept of the urban imaginary acknowledges that cities are largely "fictionalized interrelationships among strangers" (LiPuma and Koelble 2005:156). In this sense the "imaginary" captures the ambiguities of urban life, the sacrifices of crowded and dangerous living counterpoised with the continued willingness of people to participate in urban environments. These characteristics are no less true of ancient urban centers—in many cases the harshest aspects of urban life were more prevalent in ancient societies, which had little expectation of public works such as education or sanitation. Edward LiPuma and Thomas Koelble suggest that one of the characteristics of the urban imaginary is the specific nature of circulations—an overlapping set of experiences of exchange, whether of goods, stories, ideas, or ways of being that lead to a unique and specific everyday understanding, an identity of being "from there." Each time a person states that he or she is headed to the savanna or coast, for example, the individual is reasserting a position in a shared imaginary urban space and circulating this idea to those around him or her.

Obviously, one of the most important forms of circulation accessible to an archaeologist would be the circulation of goods throughout an urban space and the shared experiences this generates. At Chunchucmil, another avenue for shared participation in circulation is the movement of people to and from the coast by way of the wetland savanna (Ardren 2015; Magnoni et al. 2014). An economy built around control of salt trade and savanna products necessitated movement from the urban center to the coast by some part of the population. Based on ethnographic analogy, apparently on an annual basis a large segment of the urban population moved out to the salt flats to harvest salt, perhaps also transporting it back to the site for warehousing. Monumental architectural groups with enclosed patio areas may have been the setting for salt storage or trade. The hamlet and campsites identified within the savanna zone certainly played a part in this experience, perhaps as way stations for rest along the journey or as landmarks along the way (Ardren and Lowry 2011). To walk to the coast, one left the relatively higher ground and dense urban atmosphere of the city, moved through an often wet and grassy savanna filled with freshwater springs and wildlife, then eventually reached the coastal mangroves and estuaries of the salt flats. Workers who traveled together must have shared stories of their work and lives and returned home with stories of the landscape outside the city. This circulation of people through contrasting environs, locations of profound economic, political, and cultural significance in the economy of ancient Chunchucmil, became part of the shared circulations of stories and knowledge that helped shape the experience of the city and the urban social relations that kept it functioning (Grieco 1995:190).

While Dahlin and other members of the Pakbeh Project, including myself, argued often that the urban settlement of Chunchucmil was located at the westernmost point of inhabitable land on the peninsula, I wish to clarify that the savanna and estuary zones were not in any way marginal to the complex history of this ancient city (Dahlin and Ardren 2002). The unique and abundant resources of the savanna were central to Chunchucmil's trajectory and contributed to its immense growth despite the poor agricultural potential of its location. The multitude of natural resource assets the savanna provided were an inescapable component of not only the local economy but the local identity as well.

As Monica Smith (this volume) points out, abundance is implicated in many social processes that were fundamental to ancient complex cultures. The abundance of the savanna may have contributed to the unique nature of Chunchucmil in the key arenas of adaptability, collective engagement, and mass trade. The rich resource diversity of the savanna coupled with poor agricultural potential presented an opportunity for rapid adaptation to an "abundance of variants" (Smith, this volume). It may have been the accumulated advantages of long-term adaptation to the multiplicity of challenges and opportunities presented by life adjacent to the savanna that predisposed Chunchucmileños to venture into long-distance trade in salt and savanna products. The diversity of goods sourced and managed locally in the savanna likely provided a very different set of skills than were necessary at inland centers or small coastal hamlets more characteristic of Classic Maya settlement patterns. Those typical centers were supported by large resident farming populations, while Chunchucmil was filled with a wider range of specialists (as documented in craft production debris, the absence of agricultural land, and an architectural corpus that mutes hierarchical difference). For many reasons Chunchucmil was not a typical Maya city, although a similar pattern of muted social hierarchy as demonstrated in relative architectural homogeneity can also be seen in other Maya sites active in natural resource trade, such as the cacao-producing sites of the Sibun Valley in Belize and the chert-producing site of Colha—but the opposite is true for the jade ornament production site of Cancuen, which is located far from the jade sources (Kovacevich 2007; McAnany et al. 2002; Shafer and Hester 1983). Maya settlements in areas with abundant and valuable natural resources were organized in variable ways, although more work remains to be done to assess the role of such resource hot spots in the evolution of Classic period polities.

ABUNDANCE AND LOCAL IDENTITY

The "acquisition of repetitive objects from a particular place constitutes another form of collective engagement" (Smith, this volume), and, as discussed, circulation between the city and coast through the resource-rich wetlands was likely a key component of how a sense of place and identity was perpetuated at Chunchucmil. When the importance of plant fibers is introduced into these circulations, the numbers needed to provide adequate roofing material argue that hundreds of thousands of palm fronds were cut every year. The abundance provided by the savanna but also the physical act of harvesting that abundance was certainly a repetitive activity that large numbers of ancient Maya people experienced. The visual impact of leaving a city covered in palm thatch to individually harvest hundreds of such fronds and then return with them to the collectivity is a clear example of the materialization of collective engagement and place-making rooted in the principle of abundance.

As a port of trade with a central market, Chunchucmil was marked as a place of plenty (Dahlin et al. 2007; Hutson 2016). A greater diversity of trade goods from elsewhere, larger-than-average percentages of commodities such as obsidian, and a huge resident population all demonstrate the unusual access this city had to economic resources. The lack of typically Maya signatures of dynastic rule at the site, such as funerary pyramids and rich elite burials, has long perplexed us but can be explained as the result of the leveling effect of an economic alliance of relative equals. Traders who were made wealthy through the movement of a wide variety of goods seem to have set up individual compounds with private areas for viewing materials or related negotiations. These patio quadrangles were linked to the central market area by clear administrative features such as raised roads and walkways. Abundance muted the highly stratified expressions of power usual in the Maya area and problematized typical hierarchies of elites versus commoners, perhaps engendering a form of social cooperation between quadrangle occupants and their nearby domestic groups (Hutson, Dahlin, and Mazeau 2010). The city was sustained not through the movement of exotic goods alone but through an ongoing and pervasive trade in daily goods such as marine products, salt, plant fibers, and other goods that acquired distance-value through transportation (Smith 2013:155).

What we find instead at Chunchucmil is a huge population living in relatively comparable conditions with similar levels of access to goods. The city was premised on the movement of a profusion of goods that required a more extensive trading machinery than found at many typical Maya centers, where a very limited number of elites controlled access to long-distance prestige items and goods. Such a system was not functional at a location where the economy was based on exchange of a rich abundance of natural resources from the savanna and coast coupled with a high-volume trade in non-local ceramics, obsidian, and foodstuffs. In fact, the development of urbanism at an interaction zone like Chunchucmil may have been substantially different than at most Classic Maya centers because the latter grew in size largely as a result of rituals of inclusion and trust performed between rulers and subordinate elites (Golden and Scherer 2012). While in those centers the perception of abundance was reliant on the generosity of a royal dynasty, Chunchucmil's immense size and density was largely the result of a shared perception of resource abundance and the potential for exchange. The multiple elite compounds of similar size and configuration, the open marketplace at the center of the city, and the absence of iconography reinforcing restricted access to trade goods all demonstrate how abundance was performed as a guiding principle of the city's identity. These features underscore not only an abundance of raw materials but an abundance of access to resources across the population.

CONCLUSION

Plant fiber technology has been overlooked in models of ancient Maya resource diversity and craft production, despite the availability of relevant artifactual and ethnographic information. This omission marginalizes a key component of the economy in the Maya region, which like other tropical areas enjoys a profusion of usable plant materials. Forested areas tended by Maya people today are characterized as species-rich, with a complex structure of highly valued native species. Research has demonstrated that the diversity of tree species parallels the diversity in their economic value to the people who manage them in this region today (Thompson et al. 2015:126). The use and management of non-timber forest products in the Maya area is a topic of great current interest in the fields of ecology and environmental management, and archaeologists should contribute to those conversations more often, given our rich data on populations that were even more dependent on natural resources than those of today (Ford and Nigh 2015; Martinez-Ballesté, Martorell, and Caballero 2008; Ross 2011; Thompson et al. 2015).

While many other aspects of traditional Maya ethnobotany are lost to us, plant fiber technology remains a vibrant and self-perpetuating body of specialized knowledge and skills to which we have ready access. A consideration of the abundance of savanna resources provides a new perspective on initial settlement and eventual urban migrations to this unusual ancient center. Urban neighborhood networks may have facilitated annual migrations to the coast for littoral resources where social or kinship relations were deployed for the recruitment of labor. Rather than agricultural scarcity, natural resource abundance may be a more salient characteristic for the initial settlement and later success of Chunchucmil and other ancient Maya trade centers located in environments marginal for agriculture but rich in opportunities.

REFERENCES CITED

Abrams, Elliot M., and David J. Rue. 1988. "The Causes and Consequences of Deforestation among the Prehistoric Maya." *Human Ecology* 16 (4): 377–95. http://dx.doi.org/10.1007/BF00891649.

Adovasio, James M. 1977. *Basketry Technology: A Guide to Identification and Analysis.* Chicago: Aldine.

Álvarez, Héctor Hernández, and Nancy Peniche May. 2012. "Los malacates arqueologicos de la peninsula de Yucatan." *Ancient Mesoamerica* 23 (2): 441–59. http://dx.doi.org/10.1017/S0956536112000284.

Ardren, Traci. 2015. *Social Identities in the Classic Maya Northern Lowlands.* Austin: University of Texas Press.

Ardren, Traci, and Justin Lowry. 2011. "The Travels of Maya Merchants in the Ninth–Tenth Centuries: Investigations at Xuenkal and the Greater Cupul Province, Yucatan, Mexico." *World Archaeology* 43 (3): 428–43. http://dx.doi.org/10.1080/00438243.2011.607613.

Beach, Timothy. 1998. "Soil Constraints on Northwest Yucatan, Mexico: Pedoarchaeology and Maya Subsistence at Chunchucmil." *Geoarchaeology* 13 (8): 759–91.

Chase, Arlen F., and Diane Z. Chase. 1998. "Scale and Intensity in Classic Period Maya Agriculture: Terracing and Settlement of the 'Garden City' of Caracol." *Culture and Agriculture* 20 (2–3): 60–77. http://dx.doi.org/10.1525/cag.1998.20.2-3.60.

Clark, John E., and Stephen D. Houston. 1998. "Craft Specialization, Gender, and Personhood among the Post-Conquest Maya of Yucatan, Mexico." In *Craft and Social Identity*, edited by Cathy Lynne Costin and Rita P. Wright, 31–46. Archeological Papers of the American Anthropological Association 8. Washington, DC: American Anthropological Association.

Dahlin, Bruce H., and Traci Ardren. 2002. "Modes of Exchange and Regional Patterns: Chunchucmil, Yucatan, Mexico." In *Ancient Maya Political Economies*, edited by Marilyn Masson and David Freidel, 249–84. Walnut Creek, CA: Altamira.

Dahlin, Bruce H., Timothy Beach, Sheryl Luzzadder-Beach, David Hixson, Scott R. Hutson, Aline Magnoni, Eugenia B. Mansell, and Daniel Mazeau. 2005. "Reconstructing Agricultural Self-Sufficiency at Chunchucmil, Yucatan, Mexico." *Ancient Mesoamerica* 16 (2): 229–47. http://dx.doi.org/10.1017/S0956536105050212.

Dahlin, Bruce H., Chris T. Jensen, Richard E. Terry, David R. Wright, and Timothy Beach. 2007. "In Search of an Ancient Maya Market." *Latin American Antiquity* 18 (4): 363–84. http://dx.doi.org/10.2307/25478193.

Demarest, Arthur. 2005. *Ancient Maya: The Rise and Fall of a Rainforest Civilization.* Cambridge: Cambridge University Press.

Dobres, Marcia-Anne. 2010. "Archaeologies of Technology." *Cambridge Journal of Economics* 34 (1): 103–14. http://dx.doi.org/10.1093/cje/bep014.

Fadiman, Maria. 2001. "Hat Weaving with Jipi, Carludovica palmata (Cyclanthaceae) in the Yucatan Peninsula, Mexico." *Economic Botany* 55 (4): 539–44. http://dx.doi.org /10.1007/BF02871716.

Faust, Betty Bernice. 1998. *Mexican Rural Development and the Plumed Serpent: Technology and Maya Cosmology in the Tropical Forest of Campeche, Mexico*. Westport, CT: Bergin and Garvey.

Flechsig, Katrin. 2004. *Miniature Crafts and Their Makers: Palm Weaving in a Mexican Town*. Tucson: University of Arizona Press.

Follensbee, Billie. 2008. "Fiber Technology and Weaving in Formative-Period Gulf Coast Cultures." *Ancient Mesoamerica* 19 (1): 87–110. http://dx.doi.org/10.1017/S095653610 8000229.

Ford, Anabel, and Ronald Nigh. 2009. "Origins of the Maya Forest Garden: Maya Resource Management." *Journal of Ethnobiology* 29 (2): 213–36. http://dx.doi.org/10 .2993/0278-0771-29.2.213.

Ford, Anabel, and Ronald Nigh. 2015. *Maya Forest Garden: Eight Millennia of Sustainable Cultivation of the Tropical Woodlands*. Walnut Creek, CA: Left Coast.

Frink, Liam, and Celeste Giordano. 2015. "Women and Subsistence Food Technology: The Arctic Seal Poke Storage System." *Food and Foodways* 23: 251–72. http://dx.doi.org/10.10 80/07409710.2015.1099906.

Gates, William. 1937 [1566]. *Yucatan Before and After the Conquest*. New York: Dover.

Golden, Charles, and Andrew K. Scherer. 2012. "Territory, Trust, Growth, and Collapse in Classic Period Maya Kingdoms." *Current Anthropology* 54 (4): 397–435. http://dx.doi .org/10.1086/671054.

Gómez-Pompa, Arturo, Michael F. Allen, Scott L. Fedick, and Juan J. Jiménez Osornio, eds. 2003. *The Lowland Maya Area: Three Millennia at the Human-Wildland Interface*. New York: Food Products Press, an imprint of Haworth Press.

Grieco, Margaret. 1995. "Transported Lives: Urban Social Networks and Labour Circulation." In *The Urban Context: Ethnicity, Social Networks, and Situational Analysis*, edited by Alisdair Rogers and Steven Vertovec, 189–212. Oxford: Berg.

Hixson, David R. 2005. "Measuring a Maya Metropolis." *Institute of Maya Studies Newsletter* 34 (1): 1–4.

Hixson, David R. 2011. "Settlement Patterns and Communications Routes of the Western Maya Wetlands: An Archaeological and Remote-Sensing Survey, Chunchucmil, Yucatan, Mexico." PhD dissertation, Tulane University, New Orleans, LA. Manuscript in the possession of the author.

Houston, Stephen D., and Takeshi Inomata. 2009. *The Classic Maya*. Cambridge: Cambridge University Press.

Hutson, Scott R., ed. 2016. *Ancient Maya Merchants: Multidisciplinary Research at Chunchucmil.* Boulder: University Press of Colorado.

Hutson, Scott R., Bruce Dahlin, and Daniel Mazeau. 2010. "Commerce and Cooperation among the Classic Maya: The Chunchucmil Case." In *Cooperation in Economy and Society,* edited by Robert C. Marshall, 81–103. Walnut Creek, CA: Altamira.

Kovacevich, Brigitte. 2007. "Ritual, Crafting, and Agency at the Classic Maya Kingdom of Cancuen." In *Mesoamerican Ritual Economy: Archaeological and Ethnological Perspectives,* edited by E. Christian Wells and Karla Davis-Salazar, 67–114. Boulder: University Press of Colorado.

LiPuma, Edward, and Thomas Koelble. 2005. "Cultures of Circulation and the Urban Imaginary: Miami as Example and Exemplar." *Public Culture* 17 (1): 153–80. http://dx .doi.org/10.1215/08992363-17-1-153.

Magnoni, Aline. 2007. "Population Estimates at the Ancient Maya City of Chunchucmil, Yucatan, Mexico." In *CAA 2006: Computer Applications and Quantitative Methods in Archaeology,* edited by Jeffrey Clark, 160–67. BAR International Series. Oxford: British Archaeological Reports.

Magnoni, Aline, Traci Ardren, Scott Hutson, and Bruce Dahlin. 2014. "Urban Identities: Social and Spatial Production at Classic Period Chunchucmil, Yucatán, Mexico." In *Making Ancient Cities: Studies of the Production of Space in Early Urban Environments,* edited by Kevin D. Fisher and Andrew D. Creekmore III, 145–80. Cambridge: Cambridge University Press. http://dx.doi.org/10.1017/CBO9781107110274.006.

Mansell, Eugenia, Robert Tykot, David Freidel, Bruce Dahlin, and Traci Ardren. 2006. "Early to Terminal Classic Maya Diet in the Northern Lowlands of the Yucatán, Mexico." In *Histories of Maize: Multidisciplinary Approaches to the Prehistory, Biogeography, Domestication, and Evolution of Maize,* edited by John E. Staller, Robert Tykot, and Bruce F. Benz, 173–85. New York: Academic. http://dx.doi.org/10.1016/B978-012369 364-8/50265-5.

Martinez-Ballesté, Andrea, Carlos Martorell, and Javier Caballero. 2008. "The Effect of Maya Traditional Harvesting on the Leaf Production, and Demographic Parameters of Sabal Palm in the Yucatan Peninsula, Mexico." *Forest Ecology and Management* 256 (6): 1320–24. http://dx.doi.org/10.1016/j.foreco.2008.06.029.

McAnany, Patricia A. 2010. *Ancestral Maya Economies in Archaeological Perspective.* Cambridge: Cambridge University Press. http://dx.doi.org/10.1017/CBO978113919 5867.

McAnany, Patricia A., Ben S. Thomas, Steven Morandi, Polly A. Peterson, and Eleanor Harrison. 2002. "Praise the Ahaw and Pass the Kakaw: Xibun Maya and the Political Economy of Cacao." In *Ancient Maya Political Economies,* edited by Marilyn Masson and David A. Freidel, 123–39. Walnut Creek, CA: Altamira.

McNeil, Cameron L., David A. Burney, and Lida Pigott Burney. 2010. "Evidence Disputing Deforestation as the Cause for the Collapse of the Ancient Maya Polity of Copan, Honduras." *Proceedings of the National Academy of Sciences of the United States of America* 107 (3): 1017–22. Medline:20018691 http://dx.doi.org/10.1073/pnas.090 4760107.

Murdock, George, and Caterina Provost. 1973. "Factors in the Division of Labor by Sex: A Cross-Cultural Analysis." *Ethnology* 12 (2): 203–25. http://dx.doi.org/10.2307/3773347.

Paine, Richard R., and AnnCorinne Freter. 1996. "Environmental Degradation and the Classic Maya Collapse at Copan, Honduras (AD 600–1250): Evidence from Studies of Household Survival." *Ancient Mesoamerica* 7 (1): 37–47. http://dx.doi.org/10.1017/S095 6536100001279.

Pulido, Maria T., and Javier Caballero. 2006. "The Impact of Shifting Agriculture on the Availability of Non-Timber Forest Products: The Example of Sabal Yapa in the Maya Lowlands of Mexico." *Forest Ecology and Management* 222 (1–3): 399–409. http://dx .doi.org/10.1016/j.foreco.2005.10.043.

Rasmussen, Christian H., Luz Elena Arroyo, and Silvia Terán. 2010. *Las artesanías en Yucatán: tradición e innovación*. Merida: Instituto de Cultura de Yucatán, Casa de las Artesanías del Estado de Yucatán.

Rathje, William L. 1972. "Praise the Gods and Pass the Metates: A Hypothesis of the Development of Lowland Rainforest Civilization in Middle America." In *Contemporary Archeology*, edited by Mark P. Leone, 365–92. Carbondale: Southern Illinois University Press.

Renfrew, Colin. 1975. "Trade as Action at a Distance: Questions of Integration and Communication." In *Ancient Civilization and Trade*, edited by Jeremy Sabloff and C. C. Lamberg-Karlovsky, 3–59. Santa Fe: School of American Research.

Rodriguez Lazcano, Catalina, and Sergio Torres Quintero. 1992. *La Cesteria Maya de Tierras Bajas*. Mexico City: Instituto Nacional de Antropologia e Historia.

Ross, Nanci J. 2011. "Modern Tree Species Composition Reflects Ancient Maya 'Forest Gardens' in Northwest Belize." *Ecological Applications* 21 (1): 75–84. Medline:21516889 http://dx.doi.org/10.1890/09-0662.1.

Sanders, William T., and David Webster. 1988. "The Mesoamerican Urban Tradition." *American Anthropologist* 90 (3): 521–46. http://dx.doi.org/10.1525/aa.1988.90.3.02a00010.

Shafer, Harry J., and Thomas R. Hester. 1983. "Ancient Maya Chert Workshops in Northern Belize, Central America." *American Antiquity* 48 (3): 519–43. http://dx.doi .org/10.2307/280559.

Smith, Monica L. 2013. "The Substance and Symbolism of Long-Distance Exchange: Textiles as Desired Trade Goods in the Bronze Age Middle Asian Interaction Sphere." In *Connections and Complexity: New Approaches to the Archaeology of South Asia*, edited by Shinu Anna Abraham, Praveena Gullapalli, Teresa P. Raczek, and Uzma Z. Rizvi, 143–60. Walnut Creek, CA: Left Coast.

Snoddy Cuellar, Elizabeth. 1993. "La cesteria en Mexico." *Artesanias de America, Revista del CIDAP* 41–42: 252–67.

Soffer, Olga, James M. Adovasio, Jeff S. Illingsworth, Hizri A. Amirkhanov, Nikolai D. Praslov, and Martin Street. 2000. "Paleolithic Perishables Made Permanent." *Antiquity* 74: 812–21.

Thompson, Kim M., Angela Hood, Dana Cavallaro, and David L. Lentz. 2015. "Connecting Contemporary Ecology and Ethnobotany to Ancient Plant Use Practices of the Maya at Tikal." In *Tikal: Paleoecology of an Ancient Maya City*, edited by David L. Lentz, Nicholas P. Dunning, and Vernon L. Scarborough, 124–51. Cambridge: Cambridge University Press. http://dx.doi.org/10.1017/CBO9781139227209.008.

7

Abundant Exotics and Cavalier Crafting

Obsidian Use and Emerging Complexity in the Northern Lake Titicaca Basin

Elizabeth Klarich, Abigail Levine, and Carol Schultze

During the Middle Formative (1300–500 BC) and Late Formative periods (500 BC–AD 300), Taraco and Pukara became major centers in the northern Lake Titicaca Basin of Peru. Recent research has revealed similar economic patterns for both sites that included the exploitation of vast trading networks through camelid caravans. These trade networks were responsible for the importation of obsidian from the Chivay and Alca sources, located approximately 200 km to the west (figure 7.1). Although it is exotic (non-local) to the basin, obsidian is over-represented in excavated contexts at both Taraco and Pukara, and its purposeful accumulation corresponds with increased investment in corporate architecture and supra-household food sharing during the Late Formative. At Taraco, an increase in relative frequency of obsidian corresponds chronologically with its apogee as a regional center. Contemporaneously, a complete analysis of lithic collections from excavated contexts at Pukara shows that obsidian was so plentiful that craftspeople made no effort to conserve or recycle it. We argue that this wasteful behavior reflects resource abundance and the status of these centers as primary nodes in region-wide obsidian exchange networks. These results highlight the role relatively rare, non-local utilitarian products might play in the formation of regional centers and multi-community polities and underscore the fluidity of value within the prestige economy during the earliest periods of social complexity.

As outlined by Monica Smith in this volume, a focus on both actual and perceived scarcity has driven archaeological research across time periods and geographical

DOI: 10.5876/9781607325949.c007

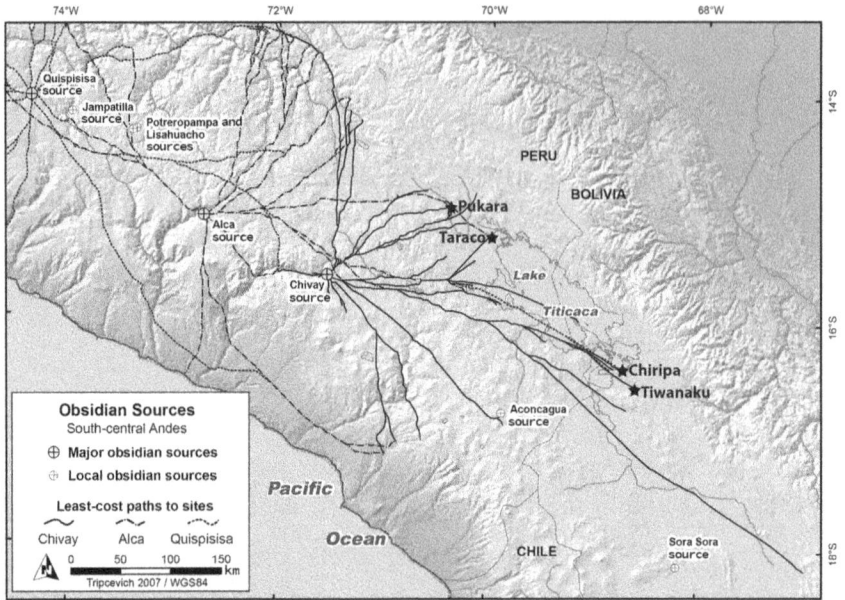

FIGURE 7.1. Major obsidian sources in the South-Central Andes (Chivay, Alca, and Quispisisa) and the least-cost paths to archaeological sites in the Lake Titicaca Basin (adapted from Tripcevich 2007:figure 3.5, p. 181).

settings. In the case of lithic raw materials, their limited geological distribution often translates to assumptions of scarcity. The presence of such materials in archaeological contexts distant from their sources triggers a series of questions related to control, conservation, and restriction at each stage of the chaîne opératoire predicated on the materials' apparent scarcity. This chapter looks at this issue in a different light and examines a case in which a geologically restricted material—obsidian—appears in relatively large percentages in burgeoning regional centers far from its sources. This unexpected abundance of an exotic good in both public and private settings at these centers presents a unique opportunity to think about perception, meaning, and decision-making in new ways. Seeking explanations for abundant non-local lithic raw materials, production debris, and finished tools can provide new insights into the nature of trade networks, the organization of craft production, the development of prestige economies through conspicuous consumption and costly signaling, and the origins of sociopolitical complexity in the Lake Titicaca Basin of highland Peru.

Andean archaeologists have traditionally focused on the relationship among resource control, interregional exchange, and sociopolitical organization because of the region's intensely vertical nature. Like other mountainous environments, there is significant variability of available natural resources in each of the "stacked" ecological niches of the Central Andes. Climatically sensitive crops such as cotton thrive in the irrigated valleys of the coastal dessert, maize is found primarily in the mid-elevation highlands, and the highest elevations are home to potatoes, quinoa, and other frost-resistant crops (Seltzer and Hastorf 1990). The diversity of this landscape has inspired decades of debate about the nature of trade and transhumanance across these vertically differentiated ecological niches. Models of vertical complementarity for subsistence exchange (Murra 1972, 1985) have inspired other models, such as horizontal complementarity (e.g., Browman 1977), and have been the subject of more generalized critiques (e.g., VanBuren 1996). While these models are of theoretical value, they often fail to consider goods that radiate diffusely across ecozones from a single source, such as salt and obsidian (Tripcevich 2007:figure 3.4; Yacobaccio et al. 2002:168; cf. Burger and Asaro 1977, 1978, 1979 and Tripcevich and Contreras 2013 for the history of Andean obsidian research).

Objects made of obsidian are extremely useful, highly visible, and chemically sourceable, and they have considerable time depth in the archaeological record of the Central Andes. Over the last two decades there has been new interest in obsidian research in the Central Andes that addresses quarrying, processing, circulation, and consumption behaviors while applying a variety of innovative methodological and theoretical approaches (Brooks, Glascock, and Giesso 1997; Burger, Chávez, and Chávez 2000; Burger et al. 1998; Craig et al. 2010; Giesso 2003; Jennings and Glascock 2002; Stanish et al. 2002; Tripcevich 2007, 2010; Tripcevich and Contreras 2011, 2013; Tripcevich and Mackay 2012). Among the most important developments were technological advances enabling the relatively rapid—and fairly low-cost—geochemical characterization of large quantities of obsidian. Technologies such as portable X-ray fluorescence (PXRF), which permit nondestructive in situ analysis of archaeological materials, have resulted in a proliferation of compositional studies in recent years and have been especially useful for monitoring patterns of quarrying and circulation of artifacts in the Andes and elsewhere (e.g., Craig et al. 2007; Shackley 2011).

This chapter integrates detailed artifact analysis with site-level contextual information and geochemical sourcing to explore the economic and social value of obsidian at Taraco and Pukara, two early regional centers in the northern Lake Titicaca Basin. Obsidian is an exotic material to this region but is found in relative abundance in recent excavations at both sites. Informed by research on regional obsidian circulation by Nicholas Tripcevich (2007:2), we use these data to assess whether obsidian was viewed as a precious commodity (like gold or lapis lazuli) or a utilitarian product (like salt) during the Middle and Late Formative periods in the northern Titicaca Basin. Together, these data further permit examination of the ways abundance figures across the multiple cooperative and competitive strategies associated with emergent social complexity.

REGIONAL CONTEXT

The Lake Titicaca Basin is a vast, high-elevation plateau ringed by the high peaks of the Andean cordilleras. Spanning the modern political borders of Peru and Bolivia, the lowest point in the basin is the lake itself, which sits at an altitude of 3,810 m above sea level. Despite a generally frigid climate and the stark conditions typical of high-altitude environments, the Titicaca Basin is a highly productive ecological zone that supports a large biomass. Tropical latitudes and a pronounced rainy season enable intensive cultivation of a variety of tubers, chenopods, and legumes on arable plains and hillsides. Expansive grasslands support large herds of both wild (vicuña and guanaco) and domesticated (llama and alpaca) camelids. The cultural developments of the Titicaca region played out in this geographical context that favored the agriculturally rich far northern and far southern areas. In the north, this region was centered in the corridor along the lake and up the rivers from Huancané through Taraco, Azángaro, and Pukara. In the south, this region is bounded through the Taraco Peninsula, Tiwanaku, and the Jesus de Machaca region.

From its earliest settlement ca. 7000 BC, wild camelid herds attracted the first nomadic foraging populations to the Titicaca Basin during the Archaic period (figure 7.2). Domesticated llamas then served as valuable pack animals, facilitating long-distance interregional exchange and contributing to the establishment of sedentary agropastoralist villages in the region. Agropastoral economies flourished in the region for millennia, leading to the development of small settled villages in the Early Formative (2000–1300 BC). A few of these settlements experienced significant growth and differentiation during the Middle Formative, a period characterized by intense political and economic expansion in the region as a whole. This competitive trend ultimately culminated with the formation of the first regionally expansive polities by the Late, or "Upper," Formative.[1]

Pukara and Taraco were at the heart of two such polities competing for regional dominance during the late Middle and early Late Formative periods. The aggregation of populations into these relatively dense political centers represents one of the most important transitions in the history of complex societies in the region (Levine 2012). In addition to their large size and the presence of corporate architecture, these centers are further distinguished by the relative abundance of specialized craft goods—primarily polychrome pottery and intricately carved stone sculptures—and of non-local objects and exotic raw materials, including obsidian

Date	Northern Titicaca Basin	Chronological Stage	Ica Sequence
AD 1500	Inka	Expansive Inka	Late Horizon
1000	Colla Late Huaña Tiwanaku	Regional period Expansive Tiwanaku	Late Intermediate period Middle Horizon
500			
AD/BC	Early Huaña Pukara	Late/Upper Formative	Early Intermediate period
500	Cusipata	Middle Formative	Early Horizon
1000	Qaluyu		
1500		Early Formatiive	
2000 BC		Late Archaic	

FIGURE 7.2. Chronological chart for the Lake Titicaca Basin (adapted from Levine 2013).

(Burger, Chávez, and Chávez 2000; see discussion in Plourde 2006). Collectively, these features constitute the Yaya-Mama Religious Tradition, a pan–Titicaca Basin elite ideology associated with the earliest complex cultures of the region (Chávez 1988; Chávez and Chávez 1975; Stanish 2003).

TARACO

As a major Middle and Late Formative period center with an uninterrupted occupational sequence, the archaeological site of Taraco in the far northern basin is ideal for studying the evolution of war and trade, two major processes associated with emergent complexity (Levine et al. 2013; Stanish and Levine 2011). The site is located along the Ramis River in the eponymous modern town approximately 15 km north of the lake, and it remained prominent in the region through subsequent Inca times, when it was mentioned in Spanish chronicles. Though few remains of the site are visible on the surface today, scholars have long noted the significance of the greater Taraco area, which is famous for the quantity and quality of its monoliths and exquisite examples of lithic art (Kidder 1943; Rowe 1942; Tschopik 1946).

Notably, these include the iconic half-male, half-female Yaya-Mama stela after which the cultural tradition was first described (Chávez and Chávez 1970, 1975).

In the systematic survey of more than 1,000 km^2 in the Huancané, Putina, Taraco, and Arapa zones, the mound at Taraco stands out because of its comparatively large size (Stanish and Umire 2004). A dense cluster of contemporary settlements, linked by a network of roads and possibly causeways, surrounds the principal mound, and together these form the Taraco site complex. As represented by survey data, the entire area of Middle and Late Formative occupation totals well over 100 hectares, making the size of the Taraco site complex several orders of magnitude greater than any of its neighbors.

Excavations in three of the eighteen mounds in the Taraco area have further revealed the importance of the site area in the history of the northern Titicaca Basin (figure 7.3). The majority of this attention has been focused on the principal mound, known as Area A (de la Vega 2005; Levine 2012, 2013). Excavations of a high-status residential area on a large (approximately 2 hectares) artificial terrace just below the highest part of the modern town exposed a stratified cultural sequence that included architectural fill episodes, midden accumulations, and buildings that were remodeled, disassembled, or destroyed. From this work, it was determined that Area A was characterized by eight occupational phases that dated from as early as 1200 BC and continued through the modern day (Levine 2012). The earliest three occupational phases (termed Phases 1, 2, and 3) date to the Formative eriod, and the latest (Phase 3), dating to approximately AD 100, corresponds with Early Pukara (Levine et al. 2013). Each of these occupations was associated with a building made of fine stone, with the two later occupations superimposed over the earlier ones. While largely domestic in character, the three Formative occupations were also associated with relatively high levels of prestige and exotic goods, including highly decorated ceramic ceremonial wares such as trumpets and braziers, as well as obsidian, indicating that they were also the locus of periodic ritual and civic-ceremonial activity (Levine 2012).

Levine's analysis of the excavation data and associated material finds indicated that Taraco achieved its political and economic status through early residents' strategic participation in long-distance trade networks used to import exotic goods, such as obsidian, from the Colca Valley (Levine 2012; Levine et al. 2013). In its earliest phases, Taraco, ideally situated along a number of trade routes, likely functioned as a "transit community" (Bandy 2005), with individual households hosting passing caravans in exchange for "presents" of exotic goods. Preferential access to these resources allowed residents to accumulate the durable wealth required for local faction building and political expansion (Levine 2012). By the middle of the Late Formative, this imported wealth was financing a thriving political economy:

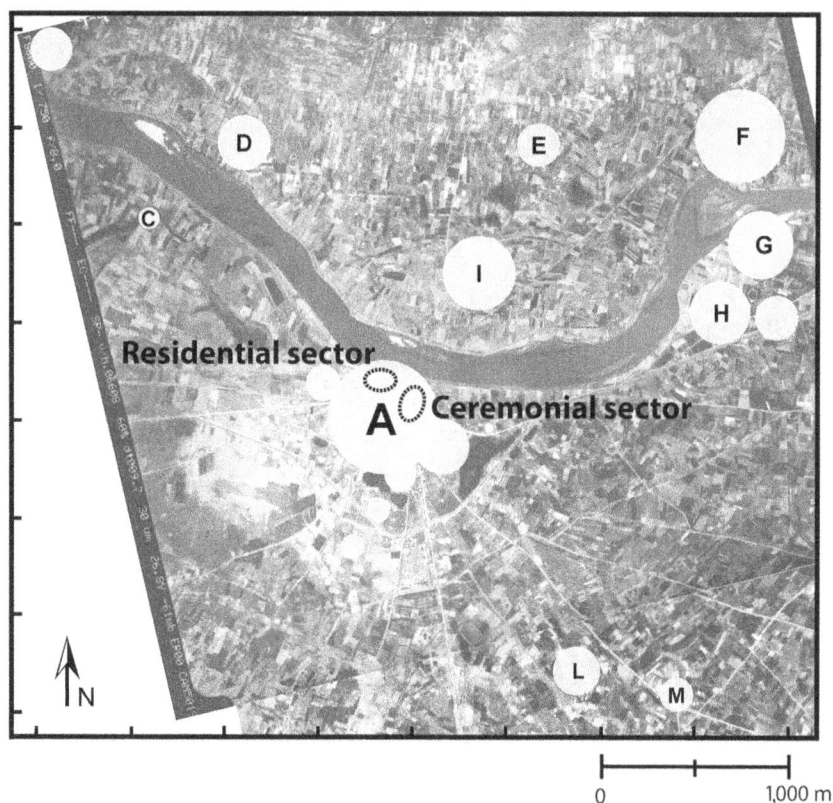

FIGURE 7.3. Taraco site map.

excavation of the terrace and the adjacent ceremonial sector (see figure 7.3 for sector locations) revealed abundant evidence of public ceremonial activities featuring music and the burning of incense and of large-scale community-sponsored feasts (Levine 2013; Levine et al. 2013). These events built and strengthened alliances among participants; attendees were granted access to exotic goods; and gifts of high-status crafted goods materialized social bonds, created indebtedness, and demonstrated hierarchy. In other words, this wealth allowed early residents of Taraco to "buy into" pan-regional ideologies, including the Yaya-Mama religious tradition. During the early Late Formative, these strategies successfully attracted populations from around the north basin and likely beyond (Levine 2012).

Taraco's economic and political success was ultimately short-lived, however, as the Phase 3 occupation was associated with a major burn event that destroyed the entire residential sector in the first century AD. Evidence of this episode was detected in all areas tested, including each of the excavation units, as well as in a profile cut along the river edge that revealed a continuous stratum of ash and architectural debris stretching for more than 35 m. Stanish and Levine (2011) have argued that this event represents evidence for intensive raiding, most likely by the Pukara polity and its allies, as the dates of this burn event correspond chronologically with dates from "pure Pucara style rubbish" excavated by Kidder at the site of Pukara.

PUKARA

By the first century AD, the majority of northern basin populations fell under the influence of the Pukara polity, with its center at the monumental site Pukara (figure 7.4). This major civic ceremonial center was approximately 80 km northwest of the lake and 50 km from Taraco. In the center of the site's core is the Qalasaya, a stone-lined platform mound topped by three sunken court complexes. It is situated at the base of a massive pink sandstone outcrop and is surrounded by a number of plazas, platforms, and artificial mounds. More modest residential architecture and dense middens of production debris and fragmentary finished goods characterize the periphery of the site. However, because of the spatial overlap of prehistoric Pukara and the modern town of Pucará, it is challenging to determine if the Formative period settlement was continuous between the core and periphery areas.

A systematic settlement survey of the Pucara River Valley provides valuable insights into the timing of the reorganization of local populations and the expansion of Pukara. Cohen (2010) documented an abrupt settlement shift as Middle Formative villages were abandoned and the majority of the population relocated to Pukara during the Late Formative. Based on intensive site-level survey, Pukara expanded to cover over 200 hectares at its apogee during the Late Formative (Klarich and Román Bustinza 2012). Excavations by Alfred Kidder II in 1939 (Chávez 1992; Franco Inojosa 1940; Kidder 1942), by UNESCO/Plan COPESCO in the 1970s (Mujica 1978, 1985, 1988, 1991; Wheeler and Mujica 1981), and most recently by the Pukara Archaeological Project (2000–present) have worked to establish the scale, spatial organization, and occupational history of Pukara, which spans from the Middle Formative to the Spanish colonial period (Abraham 2012; Klarich 2005a, 2005b, 2009; Klarich and Román Bustinza 2012; Oshige Adams 2012).

The Pukara Archaeological Project has targeted a number of areas within the civic ceremonial core and on the site periphery for intensive surveys, mapping, and excavations over the last decade. We have focused primarily on documenting the timing and directionality of site growth, and earliest dates thus far are from contexts within the civic ceremonial core. The lithic data presented in this discussion were recovered from a series of Late Formative period contexts in three excavation

Site Core
1. Qalasaya complex
2. Northern platform
3. Central Pampa (2001 excavations)
4. Lagunita mound

Site Periphery
5. Riverbank middens
6. Classic Pukara middens
7. Riverbank mounds
(highly disturbed)

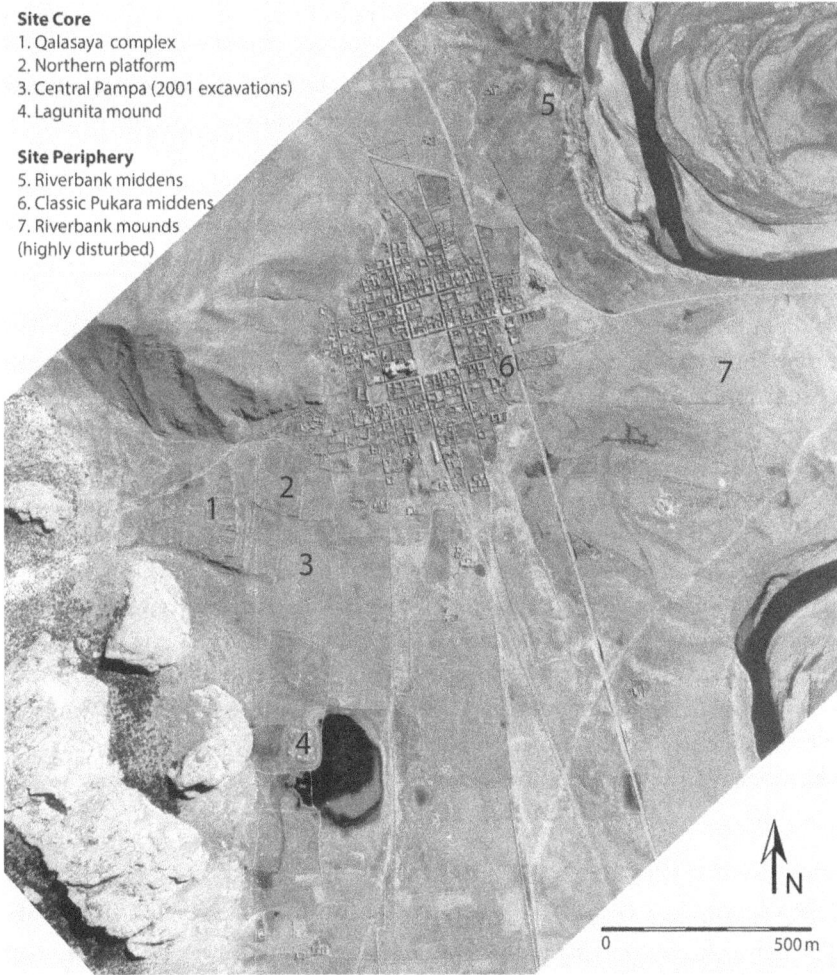

FIGURE 7.4. Pukara site map.

blocks on the Central Pampa, a large open space at the base of the Qalasaya terraces. While there was variability in the range of specific activities documented in each block, based on stratigraphic relationships and diagnostic pottery it was possible to group them broadly into initial, middle, and final occupations that all dated to the Late Formative period.[2] The initial contexts were characterized as outdoor activity areas with little evidence of long-term use. In contrast, during the middle and late occupations the pampa area was transformed into a residential sector with a diversity of architectural spaces and activity areas. Lithic materials were recovered from middens and work surfaces, reflecting a broad range of domestic and ritual activities in this non-elite residential context (see Klarich 2005a).

Based on the analysis of architectural data, activity areas, and associated artifacts, it was clear that the Central Pampa served a number of diverse functions within the civic ceremonial core during the Late Formative, a time period that can be further subdivided into Early, Middle (or Classic), and Late Pukara periods (Klarich 2005a, 2005b, 2009). In the Early Pukara period, the Central Pampa served as a plaza space used for the preparation and consumption of supra-household meals. The plaza abutted an earlier version of the Qalasaya to the west and a monumental platform to the north. During the subsequent Middle Pukara period the pampa was transformed into a residential area, with evidence of domestic activities, small-scale craft production, and ritual activities in a series of architectural compounds. During the same period the Qalasaya was significantly expanded, the platform mound was reconstructed, and sunken courts were constructed on the uppermost platforms (Wheeler and Mujica 1981). At least two secondary platform mounds were likely constructed to the north and south during this time. Klarich (2005a, 2005b, 2009) has argued that the large-scale transformations of the Qalasaya and Central Pampa reflected a shift from inclusive to exclusive leadership strategies over the course of the Late Formative period at Pukara. At a regional level, during the later part of the Late Formative there is no evidence of another center rivaling Pukara in scale or influence in the northern basin. Unfortunately, the nature of Pukara's collapse remains unclear; evidence indicates that this once-vibrant regional center was abandoned in the early centuries AD and not significantly reoccupied for several centuries.

AN ABUNDANCE OF EXOTICS: LITHIC ASSEMBLAGES AND OBSIDIAN USE

For archaeologists working in the Titicaca Basin, the presence of obsidian necessarily reflects some type of exchange relationship with individuals or networks outside the region, as no high-quality obsidian sources are available locally. There are several obsidian sources along the spine of the western Andean cordillera, but the Alca (Glascock, Speakman, and Burger 2007), Chivay (Burger et al. 1998), and Quispisisa types are the three most widely circulated in Peru and northwestern Bolivia (see figure 7.1) (Tripcevich 2007:182; see also Burger, Chávez, and Chávez 2000). Previous research in the Titicaca Basin has established that 90 percent of the obsidian recovered from prehistoric sites in the region was procured from the Chivay source, which is northwest of Lake Titicaca in the Colca Valley of Arequipa (Burger et al. 1998; Burger, Chávez, and Chávez 2000; in Tripcevich 2010:66). The import of obsidian significantly pre-dates the emergence of regional political economies; of all non-local traded goods found in pre-Hispanic contexts, obsidian is the earliest identified exotic commodity to enter the basin, appearing in small quantities as early as 8,000 years ago in Middle Archaic occupations at the site of Quelcatani (Aldenderfer 2002). Excavations on the Island of the Sun in the southern Titicaca Basin of Bolivia identified trade in obsidian from as early as the later part of the third millennium BC (Stanish et al. 2002), with nearly all of the materials imported from the Colca Valley.

Geochemical analysis of the obsidian from Pukara and Taraco indicates that nearly 100 percent was imported from the Chivay source, located in the Arequipa area approximately 200 km to the west. A random subsample (n = 58) of obsidian artifacts from Taraco's Formative contexts was selected for geochemical characterization using PXRF. Results indicated that all of the artifacts had been imported from the Chivay source with the exception of one specimen, which was traced to the Alca source (Levine 2012; Levine et al. 2013). A smaller sample was tested from recent excavations at Pukara (n = 15), with all sourced to Chivay (Tripcevich, personal communication, 2014). These results are consistent with a number of other compositional studies of obsidian in the Titicaca region and likely indicate the presence of regular trade routes and relationships that persisted for centuries (Levine et al. 2013).

Although obsidian must have been imported from sources located at a significant distance, it figured prominently in the political economy of the northern Titicaca Basin during the Formative period (Burger, Chávez, and Chávez 2000) and likely had symbolic or ritual value (Tripcevich, Eerkens, and Carpenter 2012). The recent analyses of excavated lithic materials, outlined below, are first used to characterize and quantify the relative abundance of obsidian at Pukara and Taraco. Second, the condition of the lithic debitage recovered from both sites is summarized, providing unique insights into the nature of obsidian processing during the Late Formative. Importantly, independent analyses of both the Taraco and Pukara samples indicate that craftspeople at each of the sites made few efforts to conserve obsidian, reflecting a "cavalier" treatment of an exotic raw material that merits further investigation and explanation.

PUKARA

Approximately 1,800 lithic artifacts were analyzed from Early and Middle Pukara period contexts on the Central Pampa (Schultze 2010; figure 7.5), including 15 obsidian samples subjected to geochemical analysis. The visual analysis included all Formative period lithic materials recovered from three excavation blocks, which each measured 5 m × 5 m and reached 1 m to 2 m in depth. The excavated deposits were characterized by superimposed occupation surfaces with a variety of activity areas, including primary middens associated with food preparation and disposal areas (Klarich 2005a). While the assemblage is an admittedly small sample from the expansive Central Pampa (see figure 7.3), it is the first collection of securely dated lithic materials to be analyzed from Pukara.

The classes of artifacts encountered included tools, stone-working debris (hammerstones, cores, flakes, and shatter), and raw materials. Tools (n = 166), either whole or fragmented, in this assemblage were predominately projectile points, digging-tool blades (azadones), groundstone, polishing stones (pulidores), and expedient flake-cutting tools. In addition, represented in small quantities were battleax blades (machacas), projectile stones (bolas), and burin tools. The majority of the assemblage consisted of stone-working debris, including flakes (n = 961), shatter (n = 641), and core fragments (n = 8). Unmodified materials were also recovered (n = 77). Lithic materials identified were, in order of ubiquity, chert, obsidian, basalt, quartzite, sandstone, rhyolite, possible metal ore, quartz crystal (including geodes), red ochre, a green volcanic, mica, milky quartz, and vesicular basalt. Because of the imprecision of field identification of andesite, basalt, and dacite, no attempt was made to distinguish them at this point. They are all grouped as "basalt," meaning a metavolcanic gray to black stone with or without porphyries. To quantify the relative frequency and stage of production for obsidian in the collection, flakes of all materials were weighed and then measured in two dimensions (length, width), and the presence or absence of cortex was noted. In the single lot with a prohibitively large (>100) number of small flakes, each flake was not measured; rather, they were grouped into size categories of smaller than 0.5 cm, between 0.5–1.0 cm, and larger than 1 cm. The presence or absence of cortex was noted, and the groups were weighed together.

A number of observations provide valuable insights into the organization of production and consumption of lithic materials during the Late Formative period. First, chert and obsidian are the highest-frequency lithic materials in the assemblage. When considering all flakes by count, 53 percent are chert, 33 percent are obsidian, 7 percent are basalt, and 7 percent are "other" (see list above). If we limit the comparison to only chert and obsidian present within the assemblage, 62 percent of the flakes were chert and 38 percent obsidian. While the relative frequencies of chert and obsidian do change over time and also vary across excavation blocks, local and exotic sources appear in relatively even proportions. Second, the obsidian present is unusual in that it is in an early stage of production. Much of the assemblage comprised, or showed remaining evidence of being worked from, oxidized and un-worked tabular obsidian pieces. Some of these rectangular pieces were still present in an un-worked and minimally worked form. Sizable chunks of obsidian were abandoned without further effort to rework, recycle, or conserve.

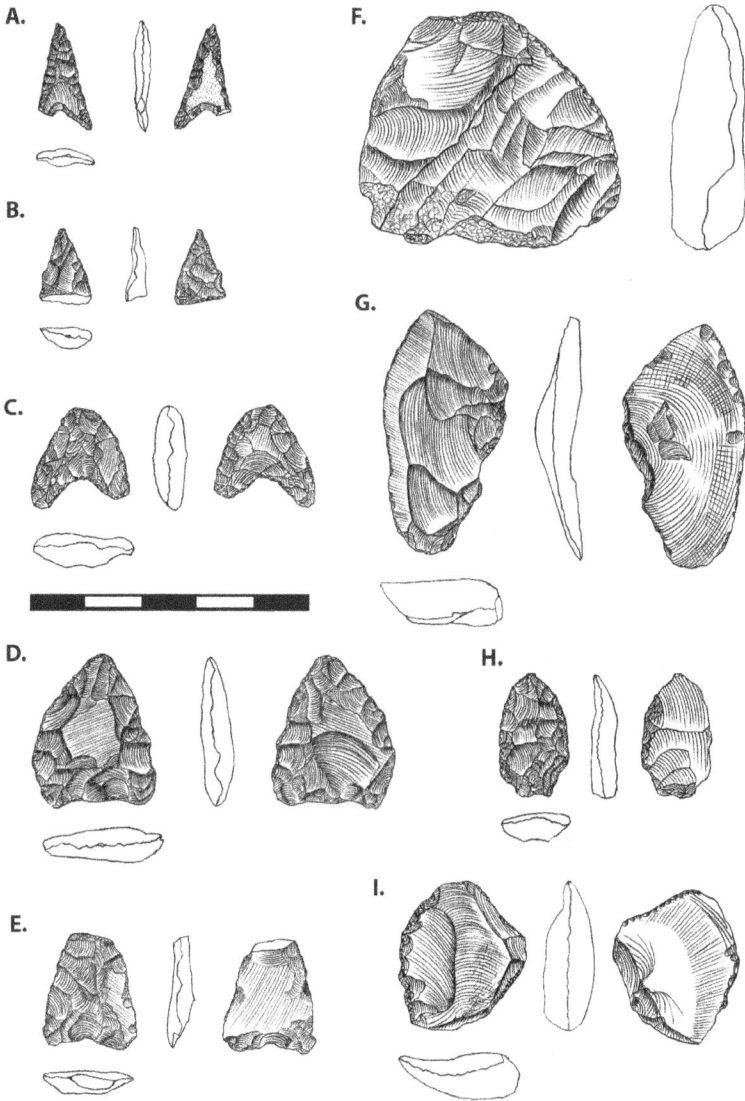

FIGURE 7.5. Obsidian artifacts from the Central Pampa at Pukara: A. concave base projectile point (Block 1; Type 5D, earliest dates 3300 BC); B. projectile point tip (Block 2); C. concave base projectile point (Block 2; Type 5C, earliest dates 3300 BC); D. bifacial knife or projectile point (Block 3); E. concave base projectile point (Block 1; Type 5D, earliest dates 3300 BC); F. bifacial preform (Block 3); G. expedient flake tool (Block 1); H. unfinished projectile point (Block 2); I. expedient flake tool (Block 1). Classification based on point types from Klink and Aldenderfer 2005 and calibrated dates from Tripcevich 2007..

Building from this observation, there is significant evidence for experimentation with different production methods, which results in many half-worked, failed, and otherwise abandoned pressure-flaked, rectangular chunks. There is a distinction to be made between oxidized un-worked surfaces and cortex, as both are present. It appears that obsidian may have been imported in the form of un-worked rectangular or tabular chunks. Craftspeople then seem to have been inexpertly experimenting with pressure flaking these tabular pieces; much of the obsidian was subjected to shallow pressure flaking along the edges. As a result, a large number of failed points were broken during manufacture rather than use. Points were made in an expedient manner by pressure flaking edges of the tabular pieces. In addition to shallow edge flaking on tabular chunks of obsidian, there were whole, broken, and nearly completed projectile points with shallow pressure flaking and un-worked surfaces (including cortex) remaining on one or both faces. Some of the projectile points and point fragments were only unifacially pressure flaked with cortex present on the un-worked face. These were noted in both obsidian and chert but more often on obsidian.

Lastly, also unusual is the use of obsidian for expedient flake tools (unmodified used flakes). These cutting tools are generally made from the most plentiful local stone available; the use of an exotic material for this type of tool is unexpected and indicates that obsidian was treated as if it were plentiful at the site. This somewhat cavalier use indicates that there was no attempt at, or perhaps need for, conservation of obsidian during the Late Formative at Pukara.

TARACO

In Area A, three random quadrants, totaling 36 m², were excavated to depths of approximately 4 m or until sterile soil was reached. In addition, two profiles along the river margin, each measuring 35 m in length, were made vertical and cleaned, providing long transects of the mound (Levine et al. 2013). A total of 4,100 lithic artifacts were recovered from these excavations across all occupational phases; obsidian artifacts comprised approximately 20 percent of this general assemblage. The majority of formal and functional categories identified for the Pukara lithic assemblage were present at Taraco (Levine 2012).

Obsidian was present in all occupational phases, and a sample (n = 76) from unmixed Formative contexts was selected for macroscopic visual analysis. Of the artifacts analyzed, only two could be classified as finished bifaces; all others were categorized as debitage or retouched flakes, and no cores were identified in the sample. The total weight of the sample was 155.4 g, indicating a relatively large average size for the flakes and debitage. While this quantity may be paltry in comparison with some well-known Mesoamerican contexts (e.g., Braswell 2003), it is nearly double the total amount of obsidian found in four seasons of excavation at Chiripa, an analogous center in the southern Titicaca Basin (Bandy 2001, 2005; Hastorf 1999). In addition, the fact that the Chiripa sample was composed primarily of bifaces and only a very small amount of debitage suggests that residents acquired obsidian in the form of finished points (Melson 2010; Perlès, Takaoğlu, and Gratuze 2011; Seddon 1994). Taraco, in contrast, was likely a locus of tool manufacture (Blomster and Glascock 2011) and, in light of the Chiripa data, almost certainly a preliminary node in a large regional exchange network (Renfrew 1975, 1977).

Importantly, analysis of the flaked tools indicated marked shifts in raw material preference over time. While obsidian is present in the earliest occupational phases, the Phase 1 assemblage is characterized by greater use of locally available raw materials for the production of flaked tools. During this time, 71 percent of flaked tools were made from a material other than obsidian—most often chert but also quartz and fine-grained volcanics such as andesite, basalt, and rhyolite (Levine et al. 2013). During subsequent phases, obsidian is imported in ever-increasing quantities, such that by the Early Pukara period (Phase 3) there is a clear preference for this expensive material over equally useful, locally available alternatives (X^2 = 19.0892, p < 0.001). During this time there is essentially a glut of obsidian, with 82 percent of flaked tools made of this exotic import (Levine 2012).

Following the burn event associated with raiding activity by Pukara, there is a steep drop in both the abundance and the average size of obsidian artifacts, two shifts that indicate a loss of access to the Chivay obsidian source. A statistically significant decline in the mean size of obsidian debitage following the burn event (p = 0.01168) suggests conservative manufacturing behaviors consistent with more limited access to resources, as well as the recycling of old materials, which results in smaller artifacts and debitage. The reuse and retouching of artifacts would also indicate new limitations or restrictions on raw material (Stanish and Levine 2011).

DISCUSSION

Based on the recent analysis of two assemblages, it is evident that tool producers at Pukara and Taraco had reliable access to obsidian and were relatively wasteful in their production techniques. As people tend to waste more when resources are abundant, the size of debitage serves as a useful proxy for access to obsidian (see Surovell 2003). The "cavalier" use of obsidian identified in the Formative contexts at both locations is likely linked with, and can indicate, regular and reliable access to the obsidian trade and traders. The ubiquitous nature of obsidian, together with its relatively careless treatment, suggests that it may have been considered an "ordinary" good (Smith 1999) by the Late Formative.

Our observation of "cavalier crafting" parallels the findings of Tripcevich's (2007, 2010) diachronic studies of obsidian circulation and utilization in the Lake Titicaca Basin. He has argued that while obsidian had served as a status marker during the earliest phases of occupation in the region (Archaic period through the Middle Formative), its meaning shifted by the middle of the Late Formative, approximately AD 1 (Tripcevich 2010). By this point in time, obsidian was widely distributed throughout the northern and western basin (Tripcevich 2010:65). It was also generally available for pastoral populations in the region, as indicated by the presence of Chivay obsidian at rock shelters and herder sites during all time periods (Tripcevich and Contreras 2013). By contrast, small relative frequencies and restriction to elite contexts are features of obsidian distribution for the southern Titicaca Basin (Couture 2003; Giesso 2003).

Tripcevich has also noted that unlike utilitarian goods such as salt, Late Formative period obsidian "continued to have meaning beyond the functional cutting properties of sharp stone" (Tripcevich 2010:66). He suggests that this particular exotic good—primarily used for the production of projectile points—could have signaled regional alliances with source areas, identified ethnic affiliations, or been a component of ritual practice (Tripcevich 2010). In other words, obsidian was a symbolically important good in the Titicaca Basin, but it was not restricted through elite control of trade networks by the Late Formative.

We propose an alternative interpretation for the abundance of obsidian identified during the Late Formative at Pukara and Taraco, which is linked to the importance of signaling abundance at influential centers. In fact, Smith (2012) has argued that the illusion of abundance (whether real or perceived) was a defining characteristic of early central places. An inherent seeking of abundance was a likely factor contributing to the growth and development of urban centers, which came to represent concentrated loci of production and consumption, particularly in nonstate contexts. In the case of obsidian, we consider that the presence and nature of production debris may provide insights outside the realm of technology. Perhaps, as proposed by Smith (this volume, 7), "Like the accumulations of manufactured objects, the heaps and scatters of waste material from production . . . presented a visible record of plenitude forming part of the community's experiential landscape." At Taraco, for example, the intensification of trade in obsidian during the Early Pukara period occurred alongside a number of other important political and economic developments. An increase in the abundance of obsidian found in the residential sector corresponds chronologically with the construction of a large platform in the ceremonial sector of Area A during the first century BC (Levine 2013), as well as increased participation in local exchange networks and supra-household food-sharing events around the site area as a whole (Levine et al. 2013).

Notably, the site-wide burn event at Taraco in the first century AD was followed by a major loss of economic and political status for site residents. As indicated by a statistically significant decrease in the size of debitage, the previously cavalier crafters became more conservative in their treatment of obsidian, perhaps retouching or reusing debitage and broken artifacts (Stanish and Levine 2011). This major shift in the treatment of obsidian prompts an important question: if obsidian had assumed an ordinary status in households across the northern Titicaca Basin by the turn of the millennium, why did Taraco's political troubles correspond to a decrease in the size of obsidian debitage (and presumably access) in the residential sector?

Parallel developments are evident at Pukara during its initial Late Formative occupations as large-scale food-sharing events were prepared and consumed in the monumental public spaces of the site's civic ceremonial core (Klarich 2005a, 2005b). Excavations on the Central Pampa recovered obsidian from virtually every Late Formative context, with chert and obsidian artifacts present in similar frequencies per context. However, obsidian is found in higher numbers than chert in the initial occupation of Block 3, an outdoor activity area with multiple hearths and primary bone middens likely used for the preparation of supra-household meals (see Warwick 2012). Future research will explore the possible relationships between obsidian artifacts and feasting activities, important public events linked to early leadership strategies at Pukara.

There are many benefits to an abundance perspective when framing the lithic data from Pukara and Taraco, but it is also important to acknowledge the lacuna in comparable regional data sets as a limiting factor at present. Based on our excavations, these northern basin centers had consistent access to obsidian and, in fact, a relative abundance of this exotic good when compared with contemporaneous centers in the southern basin, such as Chiripa and Kala Uyuni (Bandy 2001, 2005; Bandy and Hastorf 2007; Hastorf 1999), and even neighboring sites in the northern basin (Cohen 2010; Plourde 2006; Zegarra 2014). Considering the distance of the southern basin centers from these sources—Chivay is approximately 350 km to the northwest (Bandy 2005:95)—some of these differences are expected. What remains to be established is a broader pattern of obsidian artifact production and consumption at contemporaneous northern basin sites, particularly small villages and hamlets, that would have interacted with both Taraco and Pukara (Stanish 2003). Publications of field research at the Formative period sites of Huatacoa (Cohen 2010), Balsaspata (Tantaleán 2012), and Cachichupa (Plourde 2006, 2012) have all noted the presence of obsidian in excavated contexts, but detailed quantitative and qualitative descriptions of the lithic assemblages needed for comparative analyses are not readily available (cf. Schultze 2008).

The current study does, however, build upon research initiated well over a decade ago by Burger, Chávez, and Chávez (2000) in their regional study of prehistoric obsidian procurement and exchange in the Central Andes. While their primary focus was to document shifting circulation networks for Chivay and Alca obsidian, they also provided descriptions of obsidian recovered from many of the 160 sites included in the analysis. Obsidian artifacts from a number of Middle and Late Formative Titicaca Basin sites were included in their regional survey, including surface remains and excavated objects from Taraco, Pukara, and Qaluyu. Qaluyu, a mound site 4 km north of Pukara, provides preliminary insights into Middle Formative obsidian use, showing a characteristic pattern associated with the conservation of a scarce resource. The early occupations of Qaluyu are characterized by tools made of very small flakes—"no large cores or preforms, nor even large chunks of obsidian, are known to occur at the time" (Burger, Chávez, and Chávez 2000:296)—that reflect on-site manufacturing and retouching. Tools were made of very small flakes, the kind that would typically be discarded. Burger and colleagues interpret this as evidence that obsidian was a rare material being maximized through conservative production techniques. More recently, excavated lithic assemblages from sites in Puno Bay, located on the western shores of the lake, also reflect conservation of obsidian as a precious resource in Formative contexts (Schultze 2008). At Huajje, for example, the only obsidian artifacts recorded were projectiles that had been sharpened into micropoints.

A different pattern was identified at Taraco and Pukara in occupations that slightly postdate those documented at Qaluyu. Burger, Chávez, and Chávez (2000:322) note "large pieces" from the pre-Pukara levels at Taraco from the more distant Alca source. In the subsequent Pukara levels, "Slightly larger, thick chunks are more abundant, many with cortex still remaining," from the Chivay source (Burger, Chávez, and Chávez 2000:322). They note a similar pattern—the use of larger pieces of obsidian—in their analysis of Formative period obsidian artifacts excavated by Kidder at Pukara in 1939. While the inhabitants of all three Formative period sites were using exotic lithic raw materials, these earlier studies first suggested that Taraco and Pukara had access to larger pieces of obsidian while knappers at Qaluyu relied on very small flakes for tool production. These same general patterns have been identified from our recent analyses, which document the discard of large, minimally worked obsidian flakes at both Pukara and Taraco.

CONCLUSION

The proposal that waste may function as both a marker of status and a proxy for access is compelling and ties theoretically to other well-documented practices such as potlatching, in which prestige is directly correlated with how much one can give away or destroy. In these cases, it is the elimination of abundance rather than its possession or display that confers prestige: in the words of Smith (2011), "I discard, therefore I am." Under these conditions, the ability to waste becomes an important signifier of political and economic status, falling under the parallel umbrellas of conspicuous consumption and costly signaling. Cavalier treatment of imported exotics is an effective advertisement, functioning as a proxy for the strength of trade relationships and of residents' access to coveted resources.

Under different circumstances, residents of Taraco and Pukara might have opted to use their resources to produce the maximum number of artifacts. These artifacts could have been used for trade, display, or myriad other aggrandizing behaviors, and in many cases they were. However, the consistent wasting of large amounts of these resources suggests that the public discard of obsidian was likely as important as—and in some cases may have superseded—other potential uses in terms of ideological utility. Clearly, the value of obsidian was highly dependent on the time and place in which it was exploited (e.g., Levine and Carballo 2014). In light of these new data from two major regional centers in the Lake Titicaca Basin, we advocate the importance of examining patterns of use for exotic materials in archaeological context, not just simply identifying that these goods existed in relative abundance.

Acknowledgments. First, we thank Monica Smith for inviting us to participate in a thought-provoking SAA symposium and for including our case study in this publication. The authors acknowledge the extensive support provided in Peru by the Ministry of Culture (Lima and Puno), the National Institute of Culture (Lima and Puno), the Municipality of Taraco, the town of Pucará, Ruth Ttacca and Honorato Ttacca, Leny Pinto, Nancy Román, Luis Flores Blanco, David Oshige, Bárbara Carbajal, and Charles Stanish, Mark Aldenderfer, and Cecilia Chávez of the Programa Collasuyu. Finally, many thanks to the Cotsen Institute of Archaeology at UCLA, the UCLA and UCSB anthropology departments, Smith College, the National Science Foundation (BCS–0940287 and 0115233), Fulbright-Hays, Nico Tripcevich for sourcing the Pukara obsidian, and Ryan Williams for sourcing the Taraco obsidian.

NOTES

1. "Upper" and "Late" Formative are used interchangeably in the northern Lake Titicaca Basin. To maintain internal consistency, we use "Late" throughout this chapter.

2. The fifteen radiocarbon samples from the 2001 excavations range from 360 BC–AD 230, with eleven falling within the Middle/Classic Pukara period range (200 BC–AD 100), two with large ranges that span the Initial Pukara (500–200 BC) and Middle/Classic periods,

and two that span the Middle and Late Pukara (AD 100–300) periods (Klarich 2005a; see also Mujica 1988).

REFERENCES CITED

Abraham, Sarah J. 2012. "The Late Intermediate Period Occupation of Pukara, Peru." In *Advances in Titicaca Basin Archaeology—III*, edited by Alexei Vranich, Elizabeth A. Klarich, and Charles Stanish, 283–98. Ann Arbor: Museum of Anthropology, University of Michigan.

Aldenderfer, Mark S. 2002. "Late Preceramic Cultural Complexity in the Lake Titicaca Basin." Paper presented at the Annual Meeting of the Society for American Archaeology, Denver, CO, March 20–24.

Bandy, Matthew S. 2001. "Population and History in the Ancient Titicaca Basin." PhD dissertation, University of California, Berkeley.

Bandy, Matthew S. 2005. "Trade and Social Power in the Southern Titicaca Basin Formative." In *The Foundations of Power in the Prehispanic Andes*, edited by Kevin J. Vaughn, Dennis E. Ogburn, and Christina A. Conlee, 14:91–111. Archeological Papers of the American Anthropological Association. Washington, DC: American Anthropological Association. http://dx.doi.org/10.1525/ap3a.2005.14.091.

Bandy, Matthew S., and Christine A. Hastorf, eds. 2007. *Kala Uyuni: An Early Political Center in the Southern Lake Titicaca Basin*. Berkeley: Archaeological Research Facility, University of California.

Blomster, Jeffrey P., and Michael D. Glascock. 2011. "Obsidian Procurement in Formative Oaxaca, Mexico: Diachronic Changes in Political Economy and Interregional Interaction." *Journal of Field Archaeology* 36 (1): 21–41. http://dx.doi.org/10.1179/00934 6910X12707321242278.

Braswell, Geoffrey E. 2003. "Obsidian Exchange Spheres of Postclassic Mesoamerica." In *The Postclassic Mesoamerican World*, edited by Michael E. Smith and Frances Berdan, 131–58. Salt Lake City: University of Utah Press.

Brooks, Sarah O., Michael D. Glascock, and Martin Giesso. 1997. "Source of Volcanic Glass for Ancient Andean Tools." *Nature* 386 (6624): 449–50. http://dx.doi.org/10.1038 /386449a0.

Browman, David L. 1977. "The Altiplano Mode of Economic Integration in the Andes." Paper presented at the Annual Meeting of the American Anthropological Association, Houston, TX, November 29–December 4.

Burger, Richard L., and Frank Asaro. 1977. *Trace Element Analysis of Obsidian Artifacts from the Andes: New Perspectives on Pre-Hispanic Economic Interaction in Peru and Bolivia*. Berkeley: Lawrence Berkeley Laboratory, University of California at Berkeley.

Burger, Richard L., and Frank Asaro. 1978. "Obsidian Distribution and Provenience in the Central Highlands and Coast of Peru during the Preceramic Period." *Contributions of the University of California Archaeology Research Facility* 36: 61–83.

Burger, Richard L., and Frank Asaro. 1979. "Análisis de Rasgos Significativos En La Obsidiana de Los Andes Centrales." *Revista Del Museo Nacional* 43: 281–326.

Burger, Richard L., Frank Asaro, Fred Stross, and Guido Salas. 1998. "The Chivay Obsidian Source and the Geological Origin of Titicaca Basin Type Obsidian Artifacts." *Andean Past* 5: 203–24.

Burger, Richard L., Karen L. Chávez, and Sergio J. Chávez. 2000. "Through the Glass Darkly: Prehispanic Obsidian Procurement and Exchange in Southern Peru and Northern Bolivia." *Journal of World Prehistory* 14 (3): 267–362. http://dx.doi.org/10.1023/A:1026509726643.

Chávez, Karen L. Mohr. 1988. "The Significance of Chiripa in Lake Titicaca Basin Developments." *Expedition* 30 (3): 17–26.

Chávez, Sergio J. 1992. "The Conventionalized Rules in Pucara Pottery Technology and Iconography: Implications of Socio-Political Development in the Northern Titicaca Basin." PhD dissertation, Michigan State University, Lansing.

Chávez, Sergio J., and Karen L. Chávez. 1970. "Newly Discovered Monoliths from the Highlands of Puno, Peru." *Expedition* 12 (4): 25–39.

Chávez, Sergio J., and Karen L. Chávez. 1975. "A Carved Stone Stela from Taraco, Puno, Peru, and the Definition of an Early Style of Stone Sculpture from the Altiplano of Peru and Bolivia." *Nawpa Pacha* 13 (1): 45–83. http://dx.doi.org/10.1179/naw.1975.13.1.005.

Cohen, Amanda B. 2010. "Ritual and Architecture in the Titicaca Basin: The Development of the Sunken Court Complex in the Formative Period." PhD dissertation, University of California, Los Angeles.

Couture, Nicole Claire. 2003. "Ritual, Monumentalism, and Residence at Mollo Kontu, Tiwanaku." In *Tiwanaku and Its Hinterland: Archaeology and Paleoecology of an Andean Civilization,* vol. 2: *Urban and Rural Archaeology,* edited by Alan L. Kolata, 202–25. Washington, DC: Smithsonian Institution Press.

Craig, Nathan M., Robert J. Speakman, Rachel S. Popelka-Filcoff, Mark Aldenderfer, Luis Flores Blanco, Margaret Brown Vega, Michael D. Glascock, and Charles Stanish. 2010. "Macusani Obsidian from Southern Peru: A Characterization of Its Elemental Composition with a Demonstration of Its Ancient Use." *Journal of Archaeological Science* 37 (3): 569–76. http://dx.doi.org/10.1016/j.jas.2009.10.021.

Craig, Nathan M., Robert J. Speakman, Rachel S. Popelka-Filcoff, Michael D. Glascock, J. David Robertson, M. Steven Shackley, and Mark Aldenderfer. 2007. "Comparison of XRF and PXRF for Analysis of Archaeological Obsidian from Southern Perú." *Journal of Archaeological Science* 34 (12): 2012–24. http://dx.doi.org/10.1016/j.jas.2007.01.015.

de la Vega, Edmundo. 2005. *Excavaciones Arqueologicas En El Sitio de Taraco-Puno: Informe Final*. Lima: Instituto Nacional de Cultura.

Franco Inojosa, Jorge M. 1940. "Informe Sobre Los Trabajos Arqueologicos de La Mision Kidder En Pukara, Peru (enero a Julio de 1939)." *Revista Del Museo Nacional* 9 (1): 128–42.

Giesso, Martin. 2003. "Stone Tool Production in the Tiwanaku Heartland." In *Tiwanaku and Its Hinterland: Archaeology and Paleoecology of an Andean Civilization*, vol. 2: *Urban and Rural Archaeology*, edited by Alan L. Kolata, 363–83. Washington, DC: Smithsonian Institution Press.

Glascock, Michael D., Robert J. Speakman, and Richard L. Burger. 2007. "Sources of Archaeological Obsidian in Peru: Descriptions and Geochemistry." In *Archaeological Chemistry: Analytical Techniques and Archaeological Interpretation*, edited by Michael D. Glascock, Robert J. Speakman, and Rachel S. Popelka-Filcoff, 522–52. Washington, DC: American Chemical Society. http://dx.doi.org/10.1021/bk-2007-0968.ch028.

Hastorf, Christine A. 1999. *Early Settlement at Chiripa, Bolivia*. Berkeley: University of California Press.

Jennings, Justin, and Michael D. Glascock. 2002. "Description and Method of Exploitation of the Alca Obsidian Source, Peru." *Latin American Antiquity* 13 (1): 107–18. http://dx.doi.org/10.2307/971743.

Kidder, Alfred, II. 1942. "Preliminary Notes on the Archaeology of Pucara, Puno, Peru." *Actas Y Trabajos Científicos de XXVII Congreso Internacional de Americanistas (Lima 1939)* 1: 341–45.

Kidder, Alfred, II. 1943. *Some Early Sites in the Northern Lake Titicaca Basin*. Cambridge, MA: Peabody Museum of American Archaeology and Ethnography, Harvard University.

Klarich, Elizabeth A. 2005a. "From the Monumental to the Mundane: Defining Early Leadership Strategies at Late Formative Pukara, Peru." PhD dissertation, University of California, Santa Barbara.

Klarich, Elizabeth A. 2005b. "¿Quiénes Son Los Invitados? Cambios Temporales Y Funcionales de Los Espacios Públicos de Pukara Como Una Reflexión Acerca de Las Estrategias de Liderazgo Durante El Periodo Formativo Tardío." In *Encuentros: Identidad, Poder Y Agencia de Espacios Públicos*, edited by Peter Kaulicke and Tom Dillehay, 185–206. Boletín de Arqueología PUCP 9. Lima: Pontificia Universidad Católica del Perú.

Klarich, Elizabeth A. 2009. "Pukara: Investigaciones de La Temporada 2001 Y Un Nuevo Modelo Para El Desarrollo Del Sitio." In *Actas Del Simposio Internacional Sobre Arqueología Del Área Centro Sur Andina*, edited by Augusto Belén Franco, Mariusz Ziolkowski, Justin Jennings, and Andrea Drusini, 23–31. Warsaw, Poland: Center for Pre-Columbian Studies, University of Warsaw.

Klarich, Elizabeth A., and Nancy Román Bustinza. 2012. "Scale and Diversity at Late Formative Period Pukara." In *Advances in Titicaca Basin Archaeology—III*, edited by

Alexei Vranich, Elizabeth A. Klarich, and Charles Stanish, 105–20. Ann Arbor: Museum of Anthropology, University of Michigan.

Klink, Cynthia J., and Mark S. Aldenderfer. 2005. "A Projectile Point Chronology for the South-Central Andean Highlands." In *Advances in Titicaca Basin Archaeology—I*, edited by Charles Stanish, Amanda B. Cohen, and Mark S. Aldenderfer, 25–54. Los Angeles: Cotsen Institute of Archaeology, University of California.

Levine, Abigail Ruth. 2012. "Competition, Cooperation, and the Emergence of Regional Centers in the Northern Lake Titicaca Basin, Peru." PhD dissertation, University of California, Los Angeles.

Levine, Abigail Ruth. 2013. "The Use and Re-Use of Ceremonial Space at Taraco, Peru: 2012 Excavations in the San Taraco Sector." *Ñawpa Pacha* 33 (2): 215–26. http://dx.doi .org/10.1179/0077629713Z.00000000010.

Levine, Abigail Ruth, Charles Stanish, P. Ryan Williams, Cecilia Chávez, and Mark Golitko. 2013. "Trade and Early State Formation in the Northern Titicaca Basin, Peru." *Latin American Antiquity* 24 (3): 289–308. http://dx.doi.org/10.7183/1045-6635.24 .3.289.

Levine, Marc N., and David M. Carballo, eds. 2014. *Obsidian Reflections: Symbolic Dimensions of Obsidian in Mesoamerica*. Boulder: University Press of Colorado.

Melson, Megan. 2010. "Trade and Exchange in the Neolithic Near East: Implications of Obsidian Remains from Ais Yiorkis, Cyprus." PhD dissertation, University of Nevada, Las Vegas.

Mujica, Elías. 1978. "Nueva Hipotesis Sobre El Desarrollo Temprano Del Altiplano, Del Titicaca Y de Sus Areas de Interaccion." *Arte Y Arqueologia* 5–6: 285–308.

Mujica, Elías. 1985. "Altiplano-Coast Relationships in the South-Central Andes: From Indirect to Direct Complementarity." In *Andean Ecology and Civilization*, edited by Shōzō Masuda, Izumi Shimada, and Craig Morris, 103–40. Tokyo: University of Tokyo Press.

Mujica, Elías. 1988. "Peculiaridades Del Proceso Historico Temprano En La Cuenca Norte Del Titicaca: Una Propuesta Inicial." *Boletín Del Laboratorio de Arqueología* 2: 75–122.

Mujica, Elías. 1991. "Pukara: Una Sociedad Compleja Temprana En La Cuenca Norte de Titicaca." In *Los Incas Y El Antiguo Peru: 3000 Años de Historia*, edited by Paz Cabello Carro, 1:272–97. Madrid: Sociedad Estatal Quinto Centenario.

Murra, John V. 1972. "El 'Control Vertical' de Un Máximo de Pisos Ecológicos En La Economía de Las Sociedades Andinas." In *Visita de La Provinvia de León de Huanuco En 1562*, edited by John V. Murra, 2:427–76. Documentos Por La Historia Y Etnología de Huanuco Y La Selva Central. Huánaco: Universidad Nacional Hermilio Valdizán.

Murra, John V. 1985. "'El Archipelago Vertical' Revisited." In *Andean Ecology and Civilization*, edited by Craig Morris, 3–14. Tokyo: University of Tokyo Press.

Oshige Adams, David. 2012. "The Earliest Ceramic Sequence at the Site of Pukara, Northern Lake Titicaca Basin." In *Advances in Titicaca Basin Archaeology—III*, edited by Alexei Vranich, Elizabeth A. Klarich, and Charles S. Stanish, 13–48. Ann Arbor: Museum of Anthropology, University of Michigan.

Perlès, Catherine, Turan Takaoğlu, and Bernard Gratuze. 2011. "Melian Obsidian in NW Turkey: Evidence for Early Neolithic Trade." *Journal of Field Archaeology* 36 (1): 42–49. http://dx.doi.org/10.1179/009346910X12707321242313.

Plourde, Aimée Marcelle. 2006. "Prestige Goods and Their Role in the Evolution of Social Ranking: A Costly Signaling Model with Data from the Formative Period of the Northern Lake Titicaca Basin, Peru." PhD dissertation, University of California, Los Angeles.

Plourde, Aimée Marcelle. 2012. "Variation in Corporate Architecture during the Early Middle Formative Period: New Data from Cachichupa, Northeastern Lake Titicaca Basin." In *Advances in Titicaca Basin Archaeology—III*, edited by Alexei Vranich, Elizabeth A. Klarich, and Charles S. Stanish, 91–104. Ann Arbor: Museum of Anthropology, University of Michigan.

Renfrew, Colin. 1975. "Trade as Action at a Distance: Questions of Integration and Communication." In *Ancient Civilization and Trade*, edited by Jeremy A. Sabloff and C. C. Lamberg-Karlovsky, 3–59. Albuquerque: University of New Mexico Press.

Renfrew, Colin. 1977. "Alternative Models for Exchange and Spatial Distribution." In *Exchange Systems in Prehistory*, edited by Timothy K. Earle and Jonathan E. Erickson, 71–90. New York: Academic. http://dx.doi.org/10.1016/B978-0-12-227650-7.50010-9.

Rowe, John H. 1942. "Sitios Históricos En La Región de Pucara, Puno." *Revista Del Instituto Arqueológico* 6 (10–11): 66–75.

Schultze, Carol. 2008. "The Role of Silver Ore Reduction in Tiwanaku State Expansion into Puno Bay, Peru." PhD dissertation, University of California, Los Angeles.

Schultze, Carol. 2010. "Lithic Analysis from the 2001 Excavations of the Central Pampa, Pukara." Manuscript in possession of the Pukara Archaeological Project.

Seddon, Matthew T. 1994. "Lithic Artifacts." In *Archaeological Research at Tumatumani, Juli, Peru*, edited by Charles Stanish and Lee Steadman, 65–71. Fieldiana Anthropology 23. Chicago: Field Museum of Natural History.

Seltzer, Geoffrey O., and Christine A. Hastorf. 1990. "Climatic Change and Its Effect on Prehispanic Agriculture in the Central Peruvian Andes." *Journal of Field Archaeology* 17 (4): 397–414.

Shackley, M. Steven, ed. 2011. *X-Ray Fluorescence Spectrometry (XRF) in Geoarchaeology*. New York: Springer. http://dx.doi.org/10.1007/978-1-4419-6886-9.

Smith, Monica L. 1999. "The Role of Ordinary Goods in Premodern Exchange." *Journal of Archaeological Method and Theory* 6 (2): 109–35. http://dx.doi.org/10.1023/A:10219 17318055.

Smith, Monica L. 2011. " 'I Discard, Therefore I Am': Identity and Leave-Taking of Possessions." In *Identity Crisis: Archaeological Perspectives on Social Identity*, edited by Lindsay Amundsen-Pickering, Nicole Engel, and Sean Pickering, 132–42. University of Calgary: Chacmool Archaeological Association.

Smith, Monica L. 2012. "Seeking Abundance: Consumption as a Motivating Factor in Cities Past and Present." In *Political Economy, Neoliberalism, and the Prehistoric Economies of Latin America*, edited by Ty Matejowsky and Donald C. Wood, 32:27–51. Bingley, UK: Emerald Group. http://dx.doi.org/10.1108/S0190-1281(2012)00000 32006.

Stanish, Charles S. 2003. *Ancient Titicaca: The Evolution of Complex Society in Southern Peru and Northern Bolivia*. Berkeley: University of California Press. http://dx.doi.org /10.1525/california/9780520232457.001.0001.

Stanish, Charles S., Richard L. Burger, Lisa M. Cipolla, Michael D. Glascock, and Esteban Quelima. 2002. "Evidence for Early Long-Distance Obsidian Exchange and Watercraft Use from the Southern Lake Titicaca Basin of Bolivia and Peru." *Latin American Antiquity* 13 (4): 444–54. http://dx.doi.org/10.2307/972225.

Stanish, Charles S., and Abigail R. Levine. 2011. "War and Early State Formation in the Northern Titicaca Basin, Peru." *Proceedings of the National Academy of Sciences of the United States of America* 108 (34): 13901–906. Medline:21788514 http://dx.doi.org /10.1073/pnas.1110176108.

Stanish, Charles S., and Adan Umire. 2004. *Prospección Arqueológica Del Sector Bajo de La Cuenca Del Ramís (Ríos Azángaro Y Ramís), Puno: Informe Final*. Lima: Instituto Nacional de Cultura.

Surovell, Todd. 2003. "The Behavioral Ecology of Folsom Lithic Technology." PhD dissertation, University of Arizona, Tucson.

Tantaleán, Henry. 2012. "Archaeological Excavation at Balsaspata, Ayaviri." In *Advances in Titicaca Basin Archaeology—III*, edited by Alexei Vranich, Elizabeth A. Klarich, and Charles Stanish, 49–75. Ann Arbor: Museum of Anthropology, University of Michigan.

Tripcevich, Nicholas. 2007. "Quarries, Caravans, and Routes to Complexity: Prehispanic Obsidian in the South-Central Andes." PhD dissertation, University of California, Santa Barbara.

Tripcevich, Nicholas. 2010. "Exotic Goods, Chivay Obsidian, and Sociopolitical Change in the South-Central Andes." In *Trade and Exchange: Archaeological Studies from History and Prehistory*, edited by Carolyn D. Dillian and Carolyn L. White, 59–73. New York: Springer. http://dx.doi.org/10.1007/978-1-4419-1072-1_4.

Tripcevich, Nicholas, and Daniel A. Contreras. 2011. "Quarrying Evidence at the Quispisisa Obsidian Source, Ayacucho, Peru." *Latin American Antiquity* 22 (1): 121–36. http://dx.doi.org/10.7183/1045-6635.22.1.121.

Tripcevich, Nicholas, and Daniel A. Contreras. 2013. "Archaeological Approaches to Obsidian Quarries: Investigations at the Quispisisa Source." In *Mining and Quarrying in the Ancient Andes*, edited by Nicholas Tripcevich and Kevin J. Vaughn, 23–44. New York: Springer. http://dx.doi.org/10.1007/978-1-4614-5200-3_2.

Tripcevich, Nicholas, Jelmer W. Eerkens, and Tim R. Carpenter. 2012. "Obsidian Hydration at High Elevation: Archaic Quarrying at the Chivay Source, Southern Peru." *Journal of Archaeological Science* 39 (5): 1360–67. http://dx.doi.org/10.1016/j.jas.2011.11.016.

Tripcevich, Nicholas, and Alexander Mackay. 2012. "Spatial and Temporal Variation in Stone Raw Material Provisioning in the Chivay Obsidian Source Area." In *Advances in Titicaca Basin Archaeology—III*, edited by Alexei Vranich, Elizabeth A. Klarich, and Charles Stanish, 141–62. Ann Arbor: Museum of Anthropology, University of Michigan.

Tschopik, Marion H. 1946. *Some Notes on the Archaeology of the Department of Puno, Peru: Expeditions to Southern Peru*. Cambridge: Peabody Museum of American Archaeology and Ethnology, Harvard University.

Van Buren, Mary. 1996. "Rethinking the Vertical Archipelago: Ethnicity, Exchange, and History in the South Central Andes." *American Anthropologist* 98 (2): 338–51. http://dx.doi.org/10.1525/aa.1996.98.2.02a00100.

Warwick, Matthew. 2012. "In the Shadow of the Peñon: A Zooarchaeological Study of Formative Diet, Economy, and Sociopolitics in the Río Pukara Valley, Peru." PhD dissertation, University of Wisconsin, Milwaukee.

Wheeler, Jane, and Elías Mujica. 1981. "Prehistoric Pastoralism in the Lake Titicaca Basin, Peru (1979–1980 Field Season)." Report submitted to the National Science Foundation.

Yacobaccio, Hugo D., Patricia S. Escola, Marisa Lazzari, and Fernando X. Pereyra. 2002. "Long-Distance Obsidian Traffic in Northwestern Argentina." In *Geochemical Evidence for Long-Distance Exchange*, edited by Michael D. Glascock, 167–203. Westport, CT: Bergin and Garvey.

Zegarra, Walter Michiel. 2014. *Excavaciones Arqueologicas En El Sitio de Taraco-Puno: Temporada 2013*. Informe Final. Lima: Ministerio de Cultura.

8

Coping with Abundance

The Challenges of a Good Thing

KATHERYN C. TWISS AND AMY BOGAARD

Abundance may be a generally good thing, but in a delayed-return society with any pretense to egalitarianism it also brings myriad challenges. Individuals or groups who produce or acquire an abundance of resources must determine how to physically preserve and/or socially deploy that abundance while maintaining at least some appearance of equality and integration with other members of society. In this chapter we evaluate strategies for coping with resource abundances at Neolithic Çatalhöyük in central Anatolia.

Individuals or groups who produce or acquire an abundance of resources are generally recognized as fortunate. Abundance, specifically abundant food, is recognized across anthropology as a Good Thing, with scholars documenting its pursuit across eras, cultures (e.g., Durrenberger and Gillogly 2014; Oka and Kuijt 2014a; Spielmann 2002), and even species (e.g., Houle, Chapman, and Vickery 2010; Naughton-Treves et al. 1998). We recognize its complications, of course, most notably in modern societies where consumption of abundant food is producing a range of health issues (World Health Organization 2014). Negative ramifications of abundance in prehistoric cultures are relatively rarely discussed, but they have been documented among non-human primates (e.g., Asquith 1989; Sugiyama and Ohsawa 1982): clearly, abundant food is not an unmitigated positive.

In this chapter we first outline some of the challenges posed by abundance and the problems that differentially abundant food production would have caused for early farmers. We then predict two strategies for coping with the challenges of

DOI: 10.5876/9781607325949.c008

differential abundance—concealment and dispersal of food outside of the household group—and examine the extent to which data from the early agricultural site of Çatalhöyük in Turkey exclude or confirm the employment of these strategies.

CHALLENGES OF ABUNDANCE

The complications of abundance are not limited to health issues: other difficulties may also ensue. Acquisition of abundant food entails specific challenges for members of delayed-return societies. A good harvest or a large kill cannot simply be appreciated at its moment through gluttonous consumption and then left behind (or at least this cannot always happen): in a delayed-return economy, abundance must be extended through time if it is to support its producers. Such extension entails both logistical and social challenges.

Imagine, for example, that a farming household has reaped an abundant harvest—enough to feed its members amply through the year and perhaps longer. This harvest cannot simply be left in a heap and accessed at will; it must be stored in such a way that the crop (e.g., wheat, chickpeas, millet, rice) remains edible and that at least some of it remains viable for future planting. Keeping even relatively easily storable goods such as grains and pulses edible across months requires space, time, and technical knowledge—and the complexity and challenge of the project increases with the intended duration of storage. Delayed-return societies in tropical regions, or those that rely on relatively perishable foods such as fish, face even greater challenges.

Practical challenges aside, there are potential social concerns for those who have reaped an abundant harvest. These may include not simply envy from the less fortunate but also potentially serious disapprobation for those who keep their wealth to themselves (e.g., Woodburn 1982:440–42, 447). The social costs of (temporary) "wealth" are well documented in many immediate-return foraging societies: for example, among the Ju/'hoansi, successful returning hunters face widespread derision and joking, which are intended to limit any arrogance they may feel as a result of their accomplishments; hunters also risk accusations of impropriety or stinginess if they do not distribute the meat to everyone's satisfaction (Lee 1993:55–56). Similar requirements may also exist in small-scale delayed-return societies: the eighteenth-century missionary Loskiel (2015:68) asserted that some Delaware "are so lazy that they will not plant at all, knowing that the more industrious cannot refuse to divide their store with them." In the present-day Andes, barter between families is obligatory, and a pastoral Awatimarka family must always supply a crop-farming partner family with meat, cheese, and other pastoral products, even if the farmers have had a poor harvest and have nothing to provide in return (Kuznar 1995:49). Even our emphatically non-egalitarian society disapproves of those who retain all of their wealth for themselves, as demonstrated by national media articles such as "Trump: The Least Charitable Billionaire" (thesmokinggun.com 2011), "The Mystery of Steve Jobs's Public Giving" (Sorkin 2011), and "Biden Gave an Average of $369 to Charity a Year" (Kelley 2008).

Far stronger sanctions may exist in societies with greater expectations of unity. It may, in such cultures, be socially risky to construct an atypically large storeroom or to leave food stores visible. In societies with pretenses to egalitarianism, therefore, people may prefer to conceal their food stores—defending not only against theft but also against envy and social condemnation. Thus, for example, Hansen (1974:13–14, cited in Peterson 1993) quotes a Pintupi man as saying, "After preparing [wild tobacco], let us hide it in the shelter, so the women won't grab it from us. Let us carry it in our pockets. If you keep it where people can see it, they ask you for it, and finish it all up." Loskiel (2015:68) reported that the Delaware "commonly keep the situation of [their storage pits] very secret, knowing that if they are found out, they must supply the wants of every needy neighbor." In Madagascar, Mikea foragers returning from the bush "immediately cache their goods within their house, then appear in public space as if they had been there all day" (Tucker 2004:47). Peterson (1993:864) adds that potential receivers may also hide their possessions so that they seem needy and can ask others for more, creating a complex two-sided dance of concealment and disbursement.

An alternative to physical storage of abundance is social storage (sensu Halstead 1989; Halstead and O'Shea 1982; O'Shea 1981): sharing your abundant food with others in the expectation that its recipients will repay you, either with food when you need it or with other goods or social benefits. Food can be shared out across a production group such as an extended family or neighborhood (assuming variability in production between group members), or it may be shared with broader social groups. In either situation, a household's distribution of its surplus may alleviate obvious economic distinctions and reinforce social bonds between individuals and groups; it may also function as the household's insurance against future food shortages (reciprocity) and/or as a political investment. Egalitarianism is not a standard characteristic of agriculturalists, but in many—arguably most—foraging societies, rough egalitarianism and sharing are commonly seen as key social values. However, there are several widely cited examples of hunting-and-gathering groups not adhering to egalitarian social norms, notably the hunter-gatherer-fisher groups of the Northwest and California Pacific Coasts (see Arnold 1996 for a broader discussion of complex foragers).

Like others before us, we suspect that early agricultural villages are likely to have retained elements of an egalitarian and community-oriented ethos—an ideology wherein high values were placed on social equality and on group unity. This ethos would only partially have been a relict of an ancient hunter-gatherer egalitarian imperative, however. Early farmers would have had several additional and ongoing incentives to guard social comity by minimizing social disparities. One classic and powerful motive for maintaining communal goodwill derives from the fact that small-scale, non-industrial agropastoral production is inherently risky: the amount of food available to each household is going to vary from one year to the next, to the point that "a substantial degree of domestic economic failure is characteristic of [a] primitive economy ([Sahlins] 1974:69)" (cited in Halstead 1989:70). Sahlins elaborates that in such situations, the basal economic unit may be the individual household, but these households can enjoy only short-term self-sufficiency (Halstead 1989:73; Hegmon 1991). It is the community that ensures their survival, as households in crisis are supplied by their currently successful neighbors, certain that the tables will be turned in the future (Halstead 1989:73–74; Hegmon 1991). This reality also means that some degree of surplus production should be normative among agriculturalists: production above standard household subsistence requirements is not necessarily excess production but serves as an essential buffer against annual variability (Halstead 1989; Oka and Kuijt 2014b).

Risk reduction would not have been early farmers' sole rationale for getting along with their neighbors. Crop monitoring is best done by many sets of eyes, and crop-farming neighbors would have been "in it together" when it came to maintaining viable seed stock and local crop landraces. In general, since both crop farming and pastoralism can benefit from at least periodic involvement of groups rather than solely that of scattered individuals, early agriculturalists would have had multiple reasons to emphasize social unity rather than fragmentation. At the same time, individual households—farming different plots of land, raising different numbers of children, experiencing different states of health—are likely to have produced different amounts of food in different years. In such a scenario, we hypothesize that private abundance—specifically large amounts of food produced by a single household—would have been socially fraught.

We propose (following ethnographic suggestions) that early farmers may therefore have employed the following strategies to cope with the challenges of differential abundance.

1. Concealment of private food supplies (primarily food stores but plausibly also acts associated with food, such as preparation and consumption)
2. Distribution/dispersal of food outside the household group. (Note: When we say "household group," we refer to a co-residential unit, the perhaps four–six occupants of a single Çatalhöyük structure. We recognize the existence and social importance of multiple-residence households, but for methodological and culture historical reasons we do not include them in our use of "households" here.)

Table 8.1 shows these strategies' predicted material correlates.

TABLE 8.1. Suggested strategies for negotiating the social complexities of owning abundant food and their predicted archaeological correlates

Strategy	General Archaeological Correlate	Specific Data Sets Considered
Concealment	Food storage out of general view	Built storage facilities (bins)
		Portable storage containers (phytoliths, edible ecofact concentrations)
		Food remains in situ in storage facilities
	Cooking in private (internal) rather than public (external) locations	Cooking features, in situ artifacts
		In situ food-processing debris (e.g., wheat husks)
Supra-household food distribution	Meals sized for groups of > 6	Scale of storage and cooking facilities and equipment
		Scale of plant-processing events
		Butchery reflecting division of carcasses into relatively large portions
		Bone clusters from single events representing large amounts of meat
	Commemoration of sharing events	"Trophy" food remains (e.g., bucrania)

We now use the Anatolian Neolithic site of Çatalhöyük as a case study to test our expectation that private abundance would have presented early farming households with significant social challenges.

ÇATALHÖYÜK: A CASE STUDY

Neolithic Çatalhöyük sits in the Konya Plain of central Anatolia. Famous for its extraordinary size (13.5 hectares at its greatest extent, with a population that would have numbered in the thousands of people), remarkable artistic wealth, and densely agglomerated architecture (Hodder 2006; Mellaart 1967), the site also provides rich artifactual, architectural, and ecofactual evidence (e.g., Hodder 2005a, 2005b, 2007, 2013a, 2013b) with which to assess the effects of abundance on an early agricultural population.

Predicted Coping Strategy #1: Concealment

We begin with evidence for the concealment of abundance. At Çatalhöyük, food storage facilities as well as processing equipment are typically found in the side rooms of structures. Bins, which were used for food storage, were primarily located in side rooms well out of visitors' immediate sight lines (Bogaard et al. 2009; figure 8.1). Main room bins have been found in three buildings, but in all three cases those bins— which are situated near or en route to side rooms—were added late in the buildings' use-lives and are plausibly interpreted as "overspill" facilities (Demirergi et al. 2014).

In burned Building 52 (figure 8.2), the distribution of edible ecofact concentra- tions suggests that bags of food were likewise kept in the side room (Twiss et al. 2008, 2009). Elsewhere at the site, botanical clusters, phytolith traces, and plaster impressions testify to broad use of perishable storage containers; these are found both inside and outside of bins but commonly appear in side rooms (Atalay and Hastorf 2006; Bogaard et al. 2009). Such storage is portable, and we cannot know where else food bags or baskets might also have been kept or where they may have been taken for consumption.

Food-processing traces commonly appear in main rooms but are present in side rooms as well. Intriguingly, plant-processing facilities and debris were discovered in the side rooms of the three buildings, which had atypically high proportions of side room space: whereas side rooms usually constitute 20 percent to 30 percent of a building's floor area, in these three they totaled up to 50 percent of floor area. This may indicate that when possible, Çatalhöyük's residents preferred private process- ing as well as storage of their food; direct evidence of such side room processing (de-husking) was recovered in Building 77 (Bogaard et al. 2014; Demirergi et al. 2014). In general, the data are consistent with the hypothesis that the farmers of Çatalhöyük largely concealed their domestic food resources and associated food- production activities from their neighbors.

PREDICTED COPING STRATEGY #2: DISPERSAL OF
FOOD OUTSIDE THE INDIVIDUAL HOUSEHOLD

At Çatalhöyük, food appears to have been consumed primarily at the level of the household. The scale of storage facilities—measured as bin volumes and as side room floor space—is reasonably analogous to the food "pantry" storage compo- nent of recent communities in the surrounding Konya Plain (these communities maintain additional "surplus" and fodder storage space; Bogaard et al. 2009:figure 10b). This is sufficient to feed roughly six house occupants for one-and-a-half to two years or for one year while maintaining a small surplus in case of need (Bogaard et al. 2009). As the houses are built immediately against one another, there is limited room for them to expand if over time the fields or the family should prove unusually productive: storage capacities would have been largely set at the time of construc- tion. No large-scale or outdoor storage facilities or locations have been identified. The scale of built storage is thus consistent with production of a "normal surplus"

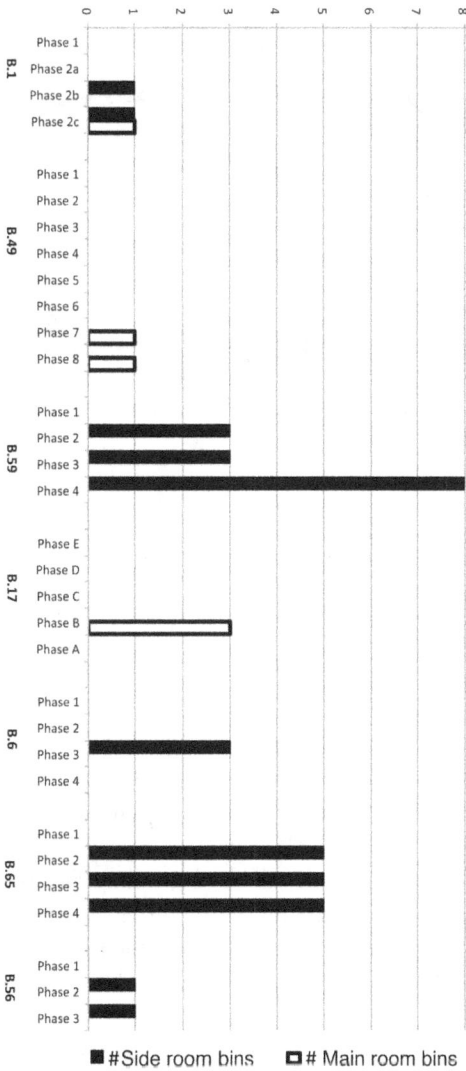

FIGURE 8.1. Side room versus main room bins in fully excavated buildings at Çatalhöyük. Modified from Demirergi et al. 2014:figure 7.5.

(Halstead 1989) only; accumulation of food above and beyond domestic subsistence needs ("excess," in the sense of Oka and Kuijt 2014b) does not appear to have been a planned-for eventuality.

Cooking and serving pots are small, suggesting primarily or entirely household-level use: no vessels suggest large-scale food distribution (Demirergi et al. 2014; Yalman, Özbudak, and Gültekin 2013). Macrobotanical, phytolithic, and

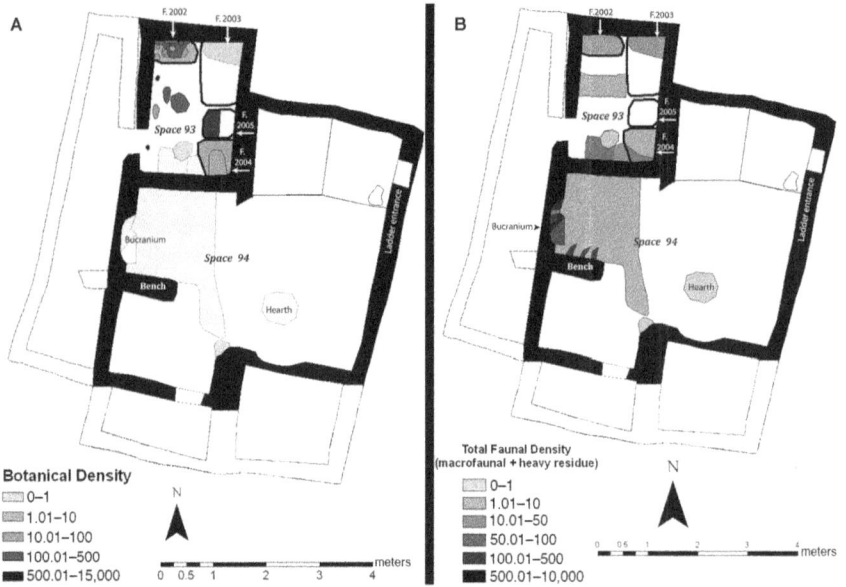

FIGURE 8.2. Primary deposits of (a) botanical and (b) faunal remains inside burned Building 52 (Bogaard et al. 2010:figure 2).

ground-stone evidence points to glume wheat being stored as spikelets, then de-husked and ground for cooking as needed (Bogaard et al. 2013; Demirergi et al. 2014). The distribution of husk waste indicates that de-husking habitually occurred indoors (in both main and side rooms) and at a scale suggesting preparation for a co-residential household-sized group. Meanwhile, all fixed grinding facilities are located indoors, and portable grinding tools are mostly found in side rooms (Wright, Tsoraki, and Siddall 2013). We cannot know if the portable tools were used or only stored in these most private of spaces: Wright (2014:15) describes the site's small planoconvex querns as "highly portable items, easily removed from bins for use anywhere. They constitute a small-scale mobile processing system, under household control, involving carefully stored private property." Nonetheless, the evidence clearly points to more interest in food concealment than in food distribution. Not all cooking was done indoors: there are small fire spots and small grinding stones in Building 65's enclosed "yard," but this is still a relatively private space. In general, we have strong evidence for food being stored, prepared, and consumed primarily at the level of the individual household or co-residential unit.

Yet evidence for dispersal of food across households does exist. Notably, there are large outdoor fire installations in "yards" in Çatalhöyük's Level South P (Bogaard et al. 2014; Demirergi et al. 2014; Regan and Taylor 2014). Ashy deposits from these large outdoor hearths and ovens contain plant food preparation/processing residues, indicating that they were in fact used for cooking at least some of the time (Bogaard et al. 2013, 2014), and their sheer scale and positioning strongly suggest the involvement of relatively large groups. Located at the edge of one of the largest unenclosed areas yet found at Çatalhöyük, these fire installations were surely in visible use by multiple houses.

Additional and much more widespread evidence comes from numerous clusters of bones that we infer were deposited in individual events: that is, we interpret them as piles of leftovers from single meals. G. Arzu Demirergi (in Demirergi et al. 2014) has evaluated the amount of meat represented by these bone clusters to estimate the number of people plausibly involved in (some) meat-sharing events. Using bone weight as a proxy for meat weight and averaging multiple authors' suggested dry-bone-to-meat-weight conversion factors, Demirergi calculates that the largest cluster would represent more than 40 kg of usable meat (40,990 g) and the smallest cluster only a quarter-kilo of meat (275 g). The average cluster deposit represents more than 6.5 kg of usable meat (6,660 g). Demirergi stresses the sheer variety of scale that characterizes the consumption events, modeling sharing events from as few as 2 to perhaps as many 1,000 people. The average cluster represents meat for between 13 and 222 people, or perhaps roughly between 2 and 44 co-residential families (Demirergi et al.)—clearly, supra-household food sharing.

The food at such meals could have been provided in a potluck fashion, with every attending household contributing a theoretically equal portion of food to the communal table (cf. Varien, Potter, and Naranjo, this volume). Such a practice would have been socially integrative, and the gracious ignoring of any inequities in contributions could have papered over smallish distinctions in household economies in a form of concealed food distribution. Alternatively, some household(s) could have hosted the event, providing the majority or all of the food. In such cases, host houses may have commemorated their generosity, displaying souvenirs of their moments of triumph or power (Twiss 2008).

At Çatalhöyük, remains of both wild and domestic cattle—symbolically prominent food animals—were displayed conspicuously in some houses. A single adult aurochs would have provided on the order of 300 kg of usable meat, and evidence for meat storage at Çatalhöyük is very limited, so supra-household distribution of meat almost certainly occurred after every aurochs hunt or cattle slaughter. Such slaughters surely occurred with some regularity, as cattle bones constitute 23 percent (NISP) of the faunal assemblage at the site (Russell et al. 2013:table 11.1). Displays such as an aurochs cranium in a centrally placed main room niche next to a bench studded with multiple aurochs horns (Building 52: Farid 2014; Twiss et al. 2008) or pairs of aurochs horns embedded in pillars directly opposite a house's main entry (Building 77: House 2014) strongly suggest that these households participated in events where meat was distributed—perhaps communal eating events such as feasts or perhaps divisions of raw meat after a kill—and indicate that these events were socially important enough to have deserved commemoration in arguably the most visible locations in each house.

Thus, data exist to support our expectations that both food concealment and food dispersal were strategies in use at Neolithic Çatalhöyük. The data further suggest that those two strategies related predominantly to plants and animals, respectively. We speculate several reasons for this pattern, from the inherent differences in basal unit size of grains versus livestock to the differences in their display potential and durability. The plant versus animal contrast might also relate at least in part to Hegmon's (1991:313–14) point that food sharing can itself be a risk in agricultural societies, as it depletes household reserves in potentially marginal situations. While the estimated proportions of plant versus animal foods in the Çatalhöyük diet will be refined through ongoing work on plant carbon and nitrogen isotope values, it is plausible that crops provided the bulk of site nutrition (cf. Pearson 2013). Habitually (but not necessarily entirely) securing those crops for domestic use might have constituted the best option for early agropastoralists, minimizing the risk of dispersing their most needed staples even as less calorically key but symbolically prominent animal foods were shared out to create and maintain social bonds that might be called upon in case of emergency (see Bogaard et al. 2009, 2010; Demirergi et al. 2014; Twiss 2012 for more discussion of plant versus animal uses and treatment at Çatalhöyük).

DIACHRONIC CHANGE?

While the patterns identified here are broadly valid throughout the site's occupation, a few mid-sequence developments might signal subtle diachronic shifts in attitudes at Çatalhöyük toward abundance and concealment. Household-scale cooking pots increase midway through the occupation, coinciding with an increase in the proportion of meat cooked off the bone rather than on it (as reflected in changing patterns of cut marks on bones): these changes may indicate an increase in meat stewing vis-à-vis roasting. Roasting is often associated with feasting in ethnographic contexts (Wandsnider 1997): a decline in roasting in favor of small-scale stewing might reflect a proportional increase in private domestic meals over supra-household food sharing. The data for this are tenuous, however, and at present no evidence suggests clearly that Çatalhöyük's occupants altered their strategies for handling abundance at any point in their centuries-long occupation of the site.

CONCLUSION

Archaeological data from the Neolithic site of Çatalhöyük in central Anatolia are consistent with our hypothesis that abundance would have been a socially complicated good in early agricultural society. We cannot reconstruct the proportions of food that were distributed across households, and it is theoretically possible that supra-household food sharing functioned at Çatalhöyük as it usually does in our society: as important social glue but not as a required element of community participation. However, it is clear that food was shared across households and that such sharing was commemorated by individual houses. It is equally clear that these houses also concealed their food stores from general sight.

Acknowledgments. We thank Monica Smith for the invitation to participate in her 2014 SAA session on surplus and for the enthusiasm, energy, and gracious efficiency with which she has assembled this volume. We thank Carola Borries and Catherine Markham for their help with the primatology literature.

REFERENCES CITED

Arnold, Jeanne E. 1996. "The Archaeology of Complex Hunter-Gatherers." *Journal of Archaeological Method and Theory* 3 (1): 77–126. http://dx.doi.org/10.1007/BF02228931.

Asquith, Pamela J. 1989. "Provisioning and the Study of Free-Ranging Primates: History, Effects, and Prospects." *Yearbook of Physical Anthropology* 32 (S10): 129–58. http://dx.doi.org/10.1002/ajpa.1330320507.

Atalay, Sonya, and Christine A. Hastorf. 2006. "Food, Meals, and Daily Activities: Food *Habitus* at Neolithic Çatalhöyük." *American Antiquity* 71 (2): 283–319. http://dx.doi.org/10.2307/40035906.

Bogaard, Amy, Michael P. Charles, Alexandra Livarda, Müge Ergun, Dragana Filipovic, and Glynis Jones. 2013. "The Archaeobotany of Mid-Later Neolithic Çatalhöyük." In *Humans and Landscapes of Çatalhöyük: Reports from the 2000–2008 Seasons*, edited by Ian Hodder, 93–128. Los Angeles: Cotsen Institute of Archaeology, University of California.

Bogaard, Amy, Michael P. Charles, and Katheryn C. Twiss. 2010. "Food Storage and Sharing at Çatalhöyük: The Botanical and Faunal Evidence." In *The Principle of Sharing: Segregation and Construction of Social Identities at the Transition from Foraging to Farming: Studies in Early Near Eastern Production, Subsistence, and Environment*, edited by Marion Benz, 14:313–30. Berlin: ex oriente.

Bogaard, Amy, Michael P. Charles, Katheryn C. Twiss, Andrew S. Fairbairn, E. Nurcan Yalman, Dragana Filipovic, G. Arzu Demirergi, Fusun Ertuğ, Nerissa Russell, and

Jennifer Henecke. 2009. "Private Pantries and Celebrated Surplus: Saving and Sharing Food at Neolithic Çatalhöyük, Central Anatolia." *Antiquity* 83 (321): 649–68. http://dx .doi.org/10.1017/S0003598X00098896.

Bogaard, Amy, Phillipa Ryan, Nurcan Yalman, Eleni Asouti, Katheryn C. Twiss, Camilla Mazzucato, and Shahina Farid. 2014. "Assessing Outdoor Activities and Their Social Implications at Çatalhöyük." In *Integrating Çatalhöyük: Themes from the 2000–2008 Seasons*, edited by Ian Hodder, 123–48. Los Angeles: Cotsen Institute of Archaeology, University of California.

Demirergi, G. Arzu, Katheryn C. Twiss, Amy Bogaard, Laura Green, Philippa Ryan, and Shahina Farid. 2014. "Of Bins, Basins, and Banquets: Storing, Handling, and Sharing at Neolithic Çatalhöyük." In *Integrating Çatalhöyük: Themes from the 2000–2008 Seasons*, edited by Ian Hodder, 91–108. Los Angeles: Cotsen Institute of Archaeology, University of California.

Durrenberger, E. Paul, and Kathleen Gillogly. 2014. "Greed in a 'Tribal' Economy? Acquisitiveness and Reciprocity in Lisu Society." *Economic Anthropology* 1 (1): 88–103.

Farid, Shahina. 2014. "Buildings 52/51." In *Çatalhöyük Excavations: The 2000–2008 Seasons*, edited by Ian Hodder. Los Angeles: Cotsen Institute of Archaeology, University of California.

Halstead, Paul. 1989. "The Economy Has a Normal Surplus: Economic Stability and Social Change among Early Farming Communities of Thessaly, Greece." In *Bad Year Economics: Cultural Responses to Risk and Uncertainty*, edited by Paul Halstead and John O'Shea, 68–80. Cambridge: Cambridge University Press. http://dx.doi.org/10.1017 /CBO9780511521218.006.

Halstead, Paul, and John M. O'Shea. 1982. "A Friend in Need Is a Friend Indeed: Social Storage and the Origins of Social Ranking." In *Ranking, Resource, and Exchange*, edited by Colin Renfrew and Steven Shennan, 92–99: Cambridge: Cambridge University Press.

Hansen, Keith C., and Lesley E. Hansen. 1974. *Pitcheri*. Papunya: SIL Bilingual Programme.

Hegmon, Michelle. 1991. "The Risks of Sharing and Sharing as Risk Reduction: Interhousehold Food Sharing in Egalitarian Societies." In *Between Bands and States*, edited by Susan A. Gregg, 309–29. Center for Archaeolgical Investigations Occasional Paper 9. Carbondale: Southern Illinois University.

Hodder, Ian. 2006. *The Leopard's Tale: Revealing the Mysteries of Çatalhöyük*. London: Thames and Hudson.

Hodder, Ian, ed. 2005a. *Changing Materialities at Çatalhöyük: Reports from the 1995–99 Seasons*. Cambridge: McDonald Institute for Archaeological Research/British Institute of Archaeology at Ankara.

Hodder, Ian, ed. 2005b. *Inhabiting Çatalhöyük: Reports from the 1995–99 Seasons.* Çatalhöyük Research Project, vol. 4. Cambridge: McDonald Institute for Archaeological Research/British Institute of Archaeology at Ankara.

Hodder, Ian, ed. 2007. *Excavating Çatalhöyük: South, North and KOPAL Area Reports from the 1995–99 Seasons.* Cambridge: McDonald Institute for Archaeological Research.

Hodder, Ian, ed. 2013a. *Humans and Landscapes of Çatalhöyük: Reports from the 2000–2008 Seasons: Çatalhöyük Research Project,* vol. 8. Los Angeles: Cotsen Institute of Archaeology Press in association with the British Institute of Archaeology at Ankara.

Hodder, Ian, ed. 2013b. *Substantive Technologies at Çatalhöyük: Reports from the 2000–2008 Seasons: Çatalhöyük Research Project,* vol. 9. Los Angeles: Cotsen Institute of Archaeology Press in association with the British Institute of Archaeology at Ankara.

Houle, Alain, Colin A. Chapman, and William L. Vickery. 2010. "Intratree Vertical Variation in Fruit Production and the Nature of Contest Competition in Frugivores." *Behavioral Ecology and Sociobiology* 64 (3): 429–41. http://dx.doi.org/10.1007/s00265 -009-0859-6.

House, Michael. 2014. "Building 77." In *Çatalhöyük Excavations: The 2000–2008 Seasons,* edited by Ian Hodder, 485–503. Los Angeles: Cotsen Institute of Archaeology, University of California.

Kelley, Matt. 2008. *USA Today,* September 12. "Biden Gave an Average of $369 to Charity a Year." Accessed September 12, 2014. http://usatoday30.usatoday.com/news/politics /election2008/2008-09-12-biden-financial_N.htm.

Kuznar, Lawrence A. 1995. *Awatimarka: The Ethnoarchaeology of an Andean Herding Community.* Fort Worth, TX: Harcourt Brace.

Lee, Richard B. 1993. *The Dobe Ju/'hoansi.* New York: Harcourt Brace.

Loskiel, George Henry. 2015. *History of the Mission of the United Brethern among the Indians in North America* (Classic Reprint). London: Forgotten Books.

Mellaart, James. 1967. *Çatal Hüyük: A Neolithic Town in Anatolia.* London: Thames and Hudson.

Naughton-Treves, Lisa, Adrian Treves, Colin A. Chapman, and Richard Wrangham. 1998. "Temporal Patterns of Crop Raiding by Primates: Linking Food Availability in Croplands and Adjacent Forest." *Journal of Applied Ecology* 35 (4): 596–606. http://dx .doi.org/10.1046/j.1365-2664.1998.3540596.x.

O'Shea, John. 1981. "Coping with Scarcity: Exchange and Social Storage." In *Economic Archaeology,* edited by Alison Sheridan and Geoff Bailey, 167–83. Oxford: British Archaeological Reports.

Oka, Rahul, and Ian Kuijt. 2014a. "Greed Is Bad, Neutral, and Good: A Historical Perspective on Excessive Accumulation and Consumption." *Economic Anthropology* 1 (1): 30–48.

Oka, Rahul, and Ian Kuijt. 2014b. "Introducing an Inquiry into the Social Economies of Greed and Excess." *Economic Anthropology* 1 (1): 1–16.

Pearson, J. 2013. "Human and Animal Diets as Evidenced by Stable Carbon and Nitrogen Isotope Analysis." In *Humans and Landscapes of Çatalhöyük: Reports from the 2000–2008 Seasons*, edited by Ian Hodder, 271–98. Los Angeles: Monographs of the Cotsen Institute of Archaeology, University of California at Los Angeles.

Peterson, Nicolas. 1993. "Demand Sharing: Reciprocity and the Pressure for Generosity among Foragers." *American Anthropologist* 95: 860–74.

Regan, Roddy, and James Taylor. 2014. "The Sequence of Buildings 75, 65, 56, 69, 44, and 10 and External Spaces 119, 129, 130, 144, 299, 314, 319, 329, 333, 339, 367, 371, and 427." In *Çatalhöyük Excavations: The 2000–2008 Seasons*, edited by Ian Hodder, 35–52. Los Angeles: Cotsen Institute of Archaeology, University of California.

Russell, Nerissa, Katheryn C. Twiss, David Orton, and G. Arzu Demirergi. 2013. "More on the Çatalhöyük Mammal Remains." In *Humans and Landscapes of Çatalhöyük: Reports from the 2000–2008 Seasons: Çatalhöyük Research Project*, vol. 8, edited by Ian Hodder, 213–58. Los Angeles: Cotsen Institute of Archaeology, University of California.

Sorkin, Andrew Ross. 2011. "The Mystery of Steve Jobs's Public Giving." *New York Times*, August 29. Accessed September 12, 2014. http://dealbook.nytimes.com/2011/08/29/the-mystery-of-steve-jobss-public-giving/?_php=true&_type=blogs&_r=0.

Spielmann, Katherine A. 2002. "Feasting, Craft Specialization, and the Ritual Mode of Production in Small-Scale Societies." *American Anthropologist* 104 (1): 195–207. http://dx.doi.org/10.1525/aa.2002.104.1.195.

Sugiyama, Yukimaru, and Hideyuki Ohsawa. 1982. "Population Dynamics of Japanese Monkeys with Special Reference to the Effect of Artificial Feeding." *Folia Primatologica* 39 (3–4): 238–63. Medline:7166288 http://dx.doi.org/10.1159/000156080.

thesmokinggun.com. 2011. April 12. Accessed September 12, 2014. http://www.thesmokinggun.com/documents/celebrity/trump-least-charitable-billionaire%E2%80%93109247.

Tucker, Bram. 2004. "Giving, Scrounging, Hiding, and Selling: Minimal Food Sharing among Mikea of Madagascar." *Research in Economic Anthropology* 23: 45–68. http://dx.doi.org/10.1016/S0190-1281(04)23002-5.

Twiss, Katheryn C. 2012. "The Complexities of Home Cooking: Public Feasts and Private Meals Inside the Çatalhöyük House." *eTopoi* 2. Accessed January 10, 2017. http://journal.topoi.org/index.php/etopoi/issue/view/3.

Twiss, Katheryn C. 2008. "Transformations in an Early Agricultural Society: Feasting in the Southern Levantine Pre-Pottery Neolithic." *Journal of Anthropological Archaeology* 27 (4): 418–42. http://dx.doi.org/10.1016/j.jaa.2008.06.002.

Twiss, Katheryn C., Amy Bogaard, Doru Bogdan, Tristan Carter, Michael P. Charles, Shahina Farid, Nerissa Russell, Mirjana Stevanović, E. Nurcan Yalman, and Lisa Yeomans.

2008. "Arson or Accident? The Burning of a Neolithic House at Çatalhöyük." *Journal of Field Archaeology* 33 (1): 41–57. http://dx.doi.org/10.1179/009346908791071358.

Twiss, Katheryn C., Amy Bogaard, Michael P. Charles, Jennifer Henecke, Nerissa Russell, Louise Martin, and Glynis Jones. 2009. "Plants and Animals Together: Interpreting Organic Remains from Building 52 at Çatalhöyük." *Current Anthropology* 50 (6): 885–95. http://dx.doi.org/10.1086/644767.

Wandsnider, LuAnn. 1997. "The Roasted and the Boiled: Food Composition and Heat Treatment with Special Emphasis on Pit-Hearth Cooking." *Journal of Anthropological Archaeology* 16 (1): 1–48. http://dx.doi.org/10.1006/jaar.1997.0303.

Woodburn, James. 1982. "Egalitarian Societies." *Man* 17 (3): 431–51. http://dx.doi.org/10.2307/2801707.

World Health Organization. 2014. "Obesity and Overweight." Accessed September 12, 2014. http://www.who.int/mediacentre/factsheets/fs311/en/.

Wright, Katherine I. 2014. "Domestication and Inequality? Households, Corporate Groups, and Food Processing Tools at Neolithic Çatalhöyük." *Journal of Anthropological Archaeology* 33 (March): 1–33. http://dx.doi.org/10.1016/j.jaa.2013.09.007.

Wright, Katherine I., Christina Tsoraki, and Ruth Siddall. 2013. "The Ground Stone Technologies of Çatalhöyük." In *Substantive Technologies at Çatalhöyük: Reports from the 2000–2008 Seasons*, edited by Ian Hodder, 365–416. Los Angeles: Cotsen Insitute of Archaeology, University of California.

Yalman, Nurcan, Duygu Tarkan Özbudak, and Hilal Gültekin. 2013. "The Neolithic Pottery of Çatalhöyük: Recent Studies." In *Substantive Technologies at Çatalhöyük: Reports from the 2000–2008 Seasons*, edited by Ian Hodder, 143–78. Los Angeles: Cotsen Institute of Archaeology, University of California.

9

Pottery

Abundance, Agency, and Choice

JUSTIN ST. P. WALSH

Pottery tends to arouse strong emotions in archaeologists: they either love it or hate it. For some it has an indefinable fascination, and is potentially full of information, which has to be teased out of it by careful and painstaking study. At the other end of the scale, it is seen as the most common of archaeological materials, whose main functions are to slow down the real business of digging, fill up stores, and behave as an archaeological "black hole" for post-excavation resources. Between these extremes there is a whole spectrum of opinion: some, for example, see pottery as an unavoidable chore, a material to be processed as quickly as possible before being reburied (either in the ground or in a store), rather like low-level nuclear waste.

ORTON AND HUGHES 2013:3

So opens one of the most influential handbooks on the study of pottery in archaeology. Although ceramicists Clive Orton and Michael Hughes believe that pottery can be extremely useful evidence for archaeologists, they still felt the need to acknowledge the negative emotions that are often prompted by this category of artifacts' most salient archaeological characteristic: its overwhelming abundance. Only in very rare circumstances (primarily in excavations of pre-ceramic societies) are any other categories of material culture better represented; most often, fragments of pottery are counted in the thousands or more per site—at my current excavation in southern Spain, just six seasons of work have generated at least 730,000 sherds, all of which have to be cleaned, sorted, counted, labeled, and stored. Some of it

DOI: 10.5876/9781607325949.c009

also has to be professionally photographed or drawn by hand. So it is unsurprising that archaeologists often feel overwhelmed when they think about how to manage, analyze, and publish this kind of material.

Attitudes about how to handle pottery and understand its meaning have changed substantially over the last 150 years. Already in Heinrich Schliemann's excavations at Mycenae, Greece, in the 1870s, stylistic differences were seen by Adolf Furtwängler and Georg Loeschke as defining distinct types (in this case, between Mycenaean and Geometric wares). Alfred Kroeber's study of pottery in the American Southwest indicated for the first time how change in decoration might be linked to chronology of site occupation (Kroeber 1916). In the archaeology of the classical Mediterranean (my area of specialization), the treatment of painted Greek pottery as fine art beginning at the end of the nineteenth century had a particular effect. J. D. Beazley's adoption of Renaissance art historian Giovanni Morelli's techniques of connoisseurship for Athenian black-figure and red-figure pottery not only elevated prosaic and quotidian pots to exalted status, it also allowed the interpretation of a series of relationships involving artistic "masters" and their workshops across multiple generations. Beazley and those who followed in his footsteps created lists attributing thousands of vases to hundreds of painters. Beazley's original printed volumes run over a thousand pages in length and have been updated several times. Other scholars have deployed the same techniques for painted pottery from Corinth, East Greece, Sicily, and multiple regions of southern Italy. The contemporary successor to Beazley's lists is a database hosted by Oxford University called the Beazley Archive; it contains over 110,000 entries from sites across the Mediterranean and throughout Europe. As a result, we are extremely well-informed about the production of painted vases in the ancient Greek world.

The concentration on Greek painted wares and their manufacture has had intellectual consequences, however. At practically every site where it is found, Greek pottery takes pride of place in publications, appearing first, with the most attention paid to it in descriptions and the greatest number of illustrations. These facts hold true equally at non-Greek or mixed-population sites as at Greek ones. The publishing hierarchy of pre-Roman Mediterranean ceramics roughly descends from Athenian figured wares to other mainland painted wares, painted wares from colonial Greek settlements, painted wares pre-dating the Archaic period (before 600 BCE) or postdating the Classical period (after about 300 BCE), unpainted but slipped wares from Athens and other mainland settlements, slipped wares from colonial sites, wares from other colonizing cultures of the Mediterranean (e.g., Phoenician), plain Greek wares, and finally, indigenous fine and plain wares from regions colonized by Greeks or on their trade routes.[1] By contrast, some scholars, notably Michael Vickers and David Gill, have argued that consideration of painted Greek wares as art objects in the modern sense obscures their actual role in ancient societies. Moreover, the modern demand for painted Greek vases, expressed in market prices of over $1 million for an individual piece in some instances, has led to the looting and destruction of archaeological sites, especially cemeteries, in pursuit of intact salable merchandise. Many Greek vases on the market and in collections—perhaps the majority of them—have find-spots that are known vaguely or not at all. Not only are these pots without context, making it difficult to understand their ancient significance, but the other material found with those that were illicitly excavated, including other pottery, is dispersed and unrecorded.

This situation raises the question of how it might be possible to undertake a post-colonialist study of the archaeology of non-Greek Mediterranean cultures, for example, in Western Europe, when the relevant excavations and publications from this region have been so biased toward Greek material. Indeed, excavations at archaeological sites in this region dating between 800 and 300 BCE have revealed an extraordinary array of Greek pottery, given their distance from Greece (Domínguez and Sánchez Fernández 2001; Jully 1982). Some of the sites were Greek colonies or were located near Greek colonies on the coast of Spain or France, where Greek traders might have been regular visitors. Others were hundreds of kilometers from Greek colonies—not only in Spain and France but also in Portugal, Switzerland, and Germany—often far inland along routes that followed river valleys, where it is far less likely that Greeks arrived on anything more than the most sporadic basis (if they were present at all; Arafat and Morgan 1994).

Might it be possible to identify patterns in the evidence from pottery that correlate to relationships between groups of people or between places that are either politically or geographically similar? Is there a way, in other words, to turn this bias, the sheer number of published Greek vases, to our benefit? Everyone who acquired Greek pottery—even Greeks—had access to other kinds as well, especially locally produced, so there must have been some reason or reasons why ancient consumers, whatever their cultural background, decided to select Greek vases in addition to or instead of other kinds. These reasons may have been the same across regions, or they could have varied even from one town to the next.

I have gathered data for 23,928 Greek vases or fragments of vases found at 233 sites scattered across the five countries listed above. The information was entered into a relational database, organized, and queried to select for vessel dates, functional types (drinking, eating, household, storage, and transport), and some individual shapes. The results of the queries were mapped in ArcGIS. By using a geostatistical method called "kriging," it was possible to make predictions about what patterns might appear in the areas between sampled sites, thereby enabling a picture to be constructed region by region of ancient patterns of consumption.[2]

LOCATIONS, PEOPLES, GREEK POTTERY

This chapter focuses on the coastal area between two Greek colonies, Massalia (modern Marseille) in southeastern France and Emporion (modern Empúries or Ampurias) in northeastern Spain. The 64 sites in these regions accounted for 12,391 vases or fragments of vases (or almost 52% of the total number in the database). It is unknown when traders of Greek goods first started coming to this area; they had certainly arrived by the end of the sixth century BC, shortly before Massalia's foundation. None of the Greek pottery cataloged for the province of Girona in Spain and the *départements* of Pyrenées-Orientales, Aude, Hérault, Gard, and Bouches-du-Rhône has a median production date earlier than 650, and only 96 pieces date to the half-century between 650 and 600 (figure 9.1).[3] The presence of Etruscan and Phoenician goods indicates that there was probably competition between traders from different backgrounds in this area. With the foundation of Massalia around 600 and Emporion around 580–50, however, the consumption of Greek pottery grew dramatically, with 2,471 examples dating to between 600 and 550. Similarly high numbers of exports persisted throughout the sixth and fifth centuries, reaching a peak of 3,567 produced between 400 and 350, before the market for Greek imports seems to have collapsed. Only 265 examples in the catalog were produced between 350 and 300. It is not entirely clear what indigenous groups offered in compensation for the goods they consumed. Agricultural produce was probably an important component of the trade. Salt, readily available in the pans and lagoons of the Rhône delta region, was likely also a valuable commodity (Bouloumié 1984).

The identities of the non-Greek inhabitants of this coastal region also require clarification if we are to examine their relevance for understanding the distribution of vases. For our purposes, identity will be defined as claimed or real membership in a group. We do not have direct access to non-Greeks' characterization of their own ethnic identity because we lack any firsthand accounts that would elucidate it. Only Greek and Roman descriptions survive, and they are problematic. Greek and Roman writers identified several different ethnic groups in the area covered by the study, particularly Celts and Iberians. The issues associated with interpreting the treatment of foreigners in ancient literature include three points: first, such accounts are often self-justifying and biased in other ways toward the authors' own cultures and against those of the foreigners; second, they are frequently based on second- or third-hand reports of interactions with foreigners; third, the date of their composition is often centuries later than the events they purport to describe (Antonaccio 2003, 2005, 2009; Dietler 2010; Hodos 2006, 2009). It is not clear, for example, how accounts that define or describe ancient cultural groups reflect the actual ways in which people attributed to those groups would have identified themselves and their similarities to or differences from other groups. Did Celts—whose name, in any case,

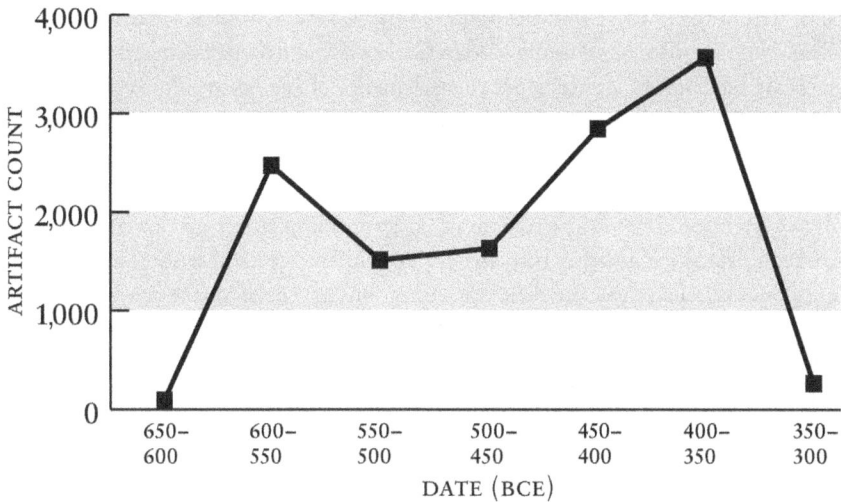

FIGURE 9.1. Number of imported Greek vases found in coastal northeastern Spain and southern France, by median production date, 650–300 BCE.

seems to have belonged only to a group in southeastern France but was applied by Greeks to people living from Central Europe to Provence and perhaps even farther west and south—think of themselves as belonging to a unified group, or were there distinctions (subtle or otherwise) made on a regional or local level?

With regard to the archaeological record, answers to this question have so far been mixed. Archaeologists have identified a cultural group spanning Central and Western Europe between roughly 800 and 450, referred to by the name of an Austrian type-site, Hallstatt. The Hallstatt culture was succeeded by a related one, named for the Swiss site La Téne, which persisted until the Roman conquests in the first century BCE. Hallstatt culture was characterized by a highly stratified society centered on hilltop settlements (the so-called princely sites, or *Fürstensitzen*), as well as prominent burials containing rich arrays of grave goods and marked by tumuli. The best-known and most extensively studied sites are Heuneburg in southwest Germany (Bittel and Rieth 1951; Kimmig 1983; Kimmig and Böhr 2000) and Vix (Mont Lassois) in eastern France (Chaume and Brun 1997; Chaume, Mordant, and Allag 2011; Chaume, Nieszery, and Reinhard 2012; Chaume, Olivier, and Reinhard 2000; Chaume, Reinhard, and Nieszery 2007). The La Téne period seems to have resulted from a collapse of Hallstatt sites, perhaps because of social strife. It was characterized by fortified towns still identified by the word Roman writers used to describe them: *oppida*. In general, scholars have equated these two cultures with the "Celts" first named by the Greek historians Hekataios (Jacoby 1923–98 1:F 54–55) and Herodotos (2.34, 4.48), although the precise range of their settlements is not clear. Hallstatt sites have been found in Galicia and northern Portugal, and several scholars have noted affinities between elements of Hallstatt culture such as jewelry and local products found as far away from Austria as El Carambolo, outside Seville in southwestern Spain, leading to the theorization of a hybrid group of "Celt-Iberians" (Almagro-Gorbea 1997; Lenerz-de Wilde 1995).[4] This formulation draws attention to another problem in understanding ethnic groups from literary sources: discerning whether similarities in the material record reflect cultural influence or cultural connections. The same questions also exist for the other major ethnic group mentioned in this region: the Iberians (whose name comes from the one given by ancient authors for the Ebro River; Almagro-Gorbea 1988; Buxó and Pons i Brun 2000; Rouillard 1991; Sanmartí-Grego 1992; Vives-Ferrándiz 2010).

Similar to the Hallstatt and La Téne cultures, the material culture throughout most of the Iberian Peninsula, especially the eastern half, was socially stratified and controlled from a few major centers, such as Ullastret in Catalonia and Cástulo in Andalusia. These centers controlled territories of up to 2,000–3,000 km² (larger than most Greek city-states) through a network of smaller settlements ranging from individual farmsteads to small towns scattered across the landscape (Plana i Mallart and Martín Ortega 2001; Sanmartí and Santacana 2005). Just as the Hallstatt/La Téne cultures have been connected to the "Celts" described in literature, so, too, the culture of eastern Iberia has been linked with the literary "Iberians." Connecting the material record to ethnicity has been a matter of some debate in studies of the Greek world, though, and so the opportunity to explore a possible relationship between the archaeological evidence and the concept of ethnicity is an important one (Antonaccio 2001, 2005, 2009; Hall 2000, 2005; Ruby 2006).

It is perhaps already clear that a distinction between Celts and Iberians is not easy to make. For example, where did the territory of one begin and the other end? In the late first century BCE, Strabo wrote that "historians of former times, it is said, gave the name of Iberia to all the land beyond the Rhodanos (Rhône) and that isthmus between the Galatic gulfs [i.e., the modern Iberian Peninsula]" (Jacoby 1923–98 3.4.19, trans. Jones). This statement seems to indicate that Iberians controlled a significant area north of the Pyrenees, including the modern regions of Rousillon and Languedoc. The mountains are less of a barrier than they might seem, however. Rousillon was part of the Principality of Catalonia until 1659, and even today, many inhabitants of that area speak Catalan in addition to French. Was Strabo therefore correct in suggesting that, in some period prior to his writing, a boundary did exist between non-Greek populations in the region between Massalia and Emporion? If such a boundary can be shown to have existed, where was it located? More specifically for the purposes of this chapter, to what extent can the consumption of imported pottery in large quantities (since the acquisition of these objects involved a clear act of choice by consumers) be used as a sign of ethnic boundaries? Some evidence collected over the last two decades already suggests that Iberian populations lived north and east of the Pyrenees (Dietler 1997, 2010:80). One sign of a difference may be the use of different alphabets in inscriptions (Untermann 1992). Material differences seem to have existed as well, at least early on. Local ceramic assemblages were different at the transition from the Bronze Age to the Early Iron Age in the seventh and sixth centuries, composed of two sets of material culture: to the east the so-called Suspendian type, similar to those of the Iberian Peninsula, and to the west the Mailhac II/Grand Bassin II type, which resembled Hallstatt styles (Dietler 1997:277; Garcia 1993:316; Py 1992:29–30). In the cases of both the writing systems and the cultural assemblages, however, the dividing line does not seem to have been found at the Rhône River but rather to the west, at the Hérault. The effort that follows tries to show how imported pottery might clarify the situation.

POTTERY DISTRIBUTIONS

A kriging analysis of the total number of imported vessels (or fragments of vessels) in the area between Massalia and Emporion between 650 and 300 BCE shows several patterns (figure 9.2). First, the zone with the greatest quantity of Greek imports is, perhaps unsurprisingly, around the colony of Massalia itself. This area also stretches about 50 km west to include a major site where thousands of fragments have been found, Saint-Blaise (Bouloumié 1992). This settlement, adjacent to the mouth of the Rhône, was largely inhabited by an indigenous population, to judge from its architecture, and it seems to have been a significant point of interaction and exchange between Greeks and non-Greeks.

The territory around Emporion also featured high numbers of Greek imports but in a much smaller area (in fact, the intensity of the kriging prediction for this area is almost entirely a result of Emporion's very large quantity of published material, while its neighboring sites contributed very little). Somewhat high levels of consumption spread along the coast to the north before dropping off precisely at the Hérault River. The kriging prediction does not take topographic features into account, so the fact that the river coincides with one of the contour edges is not only a striking marker of different patterns of consumption but also possibly an independent marker of a boundary between groups. Along the coast of eastern Languedoc, between the Hérault and Rhône Rivers, there is a noticeable decline in the level of consumption of Greek imports, a pattern similar to what is found in the hinterland of western Languedoc and Rousillon, 50 km or more inland. At the same time the quantity of vessels was lower in this area, though, on average

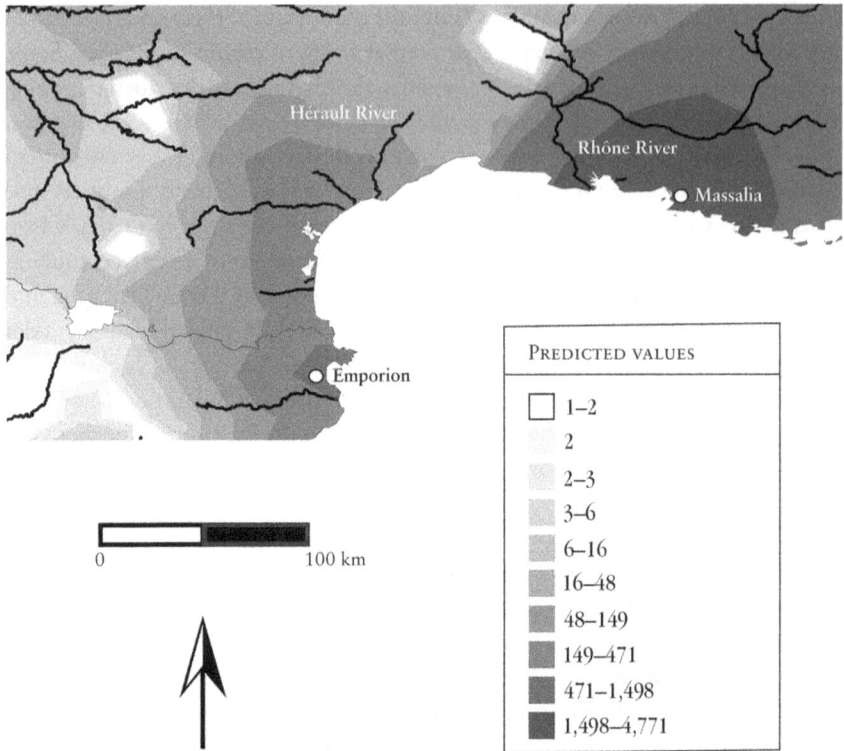

FIGURE 9.2. Kriging results for the distribution of Greek vases, 650–300 BCE.

the range of functional types (drinking, eating, household, storage, and transport) present at sites in eastern Languedoc was richer than at sites elsewhere, particularly to the west and south. Using a statistical measure known as Simpson's Index of Diversity, which calculates how evenly distributed individual vessels are across categories (the index ranges from 0 to 1; a higher number means a greater evenness), it can be shown that sites between the Hérault and Rhône tended to have higher index scores of between 0.5 and 0.6.[5] West of the Hérault, by contrast, sites showed less diversity, with scores ranging from 0.29 to 0.39. In other words, despite lower overall consumption of Greek imports in eastern Languedoc, people tended to buy a broader range of functional types of vessels when compared with their neighbors, either to the east in Saint-Blaise and Massalia or to the west.

A closer look at certain aspects of the pottery distribution can be equally illuminating—for example, individual functional types. The consumption patterns associated with vessels used for drinking—cups, jugs, mixing vessels—were essentially identical to the ones already noted for the complete set of vessels, since drinking vessels formed 74 percent of the corpus. The divergence between western Languedoc and Rousillon, on one hand, and eastern Languedoc, on the other, was quite strong, with the eastern sites showing only one-tenth the predicted values for drinking vessels as their counterparts on the other side of the Hérault. The range of drinking shapes was slightly higher in western Languedoc, but the diversity of drinking assemblages was again higher to the east. The spread of one specific type of drinking vessel, the krater, may be of special importance for understanding local interest in Greek pottery. This very large and distinctive shape, used for mixing wine and water prior to drinking, was emblematic of the Greek symposium, as it often appeared in depictions of symposia. It may even be seen as symbolic of Greekness itself, since Greek authors claimed the dilution of wine was the epitome of civilized behavior, while the drinking of unmixed wine, by contrast, was a behavior attributed to uncivilized foreigners (in some literary discussions, unmixed wine was seen as dangerous or even deadly). When kraters are found in non-Greek contexts, it is not possible to be certain that they were used for mixing, particularly when they are found outside of domestic spaces (e.g., in tombs). In keeping with all the other kinds of Greek pottery except transport amphorai, consumption of kraters at non-Greek sites between Massalia and Emporion was concentrated in western Languedoc (figure 9.3). Almost 250 were found at one site, Nissan-lez-Ensérune. Only the Greek colony Emporion, with 549 kraters, revealed more examples. But the vessels that appeared in western Languedoc were concentrated at only a few major centers rather than evenly distributed across all towns. East of the Hérault, by contrast, relatively few kraters appeared outside of Saint-Blaise and Massalia.

Where vessels used for eating (primarily bowls and, to a lesser extent, plates) are concerned, a somewhat different pattern emerges. In the corpus as a whole, eating vessels comprised only 14 percent of the total, and they were most associated with Greek colonies (figure 9.4). Few sites in eastern Languedoc acquired much pottery used for eating—only one had more than 14 examples (Saint-Gilles-du-Gard, with 46). West of the Hérault, too, there was little apparent widespread interest in Greek eating vessels—large quantities were found only at a few major centers, especially in close proximity to the coast. Four of these sites ranked highest in the entire corpus of 233 sites for their range of eating vessels, and another 4 sites fell among the top 13. In this case, the important western sites not only showed a wider range of eating vessels, but there is also no difference in the diversity of eating assemblages between sites on either side of the Hérault. The eating function therefore seems to have been the subject of a particular lack of emphasis or interest for consumers of Greek pottery in the east, while it was more important west of the Hérault than anywhere else in Western Europe except for Massalia, Saint-Blaise, and Emporion.

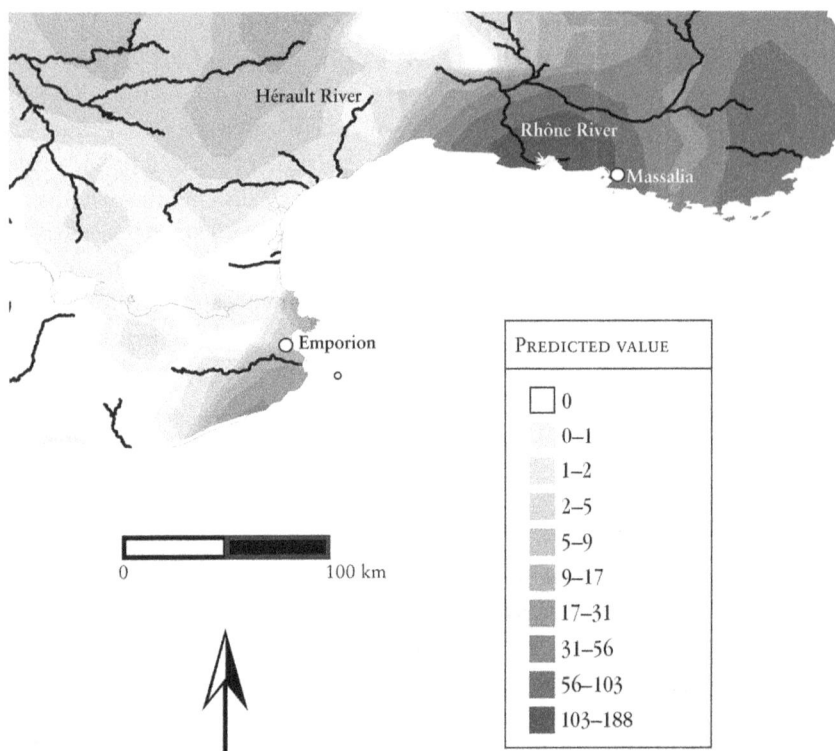

FIGURE 9.3. Kriging results for the distribution of kraters (mixing vessels for wine), 650–300 BCE.

Transport amphorai might be considered a particularly important functional category for understanding differences between groups because their presence is assumed by scholars to imply the presence of wine as well. Although it is far from clear that non-Greeks consumed wine the way Greeks did at their symposia—that is, with water mixed in large quantities for a group of men to consume over several hours while reclining, often in a highly ritualized fashion—it has been argued that wine was first introduced to this region by Greek traders.[6] The number of amphorai might suggest the interest of non-Greeks in a new beverage for banquets that had previously included beer or mead. It is clear that in the seventh century and early sixth century, Etruscan amphorai were dominant in this region, but within a few generations of the foundation of Massalia, that city's products became the most popular (it was the source for 41% of all transport amphorai in this survey). As the kriging map for transport vessels shows (figure 9.5), Saint-Blaise and Massalia were again the largest consumers, but now they were joined by several other sites nearby

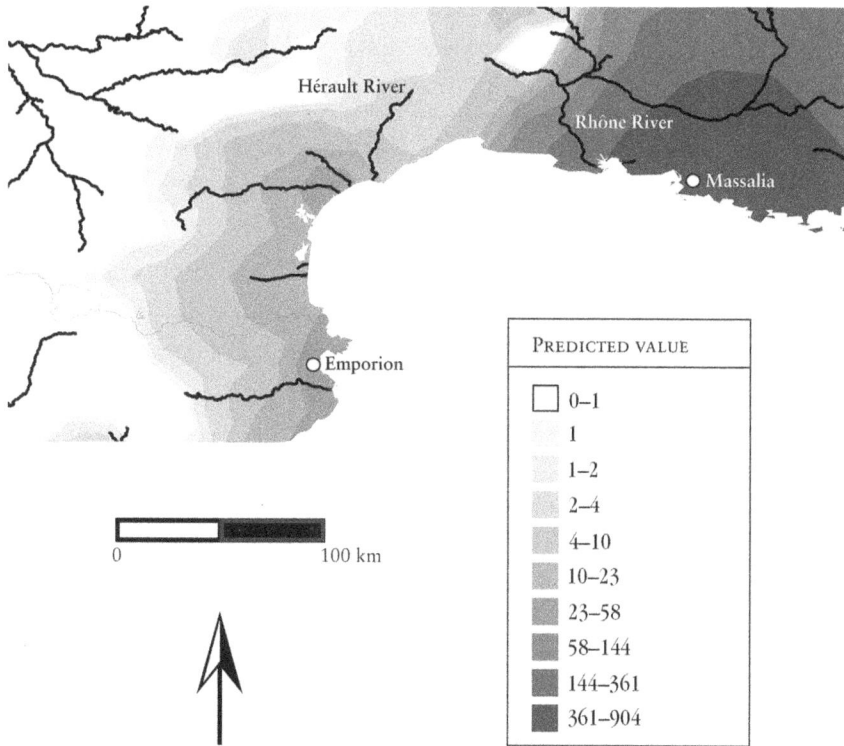

FIGURE 9.4. Kriging results for the distribution for Greek vessels for eating, 650–300 BCE.

that had many amphorai, especially Beaucaire and Saint-Gilles-du-Gard. The number of amphorai declined sharply—seemingly almost as a function of their distance from Massalia—so that in southwestern Languedoc and Rousillon, there seem to have been few to none present at any site. Proximity to Emporion seems to have been unrelated to wine consumption, suggesting that importation of wine was not caused merely by contact with Greeks.

Some consideration of the find-spots of Greek imports within a site is also worthwhile for ascertaining cultural differences between various regions. As noted, a vase would likely have had a very different meaning if found in a tomb, a sanctuary, or a house. In the period discussed here, when Greeks buried their dead, they might have placed a few small vases (especially in the oil-flask shape known as the lekythos) and occasionally cups, bowls, or plates inside or near a tomb. They rarely placed larger shapes or shapes associated with commensal banqueting (such as table amphorai or kraters) with the dead. At non-Greek sites in the south of France, practices seem to have been variable in these regards.[7] In western Languedoc and

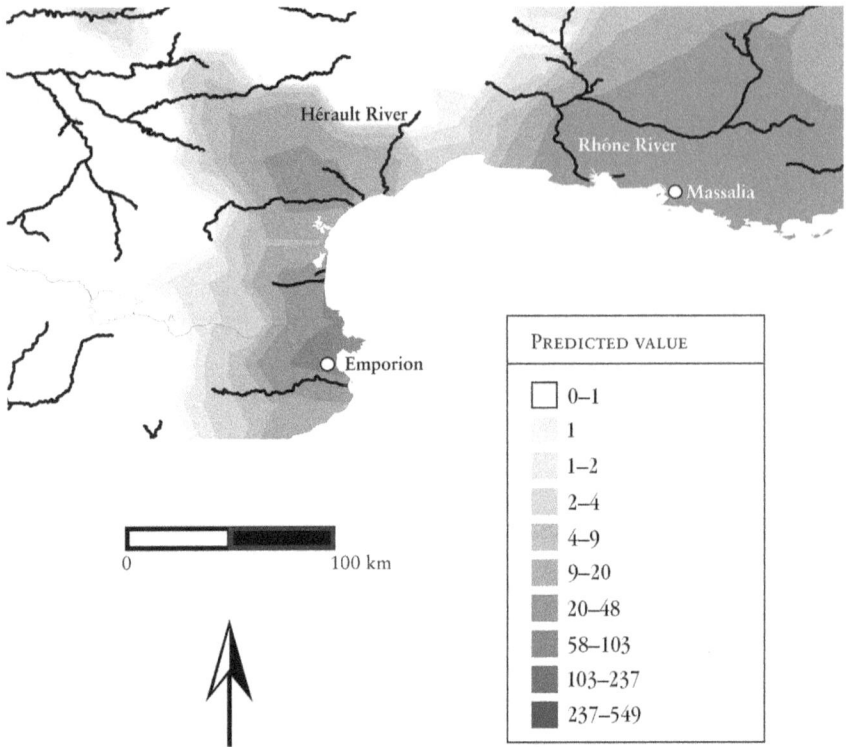

FIGURE 9.5. Kriging results for the distribution of Greek transport amphorai, 650–300 BCE.

Rousillon, Greek vases were placed in tombs in significant numbers at a few sites (Nissan-lez-Ensérune, with 515 vessels, and Pézenas, with 339 vessels comprising all the Greek vases found at the site), while at most other sites (such as Sigean [Pech Maho] and Mailhac), they were found only within settlements. Only 3 sites east of the Hérault showed vases in tombs; of these, 2 were located along the river, and only 1 had more than 1 vase from a grave context (Agde, which had just 4 vessels dating to the seventh century, prior to its settlement by Greeks).

INTERPRETING THE DISTRIBUTION PATTERNS

Pottery assemblages clearly demonstrate the agency of consumers to make choices about what goods to acquire based on locally determined value systems and interests (Cook, Yamin, and McCarthy 1996; Dietler 1999; Marshall and Maas 1997). Generally speaking, there were notably different patterns on either side of the Hérault River. For the most part, there was higher consumption of Greek imports to the west and lower consumption to the east. The higher interest in Greek wares was pervasive across almost all categories in western Languedoc and, to a lesser extent, Rousillon. There were variations in practice not only between regions but also within them. To the west, major centers were the biggest consumers of Greek pottery, where much less was found at smaller sites; to the east, there was less differentiation among sites. Moreover, non-Greeks west of the Hérault did not seem to be concerned about using Greek vessels exactly the way Greeks did—for example, occasionally placing large vessels associated with commensal banqueting in tombs. In perhaps the most striking pattern, to the east of the Hérault, particularly in the area close to the mouth of the Rhône, consumers appear to have been more interested in Greek wine than in the vessels Greeks used to drink it.

CONCLUSION

The use of a geostatistical technique, kriging, allows the interpretation of a rich data set from a geographical perspective. Kriging also allows the analyst to plot the amount of error associated with the prediction. In the case of imports of Greek pottery to southern France and northeastern Spain, clear variations can be identified between regions, and the associated prediction error is very low because of the large number of sampled sites in a relatively small area. The identified variance seems to offer an independent confirmation of the distinction made by previous scholars between two non-Greek cultural groups in these regions. In contradiction of Strabo's claim that the Rhône River formed the boundary between Iberians and Celts, the most significant geographical feature that can be associated with the pottery distribution patterns is instead the Hérault River. Even in analyses where the predicted distribution contours do not precisely align with the river, they typically fall within 10 km of it. It is therefore possible, based on the array of evidence now assembled from literary and material sources, to identify the two cultural groups with the Iberians and the Celts, although some caution should be exercised in using this terminology, since cultural mixing seems to have been a frequent occurrence; in addition, there are problems associated with taking ancient reports of ethnonyms at face value.

With regard to this question of cultural identity, it is perhaps of some interest to compare consumption patterns in western Languedoc with the rest of the Iberian Peninsula. In fact, a wide variety of patterns can be identified throughout Iberia, depending on the period and location. For example, in the earliest days of contact and trade, in the eighth through sixth centuries BCE, most consumption of Greek goods by indigenous groups happened in the southwest of Spain, in the area identified by many scholars as ancient Tartessos, around modern Huelva. This region was legendary for its wealth, purportedly derived from silver production (Jacoby

1923–98 3.2.8, 3.2.11, 4.155). Elsewhere on the Iberian Peninsula, however, there was hardly any interest in Greek vases during this period, either from indigenes or from Phoenicians who had founded their own emporia. Following the foundation of Emporion, there was strong interest in Greek pottery at the nearby regional center of Ullastret but not elsewhere, until new mines opened in eastern Andalusia in the fifth century around the town of Cástulo. The surrounding province of Jaén became the largest importer of Greek pottery in Iberia through the fourth century. These general trends show that Iberians generally were not enamored of Greek pottery but that in situations where increased wealth could spur status competitions, consumption of imports was one way distinctions might be made between individuals (Walsh 2014). Such an explanation also seems appropriate for the concentration of Greek vases at the major centers of Ibero-Languedoc. Likewise, the consumption of wine in eastern Languedoc may have been associated with status competitions in arenas of commensality (Dietler 1997, 2005, 2010).

Beyond these specific conclusions, this chapter has also demonstrated how the richness of the publications regarding pottery from one region relative to those on other wares can be used to identify important patterns of indigenous behavior following local principles. The modern colonialist bias toward objects associated with ancient Greeks, the desire of people in southern France and northeastern Spain for those products, and perhaps especially the abundance of pottery as a category of artifacts recovered through excavation (resulting from the utility of fired clay for creating containers and the durability of ceramics over very long periods of time) have combined with a new perspective on the agency of consumers to allow the development of significant new insights into ancient behaviors. The acquisition of imported pottery must have been more costly—however that cost was reckoned, whether in coined money, non-currency resources, or some other capacity to make choices—than locally produced options, and thus it represented a kind of luxury.[8] It therefore seems probable that the varying patterns identified are reflective of status competitions operating within the rules of the local cultural context. Greater consumption, demonstrated by a greater abundance of imports, thus likely indicates more intense competitions.

NOTES

1. At least one major publication has purposely subverted this practice, creating typologies first by shape, then by ware (Blondé 2007). Her work thus emphasized how different production centers were producing vessels in the same shapes at the same time.

2. Kriging creates a mathematical prediction for regional patterns that is derived from reported samples and the relative distance of sampled locations from each other (Wheatley

and Gillings 2002). Using ArcGIS, these predictions can be displayed visually on a map as shaded regions showing ranges of similar values.

3. There are, admittedly, real problems with interpreting pottery distributions from sherd counts (Orton and Hughes 2013). The analysis below is based on three methods, of which the counting of sherds forms only one. The other methods depend on identifying the presence or absence of types and on a statistical measure of population diversity known as Simpson's Index of Diversity (Simpson 1949). For a full discussion of these methods, see Walsh 2014:99–103.

4. This name was known in antiquity, too, but Strabo (Jacoby 1923–98 1.2.27) thought it was incorrect.

5. Another way of understanding Simpson's Index of Diversity is to see it as describing the chances that two consecutive selections from a set will turn up individuals of different types; a higher index score indicates a greater chance and thus greater diversity.

6. The earliest direct evidence for the presence of wine in France has recently been identified in scientific testing of residues from an Etruscan amphora dating to 500–475, which was found at Lattes (ancient Lattara; McGovern et al. 2013).

7. Find-spots were not always reported or clarified in the publications used as sources for this study (e.g., Domínguez and Sánchez Fernández 2001; Jully 1982), so the conclusions derived from this analysis must necessarily be regarded as somewhat tentative.

8. Walsh 2013, 2014. I am pleased to note that similar points have been raised independently in a Mesoamerican context by Hector Neff (2014).

REFERENCES CITED

Almagro-Gorbea, M. 1988. "Société et Commerce Méditerranéen dans la Peninsula Ibérique aux VIIe–Ve Siècles." In *Les Princes Celtes et la Méditerranée*, edited by J. P. Mohen, A. Duval, and C. Eluère, 71–80. Paris: La Documentation Francaise.

Almagro-Gorbea, M. 1997. "Die Kelten auf der Iberischen Halbinsel." In *Die Welt Der Kelten: Dia-Vortragsreihe in Hochdorf/Enz 1991–1997: 30 Vorträge–Zusammenfassung*, edited by T. Bader, 73–83. Hochdorf an der Enz, Germany: Keltenmuseum.

Antonaccio, C. M. 2001. "Ethnicity and Colonization." In *Ancient Perceptions of Greek Ethnicity*, edited by I. Malkin, 113–57. Washington, DC: Center for Hellenic Studies.

Antonaccio, C. M. 2003. "Hybridity and the Cultures within Greek Culture." In *The Cultures within Ancient Greek Culture*, edited by C. Dougherty and L. Kurke, 57–74. Cambridge: Cambridge University Press.

Antonaccio, C. M. 2005. "Excavating Colonization." In *Ancient Colonizations: Analogy, Similarity, and Difference*, edited by H. Hurst and S. Owen, 97–114. London: Duckworth.

Antonaccio, C. M. 2009. "(Re)defining Ethnicity: Culture, Material Culture, and Identity." In *Material Culture and Social Identities in the Ancient World*, edited by S. Hales and T. Hodos, 32–53. Cambridge: Cambridge University Press.

Arafat, K., and C. Morgan. 1994. "Athens, Etruria, and the Heuneburg: Mutual Misconceptions in the Study of Greek-Barbarian Relations." In *Classical Greece: Ancient Histories and Modern Archaeologies*, edited by I. Morris, 108–34. New Directions in Archaeology. Cambridge: Cambridge University Press.

Bittel, K., and A. Rieth. 1951. *Die Heuneburg an der oberen Donau: Ein Frühkeltischer Fürstensitz z: Vorläufiger Bericht Über die Ausgrabungen 1950*. Stuttgart: Kohlhammer.

Blondé, F., with Maurice Picón. 2007. *Les céramiques d'usage quotidien à Thasos au IVe siècle avant J.-C. (Études Thasi-ennes XX)*. Athens: École Française d'Athènes.

Bouloumié, B. 1984. "Saint-Blaise, Oppidum du Sel." *Dossiers D'archéologie* 84: 5–96.

Bouloumié, B. 1992. *Saint-Blaise, Fouilles H. Rolland: L'habitat Protohistorique: Les Céramiques Grecques: Travaux du Centre Camille Jullian 13*. Aix-en-Provence: Publications de l'Université de Provence.

Buxó, R., and E. Pons i Brun, eds. 2000. *L'hàbitat protohistòric a Catalunya, Rosselló i Llenguadoc occidental: Actualitat de l'arqueologia de l'edat del ferro: Actes del XXII col·loqui internacional per a l'estudi de l'Edat del Ferro*. Girona, Spain: Museu d'Arqueologia de Catalunya.

Chaume, B., and P. Brun, eds. 1997. *Vix et les Éphèmères Principautés Celtiques: Les 6e et 5e Siècles avant J.-C. en Europe Centre-occidentale. Actes du Colloque de Châtillon-sur-Seine, 27–29 Octobre 1993*. Archéologie Aujourd'hui. Paris: Éditions Errance.

Chaume, B., C. Mordant, and C. Allag. 2011. *Le complexe aristocratique de Vix: nouvelles recherches sur l'habitat et le système de fortification et l'environnement du Mont Lassois*. Dijon: Editions universitaires de Dijon.

Chaume, B., N. Nieszery, and W. Reinhard. 2012. "Ein Frühkeltischer Fürstensitz im Burgund: Der Mont Lassois." In *Die Welt der Kelten—Zentren der Macht, Kostbarkeiten der Kunst*, edited by Archäologisches Landesmuseum Baden-Württemberg, 132–38. Stuttgart: Thorbecke.

Chaume, B., L. Olivier, and W. Reinhard. 2000. "L'enclos Cultuel Hallstattien de Vix, Les Herbues." *Ocnus: Quaderni della Scuola di Specializzazione in Archeologia* 8: 229–49.

Chaume, B., W. Reinhard, and N. Nieszery. 2007. "Le Palais de La Dame de Vix." *Bulletin Archéologique et Historique du Châtillonnais* 6: 23–27.

Cook, L. J., R. Yamin, and J. P. McCarthy. 1996. "Shopping as Meaningful Action: Toward a Redefinition of Consumption in Historical Archaeology." *Historical Archaeology* 30 (4): 50–65. http://dx.doi.org/10.1007/BF03373596.

Dietler, M. 1997. "The Iron Age in Mediterranean France: Colonial Encounters, Entanglements, and Transformations." *Journal of World Prehistory* 11 (3): 269–358. http://dx.doi.org/10.1007/BF02221134.

Dietler, M. 1999. "Consumption, Cultural Frontiers, and Identity: Anthropological Approaches to Greek Colonial Encounters." In *Confini e Frontiere nella Grecità d'Occidente* 1:475–501. Naples: Arte tipographica.

Dietler, M. 2005. *Consumption and Colonial Encounters in the Rhône Basin of France: A Study of Early Iron Age Political Economy*. Monographies d'Archéologie Méditerranéenne 21. Lattes, France: CNRS.

Dietler, M. 2010. *Archaeologies of Colonialism: Consumption, Entanglement, and Violence in Ancient Mediterranean France*. Berkeley: University of California Press. http://dx.doi .org/10.1525/california/9780520265516.003.0002.

Domínguez, A. J., and C. Sánchez Fernández. 2001. *Greek Pottery from the Iberian Peninsula: Archaic and Classical Periods*. Edited by G. R. Tsetskhladze. Leiden: Brill.

Garcia, D. 1993. *Entre Ibères et Ligures: Lodécois et Moyenne Vallée de l'Hérault Protohistoriques*. Revue Archéologique de Narbonnaise Supplément 26. Paris: CNRS.

Hall, J. M. 2000. *Ethnic Identity in Greek Antiquity*. Cambridge: Cambridge University Press.

Hall, J. M. 2005. *Hellenicity: Between Ethnicity and Culture*. Chicago: University of Chicago Press.

Hodos, T. 2006. *Local Responses to Colonization in the Iron Age Mediterranean*, 1st ed. London: Routledge.

Hodos, T. 2009. "Local and Global Perspectives in the Study of Social and Cultural Identities." In *Material Culture and Social Identities in the Ancient World*, edited by S. Hales and T. Hodos, 3–31. Cambridge: Cambridge University Press.

Jacoby, F. 1923–98. *Die Fragmente der Griechischen Historiker*, 4 parts. Berlin and Leiden: Weidmannische Buchhandlung and Brill.

Jully, J.-J. 1982. *Ceramiques Grecques ou de type Grec and Autres Ceramiques en Languedoc Mediterraneen, Roussillon and Catalogne*. 2 vols. Besançon, France: Presses Universitaires de Franche-Comté.

Kimmig, W. 1983. *Die Heuneburg an der oberen Donau*, 2nd ed. Führer Zu Archäologischen Denkmälern in Baden-Württemberg 1. Stuttgart: Theiss.

Kimmig, W., and E. Böhr. 2000. *Importe und mediterrane Einflüsse auf der Heuneburg*. Heuneburgstudien 11; Römisch-germanische Forschungen Bd. 59. Mainz am Rhein: V. Zabern.

Kroeber, A. 1916. "Zuñi Potsherds." *Anthropological Papers of the American Museum of Natural History* 18: 1–38.

Lenerz-de Wilde, M. 1995. "The Celts in Spain." In *The Celtic World*, edited by M. J. Green, 533–51. London: Routledge.

Marshall, Y., and A. Maas. 1997. "Dashing Dishes." *World Archaeology* 28 (3): 275–90. http://dx.doi.org/10.1080/00438243.1997.9980348.

McGovern, Patrick E., Benjamin P. Luley, Nuria Rovira, Armen Mirzoian, Michael P. Callahan, Karen E. Smith, Gretchen R. Hall, Theodore Davidson, and Joshua M. Henkin. 2013. "Beginning of Viniculture in France." *Proceedings of the National Academy of Sciences of the United States of America* 110 (25): 10147–52. Medline:23733937 http:// dx.doi.org/10.1073/pnas.1216126110.

Neff, H. 2014. "Pots as Signals: Explaining the Enigma of Long-Distance Ceramic Exchange." In *Craft and Science: International Perspectives on Archaeological Ceramics*, edited by M. Martinón-Torres. UCL Qatar Series in Archaeology and Cultural Heritage 1: 1–11. Doha: Bloomsbury Qatar Foundation. http://dx.doi.org/10.5339/uclq.2014.cas.ch1.

Orton, C., and M. Hughes. 2013. *Pottery in Archaeology*, 2nd ed. Cambridge: Cambridge University Press. http://dx.doi.org/10.1017/CBO9780511920066.

Plana i Mallart, R., and M. A. Martín Ortega. 2001. "L'Organitzacio de L'espai Rural Entorn de L'oppidum d'Ullastret: Formes i Dinamica Del Poblament." In *Territori Polític i Territori Rural Durant L'edat del Ferro a La Mediterrània Occidental: Actes de La Taula Rodona Celebrada a Ullastret*, edited by A. Martín and R. Plana i Mallart, 157–76. Girona, Spain: Museu d'Arqueologia de Catalunya and Generalitat de Catalunya, Departament de Cultura i Mitjans de Comunicació.

Py, M. 1992. *Les Gaulois du Midi: De la Fin de l'Âge du Bronze à la Conquête Romaine.* Paris: Hachette.

Rouillard, Pierre. 1991. *Les Grecs et la péninsule ibérique Péninsule Ibérique du VIIIe au IVe Siècle avant Jésus-Christ.* Publications du Centre Pierre 21. Talence, France: Université de Bordeaux III and Diffusion De Boccard.

Ruby, P. 2006. "Peuples, Fictions? Ethnicité, Identité Ethnique et Sociétés Anciennes." *Revue des Études Anciennes* 108 (1): 25–60.

Sanmartí, J., and J. Santacana. 2005. *Els Ibers del Nord.* Barcelona: Rafael Dalmau.

Sanmartí-Grego, E. 1992. "Massalia et Emporion: Une Origine Commune, Deux Destins Differents." In *Marseille Grecque et la Gaule: Actes du Colloque Interntaionale D'histoire et de Archéologie et du Ve Congrès Archéologique de Gaule Meridionale*, edited by M. Bats, G. Bertucchi, G. Congès, and H. Tréziny, 27–41. Études Massaliètes 3. Lattes/Aix-en-Provence, France: ADAM-PUP.

Simpson, E. H. 1949. "Measurement of Diversity." *Nature* 163 (4148): 688. http://dx.doi .org/10.1038/163688a0.

Untermann, J. 1992. "Quelle Langue Parlait-on dans l'Hérault Pendant l'Antiquité?" *Revue Archéologique Narbonnaise* 25 (1): 19–27. http://dx.doi.org/10.3406/ran.1992.1396.

Vives-Ferrándiz, J. 2010. "Mobility, Materiality, and Identities in Iron Age East Iberia: Appropriation of Material Culture and the Question of Judgement." In *Material Connections in the Ancient Mediterranean: Mobility, Materiality, and Identity*, edited by P. van Dommelen and A. B. Knapp, 190–209. New York: Routledge.

Walsh, J.S.P. 2013. "Consumption and Choice in Ancient Sicily." In *Regionalism and Globalism in Antiquity: Exploring Their Limits*, edited by F. de Angelis, 229–46. Colloquia Antiqua 7. Leuven, Belgium: Peeters.

Walsh, J.S.P. 2014. *Consumerism in the Ancient World: Imports and Identity Construction*. Routledge Monographs in Classical Studies 17. New York: Routledge.

Wheatley, D., and M. Gillings. 2002. *Spatial Technology and Archaeology: The Archaeological Applications of GIS*. New York: Taylor and Francis. http://dx.doi.org/10.4324/9780203302392.

"Excessive Economies" and the Logics of Abundance

Genealogies of Wealth, Labor, and Social Power in Pre-Colonial Senegal

FRANÇOIS G. RICHARD

Elite control over property, production, economic surplus, and long-distance trade has been a central feature in archaeological scenarios of political complexity. Such was not always the case, however; in many parts of pre-colonial West Africa, where the widespread availability of land combined with relatively small, mobile populations posed headaches for would-be rulers (McIntosh 1999) and where conventional notions of dispossession, scarcity, and accumulation fall short of capturing the subtleties of political economy. Rather, mechanisms rooted in a broad ethos of abundance—collective ownership, horizontal redistribution, wealth in people/ knowledge, compositional forms of consumption—subtended the economic strategies of peasants and aristocrats alike. Using elements of Georges Bataille's (1991) "general economy," which draws on ideas of excess, dissipation, waste, and sacrifice, I examine broad trends in the organization of labor, wealth, and social power in northern Senegal during the past millennium and how those relationships were materialized in archaeological landscapes.

The account I present here is shaped by the partialities of available archaeological evidence. It follows the grooves of Senegal's archaeological record and reproduces its gaps. Archaeological remains are patterned unevenly in time, space, scale, and kind; altogether, they paint a discontinuous picture of long-term economic dynamics in Senegambia (see Richard 2009 for a history of archaeological research in Senegal). An earlier generation of scholars turned the bulk of their attention on the monumental funerary vestiges covering the northern half and coastal portions

DOI: 10.5876/9781607325949.c010

of the country (e.g., Descamps and Thilmans 1979; Thilmans and Descamps 2006; Thilmans, Descamps, and Khayat 1980). Excavations at a number of these megaliths and tumuli offer a slanted look into the living world of pre-Atlantic-era socioeconomic relations from the standpoint of those resting in death. Subsequent work at the end of the 1980s opened a new chapter in regional archaeology, driven by concerns for region-wide coverage, systematic research designs, and long-term material sequences. Scholarly focus shifted from the analysis of tombs and funerary remains to the study of settlement patterns, residential and craft production sites, and mundane artifact assemblages. This evidence has afforded a more robust sense of local economies and their articulation with wider worlds of exchange (e.g., Bocoum 2000; Bocoum and McIntosh 2002; Deschamps 2013; Gokee 2016; McIntosh, McIntosh, and Bocoum 1992; Richard 2007; Thiaw 1999). Recent research also extends pre-European contact data sets into the Atlantic and colonial periods, providing a chronicle of long-term changes and continuities over the past two millennia. Residential data and monumental landscapes, however, articulate with each other awkwardly; only in rare circumstances do both sets of vestiges overlap, spatially and temporally (see Magnavita and Thiaw 2015; McIntosh and McIntosh 1993 for explicit attempts to map these connections). The resulting tableau is a mosaic one: pockets of high evidential focus alternate with yawning zones of obscurity, with partial linkages loosely stringing sites, regions, and historical periods together.

While monumental and habitation data sets in Senegambia are not always evenly matched, they do condense different aspects of the historical construction of wealth in the region; more specifically, they preserve in material form the changing relationships among people, labor, and objects and their entwinement in trans-regional circuits of trade. What archaeological evidence suggests, in tandem with historical and ethnographic sources, is the centrality of *people* in economic calculi and value production in Senegal's past (Guyer 1993, 1995; Stahl 2004). As in other parts of West Africa, where commoners, juniors, and dependents often could and did "vote with their feet," people were precious economic resources. Their productive (and reproductive) capacities were harnessed, showcased, and mobilized toward elite projects. Through the amassment of abundant labor and its public dissipation, persons of authority defied the logics of utility to convert people symbolically and materially into political wealth.

As African societies grew entangled with local, regional, and intercontinental commerce, people near the coasts and far inland were traded for foreign, exotic goods, which were reinvested in the maintenance of social hierarchy and production of social relationships. Historically, human bondage was a fixture of regional labor systems, though the intensity of enslavement and the role of captives in economic production oscillated considerably over time. From ethnohistoric evidence

(Boulègue 2013; Pélissier 1966), we know that enslaved people were attached to elite households and tasked with domestic labor, military functions, concubinage, cultivation, and crafts production. They were also turned into human commodities that fed the voracious channels of Saharan and Atlantic commerce. Food growing, however, fell largely to free peasants. Among the latter as well, people (along with cattle) were a form of social capital, mobilized within and across lineages to leverage social debt and credit, consolidate group wealth, carry out collective projects, and accrue individual prestige (e.g., Gastellu 1981; Meillassoux 1975). And as peasant communities became implicated in external trade, then so did foreign objects begin to reframe local constructions of personhood, taste, and value (e.g., DeCorse 2001; Ogundiran and Falola 2007; Stahl 2001; Thomas 1991).

In what follows, I outline trends underwriting the ways configurations of people/labor/wealth have been made and remade in Senegal and the role that matters of abundance played in these long histories. By "abundance," I refer mostly to cultural orientations valuing plenitude and excess, rather than expectations of sparseness or finitude, in economic strategies. Ideas of abundance and scarcity are not necessarily exhaustive or mutually exclusive; rather, they cohabit with each other and are contingently called upon by different casts of actors to meet historical situations. "Abundance" also points to periods in Senegalese history where political economic circumstances fostered conditions of relative material prosperity.

To illustrate how ideas and conditions of abundance were mutually implicated and how those concepts informed economic history in Senegal, I zero in on three "moments" in the region's past, each providing a window into the workings of what, following Bataille, I call Senegal's "excessive economy." I first focus on the pre–contact era and how a central elite strategy of building wealth-through-people rested on leaving tangible transcripts of excessive labor: in the construction of massive monuments to the dead and through the profligate destruction of value in human sacrifice. I then examine how, during the era of the Atlantic trade from the 1450s to the 1850s, elites appeared to move away from enduring materializations of wealth on the landscape to rely on more episodic, distributed, or embodied performances of value creation focused on control over labor and the acquisition of imported goods. These resources were not just accumulated and hoarded. For instance, objects originating from external commerce were shared, redistributed, and ritually expended to build social obligations. While ritual killings of captives seemingly ceased during the Atlantic period, enslaved people were subjected to a new, unprecedented scale of human sacrifice, as tragic amounts of laboring bodies were swallowed into the belly of American plantation slavery. Lastly, I shift lenses to explore the flip side of this elite story of abundance, namely, the challenges posed by the expansion of material abundance—a new and growing world of commodities—to common people between the eighteenth and twentieth centuries. I briefly examine the implications of the "democratization" of Atlantic consumption for non-elite communities and the strategies put in place by elites to ward off the increasing accessibility of consumer goods brought about by Atlantic commerce. As it hops between these different moments, my treatment is necessarily synthetic and cuts widely across the canvas of historical process. My aim, in effect, is not to provide historical detail but to map in broad brushstrokes long-term continuities—and some departures—in regional histories of wealth and excess.

MATTERS OF ABUNDANCE IN WEST AFRICA'S PAST

Archaeologists have often foregrounded scarcity and the accumulation of finite resources as a key principle of economic and political development in the past. In conventional scenarios, would-be leaders sought to secure control over limited supplies of land, labor, food, trade goods, or technology and to convert their hold on resources into wealth, prestige, social stratification, and political authority. Mirroring the tenets of classic economic theory (Dugger and Peach 2009), sparseness is here assumed to be a basic fact of political economy. As indicated by Monica Smith (2012, this volume), however, scarcity is not a universal condition; rather, it is constructed in relation to culture, politics, and history. In this sense, scarcity only tells part of a complicated story, and equal consideration must be given to matters of abundance. Smith's observations ring particularly true for the West African past. Susan McIntosh (1999), for example, observes that the availability of land, small population levels, and human mobility imparted a distinct shape to political building in pre-colonial West Africa—such that the usual notions of dispossession, appropriation, exploitation of production, property restriction, and uneven accumulation do not quite capture the pulse of political economy (Herbst 2000). McIntosh does not discount the existence of disparity and hierarchy but suggests that they were intertwined with horizontal mechanisms rooted in a broad ethos of abundance, fertility, and complementarity. Ethnographic and historical evidence shows, for instance, that the collective management of property, strategies of wealth redistribution, an ideology of agricultural subsistence, ideas of self-sufficiency, concepts of "fair" access to resources, and the mobilization of people and knowledge played an important role in governing economic relations among different social groups in the post-contact period (Klein 1980).

Taking up Smith's challenge and McIntosh's argument, I draw on ideas of "abundance" to elucidate certain aspects of the cultural economy of Senegalese societies over the past 1,000 years or so. While conscious of archaeological phenomena and historical forces operating at the level of Senegal (and beyond), my observations are grounded in the small region of Siin (figure 10.1). Over the course of its history, the province has been variably at the forefront and background of regional cultural and economic transfers, and its archaeological record holds both central and oblique insights for our understanding of Senegal's past. The second millennium AD was an eventful, transformative period in Siin, which witnessed large-scale population movements, the emergence of centralized polities, linkages with regional and continental trading spheres, and gradual incorporation into worldwide economic networks prior to the advent of colonial rule in the 1850s and 1860s (Barry 1998; Boulègue 1987; Brooks 1993; Curtin 1975; Klein 1968, 1992; Searing 1993). If outside historical forces considerably altered the organization of local societies, they also braided with existing economic institutions to frame the experiences of resident communities. What resulted is a complex interplay of transformations and continuities in local understandings of wealth, labor, and value (e.g., Richard 2009, 2011). Because these transformations achieved various degrees of visibility in objects and architecture, archaeological evidence can shed suggestive, if impressionistic, light into the workings of West African economies. Archaeology is particularly informative about long-term, relatively stable principles of economic life that have left enduring signatures in rural landscapes. Amplified by other sources, material archives hint that a logic of abundance partly organized the circulation of people, things, riches, and power in Siin's past.

French philosopher Georges Bataille's writings on economy and sovereignty offer provocative ideas about the non-rational basis of growth and wealth, with relevance to Senegambian societies. Three points seem particularly useful for an analysis of pre-colonial West Africa: (1) the elevation of expenditure to a general foundation of political economy, or at least a set of processes critical to its operation; (2) the importance of destruction, sacrifice, and consumption in the making of social power; and (3) the fact that the principle of excess is not a primitive phenomenon but is found in ancient and modern economies alike.

"EXCESSIVE ECONOMIES": EXPENDITURE, DESTRUCTION, AND CONSUMPTION

Bataille's musings on "general economy" offer a provocative entrée into the workings of abundance and its relationship to the economic process. In his quirky book *The Accursed Share*, Bataille (1991) proposes a theory of political economy that starts not from the common premises of scarcity, utility, production, and rational calculation but from the opposite premises of excess seen in expenditure, profitless squandering, and consumptive waste. Bataille theorizes that social systems

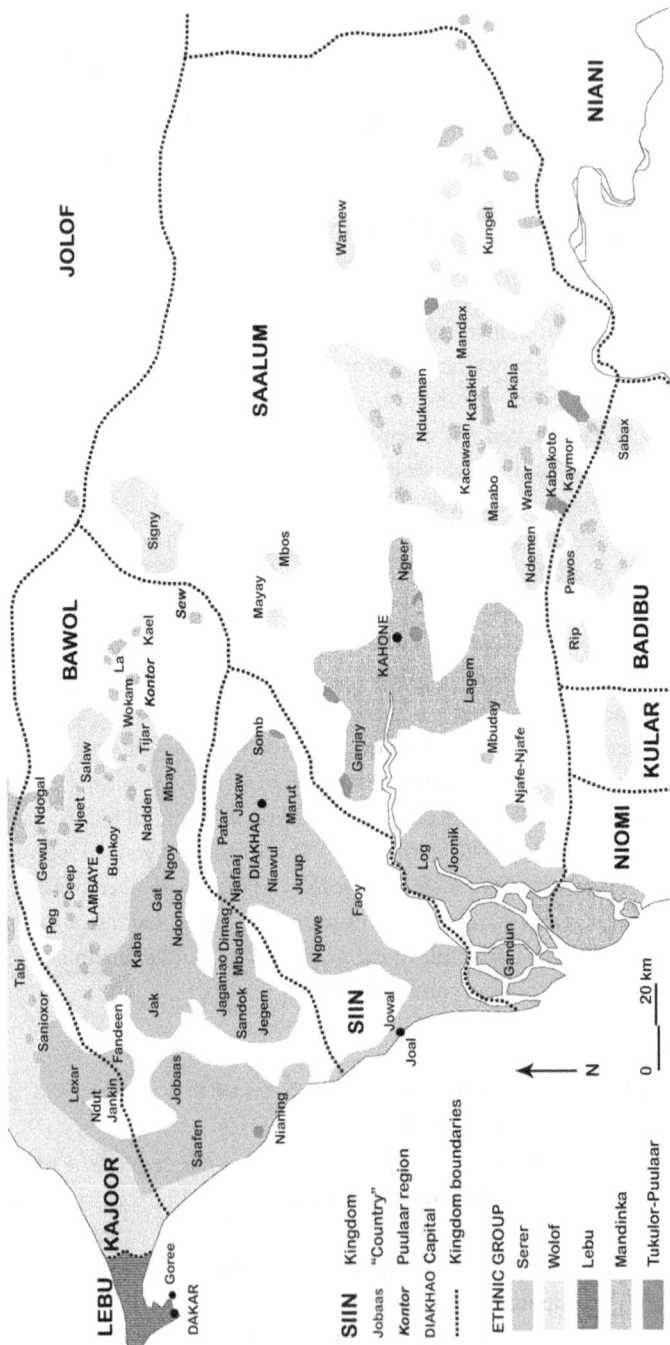

FIGURE 10.1. West-central Senegal, mid-nineteenth century: ethnic groups and kingdoms.

generate surpluses—of energy, goods, and even life. This abundance cannot be completely absorbed and must imperatively be dissipated instead. In a fairly sweeping ethnological gesture, which leapfrogs from pre-Columbian Mexico to the Marshall Plan, Bataille identifies historical examples of economic excess and various modes of release: ritual human sacrifice, the social obligations of gift exchange and reciprocity, potlatch-style tournaments of value, war and destruction, and conspicuous consumption.

I cannot review the subtleties of Bataille's model here, let alone its sometimes bizarre mix of economic analysis, metaphysics, ethics, and aesthetics or its philosophical closeness to and distance from other social thinkers. (For instance, while Bataille's work shows a passing resemblance to Veblen's interest in non-rational forms of consumption, he did not view excessive forms of waste as pernicious deviations from economic progress but instead as productive, possibly revolutionary activities unto their own; likewise, the importance he accorded to destruction, alongside production, departed from Marxist views; see Brantlinger and Higgins 2006; Stoekl 1985). At a very general level, however, Bataille's intuitions about the generative nature of expenditure *do* hit the mark for pre-colonial Senegal, where the destruction, discard, transfer, ostentation, and consumption of material riches played a key role in the economic life of indigenous societies.

While Senegambian political fields were structured in part around elite attempts to hoard precious resources and restrict their movement, these efforts were counterbalanced by strategies of wealth creation centered on the management and display of abundance. What emerges is a complex economy structured along a number of principles, whose most important axioms include: (1) ideologies of wealth based on material investments in labor, social relations, knowledge, and skills—what Africanists have called "wealth in people" (Guyer 1995; Miers and Kopytoff 1977; Miller 1988); (2) regimes of value structured not just on the quantitative accumulation of rare resources but also on the qualitative *composition* of diverse and abundant resources (Guyer 1993, 1996, 2004; Guyer and Belinga 1995); (3) a system of debt-credit relations, in which goods and services linked people together across social classes into a layered ecology of mutual obligations, reciprocity, and dependence (Searing 1993; see also Shipton 2007); and (4) an aesthetics of spectacle that revolved on public, ostentatious displays and consumptions of wealth that served the interests of power (Norman 2010; more generally, Inomata and Coben 2006). If, over time, elites proved largely successful in playing by the rules of the game and accruing economic clout, the nature of economic institutions introduced a degree of unpredictability into political power. Elite projects sometimes backfired, as prized resources bypassed the prescribed channels of tradition to create new possibilities for non-elite actors.

FIRST MOMENT: DEBT, LABOR, AND THE
EMERGENCE OF SOCIAL STRATIFICATION

My first "episode" is a very long one, spanning the length of the first millennium AD and the first part of the following millennium. It corresponds to the building and use of monumental vestiges in Senegal. Though numbers are not precise (and likely underestimates), close to 11,000 earthen tumuli (spread among nearly 1,450 sites) and over 16,900 megalithic formations (clustered into 1,965 sites) have been inventoried in the country, making them by far its most iconic archaeological vestiges (Martin and Becker 1974). These monuments show a great deal of geographic variability (figure 10.2). Tumuli occupy a wide area draping the northwestern part of Senegal (figure 10.3), while megalithic sites tend to cluster in a more confined pocket along the Middle Gambia River Valley. Both monument types are also remarkably heterogeneous with regard to form, contents, and material expression (Cros, Laporte, and Gallay 2013; Gallay, Pignat, and Curdy 1982; Holl and Bocoum 2006; Holl et al. 2007; Joire 1955; Laporte et al. 2012; Thilmans, Descamps, and Khayat 1980). To these, we should add a prodigiously large, uncounted amount of shell mounds dotting coastal and estuarine areas. These anthropogenic formations differ from other monumental remains in that they make up complexes of residential and cemetery remains and will not be examined here (see Linares de Sapir 1971 and Thilmans and Descamps 1982 for partial overviews). Tumuli and megaliths share two key characteristics: they are funerary contexts, and they represent the most extravagant displays of labor mobilization in the pre-colonial past.

While we do not know much about the societies that produced these vestiges because systematic examination of their links to residential sites and political landscapes is often lacking (but see Gallay 2010–11; Magnavita and Thiaw 2015), researchers have interpreted monumental sites as expressions of social stratification and chiefly power connected to the intensification of commerce between Senegambian polities and the Saharan ecumene (Gallay 2006, 2010; McIntosh 2001; more generally, see Mitchell 2005). This is suggested in part by the nature of inhumations and mortuary assemblages. While some monuments are individual or mass burials, many consist of a "central" inhumation made up of one or a small number of individuals with additional peripheral ones that range from a few bodies to dozens of deceased individuals. Using broad ethnological comparisons across West African societies (Gallay 2010, 2011:114–27), scholars have viewed tomb structure and skeleton arrangements as indications that peripheral bodies likely belonged to servants, slaves, or concubines (though more conclusive evidence would require systematic examination of skeletal morphology, pathology, and trauma and possibly stable isotope analysis between central and peripheral remains). Structural

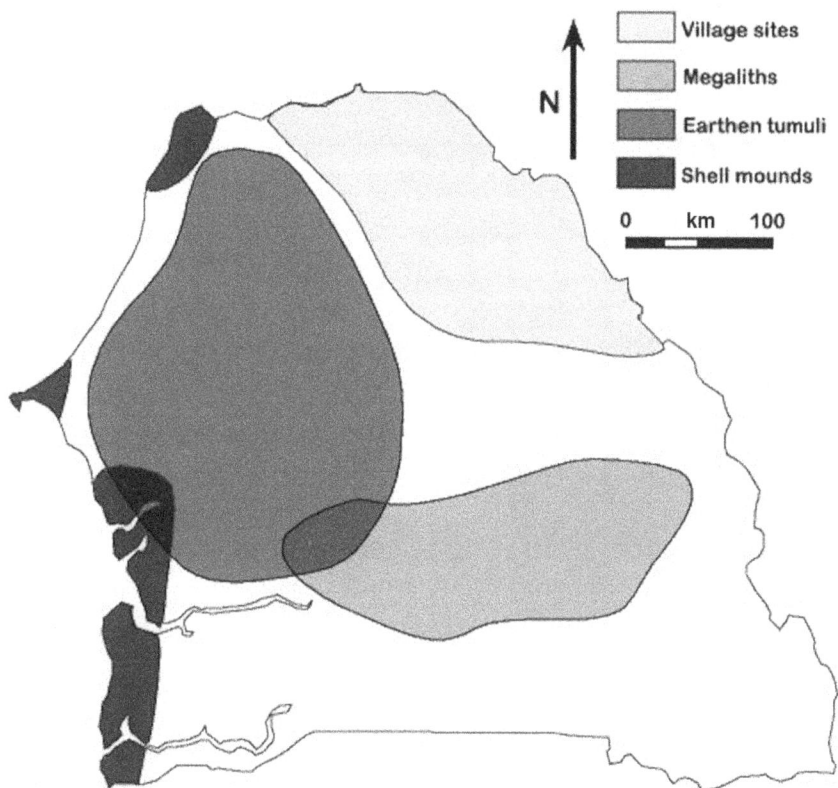

FIGURE 10.2. "Traditional" protohistoric provinces in Senegal.

remains also indicate the possible presence of "houses of the dead," huts of wood and thatch designed to protect the central interments (Cros, Laporte, and Gallay 2013). Tumulus burials often contain rich grave assemblages, including luxurious imports linked to the Saharan trade, such as copper or copper-based objects (ankle rings, bracelets, weapons), gold ornaments, and stone and glass beads (Garenne-Marot 1993; Thilmans and Descamps 2006).

The tombs' structural asymmetries and the labor involved in their construction support their function as embodiments of social power—in fact, they recall the royal sepultures described by Al-Bakrī for the famed ruler of Ghana in AD 1068 and Valentim Fernandes for Mandinka kings in the early 1500s (Becker and Martin 1982), with their lavish furnishings, human sacrifices, and wooden constructions covered by earthen mounds. The various forms of energy coiled into the tombs suggest complex strategies of power based on wealth transformation, materialization,

FIGURE 10.3. Mbacké earthen mound, McIntosh Survey 1988–89.

and ostentation. Moved by a regional "cosmology of externality" (to borrow from Newell 2012:167; also Helms 1988; Sahlins 1985), West Sahelian elites ascribed value to outside objects, locating power in their foreignness. Early leaders sought to harness the power of trade goods and convert them into the most valuable wealth of all—people—which could take the form of labor or social relations of obligation/dependence and patronage/clientelism, such as those contracted with followers, political allies, and kin (people also joined gold, salt, and textiles as the region's chief export and fueled a vibrant trans-Saharan slave trade, whose extent is still poorly known; Austen 2010). People and labor were, in turn, converted into other kinds of social power materialized through expenditures on monumental tombs, the stockpiling of trade luxuries, and the mass sacrifice of kin, servants, retainers, and slaves obligated to the king in life and death (note the similarity to scenarios presented in Bataille 1991). The conspicuous monumentalization of excess at the time of a leader's passing stamped the landscape with a most public statement of authority. Tumuli and megaliths, as material testaments of labor, wealth, and connection to a broader world associated with new elites, may have played the role of critical "places" of authority cemented through ritual ceremony at those sites (cf. MacDonald 1998).

While researchers have tended to associate funerary monuments with centralizing elites, some of these burial practices may have also taken root in relatively unstratified social settings. This may have been the case in Siin, where several seasons of survey have yielded no conclusive sign of political centralization prior to the 1400s AD. In surveyed areas, residential landscapes unfolded as (1) a highly dispersed horizon of small, relatively short-lived sites stretching thinly across the region, anchored by (2) a handful of very large, highly localized settlements clustering along the coast and river channels and occupied for long periods of time. These different levels of settlement appear to be horizontally organized rather than hierarchically ordered. Siin's political landscape at the time likely comprised shifting multi-generational village federations, formed by the coming together of residential sites and unformed as groups of residents broke off from larger communities (Richard 2007:648–49; cf. Kopytoff 1987). In these circumstances, projects of authority concentration among elites might have been counterpoised by a network of heterarchical institutions (e.g., Ehrenreich, Crumley, and Levy 1995).

Establishing clear connections between these settlement systems and monumental vestiges is difficult, however. The Siin does not have megalithic formations; tumuli are common in the countryside, though they tend to be small and widely dispersed. Local farmers distinguish between *podom* (large burial mounds built in the distant past) and *lomb* (small tombs associated with historical ancestors) (Becker and Martin 1982:282). Small tumuli are often found in the periphery of pre–Atlantic period habitation sites. A small number of surveyed settlements also featured large sand mounds. It is tempting to view the small size of tumuli and their disproportionate presence as another supporting argument for the existence of horizontally structured societies in the region. In the absence of excavated data, however, the nature of mound deposits in Siin and how they compare with tumuli elsewhere is obscure, as is the character of chronological and spatial associations with different types of residential sites.

More generally, evidence of reuse and secondary burials (Cros, Laporte, and Gallay 2013) evokes corporate funerary concessions, perhaps organized around lineage or clan principles, designed to preserve the memory and legacy of social collectivities—a practice documented historically in Siin (Corre 1883; Debien 1964). Conversely, ethnographic evidence of tumulus burial ceremonies from the late 1940s indicates that the height of the tumulus reflected the defunct's wealth in cattle or social influence—his capacity to mobilize labor in death through payments in livestock or debt/credit obligations (Lemire, in Joire 1955; see also Aujas 1925). Here again, we observe a logic of "wealth-in-people" and its materialization into visible portable goods, non-portable sections of the built landscape, and tangible manifestations of social relations.

SECOND MOMENT: THE ATLANTIC ERA AND NEW
POLITICS OF LABOR EXPENDITURE

The landing of Portuguese caravels on Senegal's shores in the 1440s sparked a reorientation in the gravity of commerce from the Sahara to the coast (Boulègue 1987; Brooks 1993). Oceanic exchanges grafted themselves onto an economy of both continuities and ruptures. One enduring feature of political worlds before and after the advent of Atlantic contacts was elites' continued reliance on long-distance trade—and the power of foreign things—for the building and consolidation of political authority. Historical archives are replete with mentions of local kings traveling to coastal trading posts to deal directly with Europeans and exchanging slaves for those precious commodities (horses, weaponry, iron, textiles, manufactured goods) inextricably entangled with practices of statecraft (e.g., Barbot 1992; Becker and Martin 1974, 1977; Thilmans 1971; Thilmans and Rossie 1969) (figure 10.4).

The most salient departure in strategies of social wealth is the abrupt decline of monumental burials, leading to their complete disappearance after the end of the fifteenth century. This disappearance is intriguing against the backdrop of the early Atlantic era, a time of state formation and concentration of royal power. What likely happened is that the new commercial order of Atlantic exchanges generated new ways of materializing wealth that replaced megaliths and tumuli. While local kings moved away from showy displays of labor and wealth hoarding, they did not abandon the logics of wealth-in-people and rituals of consumption. Instead, rulers and aristocratic families refocused their control over working bodies by investing new energy in the mobilization of human capital in the realm of the living (Miller 1988). Large slave retinues were accumulated and paraded as they took part in agriculture, craft production, and military service. At the same time, vast amounts of human life and labor *were* squandered through the channels of Atlantic slavery, in return for consumer goods (Baum 1999; Lane and MacDonald 2011; MacGaffey 1994; Palmié 1995; Shaw 2002). These new investments also adopted more qualitative expressions, manifested in the cultivation of social and political relations—a *wealth in relationships*, if you will (Piot 1991, 1996). Thus, the goods of Atlantic commerce were not simply retained and concentrated by rulers but rather were redistributed to noble families and slaves to secure alliances, loyalties, and dependencies (cf. Norman 2012).

The logic of proliferating social relations is also visible in the "bureaucratization" of political administration and the creation of a vast cadre of royal functionaries associated with the management of trade and operations of the kingdom (cf. Monroe 2007). Wealth-in-people was not just accumulative, however. It also rested on a *composition* of knowledge and skills (Guyer and Belinga 1995). Slaves were valued not just as abstract units of labor but also for their specific expertise as weavers,

FIGURE 10.4. King of Kajoor negotiating exchange fees with European merchant (Dapper, *Description de l'Afrique*, 1686) http://gallica.bnf.fr/ark:/12148/btv1b2300087h.item.f44.

potters, woodworkers, warriors, and so forth. Concurrently, at least early on, royal power also depended on the management of relationships with grassroots actors and institutions (Galvan 2004:54–59). Effective rule required the conciliation of capricious sacred and spiritual forces (Duchemin 1952), which means it required engagement with different types of expert knowledge controlled by land custodians, lineage heads, earth and rain priests, and ancestral caretakers, whose interests were not always aligned with those of the central power. This knitting together of human resources has left some archaeological traces.

Siin's residential landscape shows surprisingly little stratification during the eighteenth and nineteenth centuries, which strikes contradictory notes, since this period is described as one of ferocious state centralization (Richard 2012). What is interesting, however, is that if royal capitals do not stand out by their material grandeur, they become gravity centers of political intensity and spiritual energy. Survey around Diakhao, Siin's long-standing capital, reveals the emergence of a constellation of small satellite settlements in the eighteenth century, which oral traditions associate with craft specialists, slaves, cultivators, and various categories

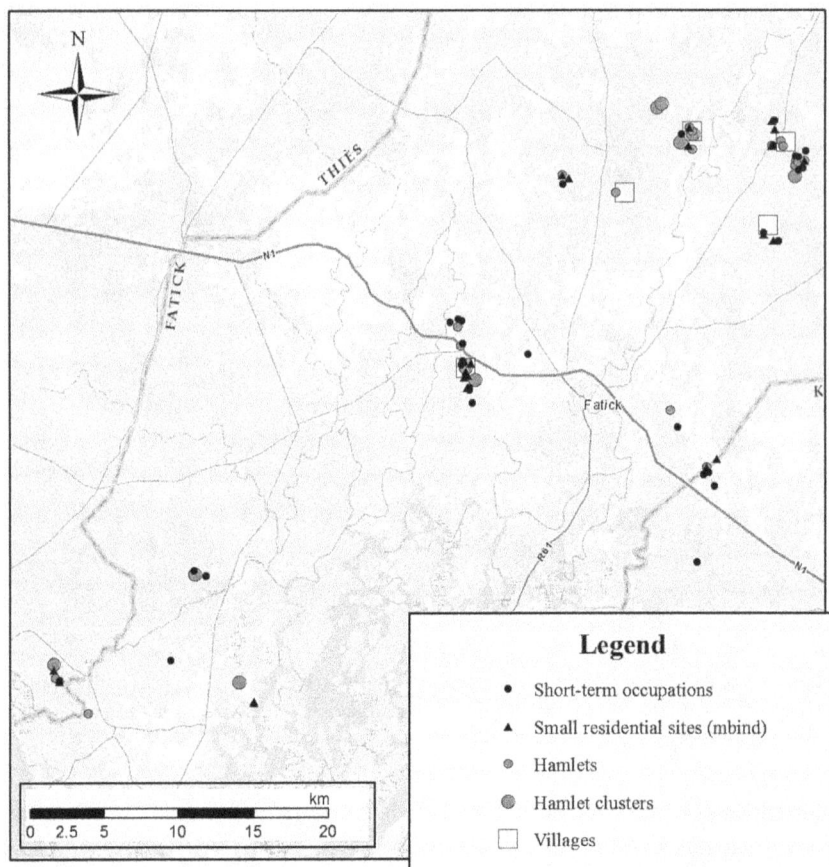

FIGURE 10.5. Residential landscapes, Central Siin, eighteenth–nineteenth centuries.

of nobles (figure 10.5). The built environment here materially translates a certain wealth-in-relations or wealth-in-composition, itself the telling sign of power. As I have argued elsewhere (Richard 2010), a similar logic of composition was at play in the reception of Atlantic commodities: African elites were less interested in the accumulation of a limited number of precious goods; rather, they reckoned value in diversity and preferred to buy assortments of different kinds of objects, illustrating the control Africans held over the terms of Atlantic exchange and consumption (Ogundiran 2002; Presholdt 2008; Stahl 2002).

Overall, the Atlantic period appears to have presided over a reconfiguration in regional economies of excess, from a visual register of power rooted partially in monumental displays and dissipations of labor to an aesthetics of statehood centered on more contingent performances and mobile signs of social wealth. Elites who took part in this new cosmology of rule converted regional forms of value (cattle hides, cotton textiles, and, later, enslaved people) into imported objects, which were in turn converted into the material, human, and symbolic substance of political power. Thus, the bounties of the Atlantic trade were translated into the accumulation of domestic captives; the constitution of slave armies, cavalry, and weapon arsenals; the acquisition of foreign exotics; practices of conspicuous consumption and feasting; the public performance of ostentatious political rituals; and the redistribution of imported goods to kin, allies, and political clients. These acts, in turn, fueled deeper participation in the slave trade, international commerce, regional diplomacy, and inter-kingdom warfare. This political aesthetics of "stateliness" (MacEachern 2015) pivoted on the "compelling visual presence" (Gates-Foster 2014) of plentiful things, people, and practices. Showy displays of slaves, objects, and followers were material signs recognized by non-elite populations as concrete emblems of authority. They also broadcast legitimate belonging in a shared economy of sovereignty to both rival and sympathetic polities.

THIRD MOMENT: PEASANTS AND THE "AMBIVALENCE" OF CONSUMPTION

Having spent a lot of time on elites, I now turn to other social classes and briefly examine how peasants experienced the changing world of goods inaugurated by the Atlantic era. Much historical literature depicts the Atlantic era as a tale of hardening aristocratic grip on the reins of power and economy (Klein 1992; Searing 1993). The seventeenth and eighteenth centuries were caught in political dynamics marked by the rise and fall of predatory kings and aristocratic families competing for the products and proceeds of trade. Peasants are often portrayed as the era's great losers, stuck in an economy of predation, enslavement, food crises, and social erosion that all but robbed them of historical agency (Barry 1998; Boulègue 2013).

My goal is not to contest this picture and the violence of the Atlantic system. There is more than enough historical—and archaeological (DeCorse 2001; Lane and MacDonald 2011)—evidence documenting the intensification of slave raiding and warfare, which led to insecurity, displacement, and famines as beleaguered peasant communities could no longer produce food to ensure social reproduction. Once defined by droughts, uneven rains, and locust infestations, food scarcity was a recurring reality after the 1740s (Becker 1986; cf. Logan 2012). What is more, a decade of archaeological surveys in Siin has produced good evidence of the atomization of social landscapes, marked in the region by unprecedented levels of short-lived residential sites, suggesting considerable human displacement and village mobility after the seventeenth century (Richard 2012).

I do, however, want to focus on aspects of the archaeological record that suggest a more resilient social world than the apocalyptic hellscape suggested in documentary archives, in which there is evidence for a dramatic rearticulation of peasant-aristocrat relations around trade and consumption. One of the great puzzles of Siin's archaeological assemblages in the eighteenth and nineteenth centuries is that they vastly increase in quantity and diversity compared to prior periods and that this increase is registered not only in settlements associated with elites but also in peasant communities. Despite the profoundly uneven character of peasant-aristocrat power relations and unquestionable expansion of royal power over time, a paradoxical effect of the Atlantic economy was that it brought about a greater "democratization" of local consumption, enabling commoners to access a world of foreign objects once restricted to aristocratic circles. Indeed, the eighteenth century witnessed European settlements' growing reliance on African communities to meet their food demands, which means that peasants would have been able to trade grain surpluses in return for iron, weaponry, dyed cloth and other manufactured goods—items that played a growing role in the making of village life (Searing 1993).

The fact that Atlantic products gradually percolated into other social strata is clear in the archaeological record, where eighteenth- and nineteenth-century village sites consistently feature abundant inventories of bottle glass, beads, metal objects, and tobacco pipes alongside local ceramics—powerful testaments of peasants' connection to a wider world. For example, the ubiquity of gin bottles on residential sites suggests the development of new non-elite tastes for certain kinds of liquor. Notwithstanding alcohol's potentially destructive impacts, empirical evidence also indicates that liquor was integrated into local practices of community and value making. The copious presence of nineteenth-century gin bottles on surveyed *pangool* (spiritual shrines) sites implies that imported liquor was invested in the propitiation of lineage ancestors, the maintenance of solidarities between the worlds of the living and the dead, and the ritual reproduction of social collectivities. More speculatively, the role alcohol plays today and in recent history in the management of services, obligations, and labor transfers suggests a similar role in pre-colonial settings (Gastellu 1981; see also Thomas 1991 on the ritual substitution of goods in colonial contexts).

The broadening of commoner consumption likely presented a threat to the architecture of aristocratic privilege, which rested on the nominal corralling of valuable connections to foreign objects and outside markets (Guyer 2004; also Frink 2009; Gregory 1982, on the role of trade goods in reconfiguring indigenous structures of authority). It provoked the development of new rituals of elite solidarity and consumption. Wary of commoners' access to relatively cheap trade liquor, the nobility seems to have reacted by regimenting the circulation of wine as a marker of elite taste.

This is suggested by deposits in a feasting pit located at the site of Ndiongolor, a known royal residence, where wine bottle sherds completely eclipsed gin bottle fragments, a reversal of usual proportions in material inventories (Richard 2010). The association of wine with performances of state making in oral traditions and with royal elites in nineteenth-century historical literature lends support to this picture.

There is, however, an ironic twist to this historical process. The "relative" climate of material prosperity created by the Atlantic economy confronted Siin's rural society with a number of contradictions—most important, among the reality (and allure) of expanded consumption, the dangers of dependence on outside markets for social reproduction (as foreign imports gradually redefined cultural, political, and spiritual practices), and a collective ethos of self-reliance and economic autonomy. If a certain abundance of goods contributed to the enhancement of material conditions for peasants during the nineteenth century—the largest villages documented archaeologically in Siin are peasant communities that emerged after the 1850s—it also created initial conditions for their subjugation to colonial rule and the erosion of economic autonomy (Klein 1968; Mbodj 1978). One of French administrators' great frustrations in the early decades of formal colonial occupation was that Siin peasants remained relatively self-sufficient food producers with very low levels of indebtedness (e.g., Noirot 1896; also Reinwald 1997). For these reasons, they remained fairly disengaged from colonial markets and relatively independent of colonial influence. For French observers, who believed the growing of cash crops and consumption of French commodities were the safest path to "civilizing the Natives," this was a problem (Galvan 2004; Richard 2011).

In subsequent decades, colonial policies relentlessly targeted agricultural subsistence in an attempt to force peasants' dependence on resources they no longer produced and obtained instead from colonial merchants. As rural social relations became gradually mediated by cash, debt, and commodities, colonial market penetration gradually eroded matrilineal holdings and kinship solidarities, disrupted subsistence economies, and reworked community relationships and generational dynamics. One disastrous legacy, still visible today, has been the dramatic rise of rural poverty. Where expanded horizons of consumption, mixed with responsible subsistence agriculture, once guaranteed a certain material abundance, a hundred years later it spelled the beginning of food insecurity, debt, and the conditions of scarcity (Lericollais 1999; cf. Twiss and Bogaard, this volume).

DISCUSSION: BRIEF NOTES ON EXCESS BEYOND SENEGAL

To what extent do Bataille's ideas of socially generative excess and expenditure advance our analysis of abundance elsewhere, and, more expansively, how might historical forms of wealth and value production observed in Africa help us think about past economies beyond the continent? Given that Bataille's views draw heavily on the ethnological literature (some of it, admittedly, a bit dated) of New World indigenous societies—chiefly, the Pacific Northwest and pre-Columbian Mexico—notions of productive waste might be usefully applied to the archaeological examination of political economy in other regions convulsed by Columbian contacts in North America, South America, and the Pacific. By extension, given the applicability to the Siin, an analysis of abundance might also complement the historical and anthropological models of value making used to flesh out the archaeological record of Atlantic Africa. I am thinking of its usefulness for understanding the relationship between materiality and social power in polities featuring rituals of human sacrifice (Monroe 2014; Rowlands 1993) and elaborate feasting spectacles (Fleisher 2010; Norman 2010); about the logics, paradoxes, and perversions of conversion among people, things, and value in times of engagement with broader economic spheres (Fleisher and Wynne-Jones 2010; Ogundiran 2002); and about debt/credit relations and their imprint on material worlds in the context of commercial slavery (Graeber 2011:chapter 6; Lane and MacDonald 2011). Conversely, African case studies can also help to fine-tune, historicize, and contextualize Bataille's general musings on the economy, if only to recognize the existence of different strategies of expenditure between social classes and their changing articulation with social principles of parsimony or frugality.

One can note interesting convergences between economic trajectories and ways of handling (conceptually and materially) the challenges of abundance in societies of Africa and Native America. Mutual insights can be found, for instance, in the domains of ritual economy (Wells and McAnany 2008), cultural mobilizations of excess labor (Pauketat 2004), and approaches to the management of surplus (see, for instance, Morehart and DeLucia 2015, including chapters by Stahl and Norman on West Africa). One may also stress the broad relevance of African orientations to value creation—especially notions of people-as-wealth and composition across quality/quantity—to the historical experiences of various Native American groups as they negotiated the travails of colonial entanglement (see Turgeon 1997, 2004; Graeber 2001:chapter 5; Loren 2009; Zedeño 2009, for a short selection).

CONCLUSION

I want to finish with two thoughts. First, what I find uniquely compelling in Bataille's account of general economy is that it does not accept scarcity as a universal condition and insists that the principle of excess is not a primitive phenomenon but is found in ancient and modern economies alike. Such insistence on the historical specificity of lack and the long-term genealogy of abundance is particularly attractive for researchers working in Africa, where the vocabulary of crisis, poverty, penury, famine, and scarcity is often elevated to a Gospel of historical and existential truth (James 2014; Makhulu, Buggenhagen, and Jackson 2012; Piot 2010; Roitman 2016). Notions of inherent scarcity are also used to naturalize Africa's anomaly in the great narrative of universal modernity. Taking a long view of economic practices, however, one equally attuned to African cultural responses and adaptations to shifts in resources, stands to historicize conventional wisdom about the continent's ailments. Such a challenge can be found in Amanda Logan's (2012, 2016) path-breaking analysis of foodways in central Ghana, which documents the dynamic fate of food practices over the past millennium to demonstrate that the food insecurity problems of the present arose only recently. In a more historical vein, geographer Michael Watts (2013) has "denaturalized" conditions of climatic hazard in Nigeria's recent past to demonstrate the colonial fashioning of shortage, famine, and lack among local peasantries.

A second point is that Africa is not a cul-de-sac of anthropological theory but instead an origin point. In their book *Theory from the South*, anthropologists Jean Comaroff and John Comaroff have argued provocatively against the common intuition that Africa has historically been divorced from the world, that the world might actually be evolving toward Africa (Comaroff and Comaroff 2012). Their point is that if in recent years Africa has been sidelined in comparative discussions of critical conceptual questions, the African continent was once a rich bed of inspiration for ethnographic thinking, and it should be recuperated as a valuable source of anthropological ideas for the rest of the world. While the argument concerns contemporary times, perhaps it can be reframed to encompass the past. In this spirit, I would like to think that some of the concepts crafted in Africanist workshops—ideas of wealth-in-people, composition, debt/credit obligations, labor expenditure—might hold useful insights about economic process in general and inspire provocative thoughts about the dynamics of abundance and scarcity in societies elsewhere.

REFERENCES CITED

Aujas, Louis. 1925. "Funérailles Royales et Ordre de Succession chez les Sérères du Sine." *Bulletin du Comité d'Études Historiques et Scientifiques de l'A.O.F.* 8: 501–8.

Austen, Ralph. 2010. *Trans-Saharan Africa in World History*. New York: Oxford University Press.

Barbot, John. 1992 [1678–1712]. *Barbot on Guinea: The Writing of Jean Barbot on West Africa 1678–1712*. London: Hakluyt Society.

Barry, Boubacar. 1998. *Senegambia and the Atlantic Slave Trade*. New York: Cambridge University Press.

Bataille, Georges. 1991. *Consumption*, vol. 1: *The Accursed Share: An Essay on General Economy*. London: Zone Books.

Baum, Robert. 1999. *Shrines of the Slave Trade: Diola Religion and Society in Precolonial Senegambia*. New York: Oxford University Press.

Becker, Charles. 1986. "Conditions écologiques, crises de subsistance et histoire de la population à l'époque de la traité esclaves en Senegambie (17e–18e siècle)." *Canadian Journal of African Studies* 20 (3): 357–76. Medline:11634787 http://dx.doi.org/10.2307/484447.

Becker, Charles, and Victor Martin. 1974. "Mémoire Inédit de Doumet (1769): Le Kayor et les Pays Voisins au cours de la Seconde Moitié du XVIIIe Siècle." *Bulletin de l'IFAN* (sér. B) 36 (1): 25–92.

Becker, Charles, and Victor Martin. 1977. "Détails Historiques et Politiques, Mémoire Inédit de J. A. le Brasseur." *Bulletin de l'IFAN* (sér. B) 39: 81–132.

Becker, Charles, and Victor Martin. 1982. "Rites de Sépulture Préislamique au Sénégal et Vestiges Protohistoriques." *Archives Suisses d'Anthropologie Générale* 46: 261–93.

Bocoum, Hamadi. 2000. *L'Âge de Fer au Sénégal: Histoire et Archéologie*. Nouakchott, Mauritania: CRIAA.

Bocoum, Hamadi, and Susan K. McIntosh. 2002. *Fouilles à Sincu Bara, Moyenne Vallée du Sénégal. Excavations at Sincu Bara, Middle Senegal Valley (Senegal)*. Dakar: CRIAA, Université de Nouakchott–IFAN / Cheikh Anta Diop.

Boulègue, Jean. 1987. *Le Grand Jolof (XIIIe–XVIe Siècle)*. Blois, France: Éditions Façades.

Boulègue, Jean. 2013. *Les Royaumes Wolof dans l'Espace Sénégambien (XIIIe au XVIIIe Siècle)*. Paris: Karthala.

Brantlinger, Patrick, and Richard Higgins. 2006. "Waste and Value: Thorstein Veblen and H. G. Wells." *Criticism* 48 (4): 453–75. http://dx.doi.org/10.1353/crt.2008.0005.

Brooks, George. 1993. *Landlords and Strangers: Ecology, Society, and Trade in Western Africa, 1000–1630*. Boulder: Westview.

Comaroff, Jean, and John L. Comaroff. 2012. *Theory from the South: Or, How Is Euro-America Evolving toward Africa*. Boulder: Paradigm.

Corre, Armand. 1883. "Les Sérères de Joal et de Portudal (Côte Occidentale d'Afrique): Esquisse Ethnographique." *Revue d'Ethnographie* 2: 1–20.

Cros, Jean-Paul, Luc Laporte, and Alain Gallay. 2013. "Pratiques Funéraires dans le Mégalithisme Sénégambien: Décryptages et Révisions." *Afrique: Archéologie and Arts* 9: 67–84.

Curtin, Philip D. 1975. *Economic Change in Precolonial Africa: Senegambia in the Era of the Slave Trade*. Madison: University of Wisconsin Press.

Debien, Gabriel. 1964. "Journal du Docteur Corre en Pays Sérère (Décembre 1876–Janvier 1877)." *Bulletin de l'IFAN* (sér. B) 26 (3–4): 532–99.

DeCorse, Christopher, ed. 2001. *West Africa during the Atlantic Slave Trade: Archaeological Perspectives*. New York: Leicester University Press.

Descamps, Cyr, and Guy Thilmans. 1979. "Les Tumulus Coquilliers des Îles du Saloum (Sénégal)." *Bulletin de l'ASEQUA* 54–55: 81–91.

Deschamps, Sandrine. 2013. "Les Groupes Culturels du Néolithique et de l'Âge du Fer des Régions de Louga, Thiès, et Saint-Louis, Sénégal (du Vième Millénaire avant J.-C. au Vième Siècle après J.-C.): Approche Taphonomique et Archéologique." PhD dissertation, Université de Paris I Panthéon–Sorbonne.

Duchemin, Georges J. 1952. "L'Organisation Religieuse et son Rôle Politique dans le Royaume Sérère du Sine (Sénégal)." *Conferencia Internacional dos Africanistas Occidentais* (2a. Conf. Bissau 1947) 5: 369–76.

Dugger, Wiliam M., and James T. Peach. 2009. *Abundance: An Introduction*. Armonk, NY: M. E. Sharpe.

Ehrenreich, Robert, Carole L. Crumley, and Janet E. Levy, eds. 1995. *Heterarchy and the Analysis of Complex Societies*. Arlington, VA: American Anthropological Association.

Fleisher, Jeffrey. 2010. "Rituals of Consumption and the Politics of Feasting on the Eastern African Coast, AD 700–1500." *Journal of World Prehistory* 23 (4): 195–217. http://dx.doi .org/10.1007/s10963-010-9041-3.

Fleisher, Jeffrey, and Stephanie Wynne-Jones. 2010. "Authorization and the Process of Power: The View from African Archaeology." *Journal of World Prehistory* 23 (4): 177–93. http://dx.doi.org/10.1007/s10963-010-9038-y.

Frink, Liam M. 2009. "The Social Role of Technology in Coastal Alaska." *International Journal of Historical Archaeology* 13 (3): 282–302. http://dx.doi.org/10.1007/s10761-009 -0081-2.

Gallay, Alain. 2006. "Le Mégalithisme Sénégambien: Une Approche Logiciste." In *Senegalia: Études sur le Patrimoine Ouest-Africain: Hommage à Guy Thilmans*, edited by Cyr Descamps and Adboulaye Camara, 205–23. Saint-Maur-des-Fossés: Éditions SÉPIA.

Gallay, Alain. 2010. "Rites Funéraires Mégalithiques Sénégambiens et Sociétés Africaines Précoloniales: Quelles Compatibilités?" *Bulletins et Memoires de la Société d'Anthropologie de Paris* 22 (1–2): 84–102. http://dx.doi.org/10.1007/s13219-010 -0010-2.

Gallay, Alain. 2010–2011. "La Nécropole de Mbolop Tobé (Santhiou Kohel, Sénégal) dans le Contexte du Mégalithisme Sénégambien." 5 vols. Unpublished Field Report.

Gallay, Alain. 2011. *Les Sociétés Mégalithiques: Pouvoir des Hommes, Mémoires des Morts*. Lausanne: Presses Polytechniques et Universitaires Romandes.

Gallay, Alain, Gervaise Pignat, and Philippe Curdy. 1982. "M'Bolop Tobé, Santhiou Kohel (Sénégal): Contribution à la Connaissance du Mégalithisme Sénégambien." *Archives Suisses d'Anthropologie Générale* 46: 217–59.

Galvan, Dennis C. 2004. *The State Must Be Our Master of Fire: How Peasants Craft Culturally Sustainable Development*. Berkeley: University of California Press.

Garenne-Marot, Laurence. 1993. "Archéologie d'un Métal: Le Cuivre en Sénégambie entre le Xème et le XIVème Siècle." PhD dissertation, Université Paris 8, Panthéon-Sorbonne.

Gastellu, Jean-Marc. 1981. *L'Égalitarisme Économique des Serer du Sénégal*. Travaux et Documents de l'ORSTOM. Paris: ORSTOM.

Gates-Foster, Jennifer. 2014. "Abundance and Innovation in the Production of Roman Tablewares." Paper presented at the Society for American Archaeology Meeting, Austin, TX, April 23–27.

Gokee, Cameron. 2016. *Assembling the Village in Medieval Bambuk: An Archaeology of Interaction at Diouboye, Senegal*. Bristol, CT: Equinox.

Graeber, David. 2001. *Toward an Anthropological Theory of Value*. New York: Palgrave. http://dx.doi.org/10.1057/9780312299064.

Graeber, David. 2011. *Debt: The First 5,000 Years*. New York: Melville House.

Gregory, Chris. 1982. *Gifts and Commodities*. New York: Academic.

Guyer, Jane I. 1993. "Wealth in People and Self-Realization in Equatorial Africa." *Man* 28 (2): 243–65. http://dx.doi.org/10.2307/2803412.

Guyer, Jane I. 1995. "Wealth in People, Wealth in Things: Introduction." *Journal of African History* 36 (1): 83–90. http://dx.doi.org/10.1017/S0021853700026980.

Guyer, Jane I. 1996. "Traditions of Invention in Equatorial Africa." *African Studies Review* 39 (3): 1–28.

Guyer, Jane I. 2004. *Marginal Gains: Monetary Transactions in Atlantic Africa*. Chicago: University of Chicago Press.

Guyer, Jane I., and Samuel M. Eno Belinga. 1995. "Wealth in People as Wealth in Knowledge: Accumulation and Composition in Equatorial Africa." *Journal of African History* 36 (1): 91–120. http://dx.doi.org/10.1017/S0021853700026992.

Helms, Mary. 1988. *Ulysses' Sail: An Ethnographic Odyssey of Power, Knowledge, and Geographical Distance*. Princeton, NJ: Princeton University Press. http://dx.doi.org/10.1515/9781400859542.

Herbst, Jeffrey. 2000. *State and Power in Africa*. Princeton, NJ: Princeton University Press.

Holl, Augustin, and Hamady Bocoum. 2006. "Variabilité des Pratiques Funéraires dans le Mégalithisme Sénégambien: Le Cas de Sine-Ngayène." In *Senegalia: Études sur le Patrimoine Ouest-Africain: Hommage à Guy Thilmans*, edited by Cyr Descamps and Abdoulaye Camara, 224–34. Saint-Maur-des-Fossés: Éditions SÉPIA.

Holl, Augustin, Hamady Bocoum, Stephen Dueppen, and Daphne Gallagher. 2007. "Switching Mortuary Codes and Ritual Programs: The Double-Monolith-Circle from Sine-Ngayène, Senegal." *Journal of African Archaeology* 5 (1): 127–48. http://dx.doi.org /10.3213/1612-1651-10088.

Inomata, Takeshi, and Lawrence Coben, eds. 2006. *Archaeology of Performance: Theaters of Power, Community, and Politics*. Lanham, MD: Altamira.

James, Deborah. 2014. *Money from Nothing: Indebtedness and Aspiration in South Africa*. Stanford, CA: Stanford University Press.

Joire, Jean. 1955. "Découvertes Archéologiques dans la Région de Rao (Bas-Sénégal)." *Bulletin de l'IFAN* (ser. B) 17: 249–333.

Klein, Martin. 1968. *Islam and Imperialism in Sine: Sine-Saloum, 1847–1914*. Stanford, CA: Stanford University Press.

Klein, Martin, ed. 1980. *Peasants in Africa: Historical and Contemporary Perspectives*. Beverly Hills: Sage.

Klein, Martin. 1992. "The Impact of the Atlantic Slave Trade on the Societies of the Western Sudan." In *The Atlantic Slave Trade: Effects in Economies, Societies, and Peoples in Africa, the Americas, and Europe*, edited by Joseph E. Inikori and Stanley L. Engerman, 25–47. Durham, NC: Duke University Press. http://dx.doi.org/10.1215/9780822382379-002.

Kopytoff, Igor. 1987. "The Internal African Frontier: The Making of African Political Culture." In *The African Frontier: The Reproduction of Traditional African Societies*, edited by Igor Kopytoff, 3–84. Bloomington: Indiana University Press.

Lane, Paul, and Kevin MacDonald, eds. 2011. *Slavery in Africa: Archaeology and Memory*. Oxford: Oxford University Press. http://dx.doi.org/10.5871/bacad/9780197264782 .001.0001.

Laporte, Luc, H. Bocoum, J.-P. Cros, A. Delvoye, R. Bernard, M. Diallo, M. Diop, A. Kane, V. Dartois, M. Lejay et al. 2012. "Megalithic Monumentality in Africa: From Graves to Stone Circles at Wanar, Senegal." *Antiquity* 86 (332): 409–27. http://dx.doi.org/10.1017 /S0003598X00062840.

Lericollais, André, ed. 1999. *Paysans Sereer: Dynamiques Agraires et Mobilités au Sénégal*. Paris: Editions de l'IRD.

Linares de Sapir, Olga. 1971. "Shell Middens of Lower Casamance and Problems of Diola Prehistory." *West African Journal of Archaeology* 1: 23–54.

Logan, Amanda. 2012. "A History of Food without History: Food, Trade, and Environment in West-Central Ghana in the Second Millennium AD." PhD dissertation, University of Michigan, Ann Arbor. http://dx.doi.org/10.1080/13545701.2012.728341.

Logan, Amanda. 2016. "'Why People Can't Feed Themselves': Archaeology as Alternative Archive of Food Security in Banda, Ghana." *American Anthropologist* 118 (3): 508–24.

Loren, Diana DiPaolo. 2009. "Material Manipulations: Beads and Cloth in the French Colonies." In *The Materiality of Individuality*, edited by Caroline White, 109–24. New York: Springer. http://dx.doi.org/10.1007/978-1-4419-0498-0_7.

MacDonald, Kevin. 1998. "Before the Empire of Ghana: Pastoralism and the Origins of Cultural Complexity in the Sahel." In *Transformations in Africa: Essays on Africa's Later Past*, edited by Graham Connah, 71–103. London: Leicester University Press.

MacEachern, Scott A. 2015. "What Was the Wandala State?" In *Ethnic Ambiguities and the African Past: Materiality, History, and the Shaping of Cultural Identities*, edited by François G. Richard and Kevin McDonald, 172–91. London: Left Coast.

MacGaffey, Wyatt. 1994. "Dialogues of the Deaf: Europeans on the Atlantic Coast of Africa." In *Implicit Understandings*, edited by Stuart Schwartz, 249–67. Cambridge: Cambridge University Press.

Magnavita, Sonja, and Ibrahima Thiaw. 2015. "Nouvelles Recherches Archeologique dans la Zone des Tumuli du Sénégal." *Nyame Akuma* 83: 3–10.

Makhulu, Anne-Maria, Beth Buggenhagen, and Stephen Jackson, eds. 2012. *Hard Work, Hard Times: Global Volatility and African Subjectivities*. Chicago: University of Chicago Press.

Martin, Victor, and Charles Becker. 1974. "Vestiges Protohistoriques et Occupation Humaine au Sénégal." *Annales de Demographie Historique* 1974 (1): 403–29. http://dx.doi.org/10.3406/adh.1974.1246.

Mbodj, Mohamed. 1978. "Un Exemple d'Économie Coloniale. Le Sine-Saloum et l'Arachide, 1870–1940." PhD dissertation, University Paris VII, Paris.

McIntosh, Susan K. 2001. "Tools for Understanding Transformation and Continuity in Senegambian Society: AD 1500–1900." In *West Africa during the Atlantic Slave Trade: Archaeological Perspectives*, edited by Christopher R. DeCorse, 14–37. London: Continuum.

McIntosh, Susan K., ed. 1999. *Beyond Chiefdoms: Pathways to Complexity in Africa*. New York: Cambridge University Press. http://dx.doi.org/10.1017/CBO9780511558238.

McIntosh, Susan K., and Roderick J. McIntosh. 1993. "Field Survey in the Tumulus Zone of Senegal." *African Archaeological Review* 11 (11): 73–107. http://dx.doi.org/10.1007/BF01118143.

McIntosh, Susan K., Roderick J. McIntosh, and Hamadi Bocoum. 1992. "The Middle Senegal Valley Project: Preliminary Results from the 1990–91 Field Season." *Nyame Akuma* 38: 47–61.

Meillassoux, Claude. 1975. *Femmes, Greniers, et Capitaux*. Paris: Maspéro.

Miers, Suzanne, and Igor Kopytoff, eds. 1977. *Slavery in Africa: Historical and Anthropological Perspectives*. Madison: University of Wisconsin Press.

Miller, Joseph C. 1988. *Way of Death: Merchant Capitalism and the Angolan Slave Trade, 1730–1830*. Madison: University of Wisconsin Press.

Mitchell, Peter. 2005. *African Connections: Archaeological Perspectives on Africa and the Wider World*. Walnut Creek, CA: Altamira.

Monroe, J. Cameron. 2007. "Continuity, Revolution, or Evolution on the Slave Coast of West Africa? Royal Architecture and Political Order in Pre-Colonial Dahomey." *Journal of African History* 48 (3): 349–73. http://dx.doi.org/10.1017/S0021853707002800.

Monroe, J. Cameron. 2014. *The Precolonial State in Africa: Building Power in Dahomey*. New York: Cambridge University Press. http://dx.doi.org/10.1017/CBO9781139628709.

Morehart, Christopher, and Kristin De Lucia, eds. 2015. *Surplus: The Politics of Production and the Strategies of Everyday Life*. Boulder: University Press of Colorado. http://dx.doi .org/10.5876/9781607323808.

Newell, Sasha. 2012. *The Modernity Bluff: Crime, Consumption, and Citizenship in Côte d'Ivoire*. Chicago: University of Chicago Press. http://dx.doi.org/10.7208/chicago /9780226575216.001.0001.

Noirot, Ernest. 1896. "Rapport Politique et Économique (10 April 1896)." Archives Nationales du Sénégal, Dakar, 13 G 327, no. 5.

Norman, Neil. 2010. "Feasts in Motion: Archaeological Views of Parades, Ancestral Pageants, and Socio-Political Process in the Hueda Kingdom, 1650–1727 AD." *Journal of World Prehistory* 23 (4): 239–54. http://dx.doi.org/10.1007/s10963-010-9037-z.

Norman, Neil. 2012. "From the Shadow of an Atlantic Citadel: An Archaeology of the Huedan Countryside." In *Power and Landscape in Atlantic West Africa: Archaeological Perspectives*, edited by J. Cameron Monroe and Akinwumi Ogundiran, 142–66. New York: Cambridge University Press. http://dx.doi.org/10.1017/CBO9780511921032.008.

Ogundiran, Akinwumi. 2002. "Of Small Things Remembered: Beads, Cowries, and Cultural Translations of the Atlantic Experience in Yorubaland." *International Journal of African Historical Studies* 35 (2–3): 427–57. http://dx.doi.org/10.2307/3097620.

Ogundiran, Akinwumi, and Toyin Falola, eds. 2007. *Archaeology of the Atlantic Africa and the African Diaspora*. Bloomington: Indiana University Press.

Palmié, Stephan. 1995. "A Taste for Human Commodities: Experiencing the Atlantic System." In *Slave Cultures and the Cultures of Slavery*, edited by Stephan Palmié, 40–54. Knoxville: University of Tennessee Press.

Pauketat, Timothy R. 2004. "The Economy of the Moment: Cultural Practices and Mississippian Chiefdoms." In *Archaeological Perspectives on Political Economies*, edited by Gary M. Feinman and Linda M. Nicholas, 25–39. Salt Lake City: University of Utah Press.

Pélissier, Paul. 1966. *Paysans du Sénégal: Les Civilisations Agraires du Cayor à la Casamance*. St. Yrieix, France: Imprimeria Fabrègue.

Piot, Charles. 1991. "Of Persons and Things: Some Reflections on African Spheres of Exchange." *Man* 26 (3): 405–24. http://dx.doi.org/10.2307/2803875.

Piot, Charles. 1996. "Of Slaves and the Gift: Kabre Sale of Kin during the Era of the Slave Trade." *Journal of African History* 37 (1): 31–49. http://dx.doi.org/10.1017/S0021853700034782.

Piot, Charles. 2010. *Nostalgia for the Future: West Africa after the Cold War*. Chicago: University of Chicago Press. http://dx.doi.org/10.7208/chicago/9780226669663.001.0001.

Presholdt, Jeremy. 2008. *Domesticating the World: African Consumerism and the Genealogies of Globalization*. Berkeley: University of California Press.

Reinwald, Birgit. 1997. " 'Though the Earth Does Not Lie': Agricultural Transitions in Siin (Senegal) during Colonial Rule." *Paideuma* 43: 143–69.

Richard, François G. 2007. "From Cosaan to Colony: Exploring Archaeological Landscape Formations and Socio-Political Complexity in the Siin (Senegal) AD 500–1900." PhD dissertation, Syracuse University, Syracuse, NY.

Richard, François G. 2009. "Historical and Dialectical Perspectives on the Archaeology of Complexity in the Siin-Saalum (Senegal): Back to the Future?" *African Archaeological Review* 26 (2): 75–135. http://dx.doi.org/10.1007/s10437-009-9050-8.

Richard, François G. 2010. "Re-Charting Atlantic Encounters: Object Trajectories and Histories of Value in the Siin (Senegal) and Senegambia." *Archaeological Dialogues* 17 (1): 1–27. http://dx.doi.org/10.1017/S1380203810000036.

Richard, François G. 2011. "We Will Find Very Desirable Tributaries for Our Commerce: Cash Crops, Commodities, and Subjectivities in Siin (Senegal) during the Colonial Era." In *The Archaeology of Capitalism in Colonial Contexts*, edited by Sarah Croucher and Lindsay Weiss, 193–218. New York: Plenum. http://dx.doi.org/10.1007/978-1-4614-0192-6_9.

Richard, François G. 2012. "Political Transformations and Cultural Landscapes in Senegambia during the Atlantic Era: An Alternative View from the Siin (Senegal)?" In *Power and Landscape in Atlantic West Africa: Archaeological Perspectives*, edited by J. Cameron Monroe and Akinwumi Ogundiran, 78–114. New York: Cambridge University Press. http://dx.doi.org/10.1017/CBO9780511921032.006.

Roitman, Janet. 2016. "Africa, Otherwise." In *African Futures: Essays on Crisis, Emergence, and Possibility*, edited by Brian Goldestone and Juan Obarrio, 23–38. Chicago: University of Chicago Press.

Rowlands, Michael J. 1993. "The Good and Bad Death: Ritual Killing and Historical Transformation in a West African Kingdom." *Paideuma* 39: 291–301.

Sahlins, Marshall. 1985. *Islands of History*. Chicago: University of Chicago Press.

Searing, James F. 1993. *West African Slavery and Atlantic Commerce: The Senegal River Valley, 1700–1860*. New York: Cambridge University Press. http://dx.doi.org/10.1017/CBO9780511572784.

Shaw, Rosalind. 2002. *Memories of the Slave Trade: Ritual and the Historical Imagination in Sierra Leone*. Chicago: University of Chicago Press.

Shipton, Parker. 2007. *The Nature of Entrustment: Intimacy, Exchange, and the Sacred in Africa*. New Haven, CT: Yale University Press.

Smith, Monica. 2012. "Seeking Abundance: Consumption as a Motivating Factor in Cities Past and Present." *Research in Economic Anthropology* 32: 27–51. http://dx.doi.org/10 .1108/S0190-1281(2012)0000032006.

Stahl, Ann B. 2001. *Making History in Banda: Anthropological Visions of Africa*. New York: Cambridge University Press. http://dx.doi.org/10.1017/CBO9780511489600.

Stahl, Ann B. 2002. "Colonial Entanglements and the Practices of Taste: An Alternative to Logocentric Approaches." *American Anthropologist* 104 (3): 827–45. http://dx.doi.org /10.1525/aa.2002.104.3.827.

Stahl, Ann B. 2004. "Political Economic Mosaics: Archaeology of the Last Two Millennia in Tropical Sub-Saharan Africa." *Annual Review of Anthropology* 33 (1): 145–72. http://dx.doi.org/10.1146/annurev.anthro.33.070203.143841.

Stoekl, Allan. 1985. "Introduction." In *Visions of Excess: Selected Writings, 1927–1939*, by Georges Bataille, ix–xxv. Minneapolis: University of Minnesota Press.

Thiaw, Ibrahima. 1999. "An Archeological Investigation of Long-Term Culture Change in the Lower Falemmé (Upper Senegal Region), AD 500–1900." PhD dissertation, Rice University, Houston, TX.

Thilmans, Guy. 1971. "Le Sénégal dans l'Oeuvre d'Olfried Dapper." *Bulletin de l'IFAN* (sér. B) 33 (3): 508–63.

Thilmans, Guy, and Cyr Descamps. 1982. "Amas et Tumulus Coquilliers du Delta du Saloum." In *Recherches Scientifiques dans les Parcs Nationaux du Sénégal*, 31–50. Mémoire de l'Institut Fondamental d'Afrique Noire 92. Dakar: IFAN.

Thilmans, Guy, and Cyr Descamps. 2006. "Fouille d'un Tumulus à Ndalane (Région de Kaolack, Sénégal)." In *Senegalia: Études sur le Patrimoine Ouest-Africain: Hommage à Guy Thilmans*, edited by Cyr Descamps and Abdoulaye Camara, 235–38. Saint-Maur-des-Fossés: Éditions SÉPIA.

Thilmans, Guy, Cyr Descamps, and Bruno Khayat. 1980. *Protohistoire du Sénégal: Recherches Archéologiques*, tome 1: *Les Sites Mégalithiques*. Mémoire de l'Institut Fondamental d'Afrique Noire 91. Dakar: IFAN.

Thilmans, Guy, and J.-P. Rossie. 1969. "Le 'Flambeau de la Navigation' de Dierick Ruiters." *Bulletin de l'IFAN* (sér. B) 31 (1): 106–19.

Thomas, Nicholas. 1991. *Entangled Objects: Exchange, Material Culture, and Colonialism in the Pacific*. Cambridge, MA: Harvard University Press.

Turgeon, Laurier. 1997. "The Tale of the Kettle: Odyssey of an Intercultural Object." *Ethnohistory* 44 (1): 1–29. http://dx.doi.org/10.2307/482899.

Turgeon, Laurier. 2004. "Beads, Bodies, and Regimes of Value: From France to North America, c. 1500–c. 1650." In *The Archaeology of Contact in Settler Societies*, edited by Timothy Murray, 19–47. New York: Cambridge University Press.

Watts, Michael J. 2013. *Silent Violence: Food, Famine, and Peasantry in Northern Nigeria*, 2nd ed. Atlanta: University of Georgia Press.

Wells, E. Christian, and Patricia McAnany, eds. 2008. *Dimensions of Ritual Economy: Research in Economic Anthropology*, vol. 27. Bingley, UK: JAI.

Zedeño, María Nieves. 2009. "Animating by Association: Index Objects and Relational Taxonomies." *Cambridge Archaeological Journal* 19 (3): 407–17. http://dx.doi.org/10.1017/S0959774309000596.

II

Production, Distribution, and Aesthetics

Abundance and Chinese Porcelain from Jingdezhen, AD 1350–1800

Stacey Pierson

Chinese ceramics, particularly the porcelains consumed worldwide from the four-teenth century onward, are an ideal case study for an examination of abundance as an economic principle. In terms of the sheer quantity and distribution of surviving material, Chinese porcelains certainly embody the concept of "more than enough." Hundreds of thousands of these porcelains were produced every year starting in the fourteenth century, and they were also transported to many locations around the world. This is impressive, yet an in-depth examination of both the material and circumstances of Chinese porcelain presents a more complicated picture of its consumption, distribution, and production, which also therefore problematizes our possibly too-narrow definition of "abundance" in economic and archaeologi-cal terms. In Chinese ceramics, for example, abundance is associated not just with economics, distribution, consumption, deposition, and production but also with cultural, aesthetic, and even textual manifestations of quantity in ways that are in fact interrelated and often interdependent.

The present study considers this problem by exploring and demonstrating the multiple representations and manifestations of abundance in Chinese porce-lains from a particular time and place—those made at Jingdezhen from the four-teenth through eighteenth centuries—as well as their numerous cultural contexts. Jingdezhen porcelains were widely distributed both within China and in the rest of the world. They are therefore well studied as both domestic products and export goods (Scott 1993; Carswell 2000; Finlay 2010; Jingdezhen Institute 1992). They

DOI: 10.5876/9781607325949.c011

also performed multiple functions within different consumer groups in the time period under consideration here, ranging widely from ritual and table vessels for the imperial court in Ming China to tomb and temple goods in fourteenth- through sixteenth-century Japan and Southeast Asia to the dining tables of members of the East India Companies in the eighteenth century. As Chinese products, they were also subject to Chinese attitudes toward material goods, including the management and taxation of products as well as the recording of such goods in detailed court records, local authority gazetteers, and connoisseurship treatises (Clunas 1991; Gerritsen 2009).

In the literature on Chinese ceramics, economic principles such as abundance are not yet considered fundamental to understanding surviving objects, apart from the bearing they have on the material analysis of production (Kerr and Wood 2004). The field is dominated instead by non-conceptual approaches such as art historical studies that focus on visual characteristics, including inscriptions; archaeological reports of sites and typologies that classify designs and forms; and anthropological studies that examine the social significance of ceramics within China (e.g., Pierson 2009; Watt and Fong 1996; Schafer 2011; Ho 1996; Liu and Lam 1993). However, when ceramics, particularly Chinese ceramics, are considered in the literature of consumption studies, economic principles and behavior are addressed, and they inform and often shape the analysis. These studies tend naturally to focus on trade ceramics and their role in consumer behavior and globalization (McCabe 2015; Batchelor 2006; Berg 2003). Yet even within these economically informed studies, abundance is not articulated as a key determining force, perhaps because ceramics are treated as neutral data and their inherent cultural and material properties are often ignored. In specialist Chinese trade ceramic studies, for example, the domestic side of consumption and production of the same or similar material is not accounted for, even though many ceramics functioned in both domestic and export markets and their production circumstances were similar (Emerson, Chen, and Gardner Gates 2000; Sargent 2012; Miksic 2009). For trade ceramic studies, the avoidance of domestic contextual issues is not entirely a result of unfamiliarity with Chinese culture or a language barrier, but nevertheless it does constrain the analysis and narrow the possibilities for new thematic approaches as attempted in this chapter.

A fundamental problem with much of the literature on Chinese ceramics in any field is a reluctance to acknowledge that forces of consumption enable porcelain vessels to be two types of objects simultaneously: daily-life functional goods as well as aesthetically pleasing works of art. This duality, as we shall see, is also a manifestation of abundance that takes us beyond the physical to consider whether quantity might also be a psycho-social principle driven by material goods. Things can be made in quantity for practical reasons, but they might also represent conceptions of quantity and their significance in a given culture. Examining Chinese ceramics through the multivalent lens of abundance should allow us to form a more inclusive picture of this product that eliminates some of the geographical and disciplinary restrictions that define current interpretations of such ceramics and their broader significance, both empirically and theoretically.

HISTORY AND DISTRIBUTION: AN OVERVIEW

Looking now specifically at abundance, with reference to the underlying principle of this concept—that is, objects in quantity—for the purposes of this chapter Chinese porcelain from Jingdezhen will be defined in terms of quantity in four main areas: production, consumption, decoration, and distribution. In their original context, these porcelains were industrial products. While today single examples of Chinese porcelain are treated as individual works of art, for most of China's history this type of object was representative of mass production and standardization at both the high and low ends of the quality scale. It was not in any way "art pottery." The main production sites were located in south China, where beginning in about AD 1000 porcelains were (and still are) made in vast quantities at Jingdezhen in Jiangxi province for domestic and foreign consumption, using large quantities of raw materials, labor, and energy.

In pre–twentieth-century China, porcelains were not used singularly or interpreted as singular items, apart from special commissions or a few rare examples that had become antiques, thus entering another category of object. At the imperial level, evidence of high-end production is visibly abundant in the huge sherd heap remains at the sites of the imperial kilns, also located at Jingdezhen from the early Ming dynasty (1368–1644). These same sherd heaps further demonstrate an abundance of waste and destruction, both intentional and consequential. For the imperial factories, numerous textual records survive from the late sixteenth century that attest to vast court orders of porcelains for specific occasions, which can often be matched to existing pieces or discarded ones at the kiln sites. In terms of aesthetics, the decoration of porcelain from both the imperial and commercial kilns indicates a cultural desire for representations of abundance through the often dense and repetitive decoration (or even the word for abundance, 富, used iconographically) that can be seen on Chinese ceramics from the fourteenth century onward.

Outside China, the development of official maritime trade from as early as the seventh century in the Tang dynasty (AD 618–906) ensured that foreign consumers could acquire large quantities of Chinese goods, including porcelain (from north China at this time), and use them in quantity. Accumulations in the Middle East and Japan from this time and later and in Europe after 1600 attest to this. The aesthetics of abundant decoration and an associated desire to display Chinese porcelain seem also to have transferred to other cultures through imitation and accumulation, demonstrating another impact of abundant porcelain. Through its appropriation in foreign cultures, most often in quantity, Chinese porcelain could take on new, locally conceived meanings (Pierson 2012).

The maritime and overland trade that distributed Chinese porcelain operated on an economic principle of abundance through economies of scale and profitability, thus providing us today with visual evidence of large-scale shipments of porcelain in the wrecked hulls of ships found worldwide and quantities of sherds found at trading ports (see Kerr 2008 for a recent overview). The function of these porcelains in trade and the vast quantities recorded in wrecks and shipping records point to abundance as a precondition for utility in this context.

Abundance is therefore an important framework for understanding key features of both the character and impact of Chinese porcelain, domestically and overseas. Through this lens, we can situate Chinese porcelain in wider discussions about material goods and global consumption. With a view to exploring this new way of looking at Chinese porcelain from Jingdezhen, this chapter considers manifestations of abundance in porcelains from three time periods and contexts: a Yuan dynasty dish, the Ming imperial factory, and a Qing dynasty shipwreck. As case studies, these examples will help illuminate both the principles of abundance as they apply to Chinese objects and the material evidence for abundance in the distribution sphere of Chinese porcelain.

A Yuan Dynasty Dish

If we consider abundance first as an economic principle with reference to objects in general, then design in terms of both formal and visual features has to be seen as part of this. Design involves a number of choices based on known variables, with the economics of production, distribution, and sale as primary factors in addition to aesthetics. Too often, design with reference to material objects tends to be analyzed through an art historical framework such that forms, visual motifs, and their arrangement are situated within a known or comparative stylistic category. In Chinese ceramic studies, for example, dishes like the one illustrated in figure 11.1 are usually classified according to several features said to be indicative of or defining style: date (Yuan dynasty, fourteenth century), color (blue and white), decoration (usually described as "Islamic"),[1] and form (large dish). Whatever the merits of these classifications, they do not consider the limitations in which producers worked, which in turn had an impact on the final appearance of the vessel.

FIGURE 11.1. Porcelain dish with underglaze blue decoration, Yuan dynasty, fourteenth century (Victoria and Albert Museum, London).

As products for sale, the ceramics needed attractive designs (decoration) and usable, sturdy forms, which were straightforward to create and repeatable to maximize profits and ensure low production costs. Thus, abundance in one sense was an aim—abundant production to maximize profits and minimize costs. In ceramic production, the maximization of profits also means, among many other things, maximizing capacity in kiln chambers as well as fuel usage while being dependent on supplies of raw materials (including fuelwood), their transportation, and their preparation. In terms of forms, once the process has been organized in an assembly line, the making of large dishes such as the one in figure 11.1, with a standard base, concave sides, and a limited number of rim shapes, is efficient yet provides some variety. The dish shown here has the straight rim shape that appears on many of these dishes. The other rim shape seen in these dishes is usually described as "bracketed" and has numerous pointed projections around the rim. Either rim shape can be made easily using a mold and a profile applied mechanically and repetitiously. Yet if efficiency and cost are important for these commercially produced wares, how then do we explain the "abundant" use of decoration on this dish—a profusion considered characteristic of this type of ware from this time period?

The decoration seen here is notably dense, with consecutive bands descending from the mouth rim, opening onto an even more densely patterned center in which one motif overlays many others on a patterned ground. The dish has been molded to emphasize the banding of the pattern, and every inch of it has been covered with hand-painted motifs in rich cobalt blue. The decorator has allowed for multiple areas of white reserve, giving the entire design a two-color appearance. Such dense and richly patterned decoration requires an abundance of materials to create, including cobalt pigment, time, and the skill required for hand-painting. The large numbers of such dishes that survive suggest that the material and labor were readily available in sufficient quantities during a possible production period of about fifty years for this type of ware. In the literature of this ware (commonly known as "blue and white"), however, studies almost always emphasize the pigment and its rarity, noting the costs assumed to be associated with the procurement of cobalt blue. Many scholars still assume that cobalt was imported into Yuan period China from Persia, where cobalt mines were located at Kashan (e.g., Vainker 2005:138; Finlay 2010:139–40; see also Häggman 2008:148). Sourcing cobalt from this location would have necessitated a number of processes, including mining, proveniencing, transportation to southeast China, and some refining

If it was true that cobalt was expensive to use at that time, especially in great quantities, then there must have been an abundance principle operating in another way—that is, in the association between costs of production and the market (though there is still much debate about the source, distribution, and costs associated with the use of cobalt blue in Chinese ceramics; for a summary, see Kerr and Wood 2004:671–80). An expensive material can be cost-effective if there are enough consumers of the product to offset the cost (cf. Klarich, Levine, and Schultze, this volume). Examples of densely decorated Yuan blue and white wares can be seen in collections formed before the present day in Istanbul (the Topkapi Palace) and Iran (the former Ardebil Shrine collection), as well as at find sites in Okinawa, Kenya, and Indonesia (Misugi 1981; Wilson 2005; Qin, Liu, and Kiriama 2012; Miksic 2009). Surviving pieces from this time period indicate that this kind of dense and abundant design was widely desirable at the time of production. It is notable that this style of decoration became much less common in the subsequent early Ming period in China when other sources of cobalt, including some in China, began to be exploited (Kerr and Wood 2004:682–84).

It is not just the decoration that is abundant on these dishes but also the number of motifs. The dense patterning is often associated in the art historical literature with "Islamic" approaches to design where a form of *horror vacui* is said to prevail, in which—in theory—no blank space is left showing (see Finlay 2010:171). While such descriptions have been somewhat discredited even in the literature on Islamic art (as summarized by Leaman 2004:40–44), as has the category of "Islamic art" as a whole (see Blair and Bloom 2003), the decoration on these Yuan blue and white dishes does have parallels with those seen on carpets and metalwork from West Asia (see Kadoi 2009 for a study of the material effects of this period of interaction between Persia and China). A closer look at the dish in figure 11.1 reveals that beyond density, a further decorative principle of abundance is operating here: that of repetitiveness. In each of the bands of decoration, similar motifs are repeated and indeed are often scrolling to give a sense of continuity. Only one motif is shown singularly—that of the "double thunderbolt" or "double *vajra*," which is associated with Tibetan Buddhism (Beer 2004). This central single motif is nonetheless circled by a band of repeated Buddhist motifs, the "flaming pearl" and the "endless knot." These are two motifs that in Chinese decorative art are part of a larger category known as the "eight Buddhist emblems" 八吉祥, a collective set of motifs ultimately derived from India (Beer 2004). In Chinese porcelain, repetitiveness in decoration reinforces a visual representation of abundance that in its wide popularity helped stimulate abundant consumption and distribution.

It could be argued that the use of cobalt pigment to paint motifs in such quantities indicates another form of abundance—that of power. If cobalt was difficult and expensive to procure, then the large-scale employment of it visually demonstrates China's power (economically and diplomatically) to acquire the material in such large quantities. The fact is that most of these blue and white wares were made in commercial kilns during the Yuan period, so this argument necessitates an assumption that commercial kilns were subject to government agendas beyond taxation. This is a complicated assumption to make about this period in Chinese history because the country was subjected to Mongol rule and was thus part of a wider federation that included the assumed source location for cobalt—Persia. Was the pigment therefore even "imported" in the political sense?

Aside from the pigment, it is interesting that the mass-market, global distribution of Yuan blue and white porcelain may also have offset the costs associated with the technique used to apply the decoration. As noted, each of these dishes, including the one in figure 11.1, was hand-painted. None of the decoration appears to have been applied using stencils or transfers; thus, the technique was very labor-intensive. However, thanks to the well-documented nature of porcelain production in China, we also know that labor was generally abundant, so expensive decorative techniques could have been economically viable; modern notions of appropriate working conditions were an undeveloped concept at that time (Kerr and Wood 2004:209–13). Certainly, this applies to the commercial kilns at Jingdezhen, the so-called porcelain city in southeast China where this dish and most porcelain was made from the early fourteenth century onward. Starting at the end of the fourteenth century, there were other producers at Jingdezhen, in addition to the commercial kilns, and their approach to abundance is in some ways similar to and in other, significant ways different from, that of the commercial kilns.

THE MING IMPERIAL FACTORY

The porcelain factory or workshop at Jingdezhen that receives the most attention in both literature and the art market is the so-called imperial factory, which was formally established during the Ming dynasty in 1392 (see Kerr and Wood 2004 for a summary of the debate about the founding date). As the official supplier of porcelain to the court, the imperial factory operated on different principles than those of the commercial factories, even when contracting out work to the latter. The market was not a concern, as the court in its widest sense was the single consumer, but that also meant there were few limits on consumption at court apart from sumptuary rules, and production was subject to quotas instead of market forces (Pierson 2013:21; Kerr and Wood 2004:202, citing Li and Shen 1963 [1587], ch. 194, p. 1a/2631). This might be viewed as a form of conspicuous consumption as defined by Mason (1981), but to be conspicuous, the consumption needs to be visible; during the Ming period, apart from public ceremonies, the court was a closed setting. Outside the court, however, conspicuous consumption was practiced by the elite to such an extent that it was eventually emulated by the merchant and aspiring classes (Clunas 1991; Burke 1993). With reference to court porcelain, abundance was therefore expressed in very different terms than those used to describe the products of the commercial factories.

During the Ming dynasty, the court required porcelain for a wide range of functions, including everyday dining, banquets, rituals, religion, gifts, and display, among others. Thus, the uses for porcelain at court were themselves abundant in their diversity. Within this abundance was the issue of reuse, as it appears that many court porcelains were only used once; therefore, every year the court sent orders for new porcelain. Certainly, when a new reign period started, new porcelains had to be ordered; since the economic status of each reign was different, the size and frequency of the orders varied accordingly. This is demonstrated by the sometimes massive orders for porcelains sent down from the court (which was based in north China starting in the 1430s) to the imperial factory. One well-known example is the more than 133,000 porcelains ordered by the Court of Imperial Entertainments in 1459 (Kerr and Wood 2004:198). On quite a few occasions, departments of the imperial palace ordered large quantities of porcelains for special events. Often, the kilns could not cope with such massive orders and production quotas were imposed, but clearly quantity was a basic requirement in many court orders. This is partly a result of the reuse issue but also a result of the necessity for large numbers of vessels to be used during state ceremonies and functions. For example, in 1528 the court ordered 189 lead-lined ice chests for the autumn offering at the Civil Temple (Kerr and Wood 2004:203, citing Li and Shen 1963 [1587], ch. 201, p. 26a/2715).

Another feature of imperial porcelains was the specificity of designs because design motifs and colors were symbolic, hierarchical, and therefore regulated. Unlike commercial kilns, whose design choices were driven by the market and economics, the court demanded propriety and appropriateness. Different departments of the imperial household also required different patterns (Kerr and Wood 2004:203). The result was a huge range of designs, colors, palettes, and styles produced by necessity at the imperial porcelain factory (or contracted out for this purpose). As an indication, during the fifteenth century imperial porcelains could be made in at least five colors, monochrome or polychrome-decorated, with hundreds of different motifs or combinations thereof and numerous decorative techniques. During the Ming dynasty, for example, the colors and decoration could be underglaze painted, overglaze painted, a combination of both, slip painted, incised, carved, or molded, sometimes in combinations on the same piece. Visually, the choice of designs for imperial porcelains in the Ming period was controlled but seemingly endless and therefore in abundance—a decorative engagement with plenitude (Smith, this volume).

In addition to decorative techniques, the repertoire of available motifs was also vast. While often used in profusion on imperial porcelains, motifs were used not only for aesthetic reasons but also to indicate distinction. Products produced for the court (including ceramics) were not made speculatively or consumed unconsciously. They were ordered in specific amounts with specific designs and colors stipulated. These designs and colors were subject to various restrictions relating to the function of the vessel, its location of consumption within and beyond the court precincts, and the status of the user within the court. For example, certain patterns were associated with different departments of the court, such as yellow and green wares with paired dragons and phoenixes, which were reserved for the Directorate for Palace Delicacies (Kerr and Wood 2004:203, citing Hucker 1985:410). At the same time, in an earlier period of the Ming dynasty, it was decreed that commoners were forbidden to use vessels with those dragon and phoenix designs (Kerr and Wood 2004:202, citing Li and Shen 1963 [1587], ch. 1, p. 21). Thus, while the repertoire of available motifs and color combinations was seemingly limitless, this abundance of choice required strict control to maintain the appropriateness, exclusiveness, and efficacy of the aesthetics. In this case, we can see that the abundance of potential designs led to a form of anxiety, necessitating imposed scarcity and informing the imposition of sumptuary laws throughout China's imperial history.

Scarcity is in fact a major consequence of the abundant designs, production, consumption, and functions of Chinese porcelain, particularly with reference to materials. In the case of Ming imperial porcelains, the two economic principles of abundance and scarcity were interrelated (cf. Moore and Schmidt, this volume; Varien, Potter, and Naranjo, this volume). Obviously, the scale of production at the imperial kilns required huge quantities of raw materials and supplies, including clays, minerals, fuels, labor, water, and equipment. The court even required labor in lieu of taxes until the sixteenth century (so-called corvée labor). It is well documented that at times the imperial factory could not cope with the often massive orders from the court and had to contract out production to private kilns (see Kerr and Wood 2004:200).

Supplies of raw materials were also noted to be nearly depleted in official records of production (Scott and Kerr 1994:8). Another factor that influenced production quantities and the use of labor and raw materials was the level of quality control and control of consumption beyond the court. Records state and archaeology confirms that in certain periods, quality control at the imperial factory was very strict and inferior pieces deemed unacceptable to court supervisors were destroyed (Scott and Pierson 1995:6). Distribution of inferior imperial factory products was also prohibited (but not closely monitored). Therefore, production was dependent not just on the receipt of orders but also on approval. For example, during the reign of the Chenghua emperor (r. 1465–87), quality control, as managed by a court official on-site, was such that it has been suggested that an exceptional number of pieces were destroyed for being inferior and not acceptable for court consumption at that time (suggested after analysis of the late Chenghua period stratigraphic level at the imperial kiln site, Jingdezhen; Liu and Lam 1993:65, 69). Today, the positive consequence of this practice has been the discovery of massive sherd heaps at the imperial kiln excavation sites in Jingdezhen. The sherd heaps are particularly capacious for the fifteenth and sixteenth centuries in general, and we therefore have abundant archaeological material to study imperial ceramic production, an advantage for both ceramic and historical analysis.

The sherd heaps further suggest that for the Ming imperial porcelain factory, waste might also have been a visual and experiential manifestation of abundance. While seemingly contradictory, destruction was an important aspect of production at this time for both consumers and producers of this category of ceramics. As the quantities of sherds demonstrate, the amount of waste is directly associated with the scale of imperial orders and the restrictions of imperial approval; the quality control system ensured that much that was produced was also destroyed. This would have been a reminder for those compelled to produce court porcelains that the end consumer of their products was somewhat capricious and that abundant production was important to ensure compliance. Multiples of each piece needed to be made to increase the likelihood of a perfect piece that would be acceptable for the court. This can be seen as an example of intentional waste, as opposed to incidental waste as in the by-products of metallurgy; therefore, it illustrates "the dynamic relationship between abundance and scarcity" (Smith, this volume). It should not be assumed that the sherd heaps were visible to those outside the factory during the Ming and Qing periods, however. Today, they are an important part of the ceramic tours of Jingdezhen, with the "finest" sherds on display in the local museum, and we might see them as symbols of waste. But for those working at the imperial factory or in the private kilns to which orders were contracted, these discards and their quantity would have been part of daily working life quickly buried by imperial decree.

A final aspect of abundance with reference to Ming imperial porcelains that needs to be addressed is the logistics of transportation, an issue that can also be considered for the earlier Yuan blue and white porcelains discussed above. Geographically, in the Ming period the only imperial porcelain factory (and its associates) was located in the southeastern part of the country, at Jingdezhen. This is over 1,500 km from the court that was eventually located in Beijing (after being moved from Nanjing, near Shanghai). Today, this route can be traveled in multiple ways, but in the Ming period, transportation was much more difficult. Jingdezhen is located in a mountainous area that was not supplied with major roads during the Ming period. Porcelains for the court would have been moved very slowly on horseback and by human power over and through steep mountains to get to the nearest major river, the Chang, then to a lake, the Poyang, and only then to the Yangtze River, which would have enabled north-south travel through a link to the Grand Canal (Dillon 1992). Thus, Jingdezhen's location was clearly favorable for raw materials but not for distribution, including court wares. Transporting imperial porcelains to the court used further labor and materials (and expense), thus contributing to the overall abundance of exploitation necessitated by the production and consumption of imperial porcelain at court.

A QING DYNASTY SHIPWRECK

Overland distribution networks would also have been necessary to transport non-imperial ceramics, but starting in the seventeenth century, those for export generally went south toward Canton to be shipped overseas. The distribution of trade porcelains from Jingdezhen began fairly early through ports first established in the Song dynasty (906–1279) and further ports, including some near Canton, in the Yuan (1279–1368) and Ming periods. The evidence for this type of movement beyond China can be traced through texts and shipwrecks, another area of ceramic archaeology where today there is abundant material for study. The export of porcelain from China started in the ninth century (earthenwares and stonewares were exported earlier), but it was in the seventeenth century that large-scale exports of porcelains began to accompany the European trade in eastern commodities such as tea and spices. Much of this trade was managed by the East India Companies, particularly those of the English (EIC) and Dutch (VOC). Tea in particular became a valuable and profitable commodity from the late seventeenth century onward, and large quantities could only be sourced in China at that time. Porcelain was a useful companion product to the tea trade that could both weight the tea ships as additional ballast and line the bottom holds to protect the tea above from dampness and odor contamination (Jacobs 2006:189). Tea was thus the profitable commodity and porcelain the additional (but desirable) product that facilitated the tea trade. Its usefulness was enhanced and to some extent determined by its abundance. No other manufactured product was readily available in the tea-producing area, mass-produced, and therefore relatively cheap, durable, and also salable in Europe after serving its shipping function.

With large-scale shipping came consequent diplomatic, political, and financial challenges in addition to frequent losses as a result of weather, mechanical failure, and human error, among other causes. Thus, a number of wrecks of East India Companies ships provide valuable (if sometimes controversial) evidence for most aspects of the trade. The Dutch East India Company ship *Geldermalsen*, which wrecked in Indonesian waters in 1752, contained the remains of over 140,000 porcelain vessels, which gives a sense of the scale of this trade in the mid-eighteenth century. Porcelain dealers at the Dutch trading port of Batavia (Jakarta) noted in the 1690s that shipments of over 2 million pieces of porcelain were received from China annually (Ledderose 2000:89, citing Jorg 1986). The cargo of the *Geldermalsen*, as well as the accompanying documents, also tell about the extensive, multi-stop journeys such porcelains made, as most goods were transhipped on either the inbound or outbound journey.

Porcelain from the wreck of the *Geldermalsen* is representative of abundance in several ways: it was produced in modular fashion, with many multiples of the same design or form; it was traded and shipped in quantity; and it was consumed in sets of many items. A copy of the packing list for the ship survives (National Archives, the Hague), which lists 171 dinner services and 16 different types of dishes, including 19,535 coffee cups with saucers, 25,921 slop bowls, and 63,623 teacups with saucers (Ledderose 2000:90, citing Jorg 1986; Sheaf and Kilburn 1986). Almost all of this porcelain was blue and white (the enamels on some having deteriorated) and was made in Jingdezhen, the porcelain town that produced the vessel shown in

FIGURE 11.2. Porcelain bowl with underglaze blue decoration, from the Nanjing Cargo, eighteenth century (British Museum, London).

figure 11.1. Thus, the quantity of the product is clearly evident, but abundance is also evident in its forms and design. For example, it is notable that there is a repetitiveness of the design patterns on the wares that come from a very limited repertoire: simple landscapes, flowers, and trees (with the occasional fish).

One scholar, Lothar Ledderose [2000], has noted an interesting feature in this limited repertoire, what he calls a modular system of design (figure 11.2). Essentially, what can be seen if a large number of these pieces is viewed is that the decoration develops in complexity through a systematic sequence of steps in which additional elements are added, starting from a single flower on one piece and leading to a more complex landscape down the line. Some pieces have the simple designs, whereas others have more complex designs representing the addition of different "modules." This reflects a production line system of manufacture, which was indeed in use at Jingdezhen, as we have seen. All of the decorative motifs can be used on their own or in combination, and they are interchangeable. The sheer abundance of the remains in this shipwreck has thus allowed us to see exactly how such mass quantities of decorated porcelain were produced and how quickly, turning hand-painting into an industrial process.

What we can also see is another representation of what was earlier called an aesthetics of abundance. The individual motifs are not in themselves abundant; rather, their repetitive use in different combinations gives rise to an almost exponential repertoire. This is a further reminder that the porcelains from Jingdezhen, both imperial and non-imperial, were made in a factory setting, using a division of labor in many stages. This resulted in many things, but standardization in particular has to be considered from both a production efficiency perspective and an aesthetic one. Efficiency may have determined the visual appearance of the wares, but the designs that resulted were widely admired outside of China. In this case, the use of a limited number of single but interchangeable motifs enabled an abundance of production and therefore consumption.

For the foreign consumer, the seemingly endless yet coordinated variety of design patterns on the wares, such as those from the *Geldermalsen* wreck, would have been very attractive, especially as the pieces were intended to be used in sets and not for the most part as individual items. Thus, their function is also reflective of quantity; most of the items were either dinner services or parts of coffee- and tea-drinking sets, as the inventory reveals. From the eighteenth-century consumer's perspective, these porcelains functioned in groups of objects, thus in quantity, and they came from a place that could apparently supply endless quantities of these desirable items. Certainly, it was cheaper to buy large quantities of porcelain from China at this time (1750s) because European and English porcelain factories were just getting started and large-scale production had not yet been achieved. In addition, the fashion for *chinoiserie* (Chinese-style designs in interiors, furnishings, and fashion) was also at its height (Pierson 2007).

The aesthetics of Chinese export porcelain, like other wares discussed, are also to some extent informed by the methods of transportation and distribution. Chinese porcelains were transported in bulk, and when they arrived at their final destination and were no longer needed as ballast, they were frequently auctioned off in major European ports such as Amsterdam and London starting in the early seventeenth century. The earliest examples were sometimes auctions of booty, including porcelains and other goods seized from downed ships of other countries. A famous example was the sale of loot from the *Santa Catarina*, a Portuguese ship captured by the Dutch off Singapore in 1603 (this event and the capture of the ship have been published widely; see Jorg 1986:15; Finlay 2010:253–54; van Ittersum 2003; Funnell and Robertson 2013:171).

The *Geldermalsen* items were lost at sea, but they, too, would have been sold in a port-side auction, a standard practice for income generation by the East India Companies. The visual aspects of these large-scale sales are of interest here as their mass presence (often upward of 100,000 pieces) would have been spectacular visually, reinforcing existing notions about the material, their manufacture, and their origins. The sale as spectacle is not a well-studied aspect of display history (the few studies that exist relate specifically to European art; see, for example, Richter 2008), but it does seem to provide another example of what Gates-Foster (2014) refers to as a "compelling visual presence." Certainly, the many visual manifestations of abundance are an important aspect of the appropriation and production of goods in general, particularly those produced on a more massive scale.

CHINESE CERAMICS AND THE CULTURE OF DISPLAY

The discovery of the *Geldermalsen* in 1985 provided a window into abundance in the past, presenting evidence for the scale of the trade and distribution as well as of manufacture and design of a particular commodity from China (for a history of the excavation and a description of the porcelains, see Sheaf and Kilburn 1986; Jorg 1986, along with the excavators' own report, Hatcher 1987). Even though it did not reach its original final destination, the ship was auctioned by Christie's in Amsterdam in 1986, bringing the goods back to the Netherlands in the end (Christie's 1986). By all accounts the sale was dramatic and therefore a spectacle, bringing an example of visual abundance from the past into the present, even using the same method of final distribution (the auction) that would have been used in the eighteenth century. This spectacle was cultivated but the methods used, including giving the cargo a name, "the Nanjing Cargo," were effective in ensuring that this was the most publicized and largest auction of porcelain in Christie's history at that time (Gould 2011:342–43; Associated Press 1986). After lying on the bed of the South China Sea for over 250 years, these pieces had an afterlife that mirrored the distribution and visual presentations of their first life. In aesthetic and design terms, too, these pieces from the Nanjing Cargo now have a well-known, shipping-related provenance. They are still widely collected and thus remain in circulation, but perhaps few are used for their intended purpose as tablewares. Instead, they have been transformed through time and consumption into objects collected in quantity—a form of abundance that for Chinese porcelain did not begin in Europe until the nineteenth century.

The display of mass quantities of Chinese porcelain (arguably a form of collecting in itself), however, began much earlier in Europe and Britain as well as outside Europe, especially in areas of West Asia that had powerful ruling dynasties. In the history of Chinese ceramics, one of the most famous "collections" outside greater China was assembled and displayed in Safavid Iran at the Ardebil Shrine, and a further assemblage was created in Ottoman Turkey at the Topkapi Palace (both sites have been extensively published and are surveyed in Misugi 1981). The Ardebil Shrine display in particular used visual abundance to reinforce the power and wealth of the sitting ruler, Shah 'Abbas (r. 1587–1629). Within a complex of buildings associated with a royal tomb, one space was converted into a *chinikhaneh*, or china hall, where royal treasures belonging to the Safavid royal family were housed after 1608. In this space, around 1,100 Chinese ceramics were displayed in niches set into the walls above displays of rare books. These foreign ceramics, many of them blue and white porcelains, were reappropriated as Safavid material culture (Pierson 2012).

The display of Chinese porcelains in architectural settings was also practiced in Europe and Britain, for similar reasons. Some of the earliest architectural displays of Chinese porcelain could be seen in Britain in the early seventeenth century in the homes of elite members of London society (Bracken 2001). In continental Europe, a number of royal palaces featured rooms designated to have lavish displays of Chinese porcelain installed on the walls. One very famous example is the porcelain room in the Charlottenburg Palace in Berlin, where mirrored walls were completely covered with blue and white Chinese and Japanese porcelain from the seventeenth and eighteenth centuries (Scharmann 2005). The scale of such displays is truly extravagant and dependent on quantity for its effect. The aesthetics and function of abundance in the interior are areas for potential future research but ones that for our purposes reinforce the significance and the role of quantity and excess in both the production and consumption of Chinese porcelain worldwide.

Display is still a significant form of representation in the archaeology of Chinese ceramics, particularly in China. A late-twentieth-century development in China gives a sense of how extensive the association of abundance with porcelain is in both archaeological and aesthetic perspectives, even in the present day. In the 1980s a number of kiln sites were excavated at Jingdezhen, and they revealed the extent and variety of production, particularly at the imperial kilns, during the Ming dynasty (e.g., Urban Council 1989; Liu 1996, 1998). Thousands of sherds were found in well-stratified layers dating from the early Ming dynasty to the sixteenth century. Interestingly, many of the sherds were exhibited and published in exhibition catalogs (Jingdezhen Institute 1992; Liu and Lam 1993). This phenomenon heralded the now familiar fashion of displaying archaeologically recovered sherds similarly to intact collected pieces—that is, aesthetically, in museum style. In China, since the advent of professional archaeology in that country in the twentieth century, archaeology has been seen as both science and a visual commodity, with entire museums built around exposed sites. The exhibitions of excavated sherds, however, visually represented a new way of thinking about ceramics in China, for the broken pots and reconstructed pieces were presented as the remains of production, were found in great quantities, and were displayed in their destroyed state. Bearing in mind that these were also wasters, viewers were invited to admire this waste, which would stand for absent perfect pieces.[2]

The great quantities of sherds on display in Jingdezhen museums, now available for study, contrast greatly with the concurrent celebration of the opposite principle of scarcity in the market for rare Chinese porcelains. This is represented by several recent spectacular auction sales of single pieces, including one small Ming cup that sold for $36 million in 2014 (Sothebys Hong Kong 2014). Porcelains like this are also from Jingdezhen, but they have been made singular through the intervention of time, collecting, and what has been called the economics of singularity (Karpik 2010). With Chinese porcelains, it seems that both abundance and scarcity are operating principles, with one informing the other, for it is clear that without the fundamental abundance in production, aesthetics, and consumption, there could be no scarcity in this case.

CONCLUSION

Examining Jingdezhen porcelains of the Yuan, Ming, and Qing dynasties through the lens of abundance allows us to reexamine and re-frame both the visual and material characteristics of these ceramics, as well as their movement and impact. In the case of the Yuan dish, we can see that production and decoration in quantity were desirable both domestically and in the trade environment with reference to taste and market forces. In contrast, in the Ming imperial factory, quantity became a liability because of cultural conventions requiring greater control and therefore limitation. While subject to different economic forces than were Yuan blue and white porcelains, Ming imperial porcelains nevertheless still required similar production support in terms of material, labor, and transportation—demonstrating the concurrent duality of quantity and scarcity operating here.

In the Qing dynasty, imperial porcelain was still produced but with different cultural forces at work, which impacted the trade ceramic industry of the time. The cargo of the vast eighteenth-century ship *Geldermalsen*, destroyed in Indonesian waters, reflected one such force: insularity. Chinese merchants overseas, who would be part of the distribution network for porcelains around the world, were effectively exiled, and much of the maritime distribution of Chinese porcelain from Canton was handled by foreign merchants such as members of the EIC, who were restricted to zoned residential areas and not permitted to live in China proper. The very successful product from China that porcelain represented was therefore strictly separated from domestic examples in the Qing dynasty. Nevertheless, this excluded porcelain also reflected the key aspects of abundance in Chinese ceramics: large-scale production, with consequently large quantities of supplies and labor; repetitive, plentiful decoration; wide distribution, including in this case beyond China; and the visual manifestations of quantity embodied in sets, display, and destruction. This single type of object reflected varying Chinese attitudes toward functional products (as well as foreign ones), which in the case of porcelain have been shown to be considered more than just physical objects but also a manifestation of ideas about things, things in quantity, and the corollary—scarcity—but also about consumption, identity, and the world as a vast market for Chinese commercial and diplomatic goods. Jingdezhen porcelain was a suitably diverse model, but other Chinese goods were also widely distributed through the same networks, and these, too, would be a mirror for both Chinese society and the societies that appropriated china.

NOTES

1. See, for example, Vainker (2005:139). So-called Islamic style is used to define and describe the densely patterned, often textile-inspired decoration on a number of Yuan dynasty blue and white porcelains. This is based on an assumption that such pieces were made for "Islamic" markets and consumers.

2. There is as yet no link made in China between the conceptual "brokenness" of the porcelains and similarly broken moral virtues, as has been demonstrated in seventeenth- and eighteenth-century England by Pennell (2010). The inherently fragile nature of Chinese porcelain is not generally acknowledged in Chinese literature. In fact, interpretations tend to favor its durability and therefore China's strength in manufacturing. Comments in Ming connoisseurship literature sometimes associate overconsumption of porcelain with greed or a lack of "elegance" 雅, however (Pierson 2013).

REFERENCES CITED

Associated Press. 1986. "Nanking Cargo Auction Sets Price Records." May 2. Accessed August 7, 2014. http://www.apnewsarchive.com/1986/Nanking-Cargo-Auction-Sets -Price-Records/id-fc7428c3e63e1d6299d2fc3dfed5d6f2.

Batchelor, Robert. 2006. "On the Movement of Porcelains: Rethinking the Birth of Consumer Society as Interactions of Exchange Networks, 1600–1750." In *Consuming Cultures, Global Perspectives: Historical Tragectories, Transnational Exchanges*, edited by John Brewer and Frank Trentman, 95–121. Oxford: Berg.

Beer, Robert. 2004. *The Encyclopedia of Tibetan Symbols and Motifs*. Chicago: Serindia.

Berg, Maxine. 2003. "Asian Luxuries and the Making of the European Consumer Revolution." In *Luxury in the Eighteenth Century: Debates, Desires, and Delectable Goods*, edited by Maxine Berg and Elizabeth Eger, 228–44. Basingstoke, UK: Palgrave Macmillan.

Blair, Shelia, and Jonathan Bloom. 2003. "The Mirage of Islamic Art: Reflections on the Study of an Unwieldy Field." *Art Bulletin* 85 (1): 152–84. http://dx.doi.org/10.2307 /3177331.

Bracken, Susan. 2001. " 'Chyna' in England before 1614." *Oriental Art* 47 (2): 8–10.

Burke, Peter. 1993. "Res et Verba: Conspicuous Consumption in the Early Modern World." In *Consumption and the World of Goods*, edited by John Brewer and Roy Porter, 148–61. London: Routledge.

Carswell, John. 2000. *Blue and White: Chinese Porcelain around the World*. London: British Museum Press.

Christie's 1986. *The Nanking Cargo: Chinese Export Porcelain and Gold, European Glass and Stoneware; Recovered by Captain Michael Hatcher from a European Merchant Ship Wrecked in the South China Seas*. Sale catalog, April 28 to May 2, 1986, Amsterdam.

Clunas, Craig. 1991. *Superfluous Things: Material Culture and Social Status in Early Modern China*. Urbana:University of Illinois Press in association with Blackwell.

Dillon, Michael. 1992. "Transport and Marketing in the Development of the Jingdezhen Porcelain Industry during the Ming and Qing Dynasties." *Journal of Economic and Social History of the Orient* 35 (3): 278–90. http://dx.doi.org/10.1163/156852092X00156.

Emerson, Julie, Jennifer Chen, and Mimi Gardner Gates. 2000. *Porcelain Stories: From China to Europe*. Seattle: Seattle Art Museum.

Finlay, Robert. 2010. *The Pilgrim Art: The Culture of Porcelain in World History*. Berkeley: University of California Press.

Funnell, Warwick, and Jeffrey Robertson. 2013. *Accounting by the First Public Company: The Pursuit of Supremacy*. London: Routledge.

Gates-Foster, Jennifer. 2014. "Abundance and Innovation in the Production of Roman Tablewares." Paper presented at the Society for American Archaeology Meeting, Austin, TX, April 23–27.

Gerritsen, Anne. 2009. "Fragments of a Global Past: Ceramics Manufacture in Song-Yuan-Ming Jingdezhen." *Journal of the Economic and Social History of the Orient* 52: 117–52.

Gould, Richard. 2011. *Archaeology and the Social History of Ships*. Cambridge: Cambridge University Press. http://dx.doi.org/10.1017/CBO9780511852060.

Häggman, Sofia, ed. 2008. *Blue and White: Porcelain from the Topkapi Palace Museum and the Museum of Turkish and Islamic Art*. Sweden: Stockholm Medelhavsmuseet.

Hatcher, Michael. 1987. *The Nanking Cargo*. Falls Village, VT: Hamish Hamilton.

Ho, Chuimei. 1996. "Social Life under the Mongols as Seen in Ceramics." *Transactions of the Oriental Ceramic Society* 59: 33–47.

Hucker, Charles O. 1985. *A Dictionary of Official Titles in Imperial China*. Stanford, CA: Stanford University Press.

Jacobs, Els M. 2006. *Merchant in Asia: The Trade of the Dutch East India Company during the Eighteenth Century*. Leiden: CNWS.

Jingdezhen Institute of Ceramic Archaeology and Fung Ping Shan Museum, University of Hong Kong. *Ceramic Finds from Jingdezhen Kilns: 10–17th Century*. 1992. Hong Kong: Fung Ping Shan Museum.

Jorg, C.J.A. 1986. *The Geldermalsen: History and Porcelain*. Groningen: Groninger Museum.

Kadoi, Yuka. 2009. *Islamic Chinoiserie: The Art of Mongol Iran*. Edinburgh Studies in Islamic Art. Edinburgh: Edinburgh University Press.

Karpik, Lucien. 2010. *Valuing the Unique: The Economics of Singularities*. Trans. Nora Scott. Princeton, NJ: Princeton University Press.

Kerr, Rose. 2008. "Porcelain Raised from the Sea: Underwater Excavations of Shipwrecks Are Making Major Additions to Our Knowledge of the Early International Trade in Chinese Ceramics as Well as Bringing to the Surface Objects of Great Beauty and Interest in Their Own Right." *Apollo* 167 (554): 47–51.

Kerr, Rose, and Nigel Wood. 2004. *Science and Civilization in China*, vol. 5. Cambridge: Cambridge University Press.

Leaman, Oliver. 2004. *Islamic Aesthetics: An Introduction*. Edinburgh: Edinburgh University Press.

Ledderose, Lothar. 2000. *Ten Thousand Things: Module and Mass Production in Chinese Art*. Princeton, NJ: Princeton University Press.

Li Dongyang and Shen Shixing. 1963 [1587]. *Da Ming hui dian (Collected Statues of the Ming Dynasty)*. Taipei: Zhong wen shu ju.

Liu Xinyuan. 1996. *Imperial Hongwu and Yongle Porcelain Excavated at Jingdezhen*. Taipei: Chang Foundation.

Liu Xinyuan. 1998. *Xuande Imperial Porcelain Excavated at Jindezhen*. Taipei: Chang Foundation.

Liu Xinyuan and Peter Yip Keung Lam. 1993. *A Legacy of Chenghua: Imperial Porcelain of the Chenghua Reign Excavated from Zhushan, Jingdezhen*. Hong Kong: Tsui Museum of Art.

Mason, Roger S. 1981. *Conspicuous Consumption: A Study of Exceptional Consumer Behaviour*. Farnborough, UK: Gower.

McCabe, Ina Baghdiantz. 2015. *A History of Global Consumption, 1500–1800*. New York: Routledge.

Miksic, John. 2009. "Research on Ceramic Trade, within Southeast Asia and between Southeast Asia and China." In *Southeast Asian Ceramics: New Light on Old Pottery*, edited by John Miksic, 70–86. Singapore: Editions Didier Millet.

Misugi, Takatoshi. 1981. *Chinese Porcelain Collections in the Near East: Ardebil and Topkapi*. Hong Kong: Hong Kong University Press.

Pennell, Sara. 2010. "'For a Crack or Flaw Despis'd': Thinking about Ceramic Durability and the 'Everyday' in Late Seventeenth- and Early Eighteenth-Century England." In

Everyday Objects: Medieval and Early Modern Material Culture and Its Meanings, edited by Tara Hamling and Catherine Richardson, 27–40. Farnham, UK: Ashgate.

Pierson, Stacey. 2007. *Collectors, Collections, and Museums: The Field of Chinese Ceramics in Britain, 1560–1960*. Bern: Peter Lang.

Pierson, Stacey. 2009. *Chinese Ceramics: A Design History*. London: V&A Publications.

Pierson, Stacey. 2012. "The Movement of Chinese Ceramics: Appropriation in Global History." *Journal of World History* 23 (1): 9–39. http://dx.doi.org/10.1353/jwh.2012.0013.

Pierson, Stacey. 2013. *From Object to Concept: Global Consumption and the Transformation of Ming Porcelain*. Hong Kong: Hong Kong University Press.

Qin, Dashu, Yan Liu, and Herman Kiriama. 2012. "The Chinese Porcelains Unearthed at Gedi Ruins in Coastal Kenya." *Wen Wu* 11: 37–60.

Richter, Anne Nellis. 2008. "Spectacle, Exoticism, and Display in the Gentleman's House: The Fonthill Auction of 1822." *Eighteenth-Century Studies* 41 (4): 543–63. http://dx.doi.org/10.1353/ecs.0.0003.

Sargent, William. 2012. *Treasures of Chinese Export Porcelain from the Peabody Essex Museum*. New Haven, CT: Yale University Press.

Schafer, Dagmar. 2011. "Inscribing the Artifact and Inspiring Trust: The Changing Role of Markings in the Ming Era." *East Asian Science, Technology, and Society: An International Journal* 5: 239–65.

Scharmann, Rudolf G. 2005. *Charlottenburg Palace: Royal Prussia in Berlin*. New York: Prestel.

Scott, Rosemary, ed. 1993. *The Porcelains of Jingdezhen*. Colloquies on Art and Archaeology in Asia 16. London: Percival David Foundation of Chinese Art / SOAS.

Scott, Rosemary, and Rose Kerr. 1994. *Ceramic Evolution in the Middle Ming Period: Hongzhi to Wanli (1488–1620)*. London: Percival David Foundation of Chinese Art / SOAS.

Scott, Rosemary, and Stacey Pierson. 1995. *Flawless Porcelains: Imperial Ceramics from the Reign of the Chenghua Emperor*. London: Percival David Foundation of Chinese Art / SOAS.

Sheaf, Colin, and Richard Kilburn. 1986. *The Hatcher Porcelain Cargoes: The Complete Record*. Oxford: Phaidon / Christie's.

Sothebys Hong Kong. 2014. "Auction Results: The Meiyingtang 'Chicken Cup.'" April 8. Accessed October 31, 2014. http://www.sothebys.com/en/auctions/2014/meiyintang-chicken-cup-hk0545.html.

Urban Council and Jingdezhen Museum of Ceramic History. *Imperial Porcelain of the Yongle and Xuande Periods: Excavations from the Site of the Ming Imperial Factory at Jingdezhen*. 1989. Hong Kong: Urban Council.

Vainker, Shelagh. 2005. *Chinese Pottery and Porcelain: From Prehistory to the Present Day.* London: British Museum Press.

van Ittersum, Martine Julia. 2003. "Hugo Grotius in Context: Van Heemskerck's Capture of the *Santa Catarina* and Its Justification in *De Jure Praedae* (1604–1606)." *Asian Journal of Social Science* 31 (3): 511–48. http://dx.doi.org/10.1163/156853103322895360.

Watt, James C.Y., and Wen C. Fong. 1996. *Possessing the Past: Treasures from the National Palace Museum, Taipei.* New York and Taipei: Metropolitan Museum of Art and National Palace Museum.

Wilson, Richard L. 2005. "Notes on Chinese Ceramics Excavated in Japan." In *Tradition and Transformation: Essays in Honor of Chu-tsing Li*, edited by Judith Smith, 472–89. Seattle: University of Washington Press.

Contributors

TRACI ARDREN
Department of Anthropology
University of Miami
Coral Gables, FL 33124

AMY BOGAARD
School of Archaeology
University of Oxford
Oxford OX1 2PG

ELIZABETH KLARICH
Department of Anthropology
Smith College
Green St. Classroom Annex 104c
Northampton, MA 01063

ABIGAIL LEVINE
Cotsen Institute of Archaeology
University of California, Los Angeles
Los Angeles, CA 90095–1510

CHRISTOPHER R. MOORE
Department of Anthropology
University of Indianapolis
Indianapolis, IN 46227

TITO E. NARANJO
Santa Clara Pueblo Elder
Española, NM 87532

STACEY PIERSON
History of Art and Archaeology
 Department
SOAS, University of London
WC1H 0XG

JAMES M. POTTER
PaleoWest Archaeology
Pasadena, CA 91114

FRANÇOIS G. RICHARD
Department of Anthropology
University of Chicago
Chicago, IL 60637

CHRISTOPHER W. SCHMIDT
Indiana Prehistory Laboratory
University of Indianapolis
Indianapolis, IN 46227

CAROL SCHULTZE
Historical Research Associates, Inc.
1904 3rd Avenue
Seattle, Washington 98101

PAYSON SHEETS
Department of Anthropology
University of Colorado
Boulder, CO 80309

MONICA L. SMITH
Department of Anthropology
University of California, Los Angeles
Los Angeles, CA 90095–1553

KATHERYN C. TWISS
Department of Anthropology
Stony Brook University
Stony Brook, NY 11794

MARK D. VARIEN
Crow Canyon Archaeological Center
Cortez, CO 81321

JUSTIN ST. P. Walsh
Department of Art
Chapman University
Orange, CA 92866

MARÍA NIEVES ZEDEÑO
School of Anthropology
University of Arizona
Tucson, AZ 85719

Index

Page numbers in italics indicate illustrations.

www.ingramcontent.com/pod-product-compliance
Lightning Source LLC
Chambersburg PA
CBHW070916030426
42336CB00014BA/2428